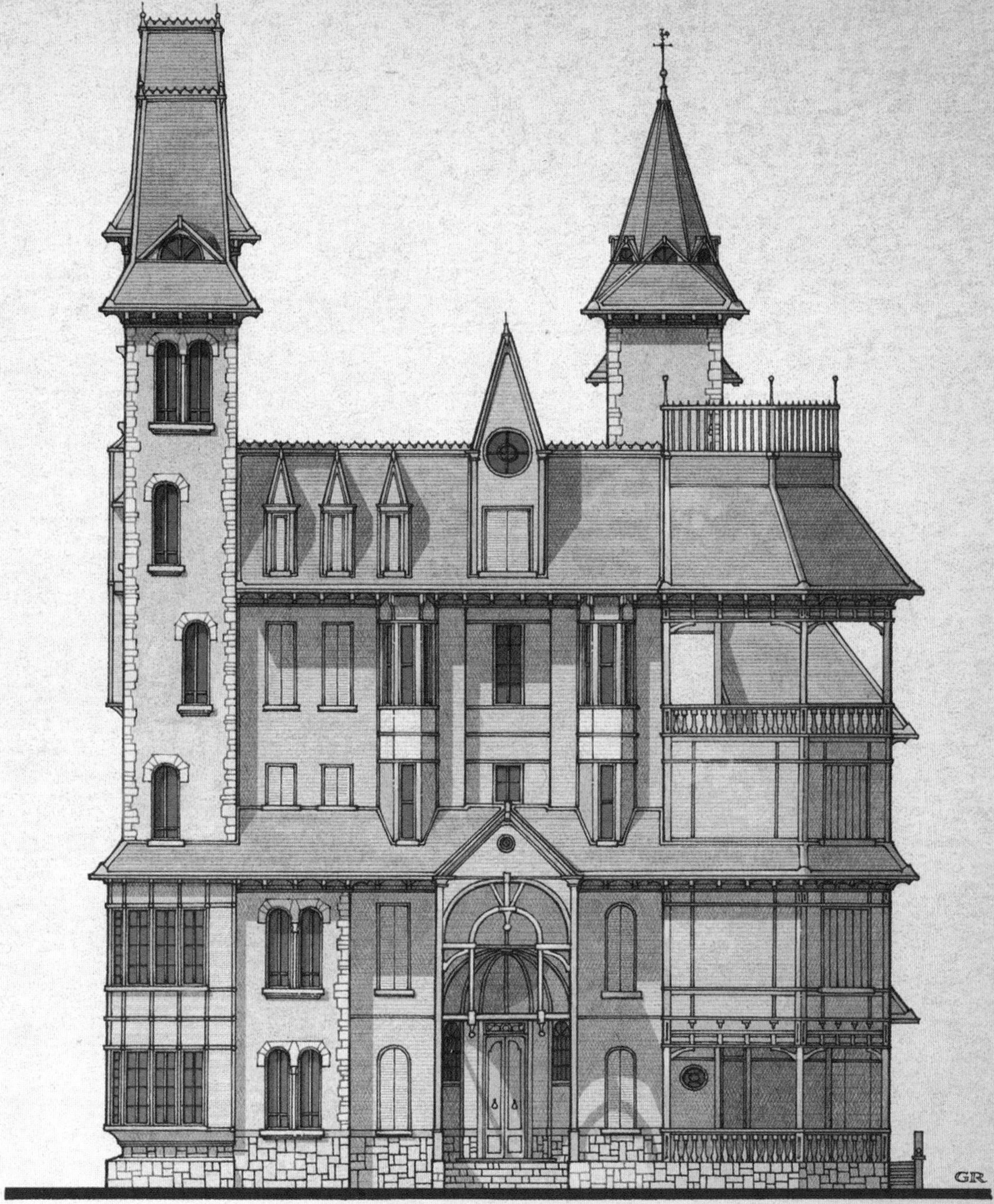
GR

Keyhouse West Elevation

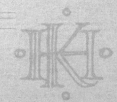

KEYHOUSE NORTH ELEVATION

HEAD GAMES

LOCKE & KEY

VOLUME 2

WRITTEN BY
JOE HILL

ART BY
GABRIEL RODRIGUEZ

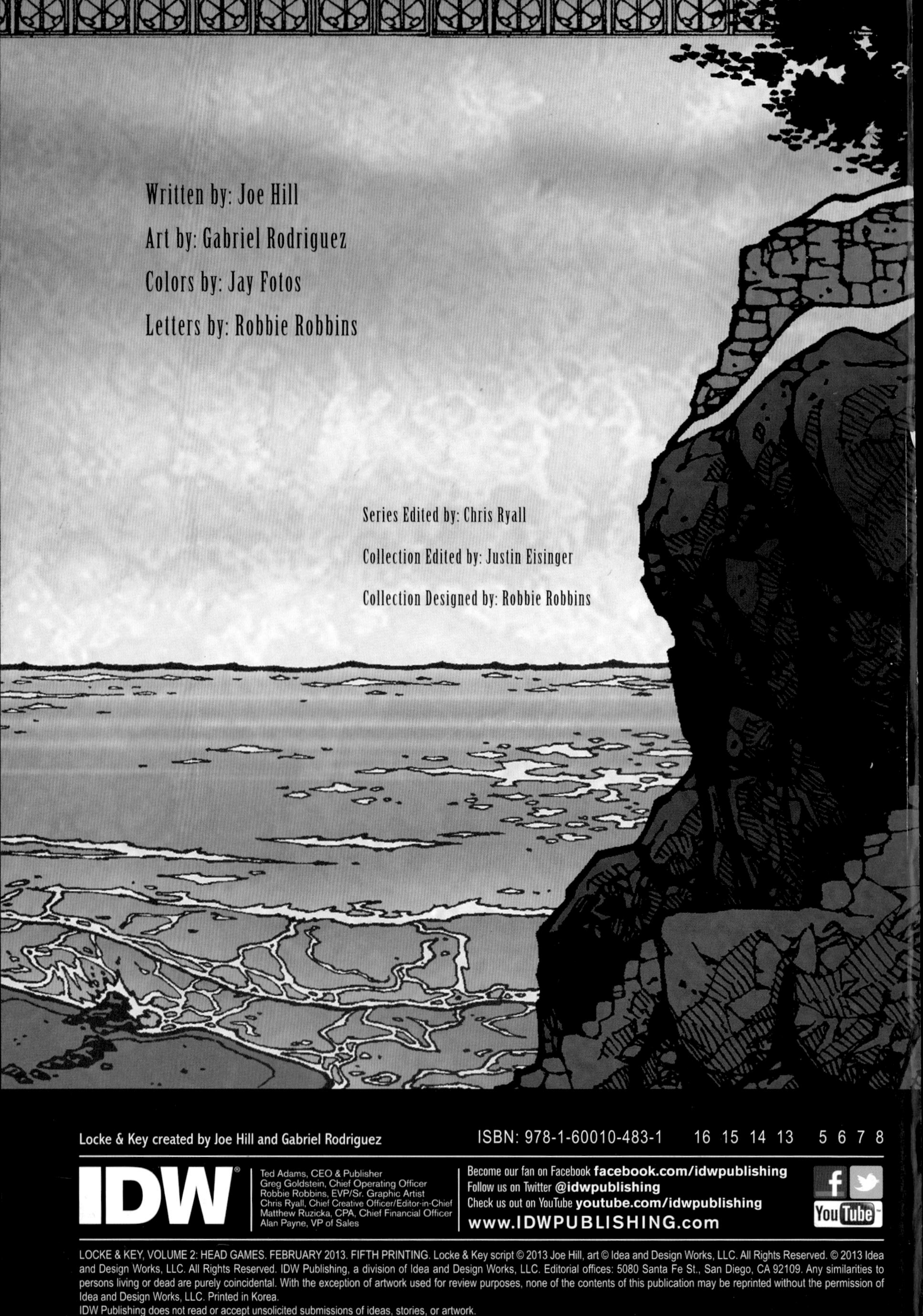

Written by: Joe Hill

Art by: Gabriel Rodriguez

Colors by: Jay Fotos

Letters by: Robbie Robbins

Series Edited by: Chris Ryall

Collection Edited by: Justin Eisinger

Collection Designed by: Robbie Robbins

Locke & Key created by Joe Hill and Gabriel Rodriguez

ISBN: 978-1-60010-483-1   16 15 14 13   5 6 7 8

IDW

Ted Adams, CEO & Publisher
Greg Goldstein, Chief Operating Officer
Robbie Robbins, EVP/Sr. Graphic Artist
Chris Ryall, Chief Creative Officer/Editor-in-Chief
Matthew Ruzicka, CPA, Chief Financial Officer
Alan Payne, VP of Sales

Become our fan on Facebook **facebook.com/idwpublishing**
Follow us on Twitter **@idwpublishing**
Check us out on YouTube **youtube.com/idwpublishing**
www.IDWPUBLISHING.com

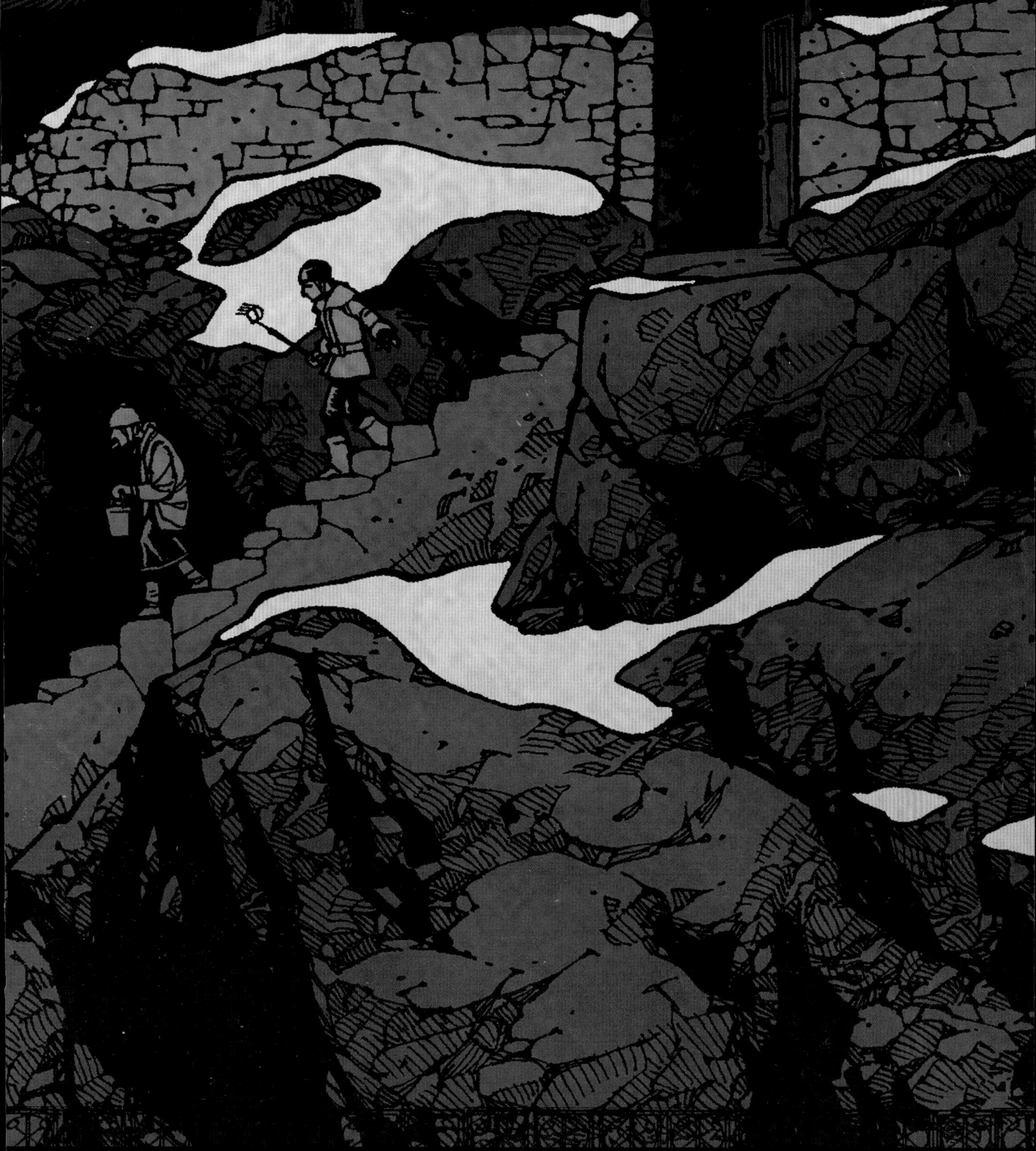

introduction
by Warren Ellis

The thing I hate most about Joe Hill is that he's cleverer than I am, and therefore has things in his head that are better than the things in my head, so what I need to do is fashion a key of some kind, very sharp, and jam it into his neck, just below the base of his skull, and twist it hard until the top of his head opens, and then rummage around in there for the clever bits, pick them out, and stuff them into a bottle, which I will fill with wine, allowing his clever bits to suffuse into the liquid, and so I will drink the then-fortified wine filled with nutritious Joe Hill headbits, and therefore will be clever enough to one day come up with the wonderful metaphorical conceit of keys to open our heads and reveal all we hide away in that dark little space, except that that's an idea Joe Hill's already had and I crudely ripped it off when I tooled my own key that I shoved into the back of Joe Hill's head, and it's not a special metaphorical magic key, it's just an old doorkey, so now there's Joe Hill's head with this manky old key that I filed a point on sticking out of the back of his neck, and he's actually made kind of a mess, and the worst thing I suppose is that he fairly obviously won't be writing any more *LOCKE & KEY* comics, which is a bloody (hah) shame because these comics are really remarkably good, among the best-written comics I've seen in the last two years, which I guess is because Joe Hill's cleverer than I am and that's why he had to die.

Sorry.

Warren Ellis
Not Telling You My Location Oh No
July 2009

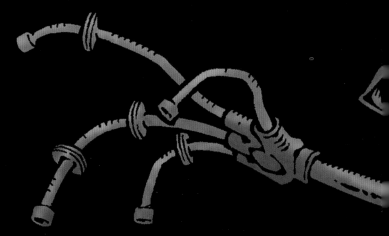

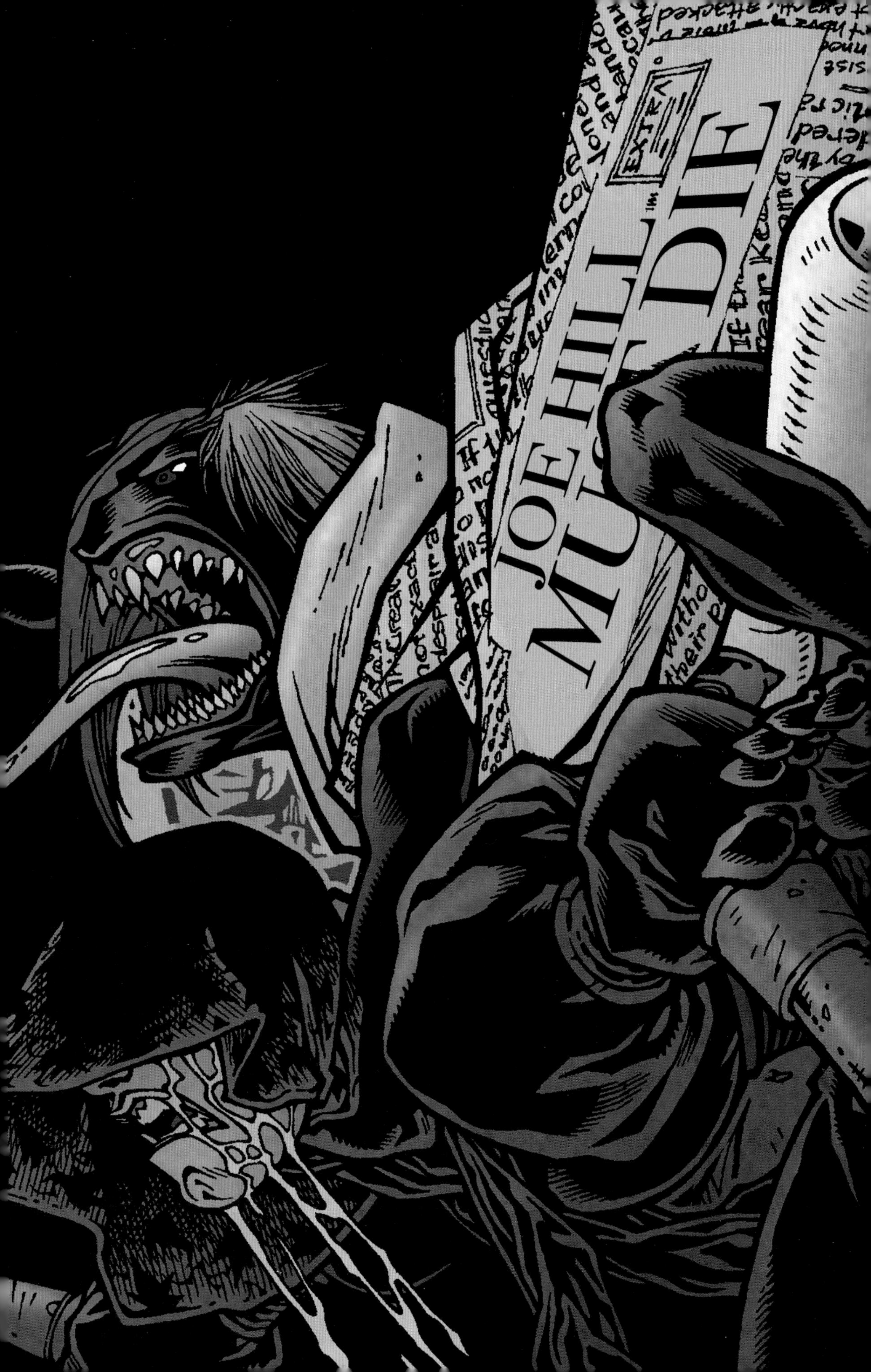
EXTRA
JOE HILL

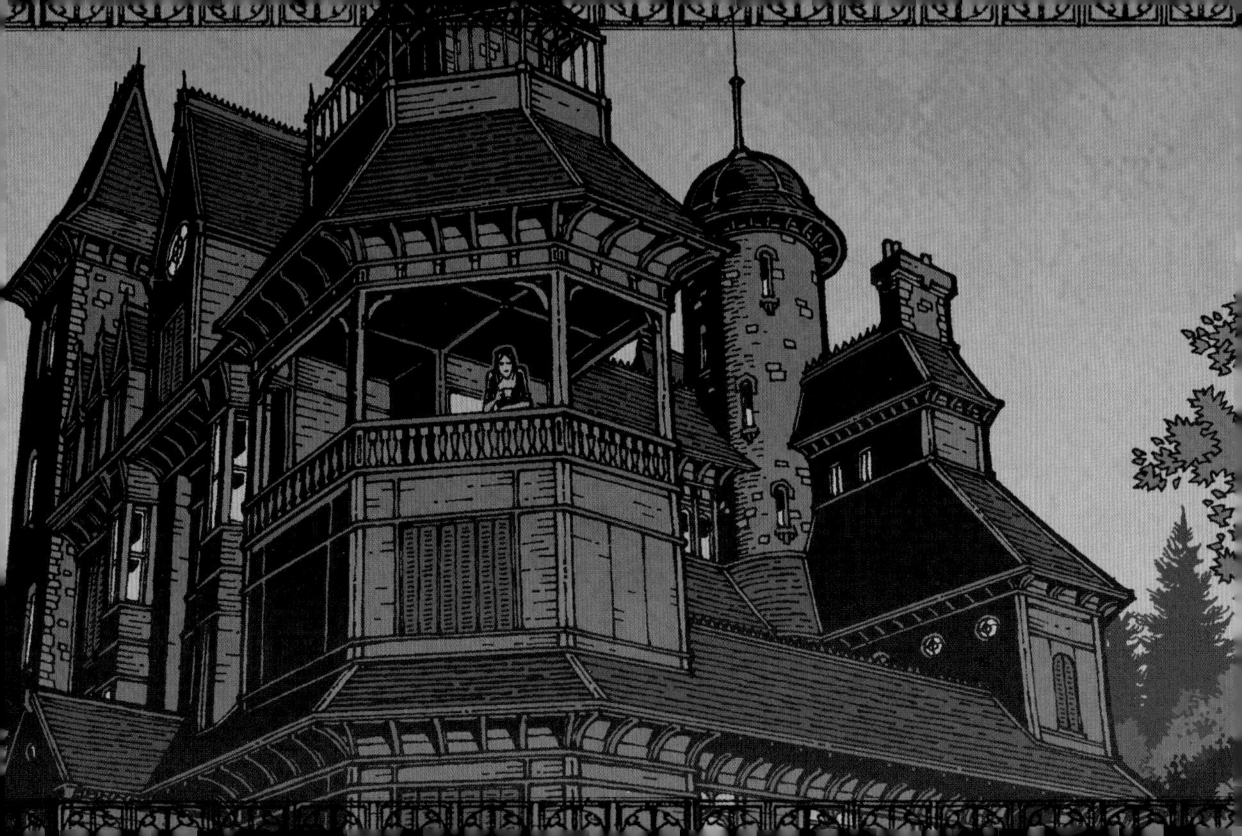

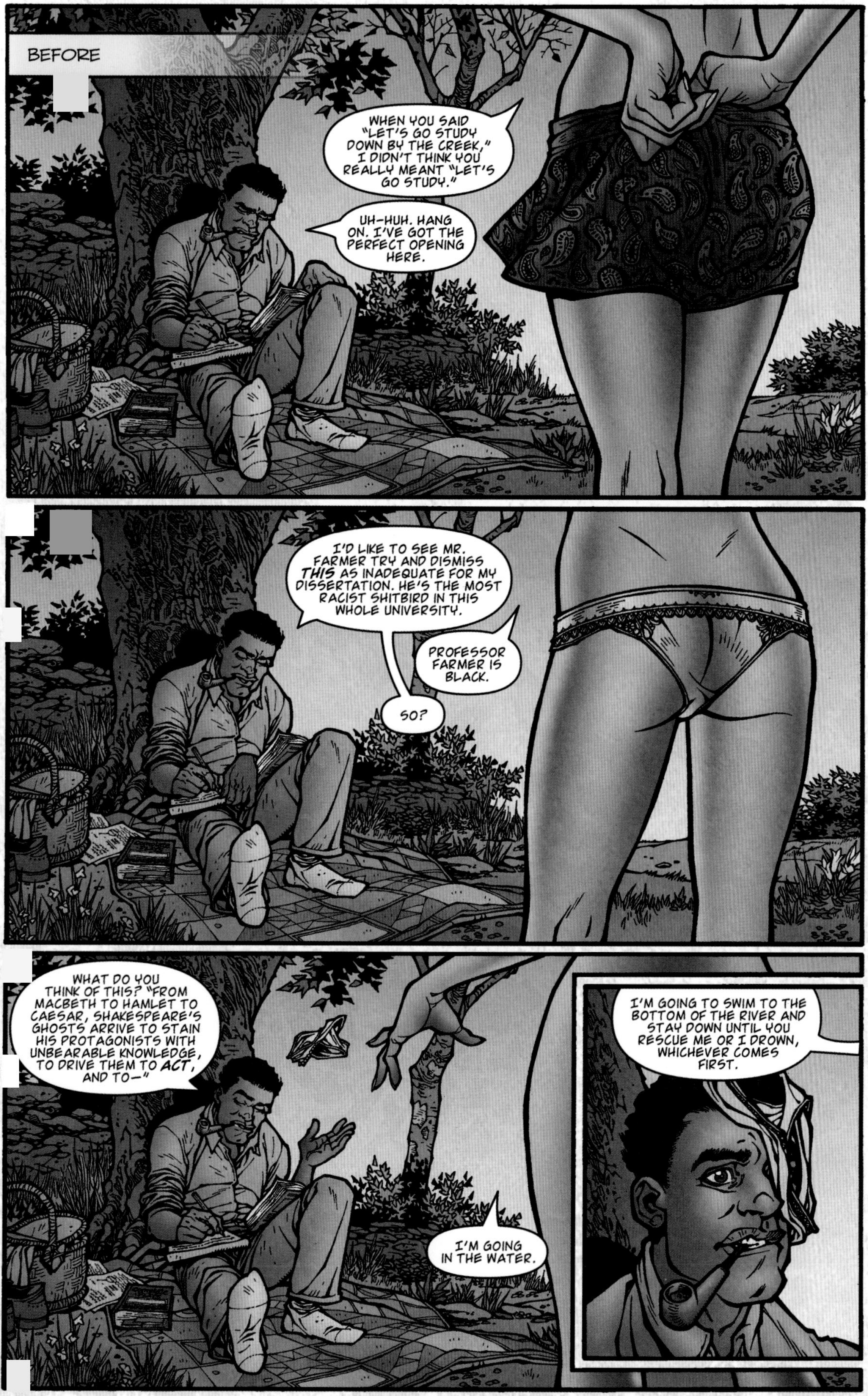
BEFORE
WHEN YOU SAID "LET'S GO STUDY DOWN BY THE CREEK," I DIDN'T THINK YOU REALLY MEANT "LET'S GO STUDY."
UH-HUH. HANG ON. I'VE GOT THE PERFECT OPENING HERE.
I'D LIKE TO SEE MR. FARMER TRY AND DISMISS THIS AS INADEQUATE FOR MY DISSERTATION. HE'S THE MOST RACIST SHITBIRD IN THIS WHOLE UNIVERSITY.
PROFESSOR FARMER IS BLACK.
SO?
WHAT DO YOU THINK OF THIS? "FROM MACBETH TO HAMLET TO CAESAR, SHAKESPEARE'S GHOSTS ARRIVE TO STAIN HIS PROTAGONISTS WITH UNBEARABLE KNOWLEDGE, TO DRIVE THEM TO ACT, AND TO—"
I'M GOING IN THE WATER.
I'M GOING TO SWIM TO THE BOTTOM OF THE RIVER AND STAY DOWN UNTIL YOU RESCUE ME OR I DROWN, WHICHEVER COMES FIRST.

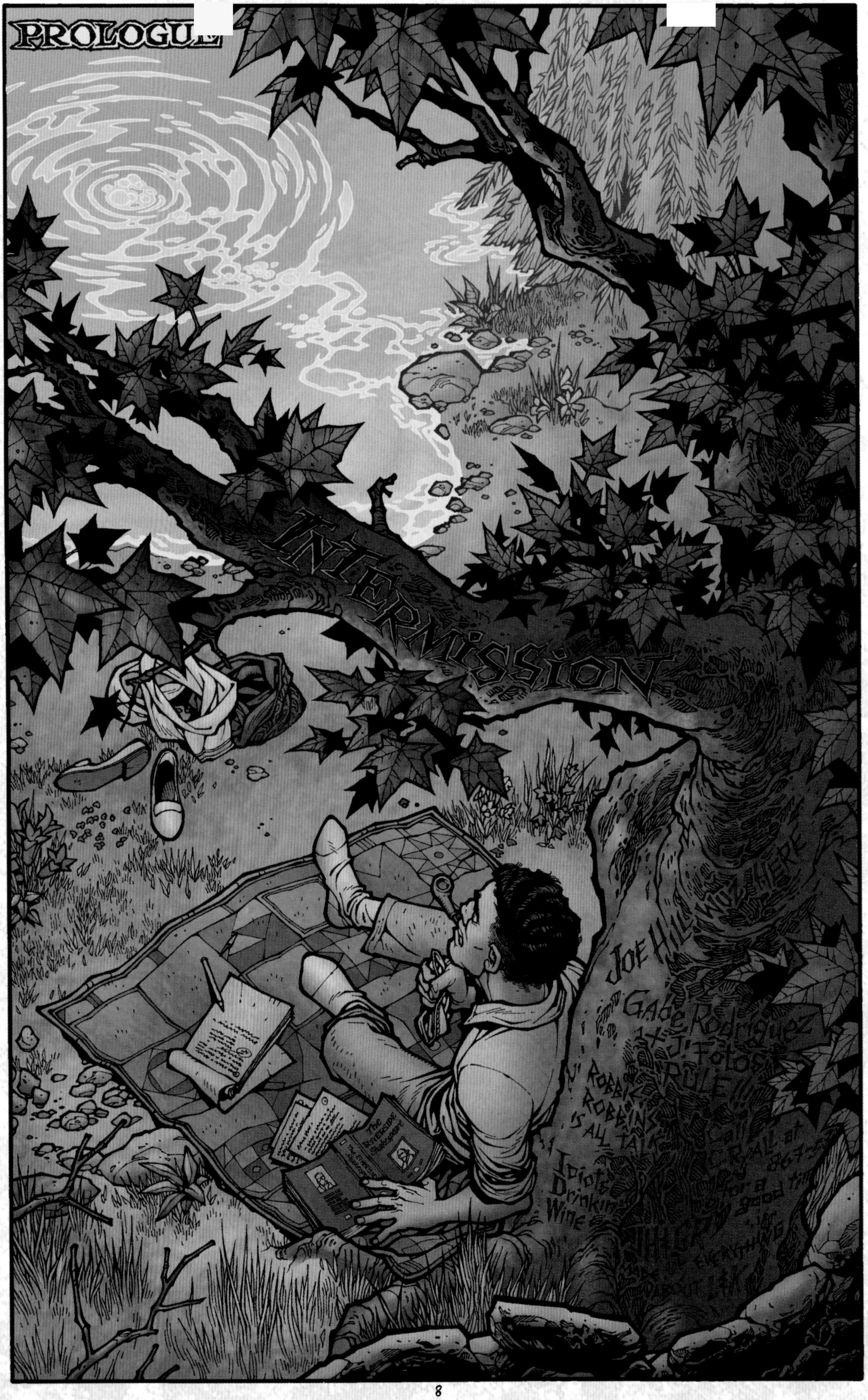
PROLOGUE
INTERMISSION
JOE HILL WUZ HERE
Gabe Rodriguez
J. Fotos
RULE
ROBBIE ROBBINS IS ALL TALK
Call
Idiots Drinkin Wine

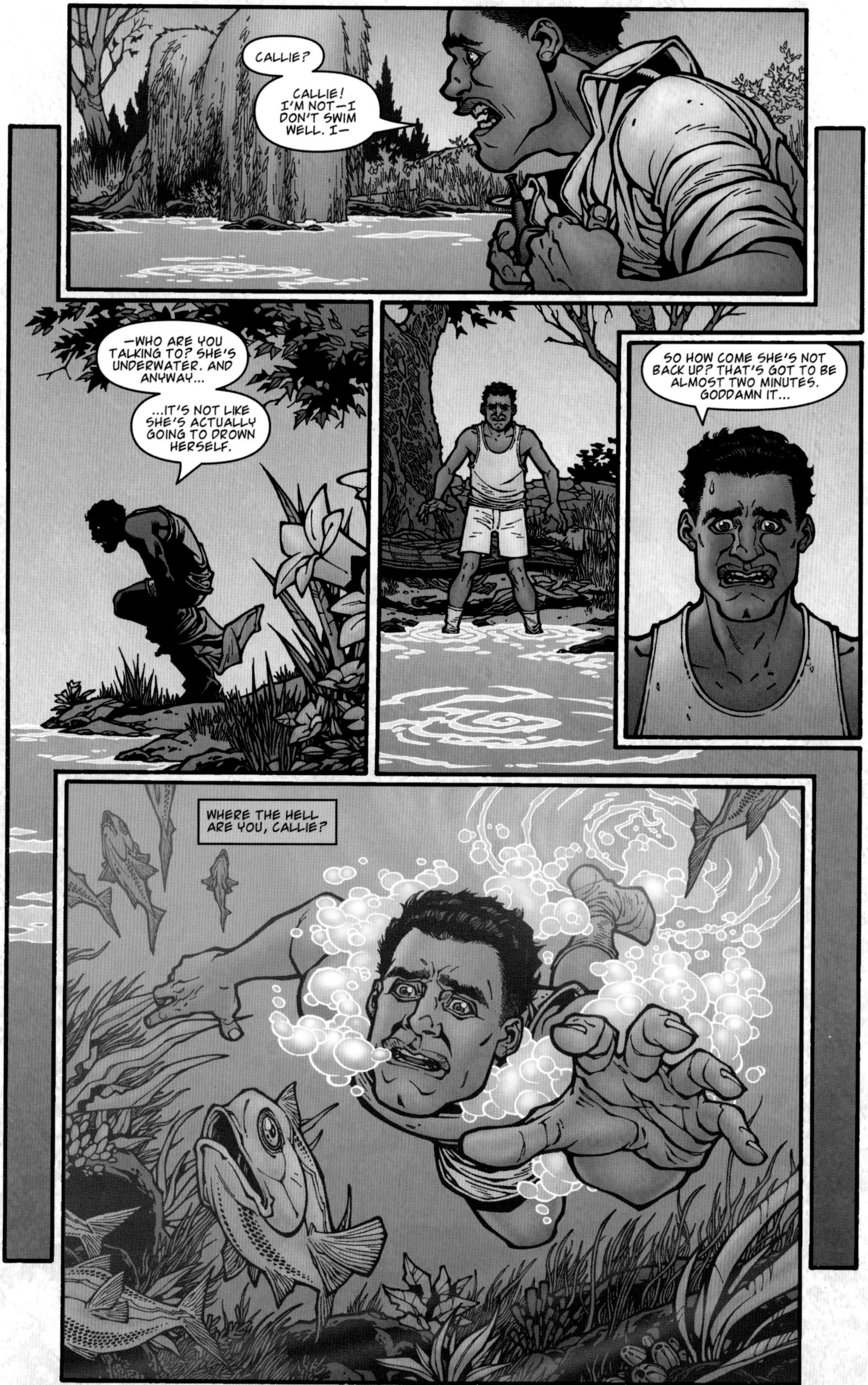
CALLIE?
CALLIE! I'M NOT—I DON'T SWIM WELL. I—
—WHO ARE YOU TALKING TO? SHE'S UNDERWATER. AND ANYWAY...
...IT'S NOT LIKE SHE'S ACTUALLY GOING TO DROWN HERSELF.
SO HOW COME SHE'S NOT BACK UP? THAT'S GOT TO BE ALMOST TWO MINUTES. GODDAMN IT...
WHERE THE HELL ARE YOU, CALLIE?

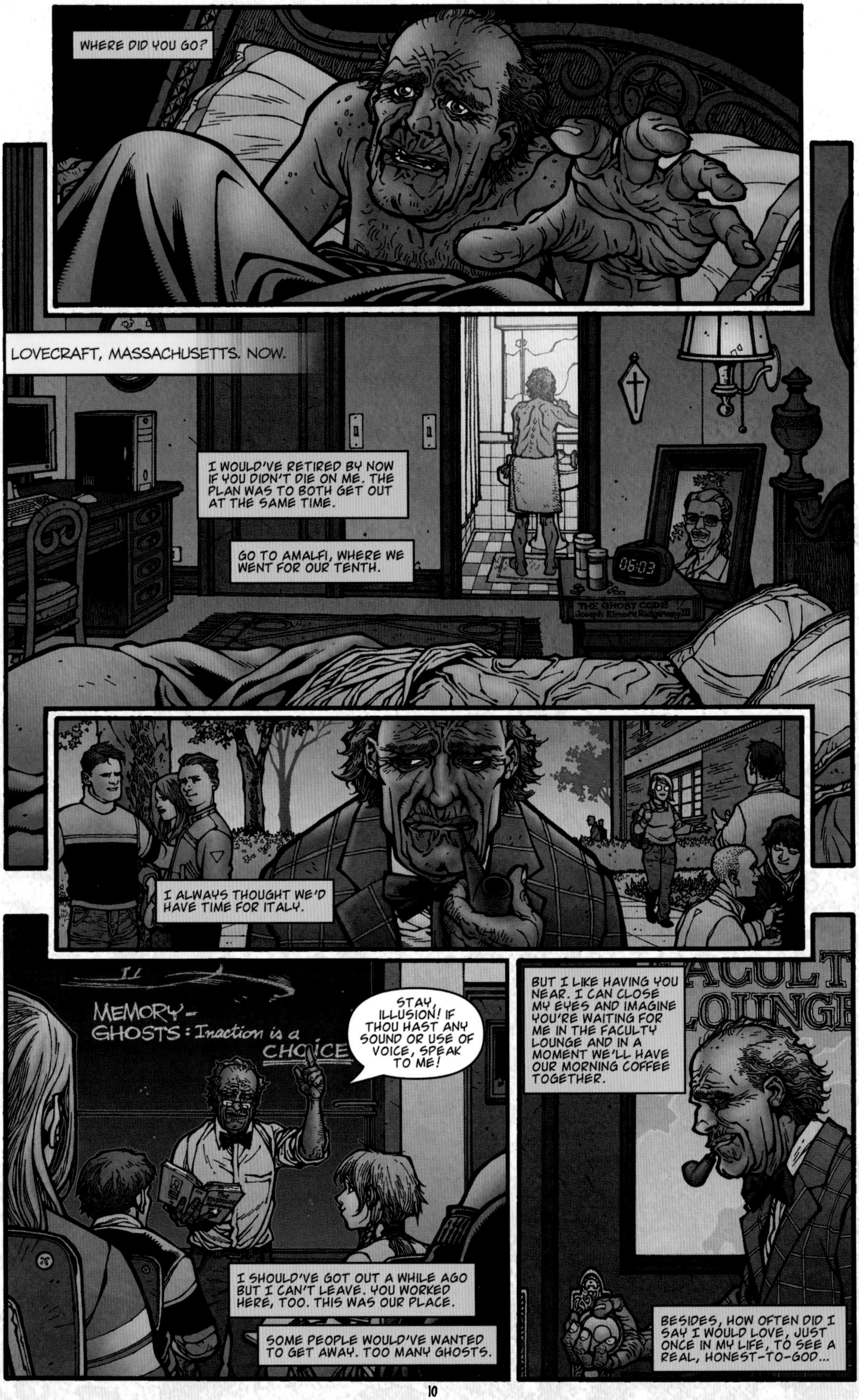
WHERE DID YOU GO?
LOVECRAFT, MASSACHUSETTS. NOW.
I WOULD'VE RETIRED BY NOW IF YOU DIDN'T DIE ON ME. THE PLAN WAS TO BOTH GET OUT AT THE SAME TIME.
GO TO AMALFI, WHERE WE WENT FOR OUR TENTH.
06:03
THE GHOST CODE
I ALWAYS THOUGHT WE'D HAVE TIME FOR ITALY.
MEMORY-GHOSTS: Inaction is a CHOICE
STAY, ILLUSION! IF THOU HAST ANY SOUND OR USE OF VOICE, SPEAK TO ME!
I SHOULD'VE GOT OUT A WHILE AGO BUT I CAN'T LEAVE. YOU WORKED HERE, TOO. THIS WAS OUR PLACE.
SOME PEOPLE WOULD'VE WANTED TO GET AWAY. TOO MANY GHOSTS.
FACULTY LOUNGE
BUT I LIKE HAVING YOU NEAR. I CAN CLOSE MY EYES AND IMAGINE YOU'RE WAITING FOR ME IN THE FACULTY LOUNGE AND IN A MOMENT WE'LL HAVE OUR MORNING COFFEE TOGETHER.
BESIDES, HOW OFTEN DID I SAY I WOULD LOVE, JUST ONCE IN MY LIFE, TO SEE A REAL, HONEST-TO-GOD...

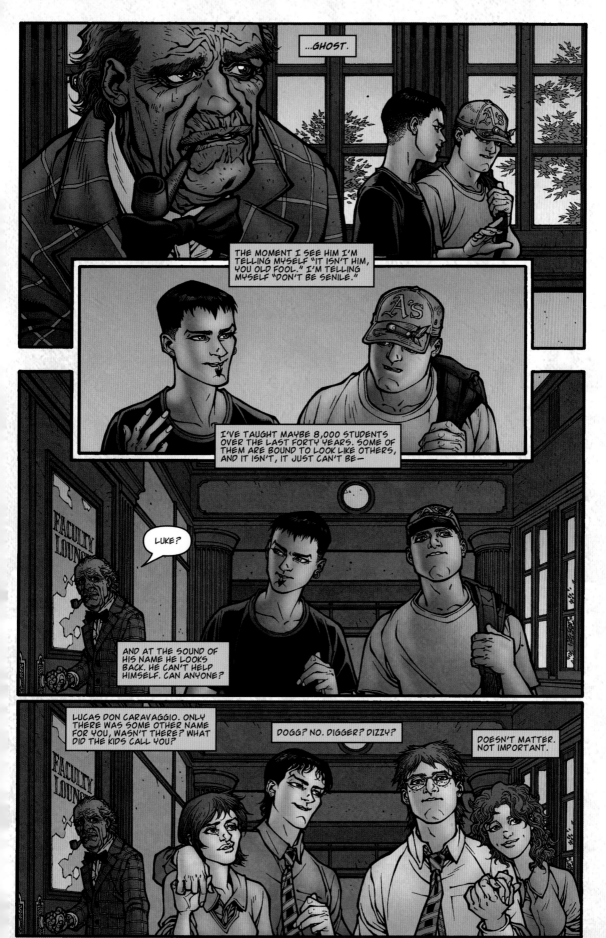

...GHOST.

THE MOMENT I SEE HIM I'M TELLING MYSELF "IT ISN'T HIM, YOU OLD FOOL." I'M TELLING MYSELF "DON'T BE SENILE."

I'VE TAUGHT MAYBE 8,000 STUDENTS OVER THE LAST FORTY YEARS. SOME OF THEM ARE BOUND TO LOOK LIKE OTHERS, AND IT ISN'T, IT JUST CAN'T BE—

LUKE?

AND AT THE SOUND OF HIS NAME HE LOOKS BACK. HE CAN'T HELP HIMSELF. CAN ANYONE?

LUCAS DON CARAVAGGIO. ONLY THERE WAS SOME OTHER NAME FOR YOU, WASN'T THERE? WHAT DID THE KIDS CALL YOU?

DOGG? NO. DIGGER? DIZZY?

DOESN'T MATTER. NOT IMPORTANT.

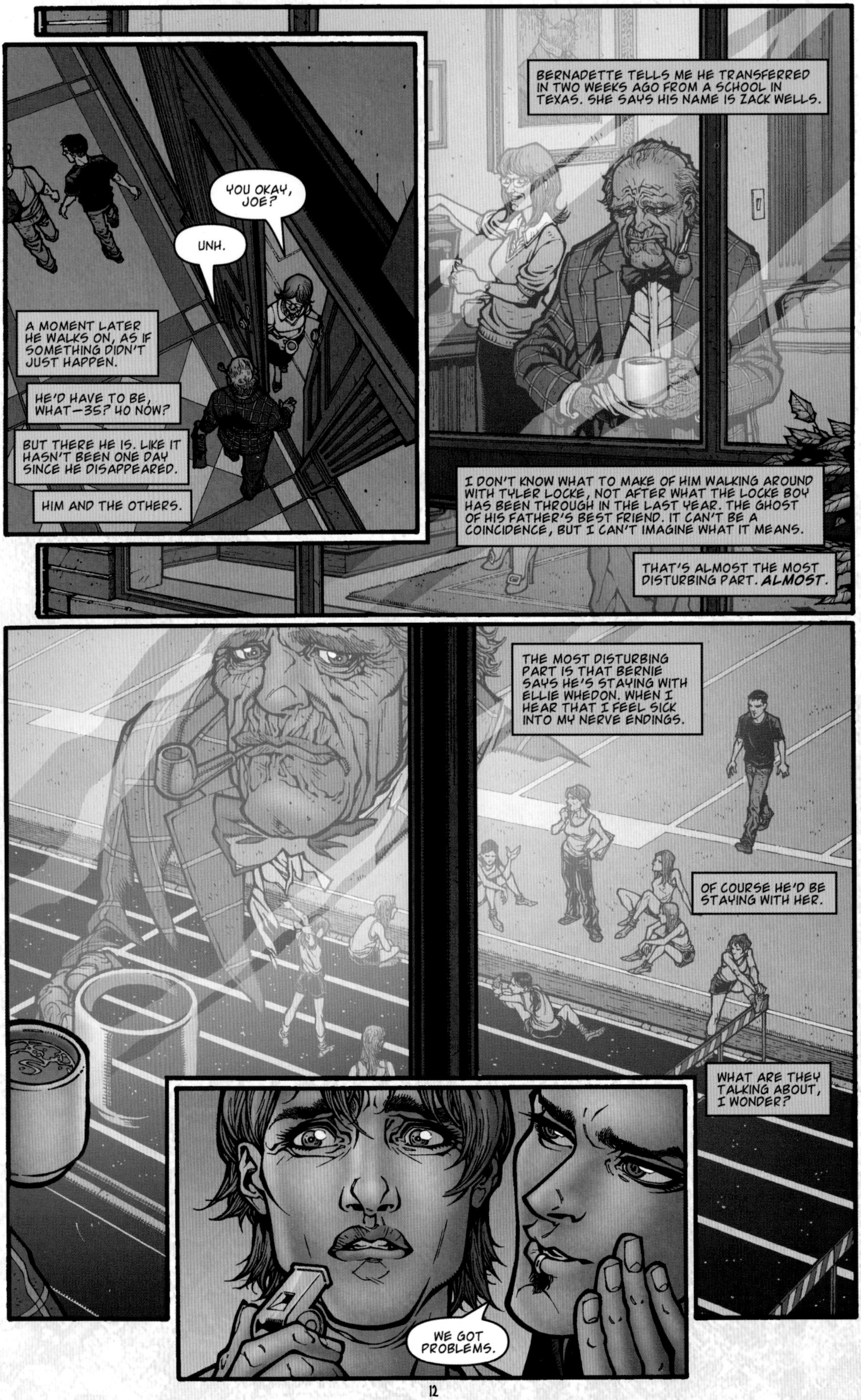
YOU OKAY, JOE?
UNH.
A MOMENT LATER HE WALKS ON, AS IF SOMETHING DIDN'T JUST HAPPEN.
HE'D HAVE TO BE, WHAT—35? 40 NOW?
BUT THERE HE IS. LIKE IT HASN'T BEEN ONE DAY SINCE HE DISAPPEARED.
HIM AND THE OTHERS.
BERNADETTE TELLS ME HE TRANSFERRED IN TWO WEEKS AGO FROM A SCHOOL IN TEXAS. SHE SAYS HIS NAME IS ZACK WELLS.
I DON'T KNOW WHAT TO MAKE OF HIM WALKING AROUND WITH TYLER LOCKE, NOT AFTER WHAT THE LOCKE BOY HAS BEEN THROUGH IN THE LAST YEAR. THE GHOST OF HIS FATHER'S BEST FRIEND. IT CAN'T BE A COINCIDENCE, BUT I CAN'T IMAGINE WHAT IT MEANS.
THAT'S ALMOST THE MOST DISTURBING PART. ALMOST.
THE MOST DISTURBING PART IS THAT BERNIE SAYS HE'S STAYING WITH ELLIE WHEDON. WHEN I HEAR THAT I FEEL SICK INTO MY NERVE ENDINGS.
OF COURSE HE'D BE STAYING WITH HER.
WHAT ARE THEY TALKING ABOUT, I WONDER?
WE GOT PROBLEMS.

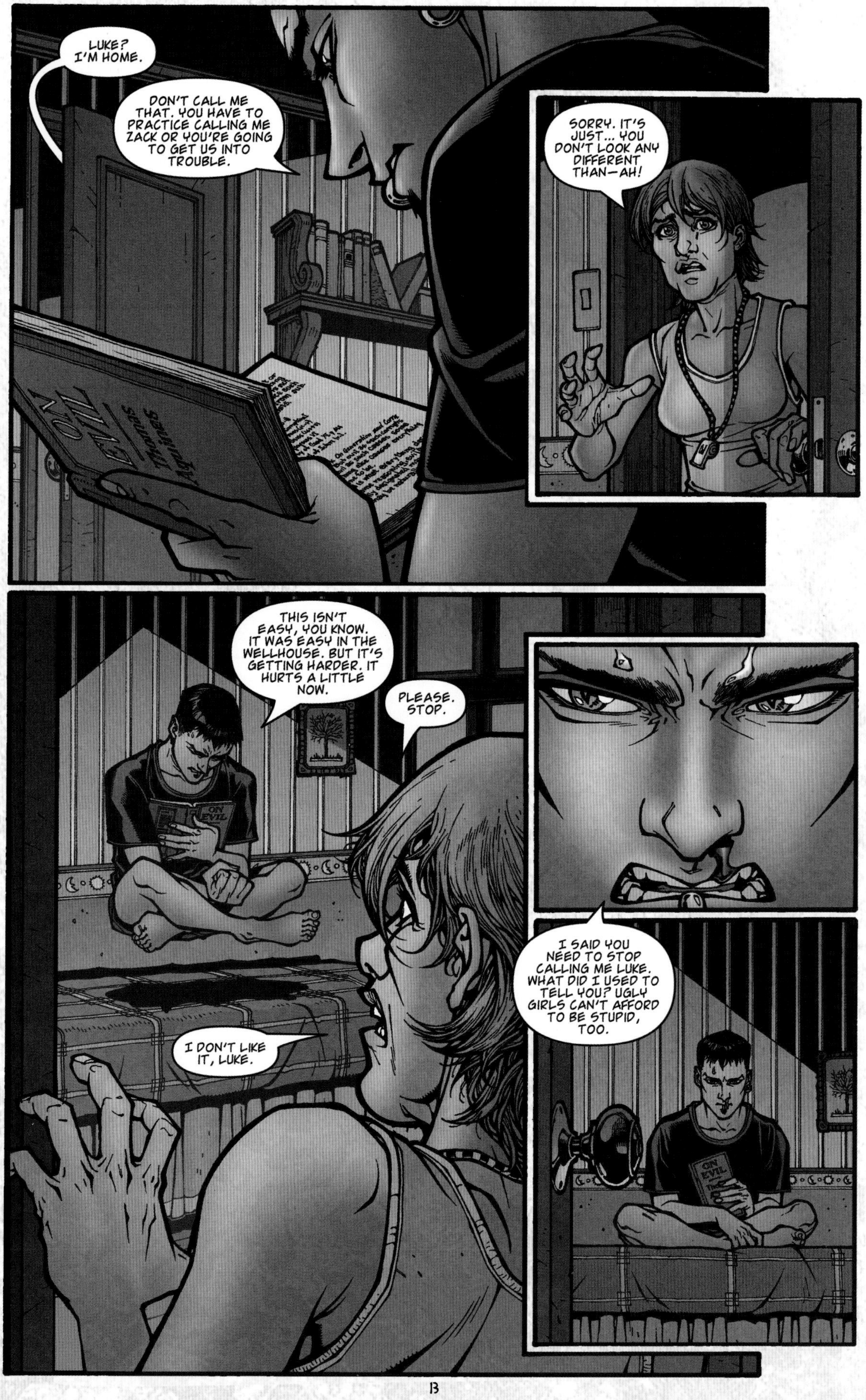
LUKE? I'M HOME.
DON'T CALL ME THAT. YOU HAVE TO PRACTICE CALLING ME ZACK OR YOU'RE GOING TO GET US INTO TROUBLE.
SORRY. IT'S JUST... YOU DON'T LOOK ANY DIFFERENT THAN—AH!
THIS ISN'T EASY, YOU KNOW. IT WAS EASY IN THE WELLHOUSE. BUT IT'S GETTING HARDER. IT HURTS A LITTLE NOW.
PLEASE. STOP.
I DON'T LIKE IT, LUKE.
I SAID YOU NEED TO STOP CALLING ME LUKE. WHAT DID I USED TO TELL YOU? UGLY GIRLS CAN'T AFFORD TO BE STUPID, TOO.

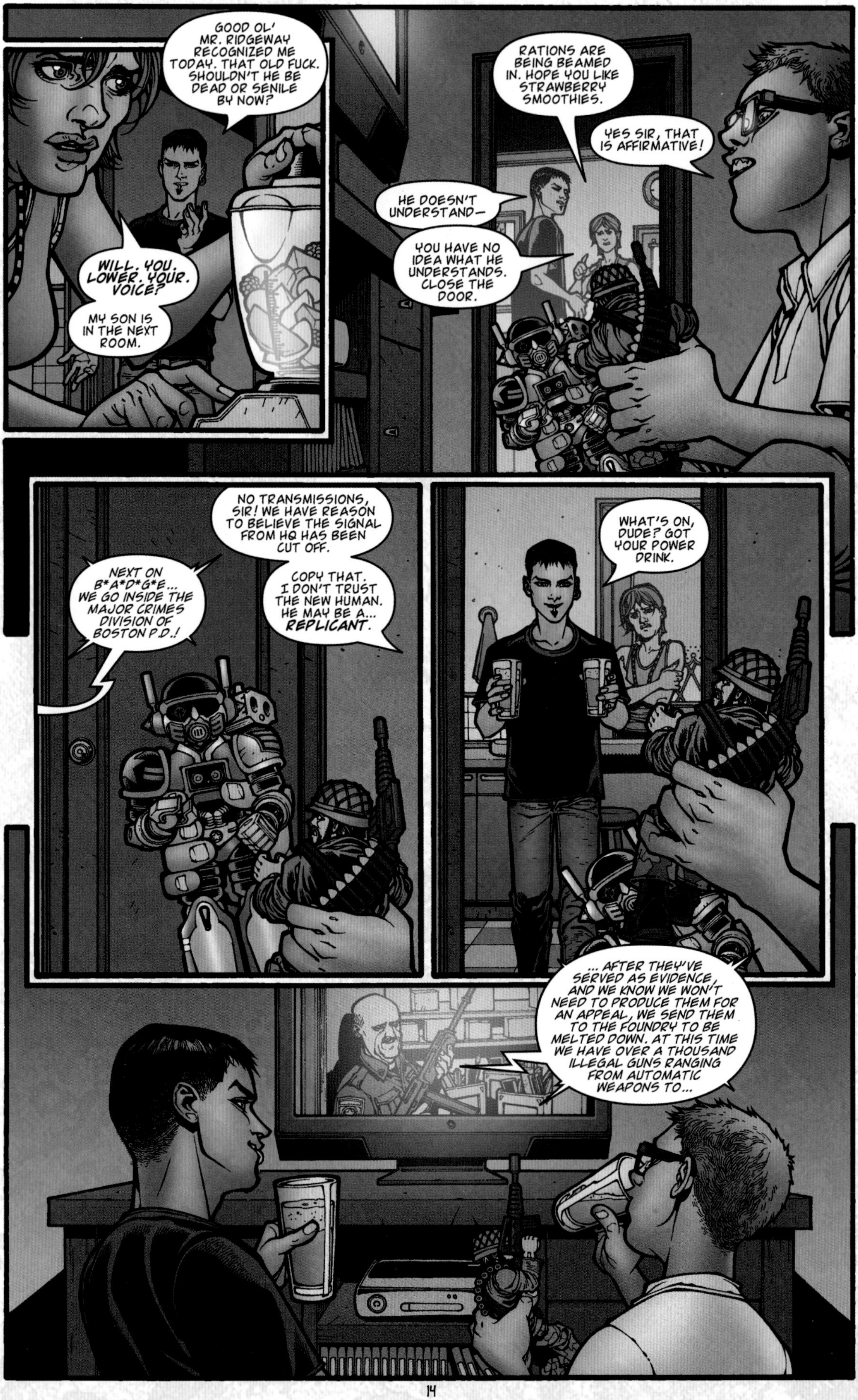
GOOD OL' MR. RIDGEWAY RECOGNIZED ME TODAY. THAT OLD FUCK. SHOULDN'T HE BE DEAD OR SENILE BY NOW?
WILL. YOU. LOWER. YOUR. VOICE?
MY SON IS IN THE NEXT ROOM.
RATIONS ARE BEING BEAMED IN. HOPE YOU LIKE STRAWBERRY SMOOTHIES.
YES SIR, THAT IS AFFIRMATIVE!
HE DOESN'T UNDERSTAND—
YOU HAVE NO IDEA WHAT HE UNDERSTANDS. CLOSE THE DOOR.
NO TRANSMISSIONS, SIR! WE HAVE REASON TO BELIEVE THE SIGNAL FROM HQ HAS BEEN CUT OFF.
COPY THAT. I DON'T TRUST THE NEW HUMAN. HE MAY BE A... REPLICANT.
NEXT ON B*A*D*G*E... WE GO INSIDE THE MAJOR CRIMES DIVISION OF BOSTON P.D.!
WHAT'S ON, DUDE? GOT YOUR POWER DRINK.
... AFTER THEY'VE SERVED AS EVIDENCE, AND WE KNOW WE WON'T NEED TO PRODUCE THEM FOR AN APPEAL, WE SEND THEM TO THE FOUNDRY TO BE MELTED DOWN. AT THIS TIME WE HAVE OVER A THOUSAND ILLEGAL GUNS RANGING FROM AUTOMATIC WEAPONS TO...

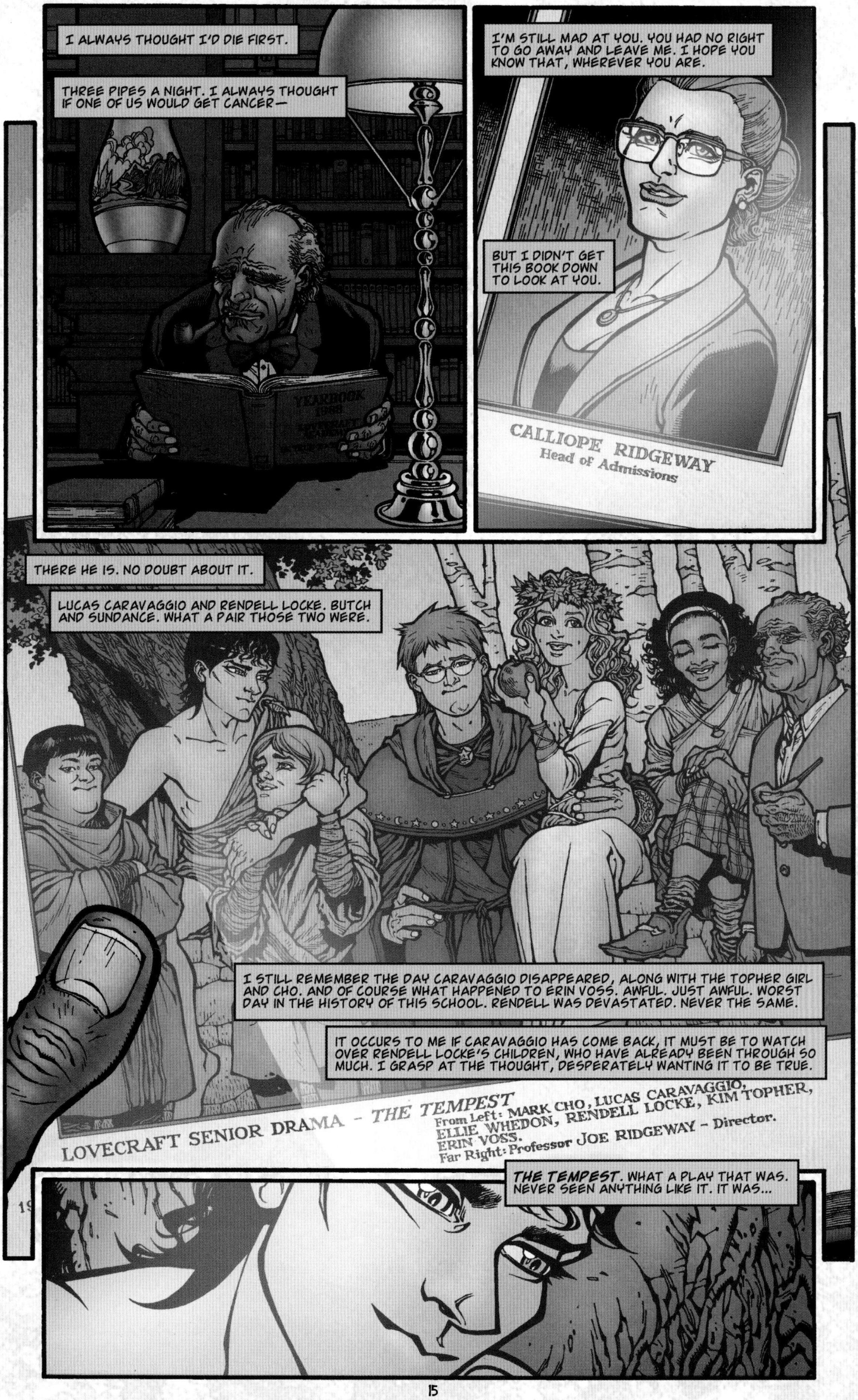
I ALWAYS THOUGHT I'D DIE FIRST.
THREE PIPES A NIGHT. I ALWAYS THOUGHT IF ONE OF US WOULD GET CANCER—
I'M STILL MAD AT YOU. YOU HAD NO RIGHT TO GO AWAY AND LEAVE ME. I HOPE YOU KNOW THAT, WHEREVER YOU ARE.
BUT I DIDN'T GET THIS BOOK DOWN TO LOOK AT YOU.
CALLIOPE RIDGEWAY
Head of Admissions
THERE HE IS. NO DOUBT ABOUT IT.
LUCAS CARAVAGGIO AND RENDELL LOCKE. BUTCH AND SUNDANCE. WHAT A PAIR THOSE TWO WERE.
I STILL REMEMBER THE DAY CARAVAGGIO DISAPPEARED, ALONG WITH THE TOPHER GIRL AND CHO. AND OF COURSE WHAT HAPPENED TO ERIN VOSS. AWFUL. JUST AWFUL. WORST DAY IN THE HISTORY OF THIS SCHOOL. RENDELL WAS DEVASTATED. NEVER THE SAME.
IT OCCURS TO ME IF CARAVAGGIO HAS COME BACK, IT MUST BE TO WATCH OVER RENDELL LOCKE'S CHILDREN, WHO HAVE ALREADY BEEN THROUGH SO MUCH. I GRASP AT THE THOUGHT, DESPERATELY WANTING IT TO BE TRUE.
LOVECRAFT SENIOR DRAMA - THE TEMPEST
From Left: MARK CHO, LUCAS CARAVAGGIO, ELLIE WHEDON, RENDELL LOCKE, KIM TOPHER, ERIN VOSS.
Far Right: Professor JOE RIDGEWAY - Director.
THE TEMPEST. WHAT A PLAY THAT WAS. NEVER SEEN ANYTHING LIKE IT. IT WAS...

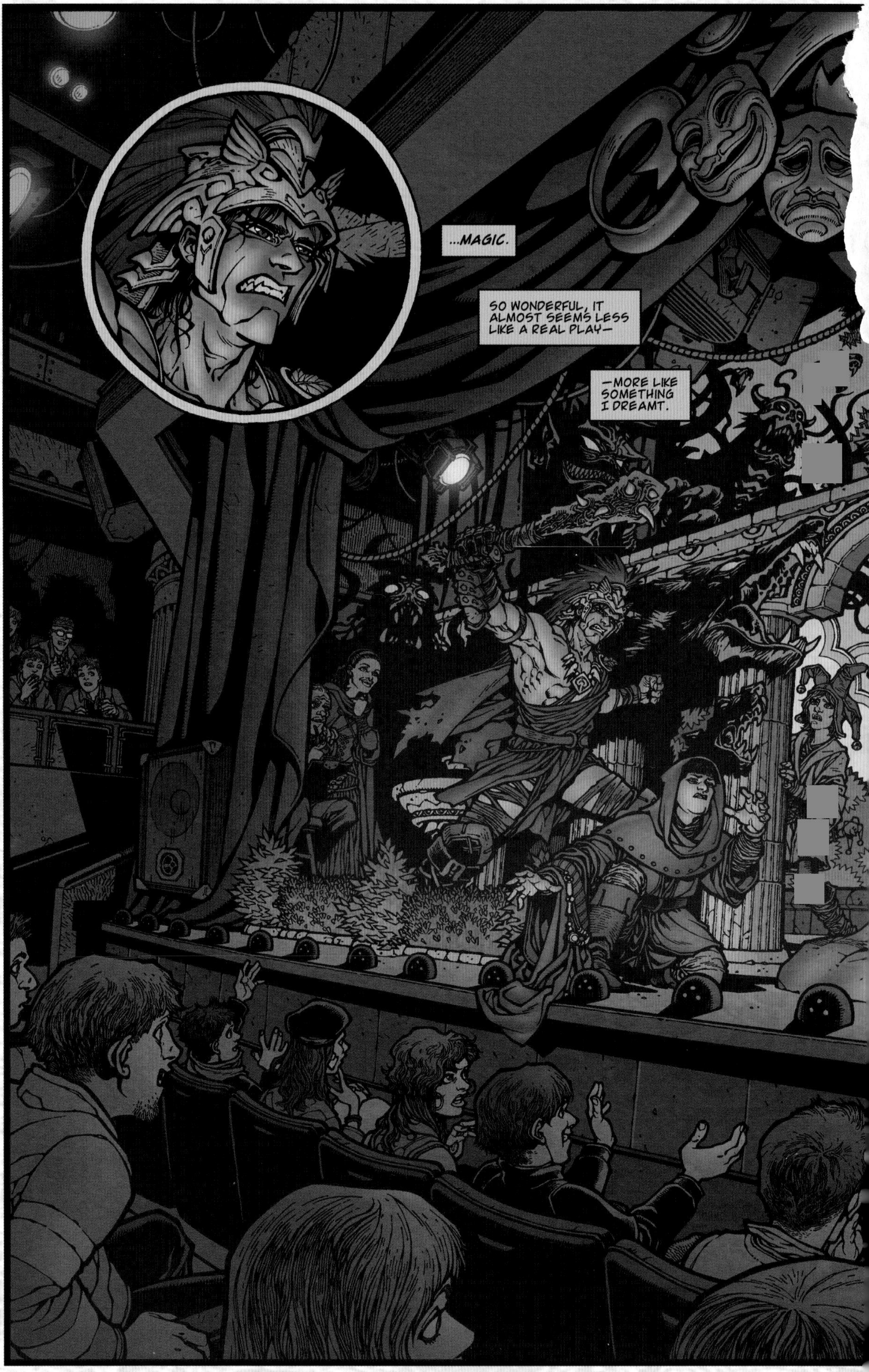
...MAGIC.
SO WONDERFUL, IT ALMOST SEEMS LESS LIKE A REAL PLAY—
—MORE LIKE SOMETHING I DREAMT.

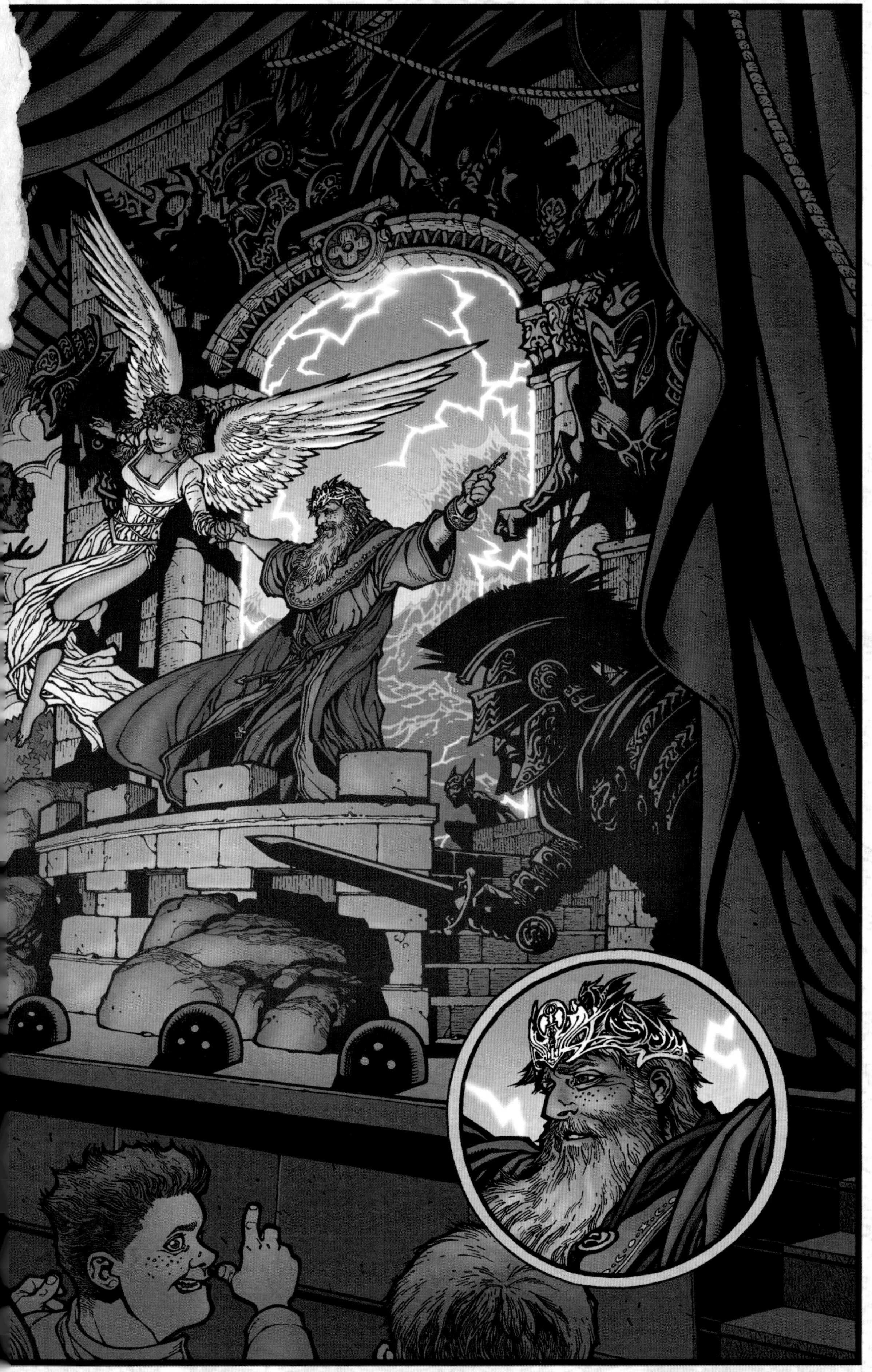

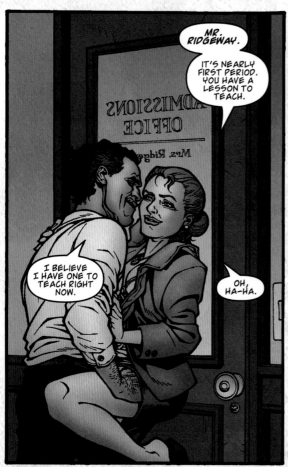

MR. RIDGEWAY.
IT'S NEARLY FIRST PERIOD. YOU HAVE A LESSON TO TEACH.
ADMISSIONS OFFICE
Mrs. Ridge
I BELIEVE I HAVE ONE TO TEACH RIGHT NOW.
OH, HA-HA.
WE TALKED ABOUT WHAT IT WOULD BE LIKE, FOR ONE OF US TO LOSE THE OTHER.
BUT THAT'S NOT HOW IT WORKS. YOU DON'T LOSE ANYONE. YOU AREN'T LOST. I CLOSE MY EYES AND THERE YOU ARE.
ADMISSIONS OFFICE
Mrs. Wood
I SHOULDN'T BE DOING THIS.
THERE ARE RULES TO PROTECT STUDENT PRIVACY.
BUT CALLIE... YOU TAUGHT ME A HEALTHY DISRESPECT FOR RULES.
BESIDES. AT MY AGE YOU CAN PRETEND TO BE A LITTLE DOTTY AND GET AWAY WITH MOST ANYTHING.
A WHITE GIRL FROM THE SOUTH LOVING A BLACK MAN IN 1967. MY GOD, YOU'RE LUCKY YOU DIDN'T GET US BOTH KILLED.
SAYS HERE HE WAS ON THE DEAN'S LIST FOR ACADEMIC ACHIEVEMENT AND CAPTAIN OF THEIR FENCING TEAM. WASN'T LUCAS CARAVAGGIO ALSO... BUT THAT DOESN'T PROVE ANYTHING.
THEN THERE'S A PERSONAL NOTE FROM ELLIE, IDENTIFYING HIM AS A COUSIN AND EXPLAINING HE'LL BE STAYING WITH HER. I DIDN'T KNOW YOU HAD KIN OUT WEST, ELLIE.
THERE'S A NUMBER FOR THE SCHOOL HE TRANSFERRED OUT OF IN TEXAS. A PART OF ME DOESN'T WANT TO CALL. A PART OF ME IS AFRAID TO... AFRAID OF WHAT I MIGHT FIND OUT.

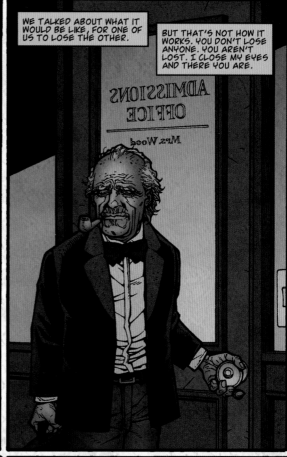

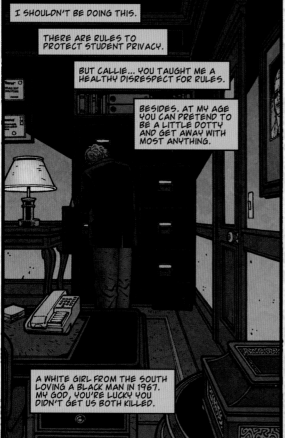

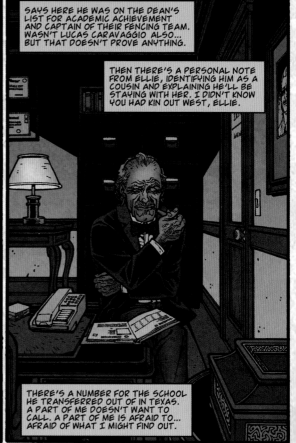

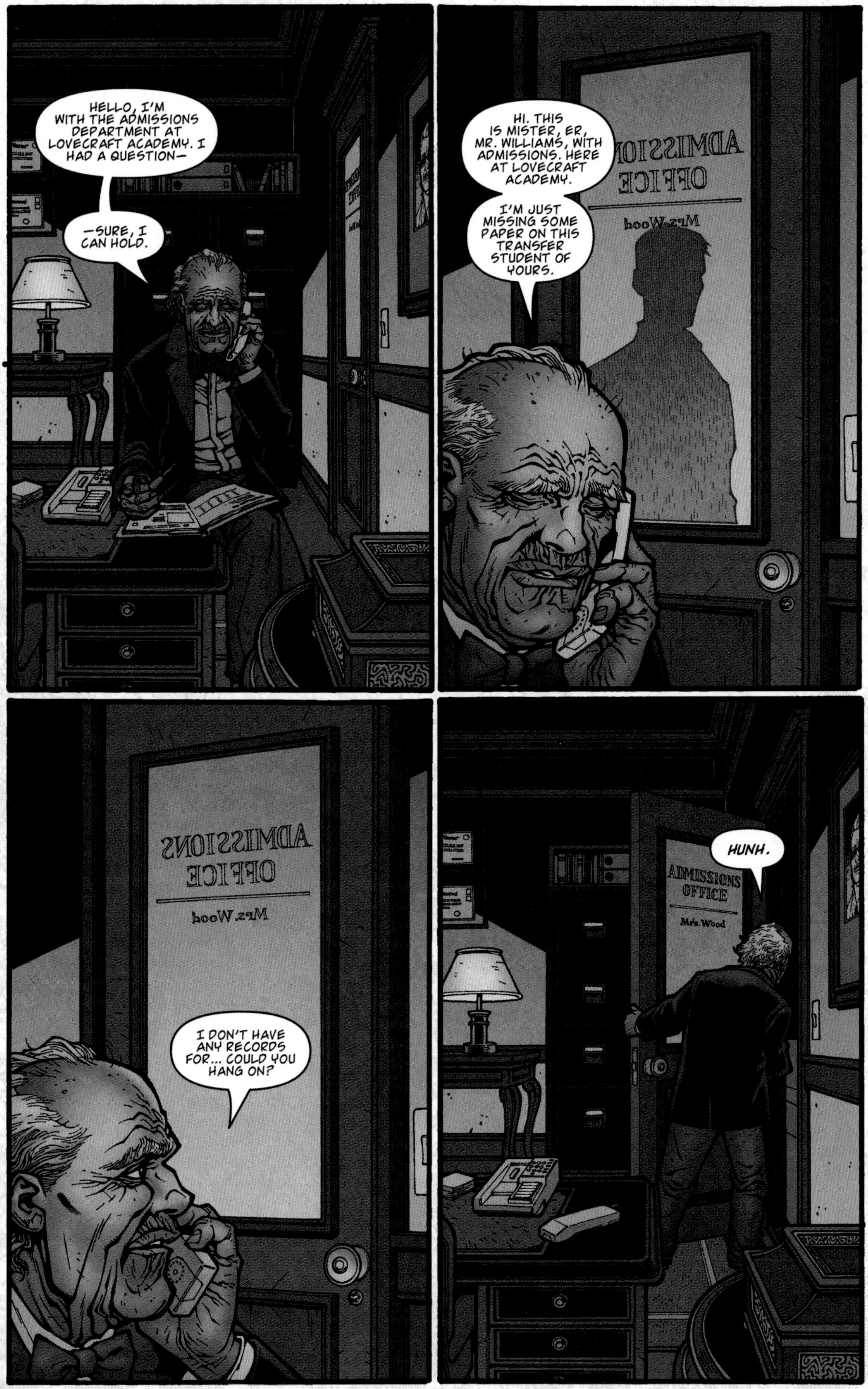
HELLO, I'M WITH THE ADMISSIONS DEPARTMENT AT LOVECRAFT ACADEMY. I HAD A QUESTION—
—SURE, I CAN HOLD.
HI. THIS IS MISTER, ER, MR. WILLIAMS, WITH ADMISSIONS. HERE AT LOVECRAFT ACADEMY.
I'M JUST MISSING SOME PAPER ON THIS TRANSFER STUDENT OF YOURS.
I DON'T HAVE ANY RECORDS FOR... COULD YOU HANG ON?
HUNH.
ADMISSIONS OFFICE
Mrs. Wood

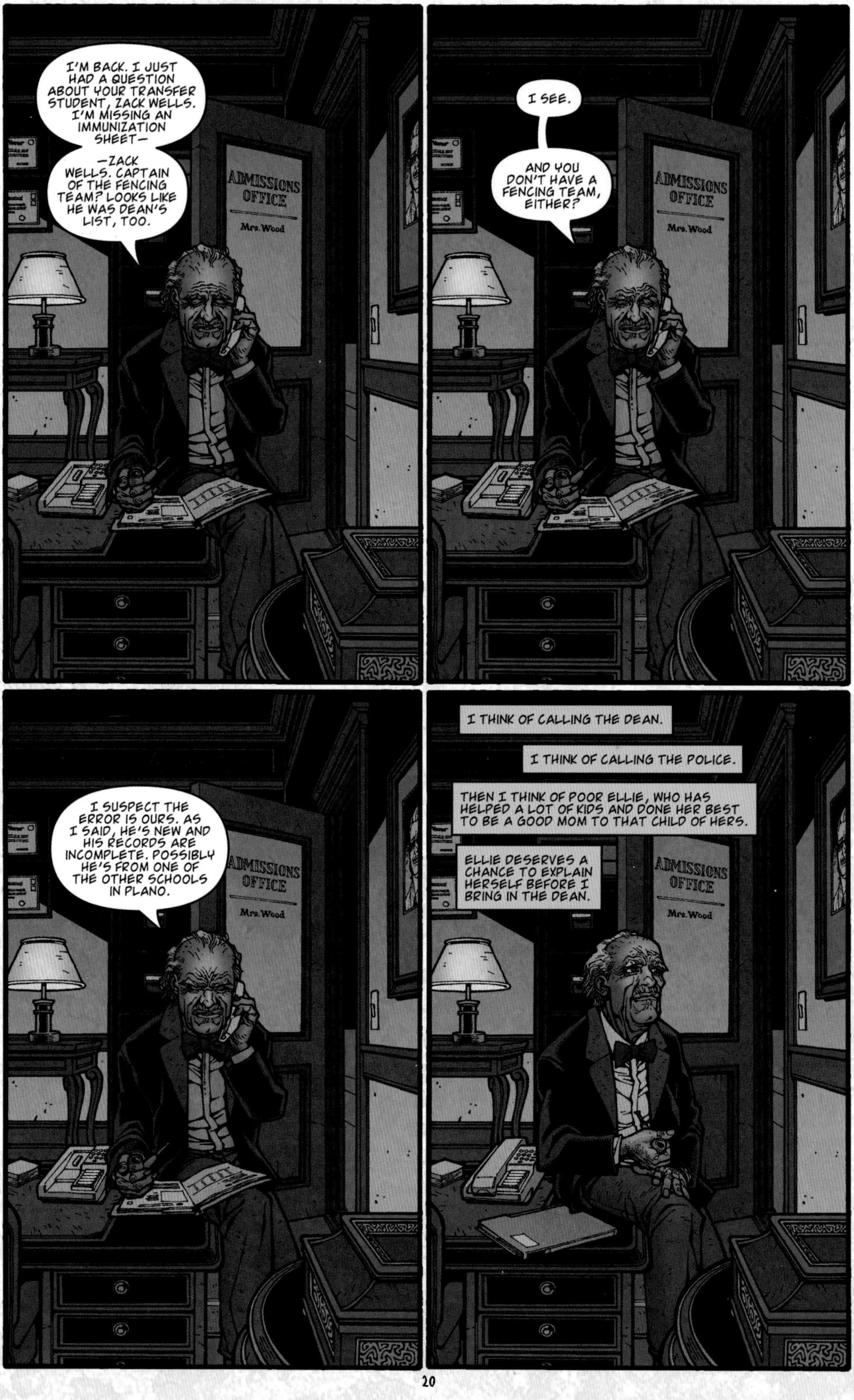
I'M BACK. I JUST HAD A QUESTION ABOUT YOUR TRANSFER STUDENT, ZACK WELLS. I'M MISSING AN IMMUNIZATION SHEET—
—ZACK WELLS. CAPTAIN OF THE FENCING TEAM? LOOKS LIKE HE WAS DEAN'S LIST, TOO.
ADMISSIONS OFFICE
Mrs. Wood
I SEE.
AND YOU DON'T HAVE A FENCING TEAM, EITHER?
I SUSPECT THE ERROR IS OURS. AS I SAID, HE'S NEW AND HIS RECORDS ARE INCOMPLETE. POSSIBLY HE'S FROM ONE OF THE OTHER SCHOOLS IN PLANO.
I THINK OF CALLING THE DEAN.
I THINK OF CALLING THE POLICE.
THEN I THINK OF POOR ELLIE, WHO HAS HELPED A LOT OF KIDS AND DONE HER BEST TO BE A GOOD MOM TO THAT CHILD OF HERS.
ELLIE DESERVES A CHANCE TO EXPLAIN HERSELF BEFORE I BRING IN THE DEAN.

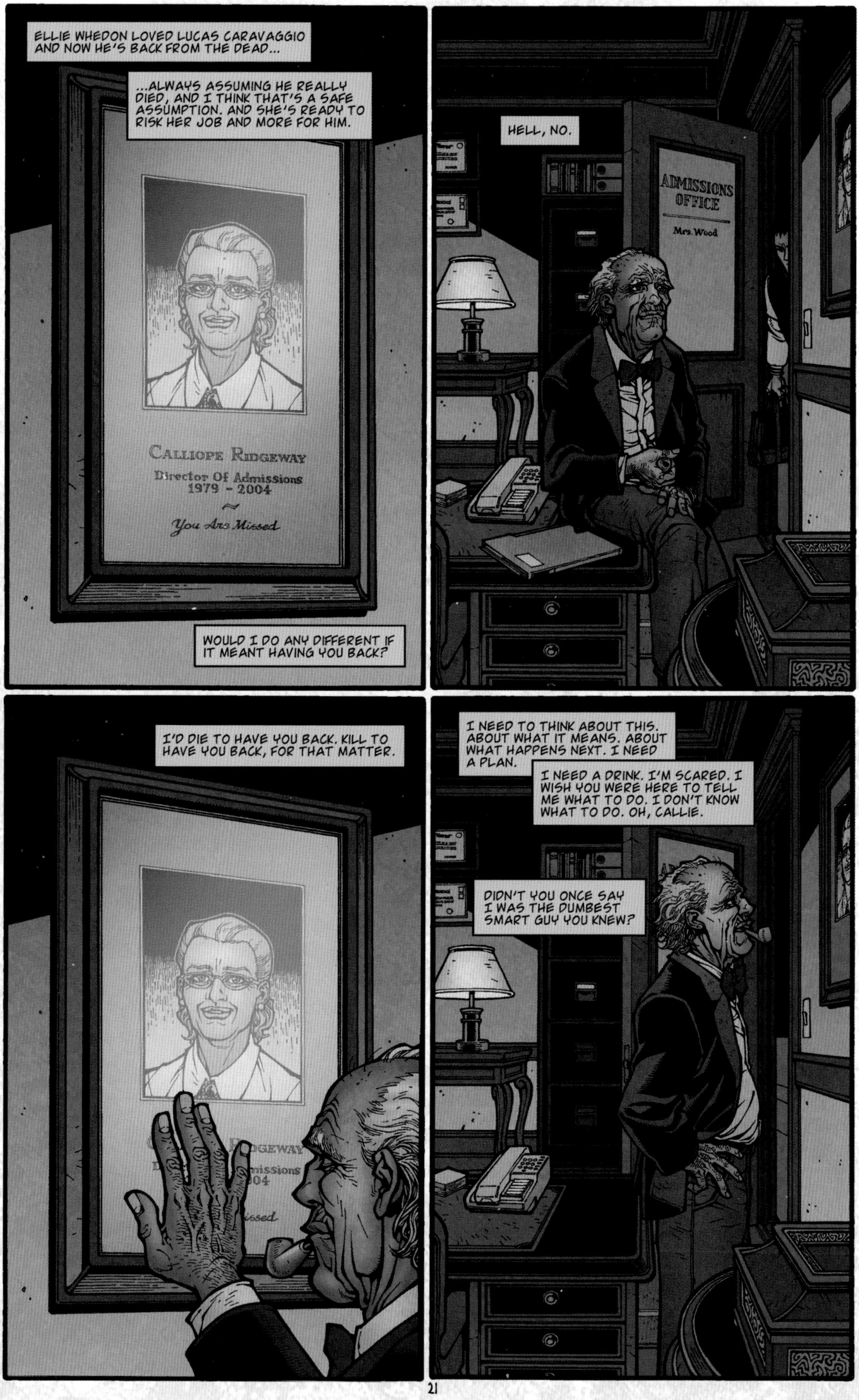
ELLIE WHEDON LOVED LUCAS CARAVAGGIO AND NOW HE'S BACK FROM THE DEAD...
...ALWAYS ASSUMING HE REALLY DIED, AND I THINK THAT'S A SAFE ASSUMPTION. AND SHE'S READY TO RISK HER JOB AND MORE FOR HIM.
CALLIOPE RIDGEWAY
Director Of Admissions
1979 - 2004
You Are Missed
WOULD I DO ANY DIFFERENT IF IT MEANT HAVING YOU BACK?
HELL, NO.
ADMISSIONS OFFICE
Mrs. Wood
I'D DIE TO HAVE YOU BACK. KILL TO HAVE YOU BACK, FOR THAT MATTER.
I NEED TO THINK ABOUT THIS. ABOUT WHAT IT MEANS. ABOUT WHAT HAPPENS NEXT. I NEED A PLAN.
I NEED A DRINK. I'M SCARED. I WISH YOU WERE HERE TO TELL ME WHAT TO DO. I DON'T KNOW WHAT TO DO. OH, CALLIE.
DIDN'T YOU ONCE SAY I WAS THE DUMBEST SMART GUY YOU KNEW?

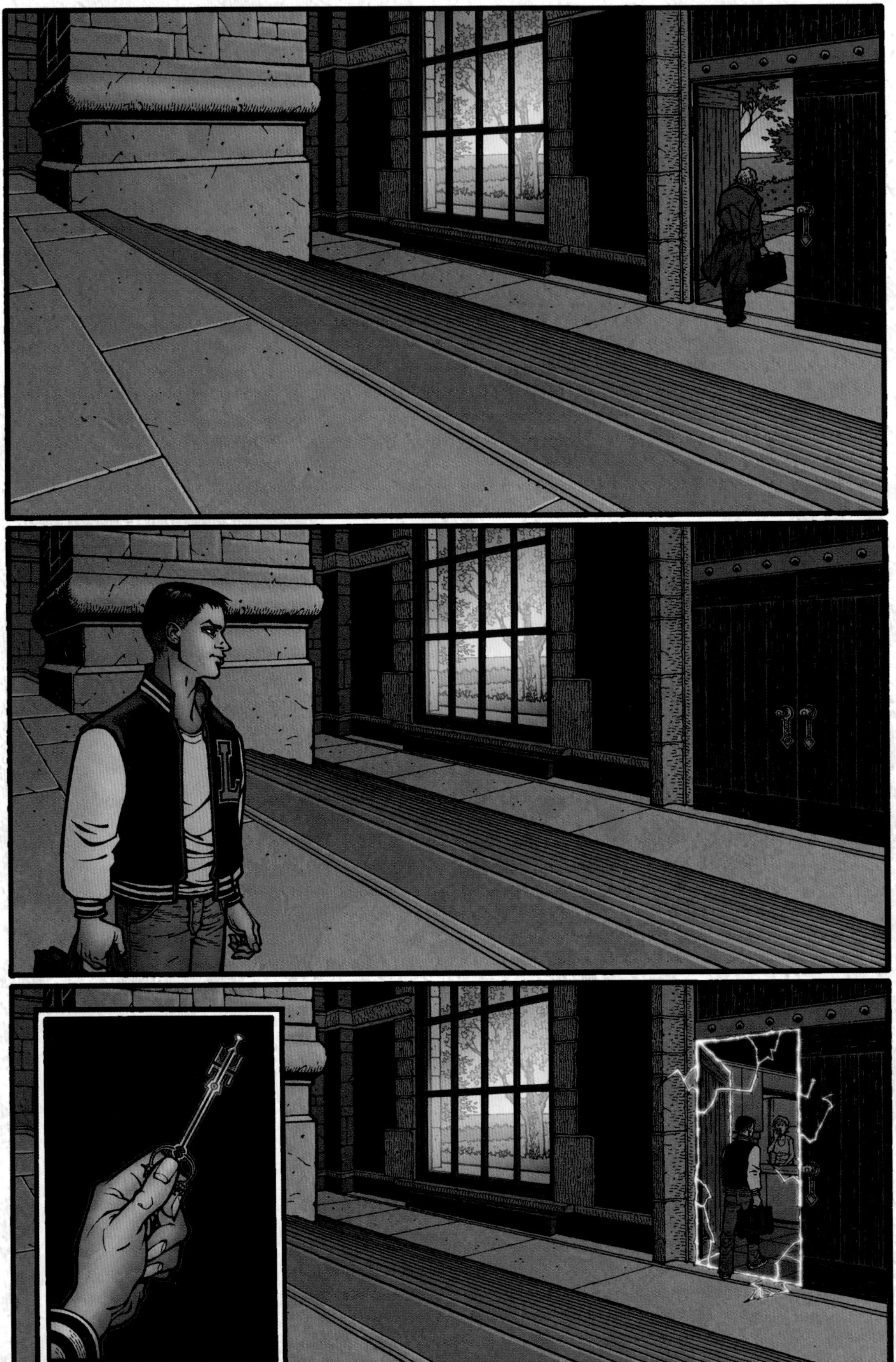

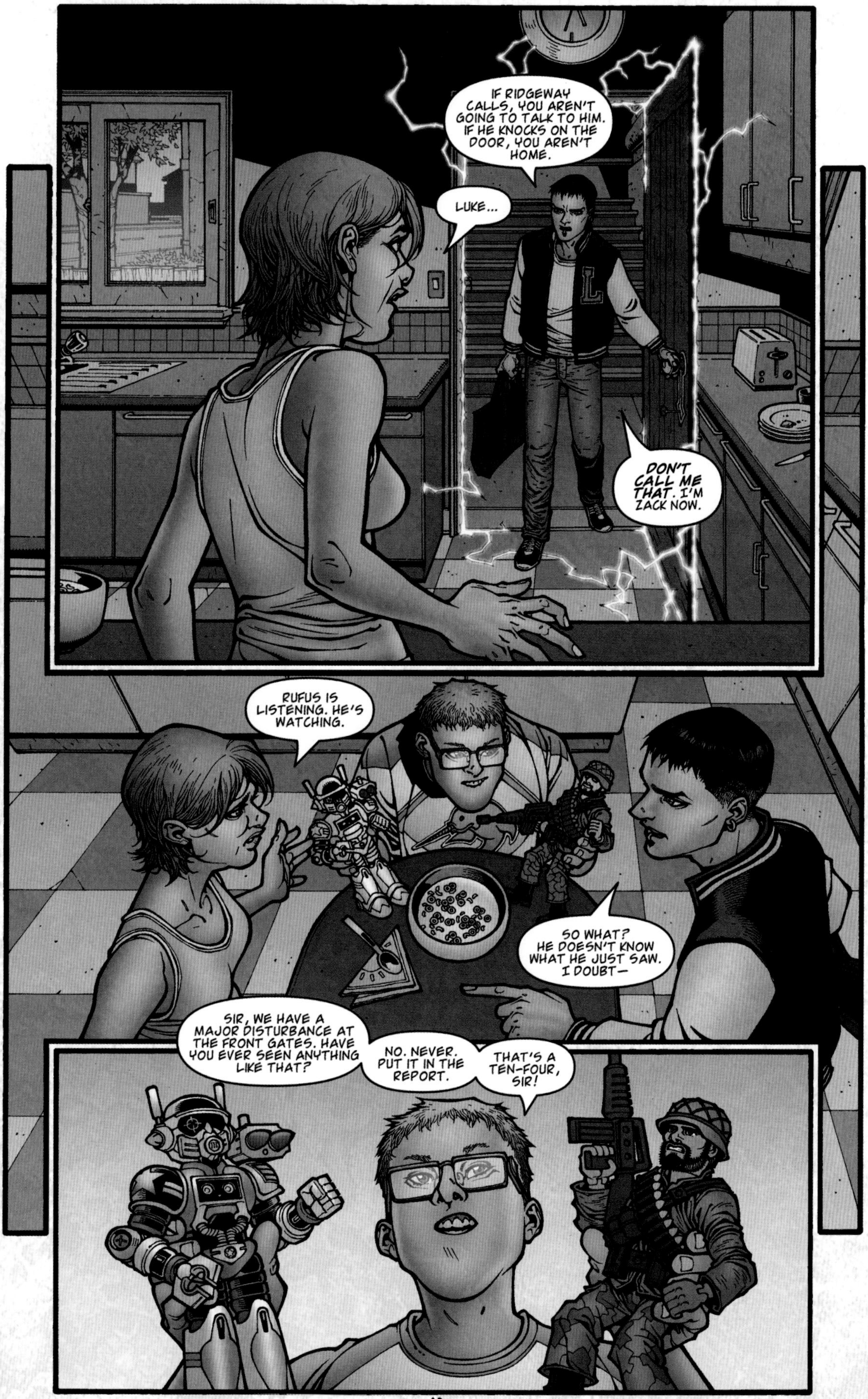

IF RIDGEWAY CALLS, YOU AREN'T GOING TO TALK TO HIM. IF HE KNOCKS ON THE DOOR, YOU AREN'T HOME.
LUKE...
DON'T CALL ME THAT. I'M ZACK NOW.
RUFUS IS LISTENING. HE'S WATCHING.
SO WHAT? HE DOESN'T KNOW WHAT HE JUST SAW. I DOUBT—
SIR, WE HAVE A MAJOR DISTURBANCE AT THE FRONT GATES. HAVE YOU EVER SEEN ANYTHING LIKE THAT?
NO. NEVER. PUT IT IN THE REPORT.
THAT'S A TEN-FOUR, SIR!

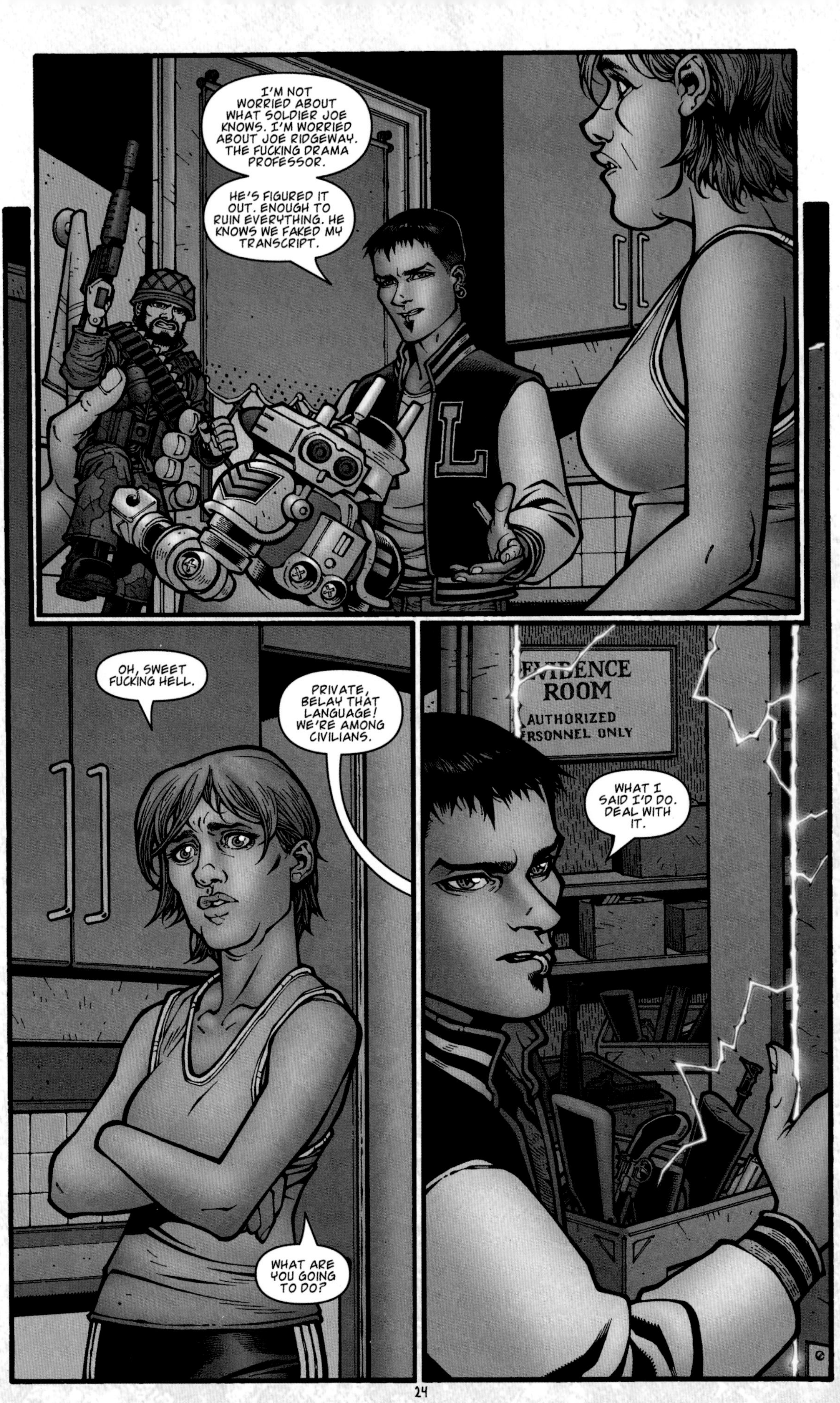
I'M NOT WORRIED ABOUT WHAT SOLDIER JOE KNOWS. I'M WORRIED ABOUT JOE RIDGEWAY. THE FUCKING DRAMA PROFESSOR.
HE'S FIGURED IT OUT. ENOUGH TO RUIN EVERYTHING. HE KNOWS WE FAKED MY TRANSCRIPT.
OH, SWEET FUCKING HELL.
PRIVATE, BELAY THAT LANGUAGE! WE'RE AMONG CIVILIANS.
WHAT ARE YOU GOING TO DO?
EVIDENCE ROOM
AUTHORIZED PERSONNEL ONLY
WHAT I SAID I'D DO. DEAL WITH IT.

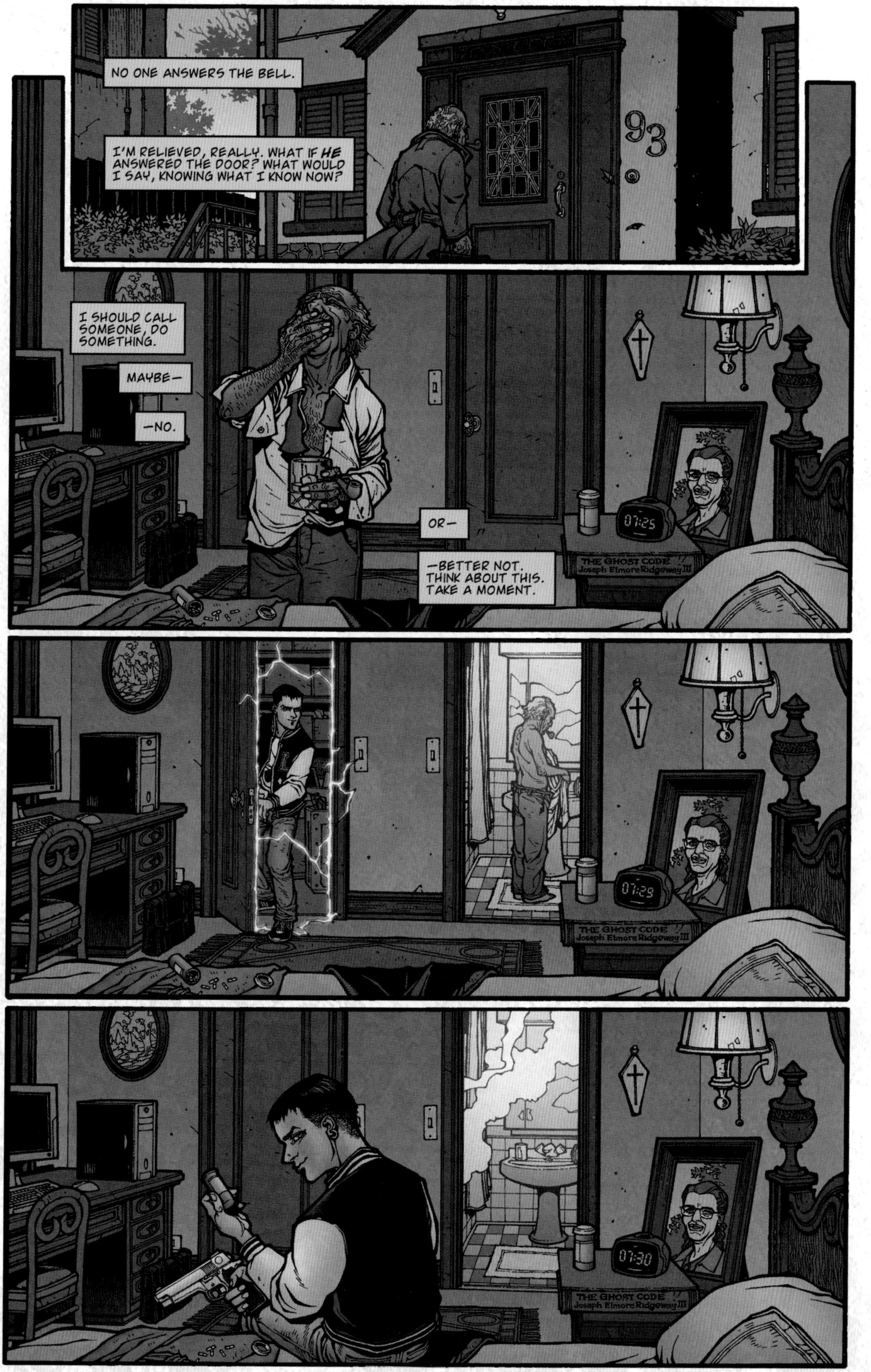
NO ONE ANSWERS THE BELL.
I'M RELIEVED, REALLY. WHAT IF HE ANSWERED THE DOOR? WHAT WOULD I SAY, KNOWING WHAT I KNOW NOW?
93
I SHOULD CALL SOMEONE, DO SOMETHING.
MAYBE—
—NO.
OR—
—BETTER NOT. THINK ABOUT THIS. TAKE A MOMENT.
07:25
THE GHOST CODE
Joseph Elmore Ridgeway III
07:29
THE GHOST CODE
Joseph Elmore Ridgeway III
07:30
THE GHOST CODE
Joseph Elmore Ridgeway III

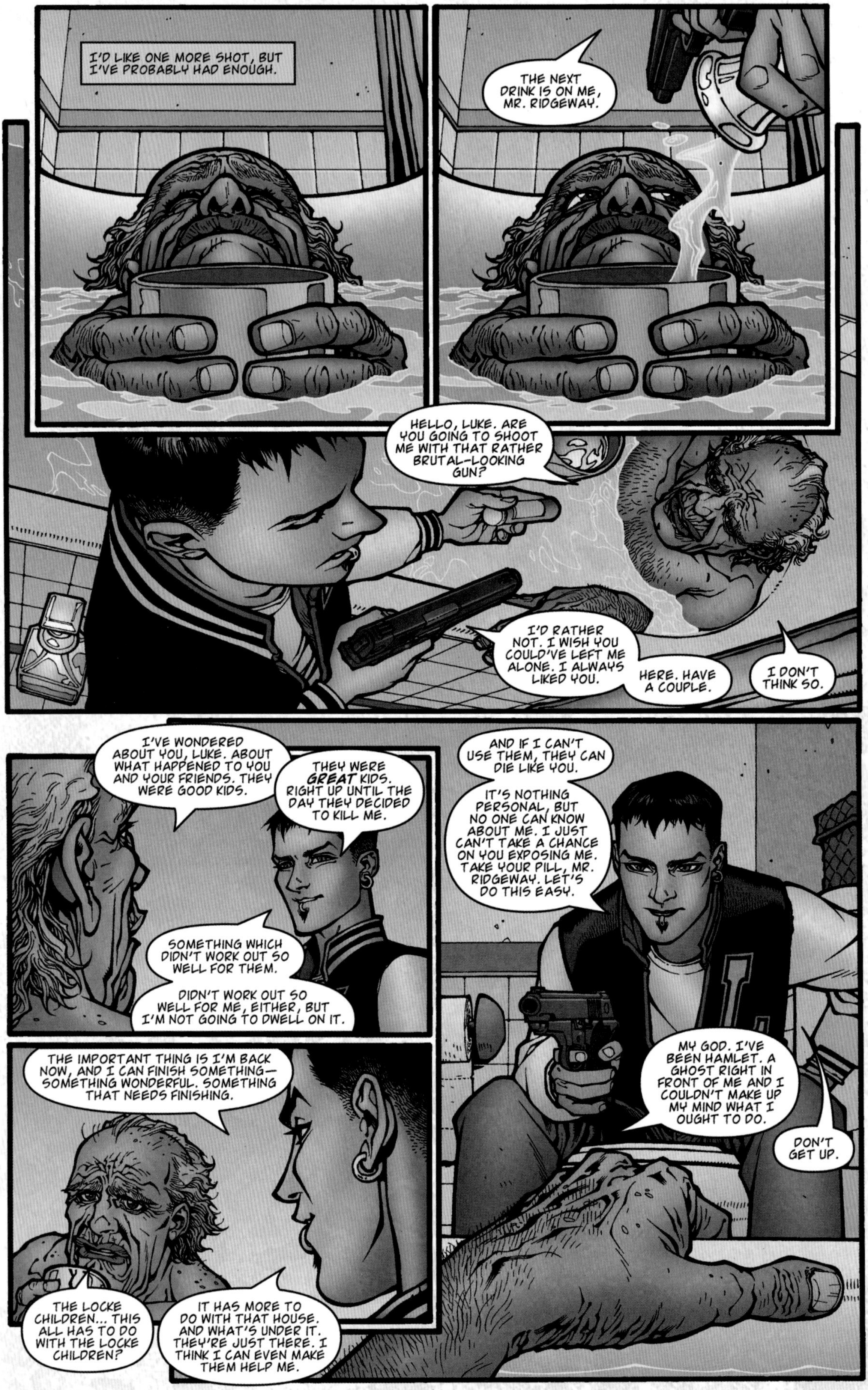
I'D LIKE ONE MORE SHOT, BUT I'VE PROBABLY HAD ENOUGH.
THE NEXT DRINK IS ON ME, MR. RIDGEWAY.
HELLO, LUKE. ARE YOU GOING TO SHOOT ME WITH THAT RATHER BRUTAL-LOOKING GUN?
I'D RATHER NOT. I WISH YOU COULD'VE LEFT ME ALONE. I ALWAYS LIKED YOU.
HERE. HAVE A COUPLE.
I DON'T THINK SO.
I'VE WONDERED ABOUT YOU, LUKE. ABOUT WHAT HAPPENED TO YOU AND YOUR FRIENDS. THEY WERE GOOD KIDS.
THEY WERE GREAT KIDS. RIGHT UP UNTIL THE DAY THEY DECIDED TO KILL ME.
SOMETHING WHICH DIDN'T WORK OUT SO WELL FOR THEM.
DIDN'T WORK OUT SO WELL FOR ME, EITHER, BUT I'M NOT GOING TO DWELL ON IT.
THE IMPORTANT THING IS I'M BACK NOW, AND I CAN FINISH SOMETHING— SOMETHING WONDERFUL. SOMETHING THAT NEEDS FINISHING.
THE LOCKE CHILDREN... THIS ALL HAS TO DO WITH THE LOCKE CHILDREN?
IT HAS MORE TO DO WITH THAT HOUSE. AND WHAT'S UNDER IT. THEY'RE JUST THERE. I THINK I CAN EVEN MAKE THEM HELP ME.
AND IF I CAN'T USE THEM, THEY CAN DIE LIKE YOU.
IT'S NOTHING PERSONAL, BUT NO ONE CAN KNOW ABOUT ME. I JUST CAN'T TAKE A CHANCE ON YOU EXPOSING ME. TAKE YOUR PILL, MR. RIDGEWAY. LET'S DO THIS EASY.
MY GOD. I'VE BEEN HAMLET. A GHOST RIGHT IN FRONT OF ME AND I COULDN'T MAKE UP MY MIND WHAT I OUGHT TO DO.
DON'T GET UP.

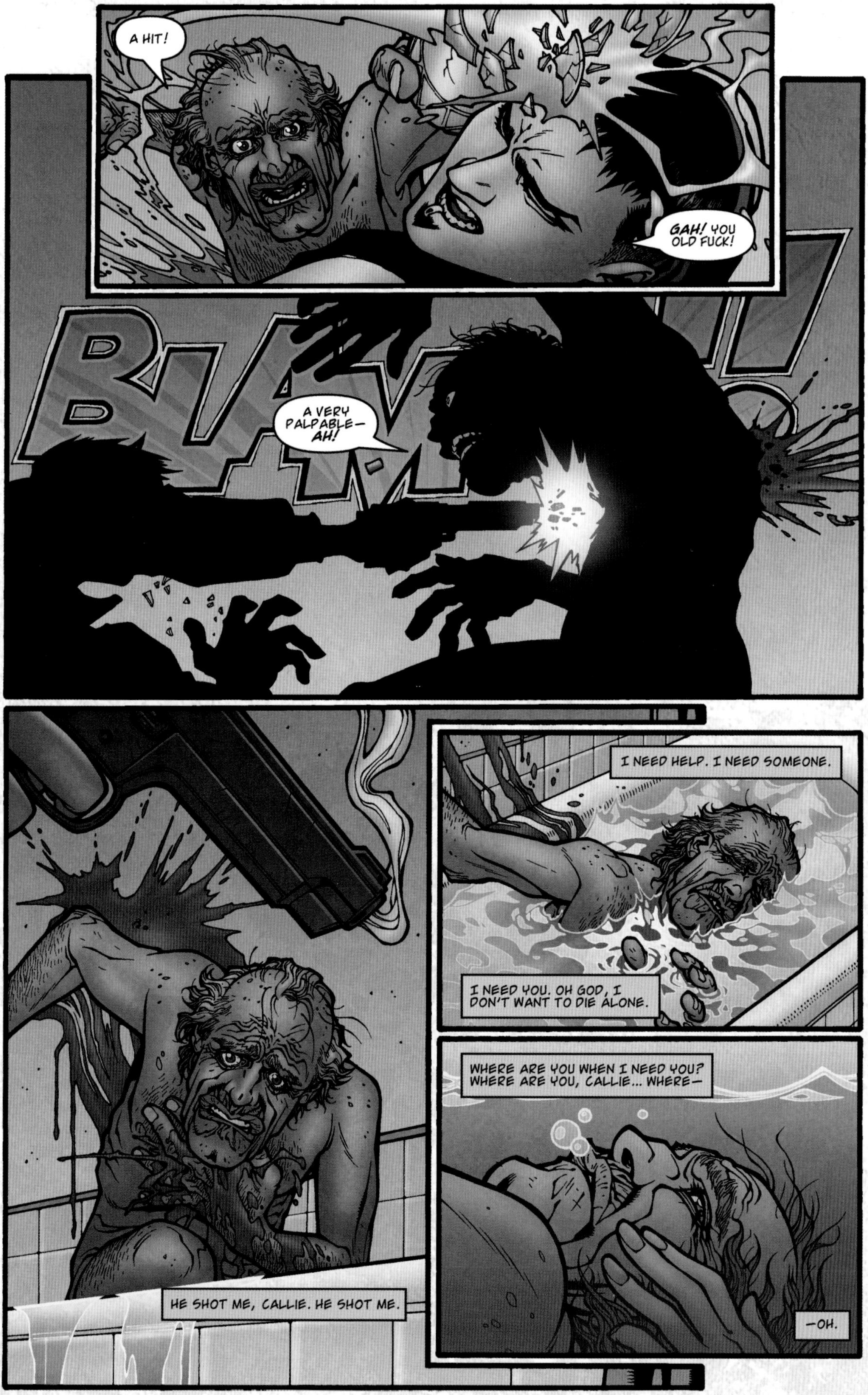

A HIT!
GAH! YOU OLD FUCK!
A VERY PALPABLE—AH!
HE SHOT ME, CALLIE. HE SHOT ME.
I NEED HELP. I NEED SOMEONE.
I NEED YOU. OH GOD, I DON'T WANT TO DIE ALONE.
WHERE ARE YOU WHEN I NEED YOU? WHERE ARE YOU, CALLIE... WHERE—
—OH.

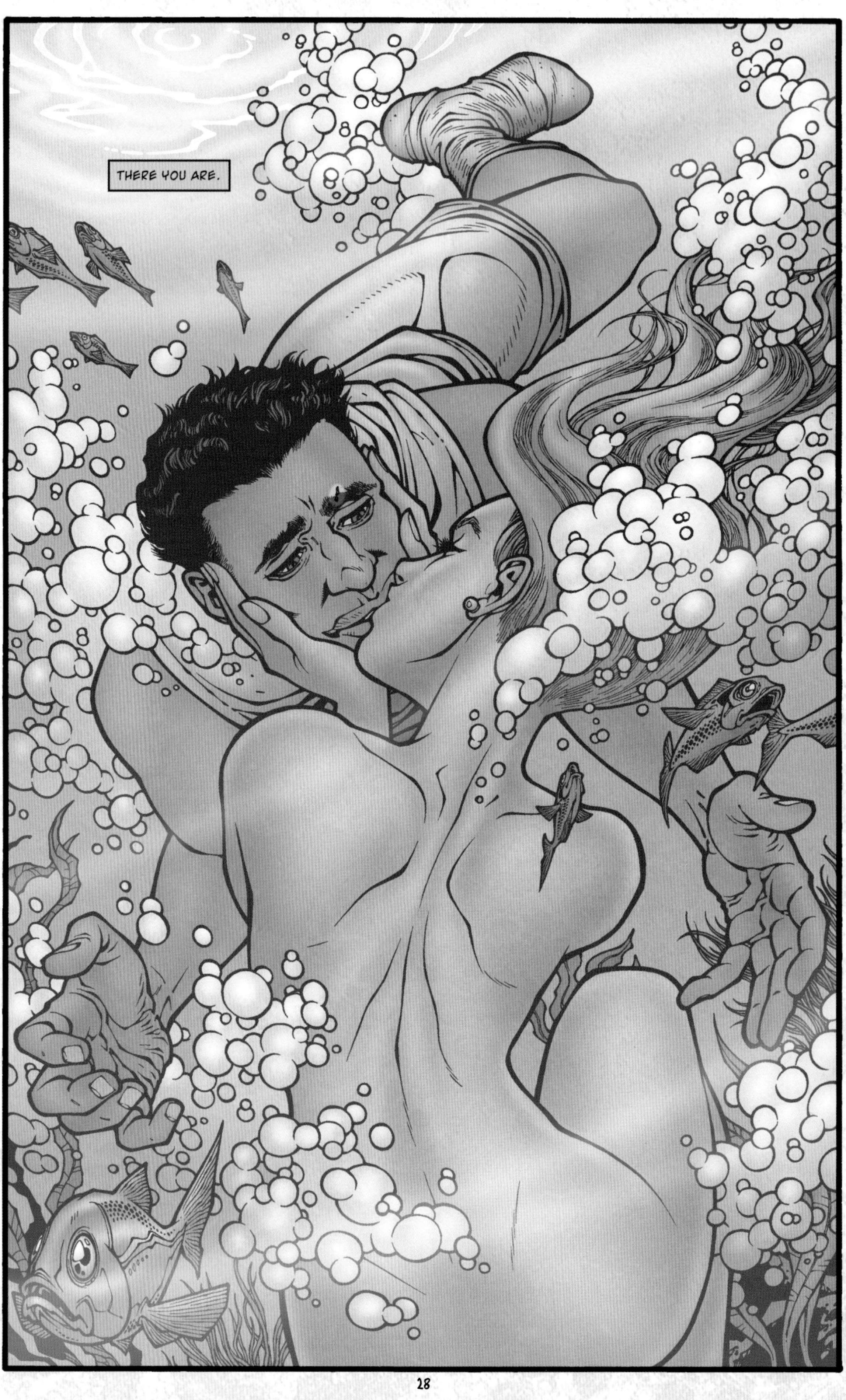
THERE YOU ARE.

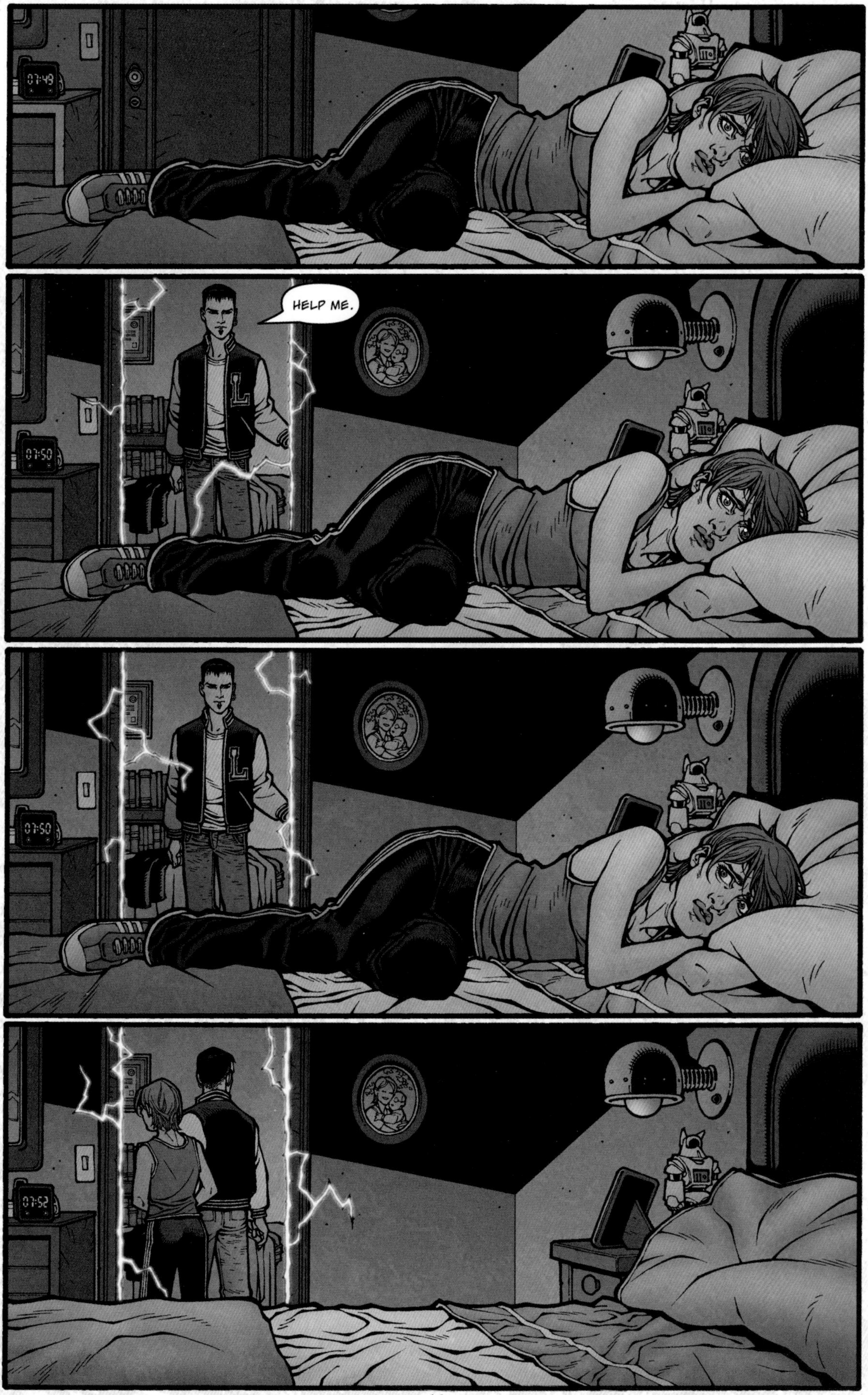
HELP ME.

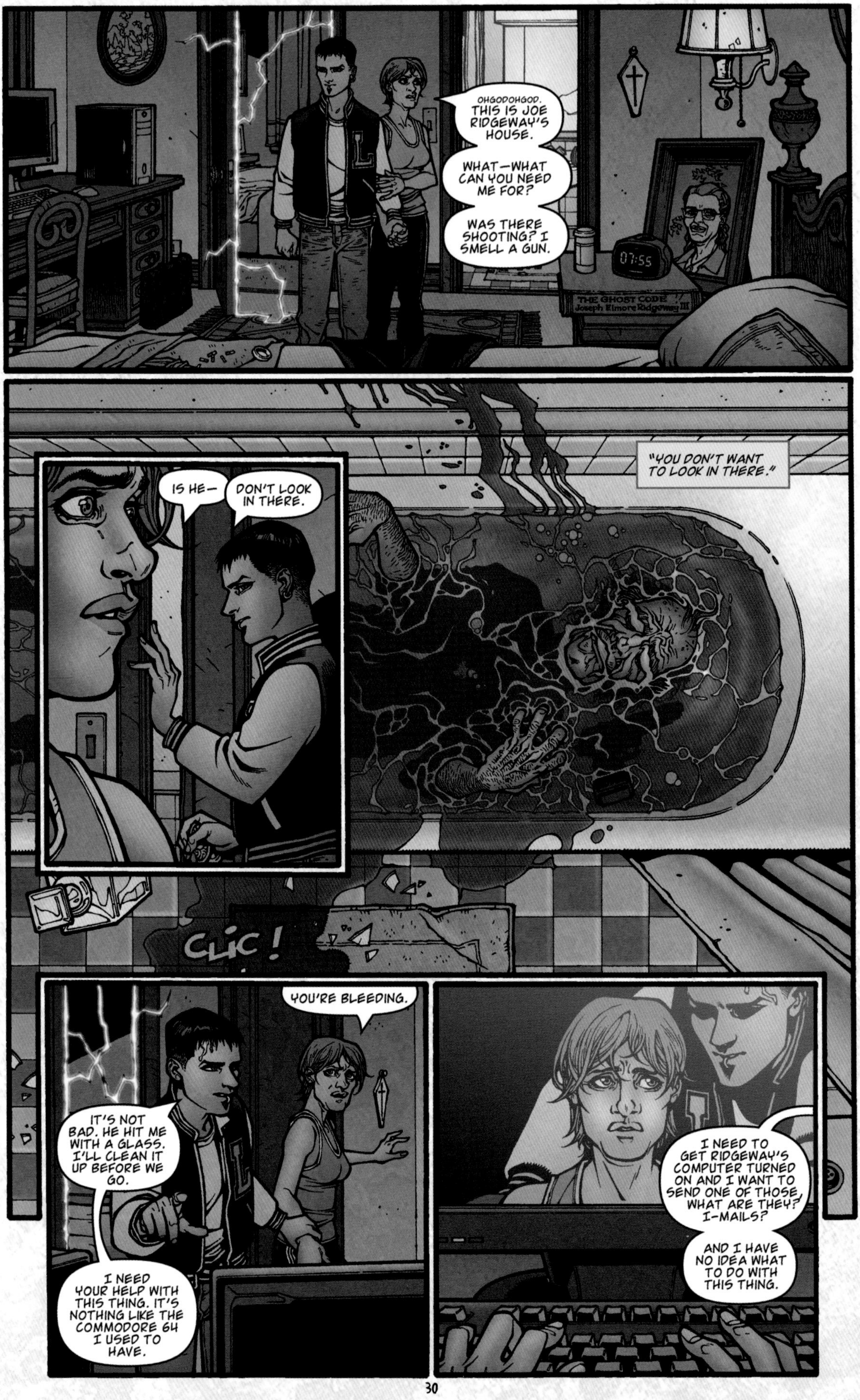
OHGODOHGOD. THIS IS JOE RIDGEWAY'S HOUSE.
WHAT—WHAT CAN YOU NEED ME FOR?
WAS THERE SHOOTING? I SMELL A GUN.
07:55
THE GHOST CODE Joseph Elmore Ridgeway III
"YOU DON'T WANT TO LOOK IN THERE."
IS HE—
DON'T LOOK IN THERE.
CLIC!
YOU'RE BLEEDING.
IT'S NOT BAD. HE HIT ME WITH A GLASS. I'LL CLEAN IT UP BEFORE WE GO.
I NEED YOUR HELP WITH THIS THING. IT'S NOTHING LIKE THE COMMODORE 64 I USED TO HAVE.
I NEED TO GET RIDGEWAY'S COMPUTER TURNED ON AND I WANT TO SEND ONE OF THOSE, WHAT ARE THEY? I-MAILS?
AND I HAVE NO IDEA WHAT TO DO WITH THIS THING.

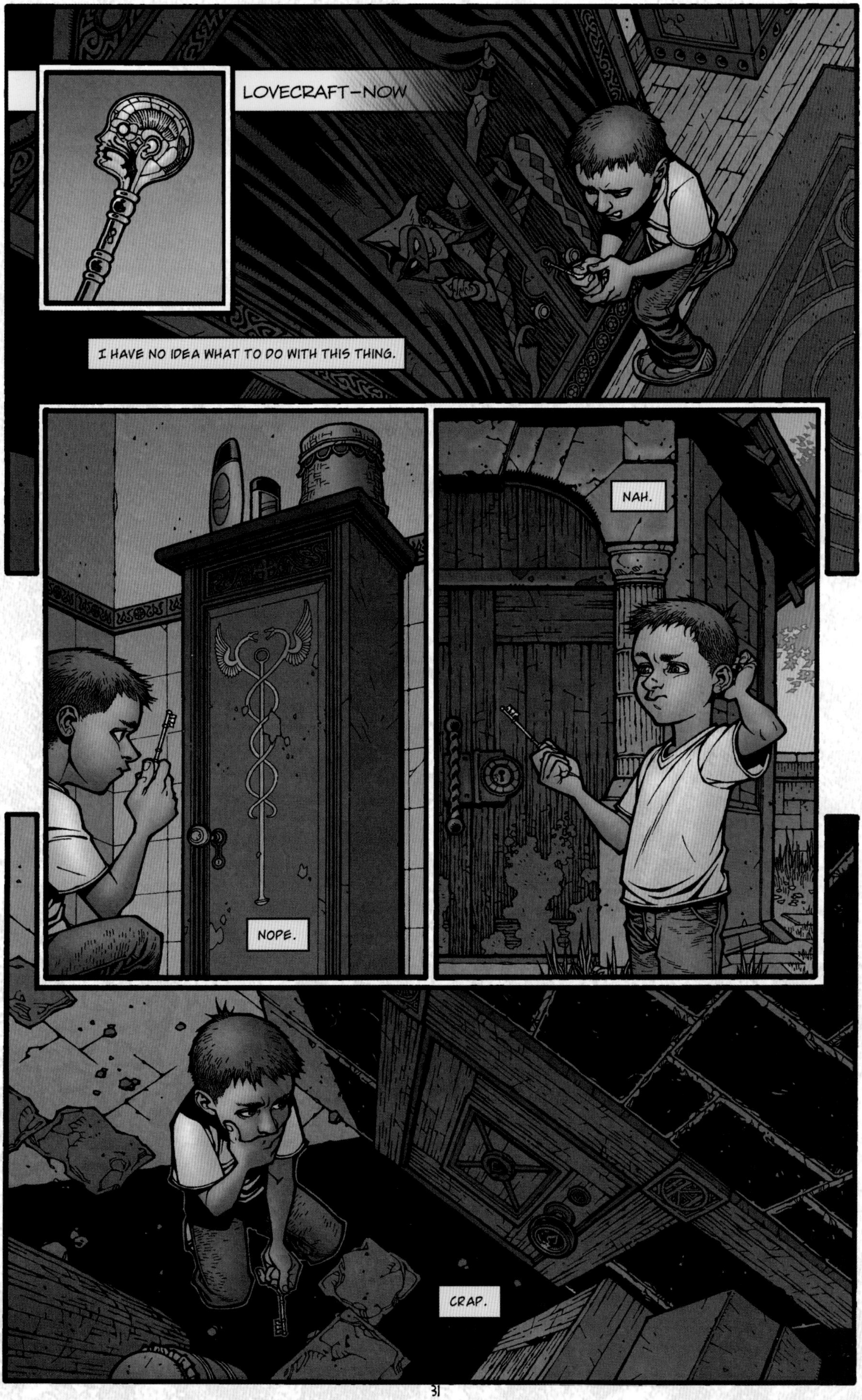
LOVECRAFT–NOW
I HAVE NO IDEA WHAT TO DO WITH THIS THING.
NOPE.
NAH.
CRAP.

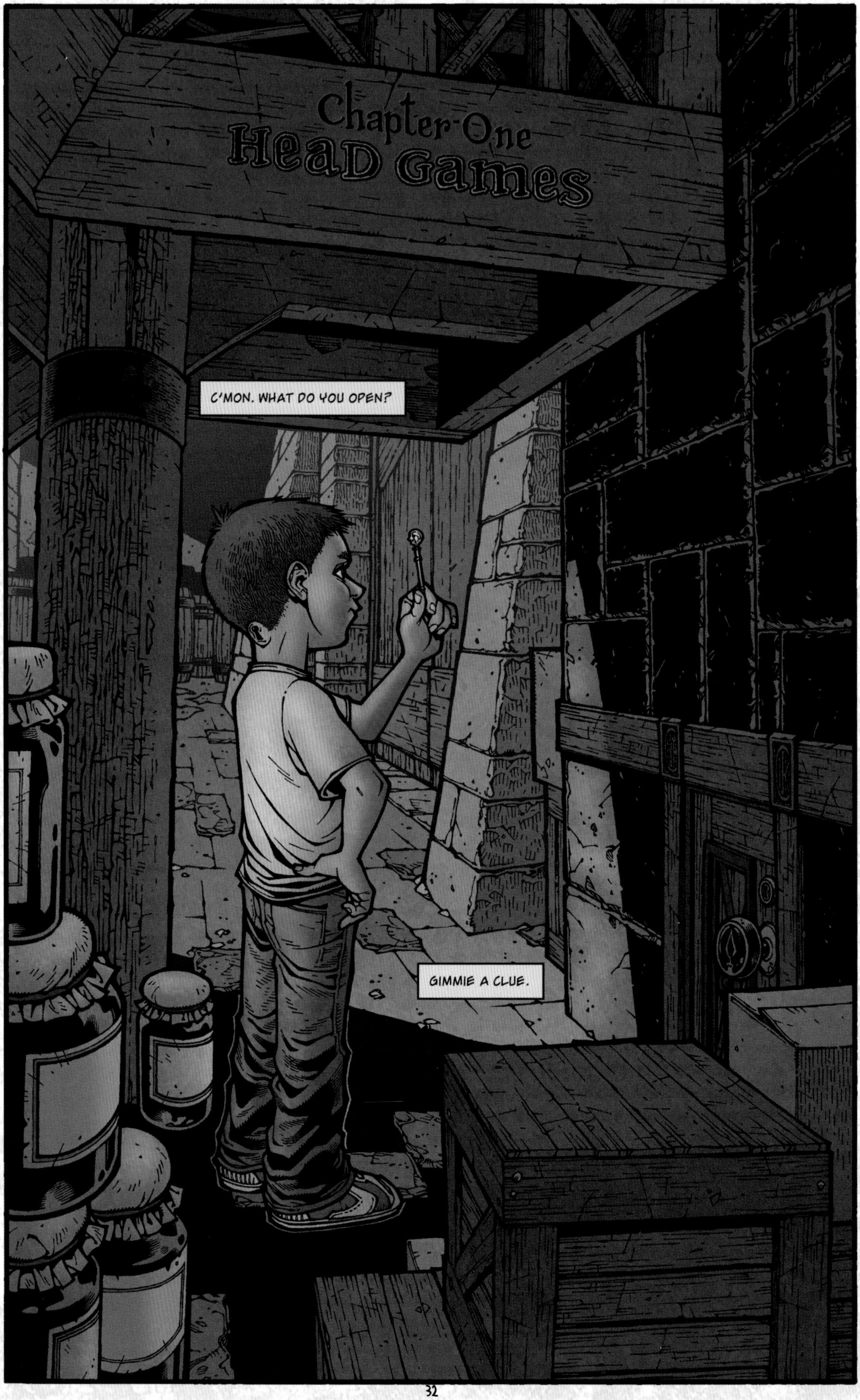
Chapter One
Head Games
C'MON. WHAT DO YOU OPEN?
GIMMIE A CLUE.

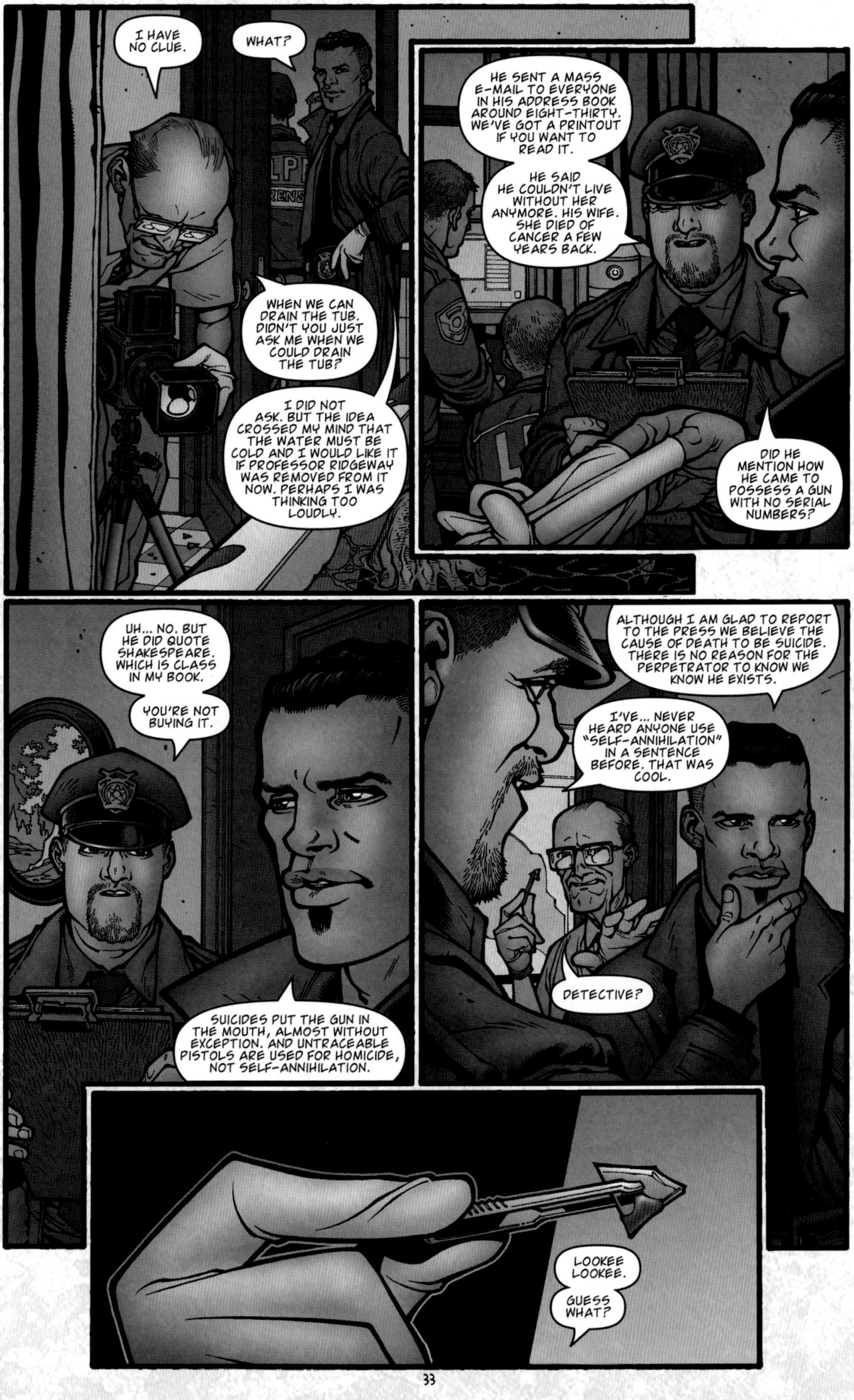
I HAVE NO CLUE.
WHAT?
WHEN WE CAN DRAIN THE TUB. DIDN'T YOU JUST ASK ME WHEN WE COULD DRAIN THE TUB?
I DID NOT ASK. BUT THE IDEA CROSSED MY MIND THAT THE WATER MUST BE COLD AND I WOULD LIKE IT IF PROFESSOR RIDGEWAY WAS REMOVED FROM IT NOW. PERHAPS I WAS THINKING TOO LOUDLY.
HE SENT A MASS E-MAIL TO EVERYONE IN HIS ADDRESS BOOK AROUND EIGHT-THIRTY. WE'VE GOT A PRINTOUT IF YOU WANT TO READ IT.
HE SAID HE COULDN'T LIVE WITHOUT HER ANYMORE. HIS WIFE. SHE DIED OF CANCER A FEW YEARS BACK.
DID HE MENTION HOW HE CAME TO POSSESS A GUN WITH NO SERIAL NUMBERS?
UH... NO. BUT HE DID QUOTE SHAKESPEARE. WHICH IS CLASS IN MY BOOK.
YOU'RE NOT BUYING IT.
SUICIDES PUT THE GUN IN THE MOUTH, ALMOST WITHOUT EXCEPTION. AND UNTRACEABLE PISTOLS ARE USED FOR HOMICIDE, NOT SELF-ANNIHILATION.
ALTHOUGH I AM GLAD TO REPORT TO THE PRESS WE BELIEVE THE CAUSE OF DEATH TO BE SUICIDE. THERE IS NO REASON FOR THE PERPETRATOR TO KNOW WE KNOW HE EXISTS.
I'VE... NEVER HEARD ANYONE USE "SELF-ANNIHILATION" IN A SENTENCE BEFORE. THAT WAS COOL.
DETECTIVE?
LOOKEE LOOKEE.
GUESS WHAT?

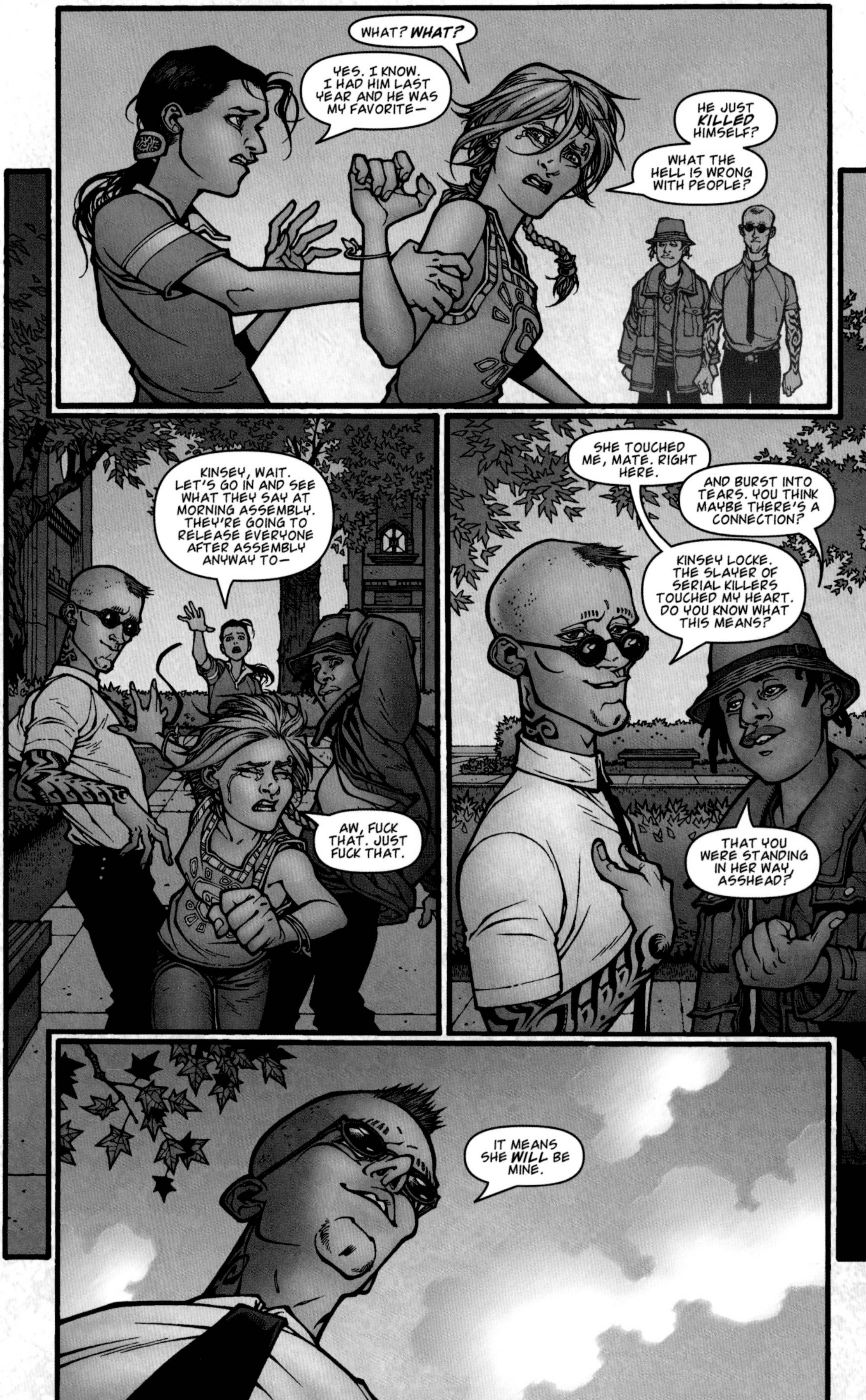
WHAT? WHAT?
YES. I KNOW. I HAD HIM LAST YEAR AND HE WAS MY FAVORITE—
HE JUST KILLED HIMSELF?
WHAT THE HELL IS WRONG WITH PEOPLE?
KINSEY, WAIT. LET'S GO IN AND SEE WHAT THEY SAY AT MORNING ASSEMBLY. THEY'RE GOING TO RELEASE EVERYONE AFTER ASSEMBLY ANYWAY TO—
AW, FUCK THAT. JUST FUCK THAT.
SHE TOUCHED ME, MATE. RIGHT HERE.
AND BURST INTO TEARS. YOU THINK MAYBE THERE'S A CONNECTION?
KINSEY LOCKE. THE SLAYER OF SERIAL KILLERS TOUCHED MY HEART. DO YOU KNOW WHAT THIS MEANS?
THAT YOU WERE STANDING IN HER WAY, ASSHEAD?
IT MEANS SHE WILL BE MINE.

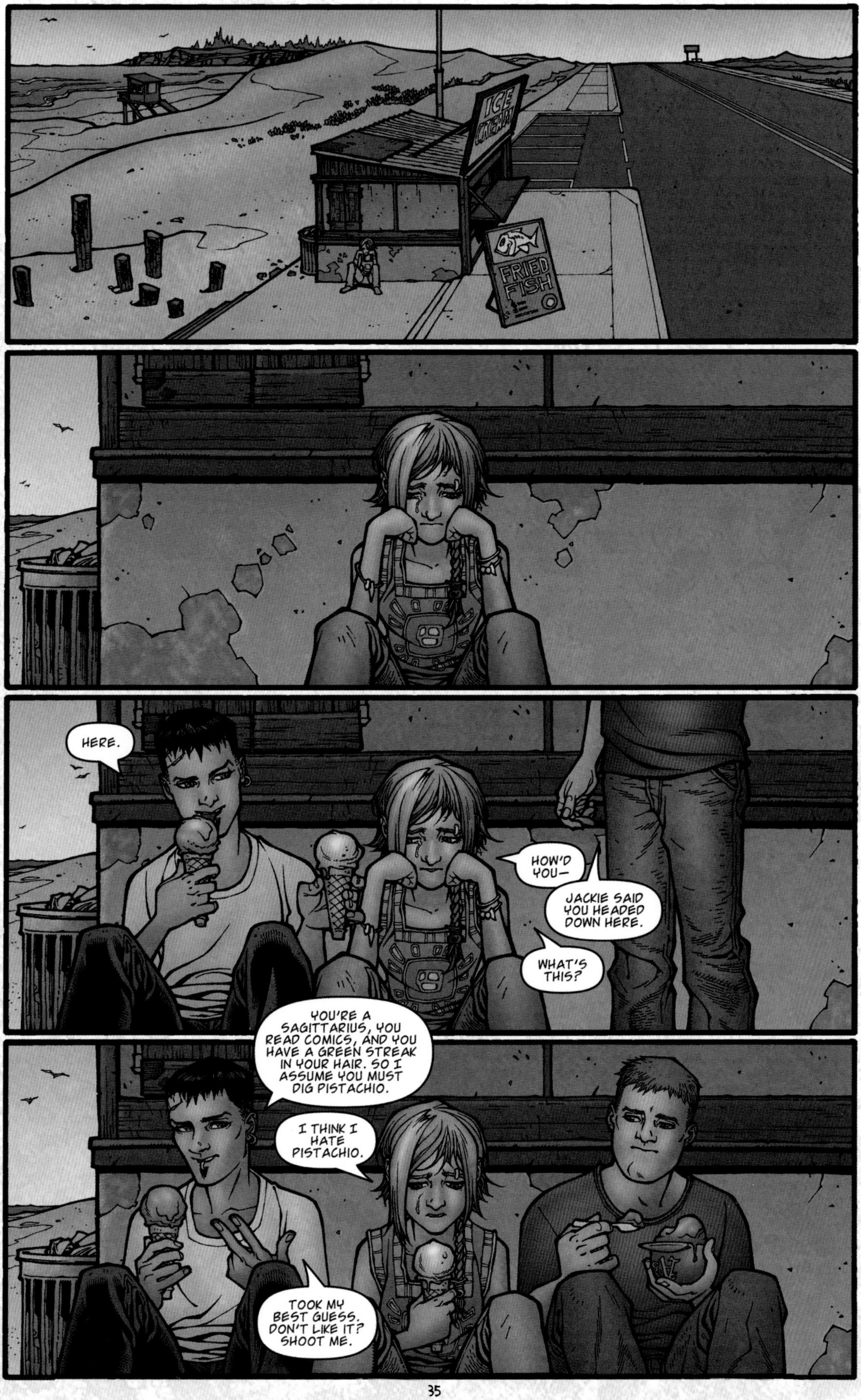
ICE CREAM
FRIED FISH
HERE.
HOW'D YOU—
JACKIE SAID YOU HEADED DOWN HERE.
WHAT'S THIS?
YOU'RE A SAGITTARIUS, YOU READ COMICS, AND YOU HAVE A GREEN STREAK IN YOUR HAIR. SO I ASSUME YOU MUST DIG PISTACHIO.
I THINK I HATE PISTACHIO.
TOOK MY BEST GUESS. DON'T LIKE IT? SHOOT ME.

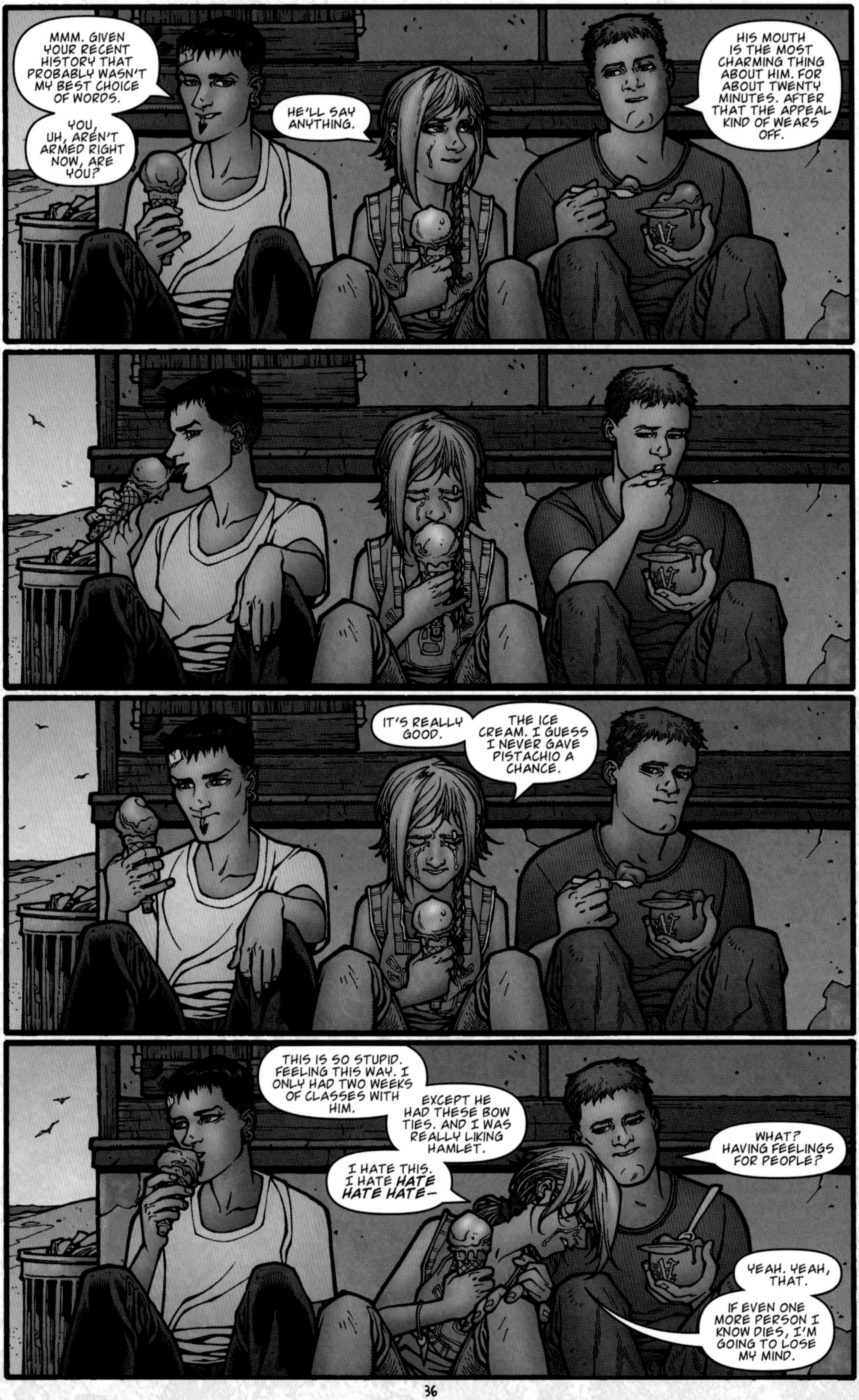
MMM. GIVEN YOUR RECENT HISTORY THAT PROBABLY WASN'T MY BEST CHOICE OF WORDS.
YOU, UH, AREN'T ARMED RIGHT NOW, ARE YOU?
HE'LL SAY ANYTHING.
HIS MOUTH IS THE MOST CHARMING THING ABOUT HIM. FOR ABOUT TWENTY MINUTES. AFTER THAT THE APPEAL KIND OF WEARS OFF.
IT'S REALLY GOOD.
THE ICE CREAM. I GUESS I NEVER GAVE PISTACHIO A CHANCE.
THIS IS SO STUPID. FEELING THIS WAY. I ONLY HAD TWO WEEKS OF CLASSES WITH HIM.
EXCEPT HE HAD THESE BOW TIES. AND I WAS REALLY LIKING HAMLET.
I HATE THIS. I HATE ***HATE HATE HATE***—
WHAT? HAVING FEELINGS FOR PEOPLE?
YEAH. YEAH, THAT.
IF EVEN ONE MORE PERSON I KNOW DIES, I'M GOING TO LOSE MY MIND.

IF YOU DON'T UNLOCK SOMETHING SOON, I'M GOING TO LOSE MY MIND.

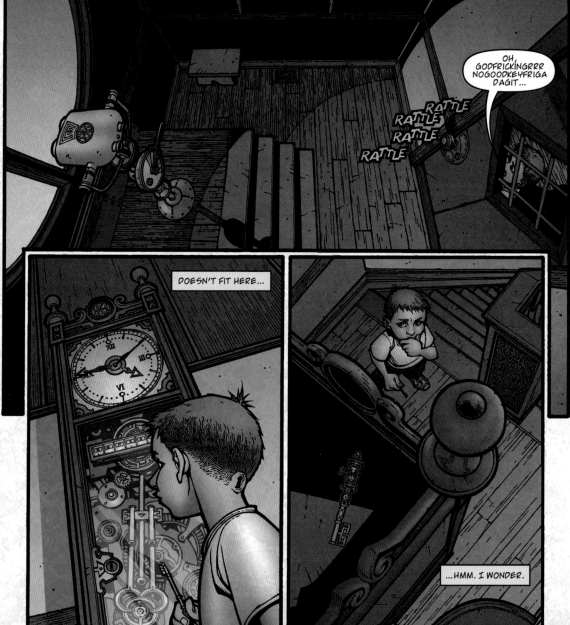

OH, GODFRICKINGRRR NOGOODKEYFRIGA DAGIT...

RATTLE
RATTLE
RATTLE
RATTLE

DOESN'T FIT HERE...

...HMM. I WONDER.

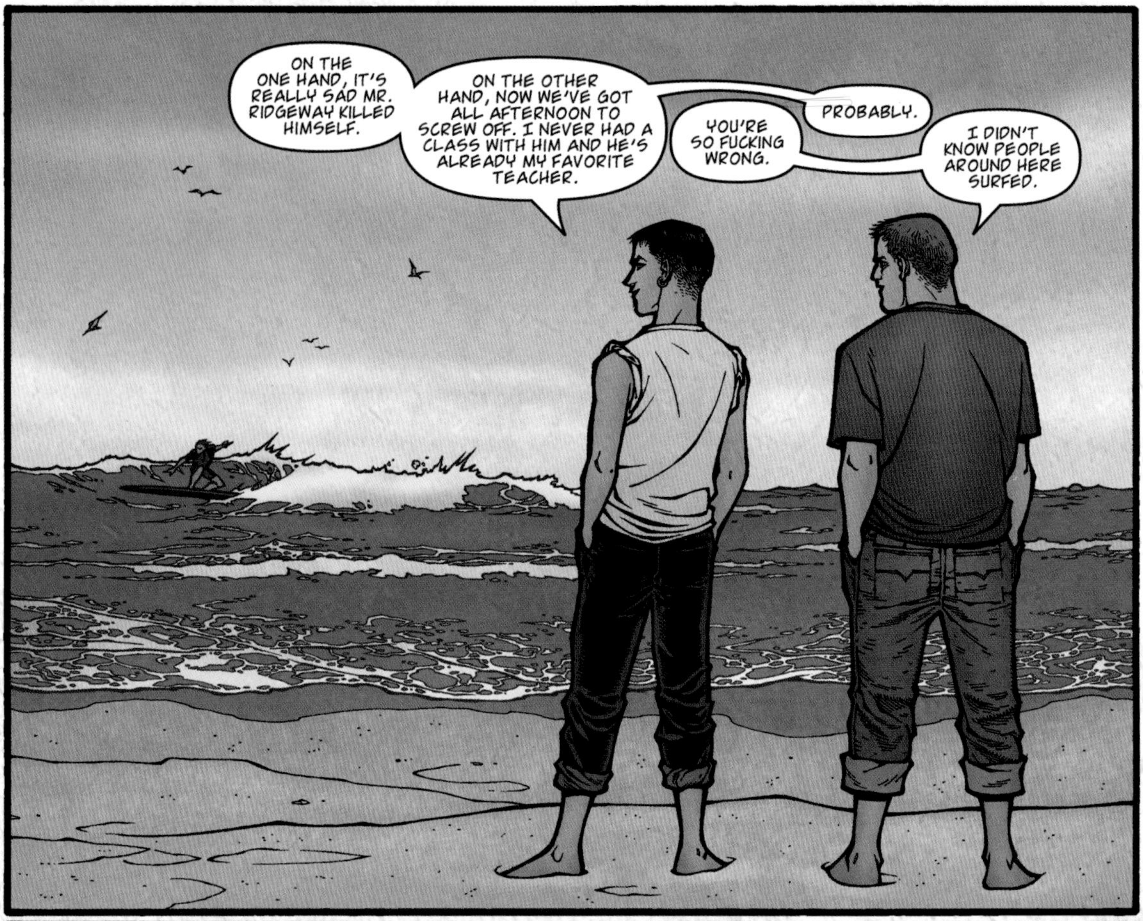
ON THE ONE HAND, IT'S REALLY SAD MR. RIDGEWAY KILLED HIMSELF.
ON THE OTHER HAND, NOW WE'VE GOT ALL AFTERNOON TO SCREW OFF. I NEVER HAD A CLASS WITH HIM AND HE'S ALREADY MY FAVORITE TEACHER.
YOU'RE SO FUCKING WRONG.
PROBABLY.
I DIDN'T KNOW PEOPLE AROUND HERE SURFED.

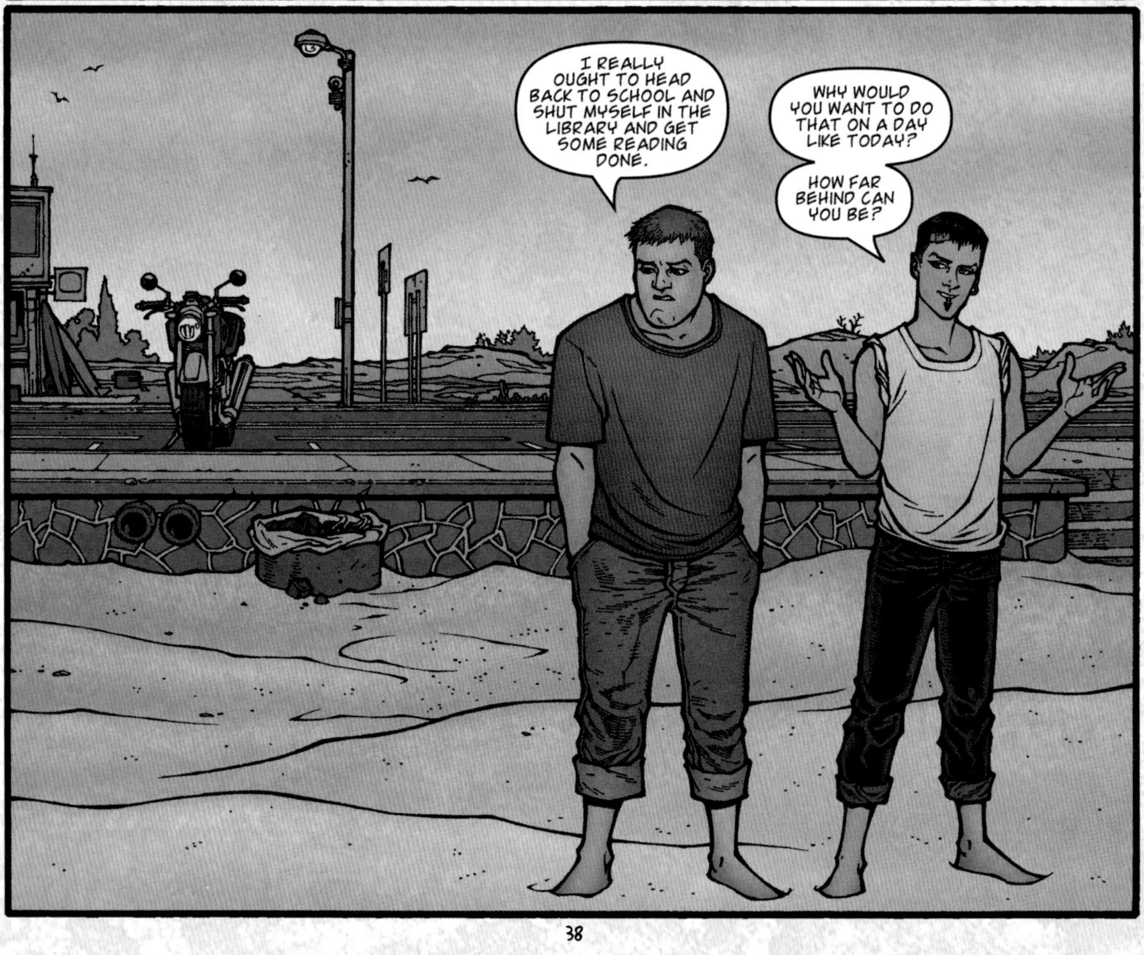
I REALLY OUGHT TO HEAD BACK TO SCHOOL AND SHUT MYSELF IN THE LIBRARY AND GET SOME READING DONE.
WHY WOULD YOU WANT TO DO THAT ON A DAY LIKE TODAY?
HOW FAR BEHIND CAN YOU BE?

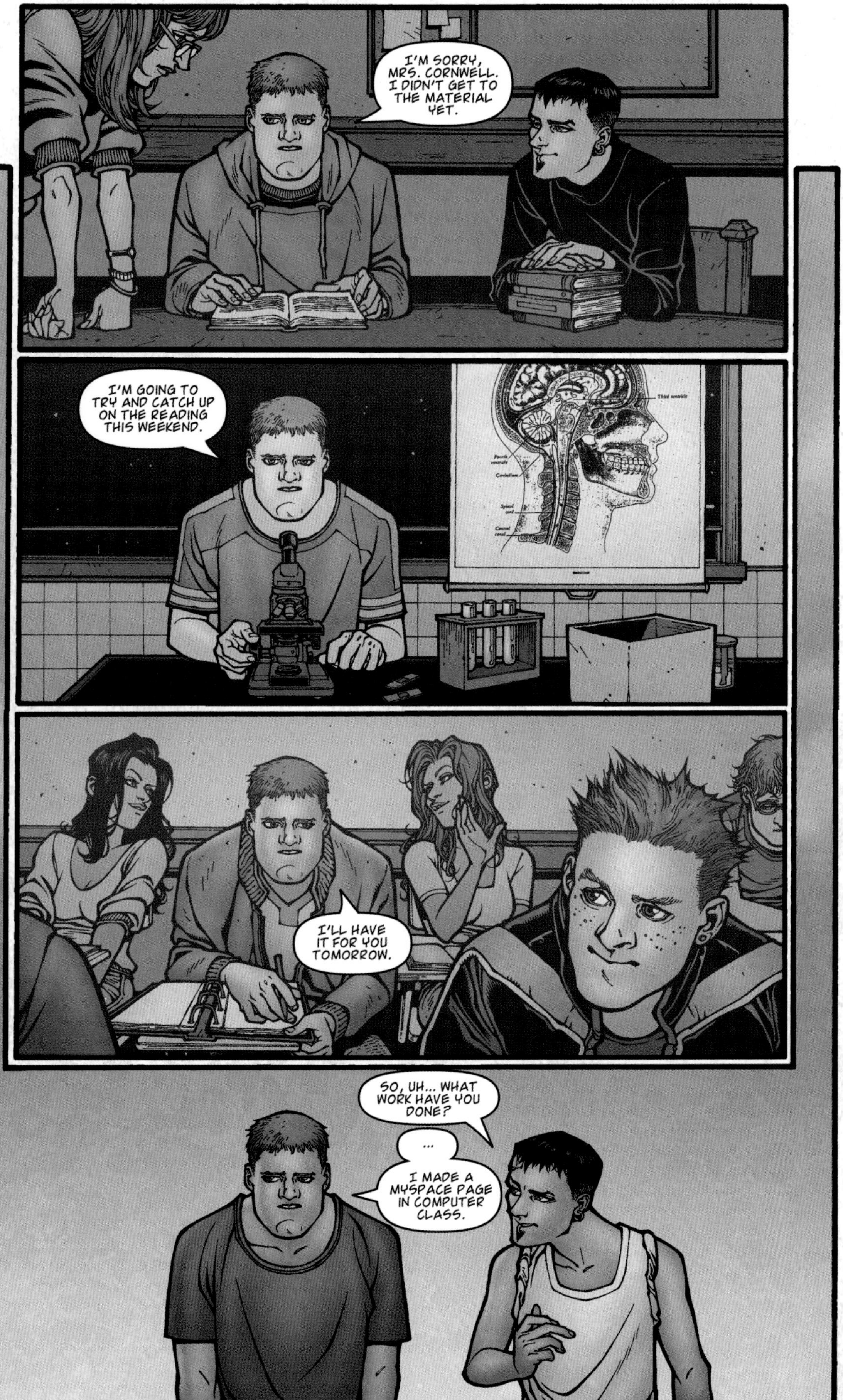

I'M SORRY, MRS. CORNWELL. I DIDN'T GET TO THE MATERIAL YET.
I'M GOING TO TRY AND CATCH UP ON THE READING THIS WEEKEND.
Third ventricle
Fourth ventricle
Cerebellum
Spinal cord
Central canal
I'LL HAVE IT FOR YOU TOMORROW.
SO, UH... WHAT WORK HAVE YOU DONE?
...
I MADE A MYSPACE PAGE IN COMPUTER CLASS.

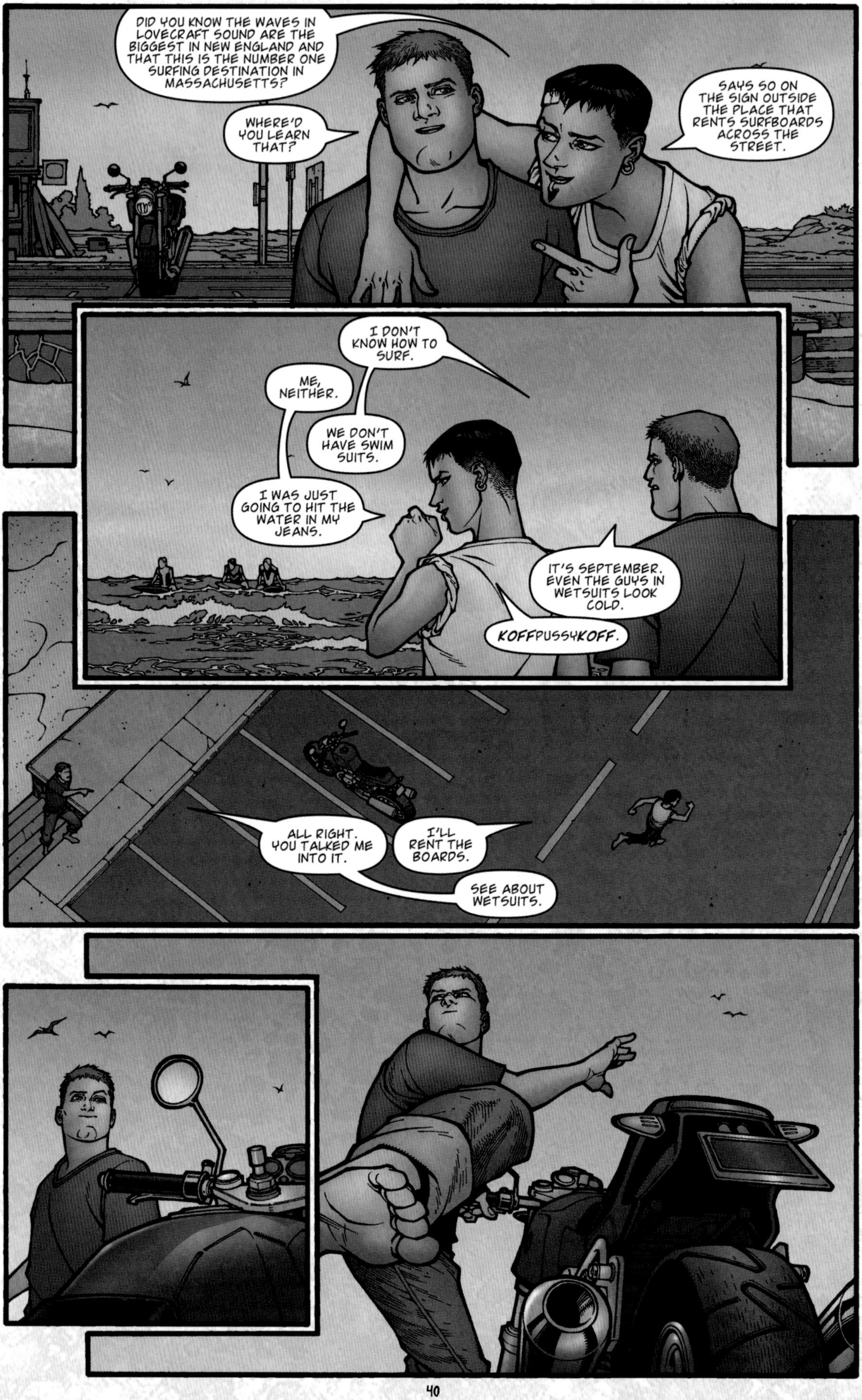
DID YOU KNOW THE WAVES IN LOVECRAFT SOUND ARE THE BIGGEST IN NEW ENGLAND AND THAT THIS IS THE NUMBER ONE SURFING DESTINATION IN MASSACHUSETTS?
WHERE'D YOU LEARN THAT?
SAYS SO ON THE SIGN OUTSIDE THE PLACE THAT RENTS SURFBOARDS ACROSS THE STREET.
I DON'T KNOW HOW TO SURF.
ME, NEITHER.
WE DON'T HAVE SWIM SUITS.
I WAS JUST GOING TO HIT THE WATER IN MY JEANS.
IT'S SEPTEMBER. EVEN THE GUYS IN WETSUITS LOOK COLD.
KOFFPUSSYKOFF.
ALL RIGHT. YOU TALKED ME INTO IT.
I'LL RENT THE BOARDS.
SEE ABOUT WETSUITS.

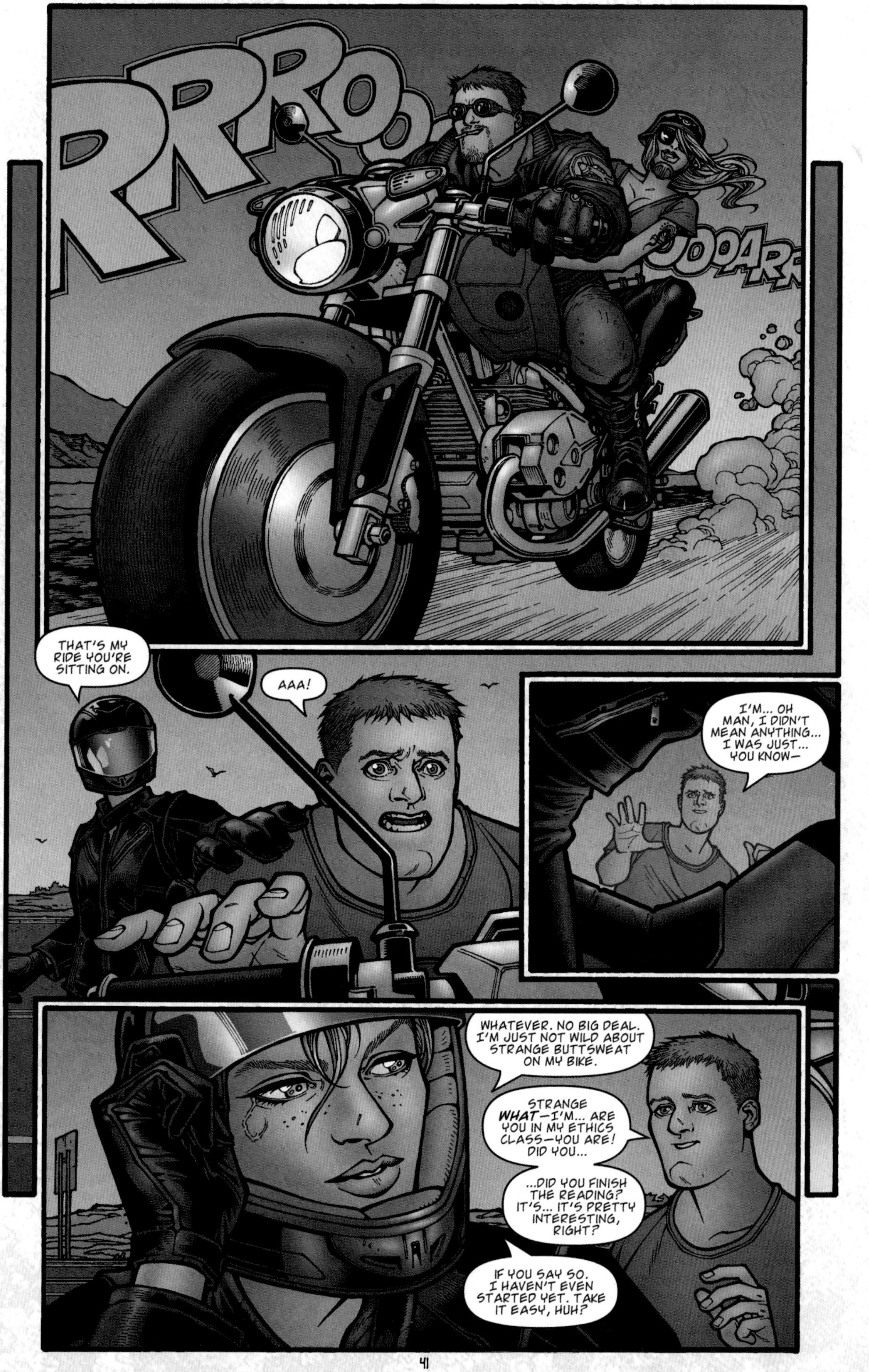
RRROOO
UOOOARR
THAT'S MY RIDE YOU'RE SITTING ON.
AAA!
I'M... OH MAN, I DIDN'T MEAN ANYTHING... I WAS JUST... YOU KNOW—
WHATEVER. NO BIG DEAL. I'M JUST NOT WILD ABOUT STRANGE BUTTSWEAT ON MY BIKE.
STRANGE ***WHAT***—I'M... ARE YOU IN MY ETHICS CLASS—YOU ARE! DID YOU...
...DID YOU FINISH THE READING? IT'S... IT'S PRETTY INTERESTING, RIGHT?
IF YOU SAY SO. I HAVEN'T EVEN STARTED YET. TAKE IT EASY, HUH?

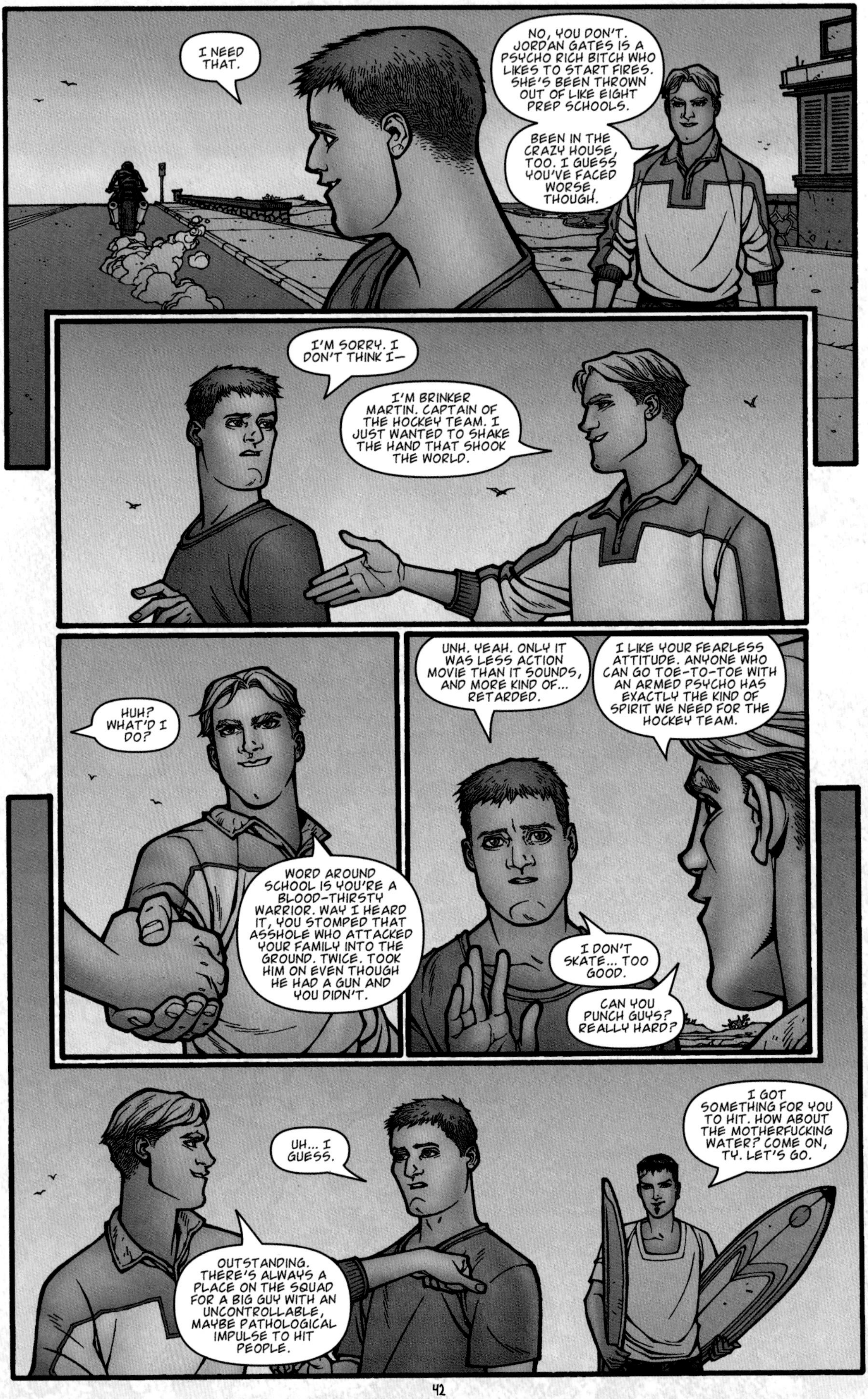
I NEED THAT.
NO, YOU DON'T. JORDAN GATES IS A PSYCHO RICH BITCH WHO LIKES TO START FIRES. SHE'S BEEN THROWN OUT OF LIKE EIGHT PREP SCHOOLS.
BEEN IN THE CRAZY HOUSE, TOO. I GUESS YOU'VE FACED WORSE, THOUGH.
I'M SORRY. I DON'T THINK I—
I'M BRINKER MARTIN. CAPTAIN OF THE HOCKEY TEAM. I JUST WANTED TO SHAKE THE HAND THAT SHOOK THE WORLD.
HUH? WHAT'D I DO?
WORD AROUND SCHOOL IS YOU'RE A BLOOD-THIRSTY WARRIOR. WAY I HEARD IT, YOU STOMPED THAT ASSHOLE WHO ATTACKED YOUR FAMILY INTO THE GROUND. TWICE. TOOK HIM ON EVEN THOUGH HE HAD A GUN AND YOU DIDN'T.
UNH. YEAH. ONLY IT WAS LESS ACTION MOVIE THAN IT SOUNDS, AND MORE KIND OF... RETARDED.
I LIKE YOUR FEARLESS ATTITUDE. ANYONE WHO CAN GO TOE-TO-TOE WITH AN ARMED PSYCHO HAS EXACTLY THE KIND OF SPIRIT WE NEED FOR THE HOCKEY TEAM.
I DON'T SKATE... TOO GOOD.
CAN YOU PUNCH GUYS? REALLY HARD?
UH... I GUESS.
OUTSTANDING. THERE'S ALWAYS A PLACE ON THE SQUAD FOR A BIG GUY WITH AN UNCONTROLLABLE, MAYBE PATHOLOGICAL IMPULSE TO HIT PEOPLE.
I GOT SOMETHING FOR YOU TO HIT. HOW ABOUT THE MOTHERFUCKING WATER? COME ON, TY. LET'S GO.

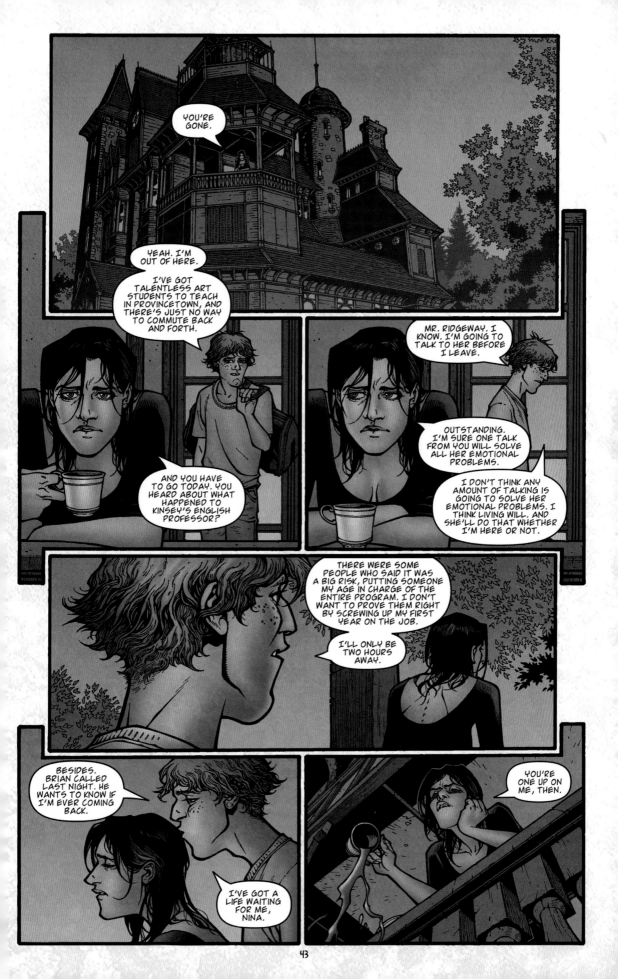

YOU'RE GONE.

YEAH. I'M OUT OF HERE.

I'VE GOT TALENTLESS ART STUDENTS TO TEACH IN PROVINCETOWN, AND THERE'S JUST NO WAY TO COMMUTE BACK AND FORTH.

MR. RIDGEWAY. I KNOW. I'M GOING TO TALK TO HER BEFORE I LEAVE.

AND YOU HAVE TO GO TODAY. YOU HEARD ABOUT WHAT HAPPENED TO KINSEY'S ENGLISH PROFESSOR?

OUTSTANDING. I'M SURE ONE TALK FROM YOU WILL SOLVE ALL HER EMOTIONAL PROBLEMS.

I DON'T THINK ANY AMOUNT OF TALKING IS GOING TO SOLVE HER EMOTIONAL PROBLEMS. I THINK LIVING WILL. AND SHE'LL DO THAT WHETHER I'M HERE OR NOT.

THERE WERE SOME PEOPLE WHO SAID IT WAS A BIG RISK, PUTTING SOMEONE MY AGE IN CHARGE OF THE ENTIRE PROGRAM. I DON'T WANT TO PROVE THEM RIGHT BY SCREWING UP MY FIRST YEAR ON THE JOB.

I'LL ONLY BE TWO HOURS AWAY.

BESIDES. BRIAN CALLED LAST NIGHT. HE WANTS TO KNOW IF I'M EVER COMING BACK.

I'VE GOT A LIFE WAITING FOR ME, NINA.

YOU'RE ONE UP ON ME, THEN.

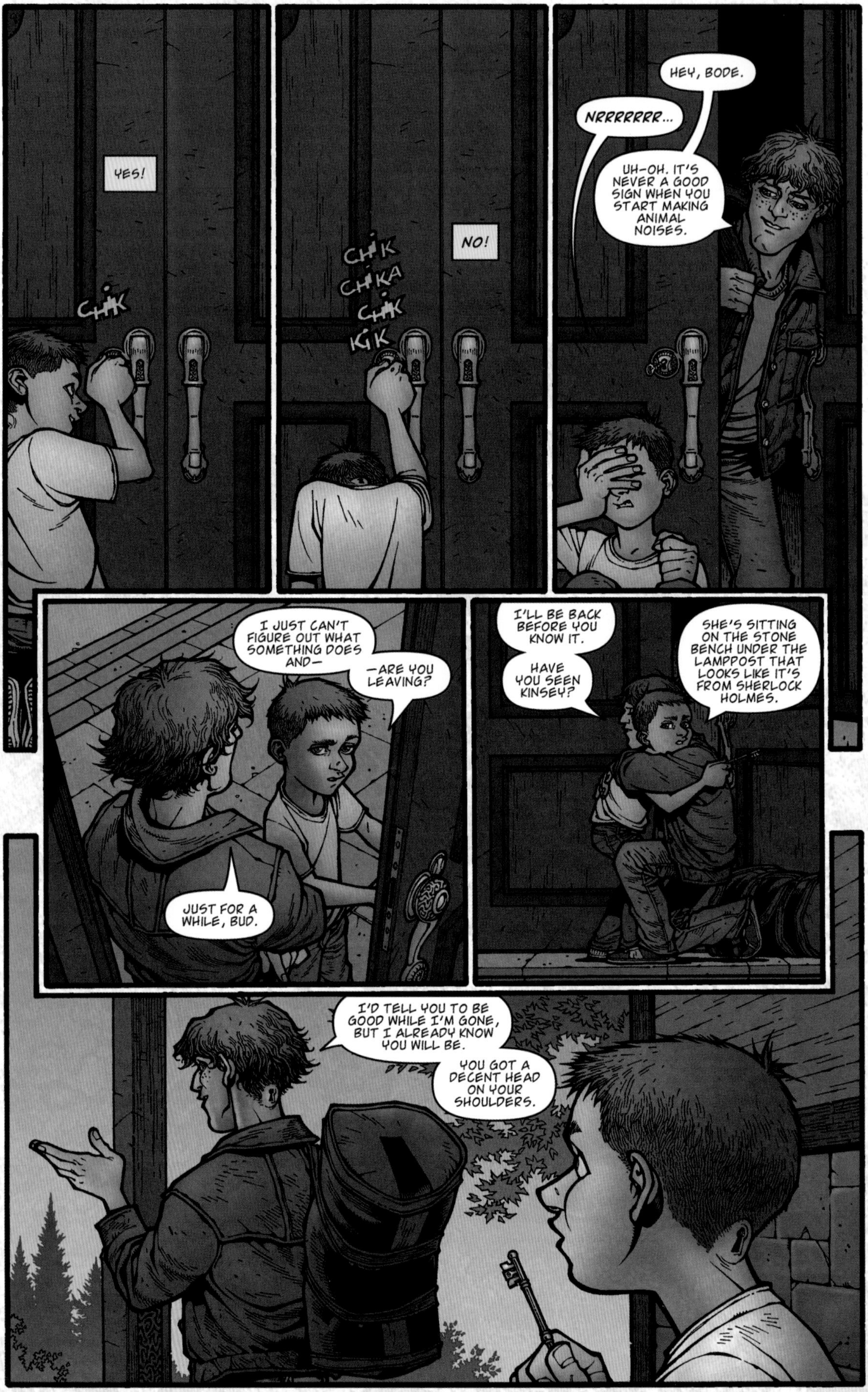
YES!
CHIK
CHIK
CHIKA
CHIK
KLIK
NO!
HEY, BODE.
NRRRRRRR...
UH-OH. IT'S NEVER A GOOD SIGN WHEN YOU START MAKING ANIMAL NOISES.
I JUST CAN'T FIGURE OUT WHAT SOMETHING DOES AND—
—ARE YOU LEAVING?
JUST FOR A WHILE, BUD.
I'LL BE BACK BEFORE YOU KNOW IT.
HAVE YOU SEEN KINSEY?
SHE'S SITTING ON THE STONE BENCH UNDER THE LAMPPOST THAT LOOKS LIKE IT'S FROM SHERLOCK HOLMES.
I'D TELL YOU TO BE GOOD WHILE I'M GONE, BUT I ALREADY KNOW YOU WILL BE.
YOU GOT A DECENT HEAD ON YOUR SHOULDERS.

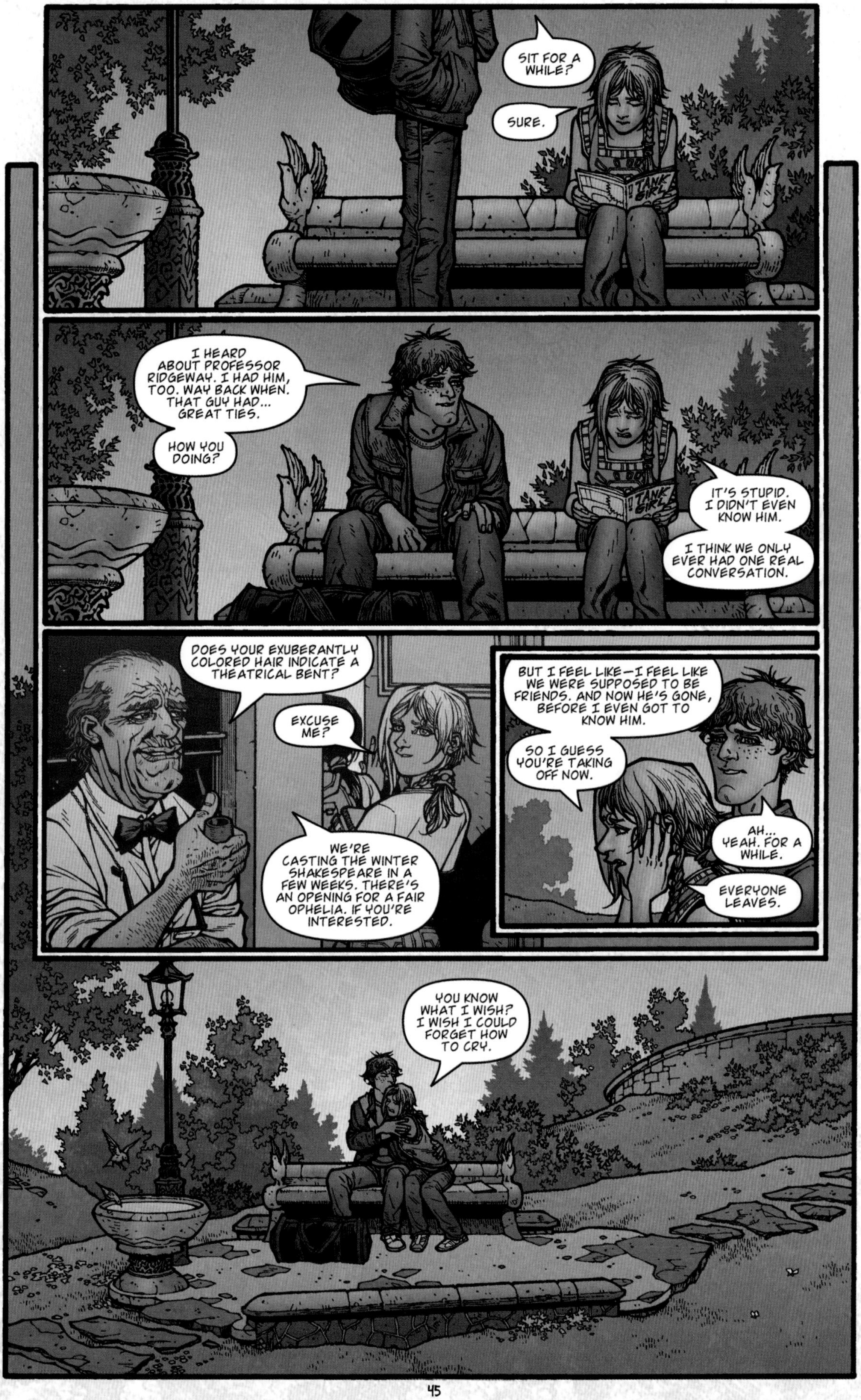
SIT FOR A WHILE?
SURE.
I HEARD ABOUT PROFESSOR RIDGEWAY. I HAD HIM, TOO. WAY BACK WHEN. THAT GUY HAD... GREAT TIES.
HOW YOU DOING?
TANK GIRL
IT'S STUPID. I DIDN'T EVEN KNOW HIM.
I THINK WE ONLY EVER HAD ONE REAL CONVERSATION.
DOES YOUR EXUBERANTLY COLORED HAIR INDICATE A THEATRICAL BENT?
EXCUSE ME?
WE'RE CASTING THE WINTER SHAKESPEARE IN A FEW WEEKS. THERE'S AN OPENING FOR A FAIR OPHELIA. IF YOU'RE INTERESTED.
BUT I FEEL LIKE—I FEEL LIKE WE WERE SUPPOSED TO BE FRIENDS. AND NOW HE'S GONE, BEFORE I EVEN GOT TO KNOW HIM.
SO I GUESS YOU'RE TAKING OFF NOW.
AH... YEAH. FOR A WHILE.
EVERYONE LEAVES.
YOU KNOW WHAT I WISH? I WISH I COULD FORGET HOW TO CRY.

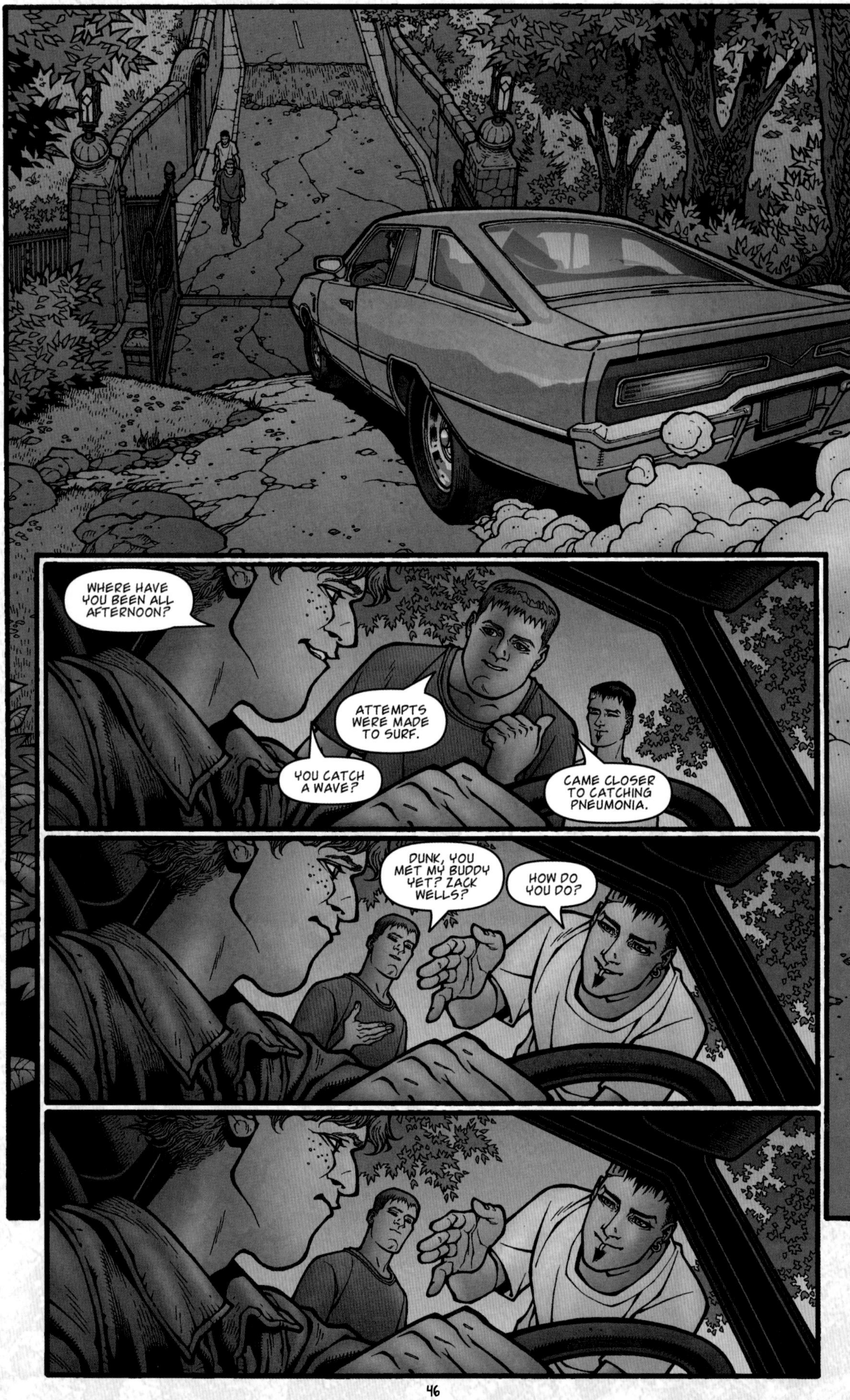
WHERE HAVE YOU BEEN ALL AFTERNOON?
ATTEMPTS WERE MADE TO SURF.
YOU CATCH A WAVE?
CAME CLOSER TO CATCHING PNEUMONIA.
DUNK, YOU MET MY BUDDY YET? ZACK WELLS?
HOW DO YOU DO?

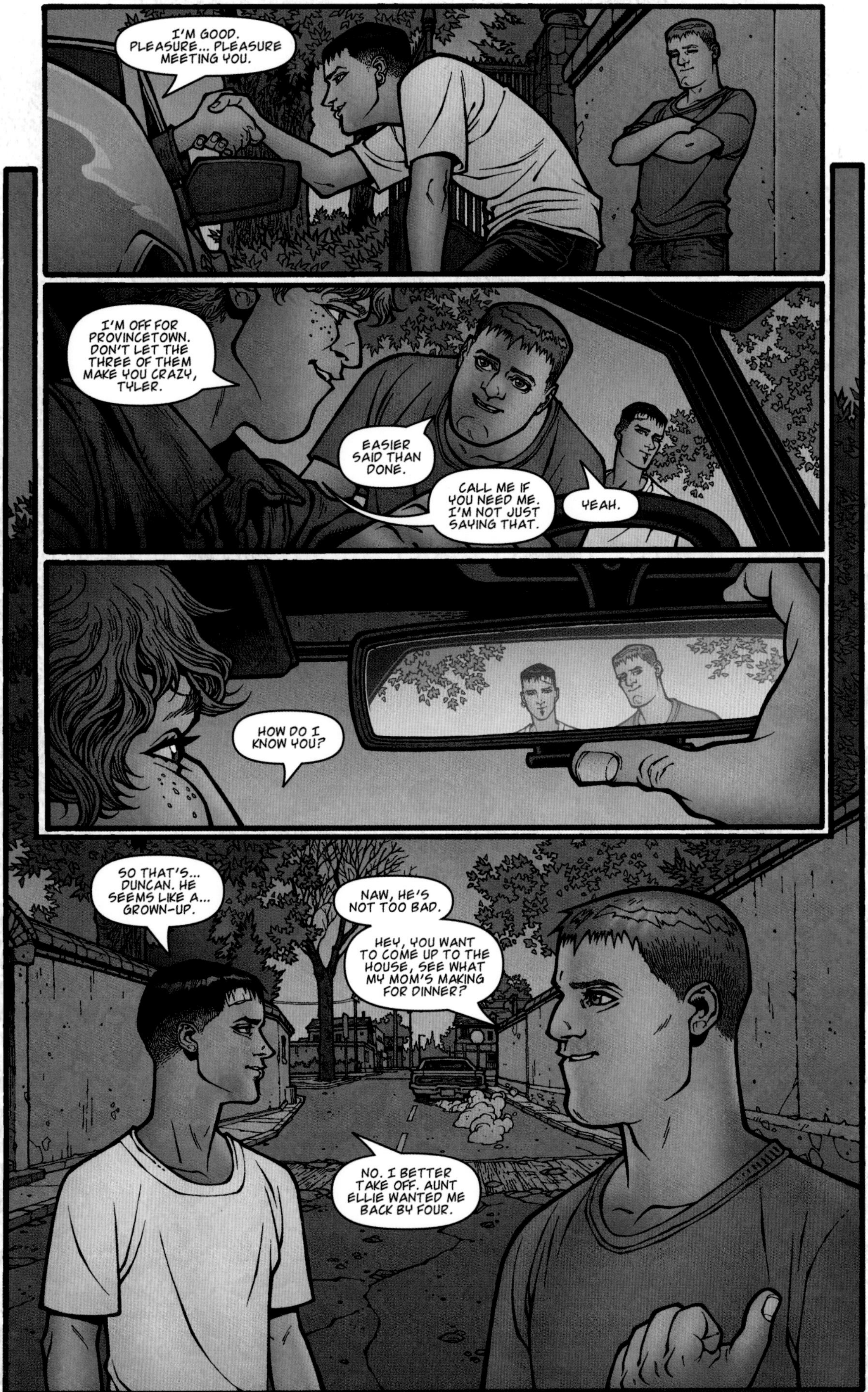
I'M GOOD. PLEASURE... PLEASURE MEETING YOU.
I'M OFF FOR PROVINCETOWN. DON'T LET THE THREE OF THEM MAKE YOU CRAZY, TYLER.
EASIER SAID THAN DONE.
CALL ME IF YOU NEED ME. I'M NOT JUST SAYING THAT.
YEAH.
HOW DO I KNOW YOU?
SO THAT'S... DUNCAN. HE SEEMS LIKE A... GROWN-UP.
NAW, HE'S NOT TOO BAD.
HEY, YOU WANT TO COME UP TO THE HOUSE, SEE WHAT MY MOM'S MAKING FOR DINNER?
NO. I BETTER TAKE OFF. AUNT ELLIE WANTED ME BACK BY FOUR.

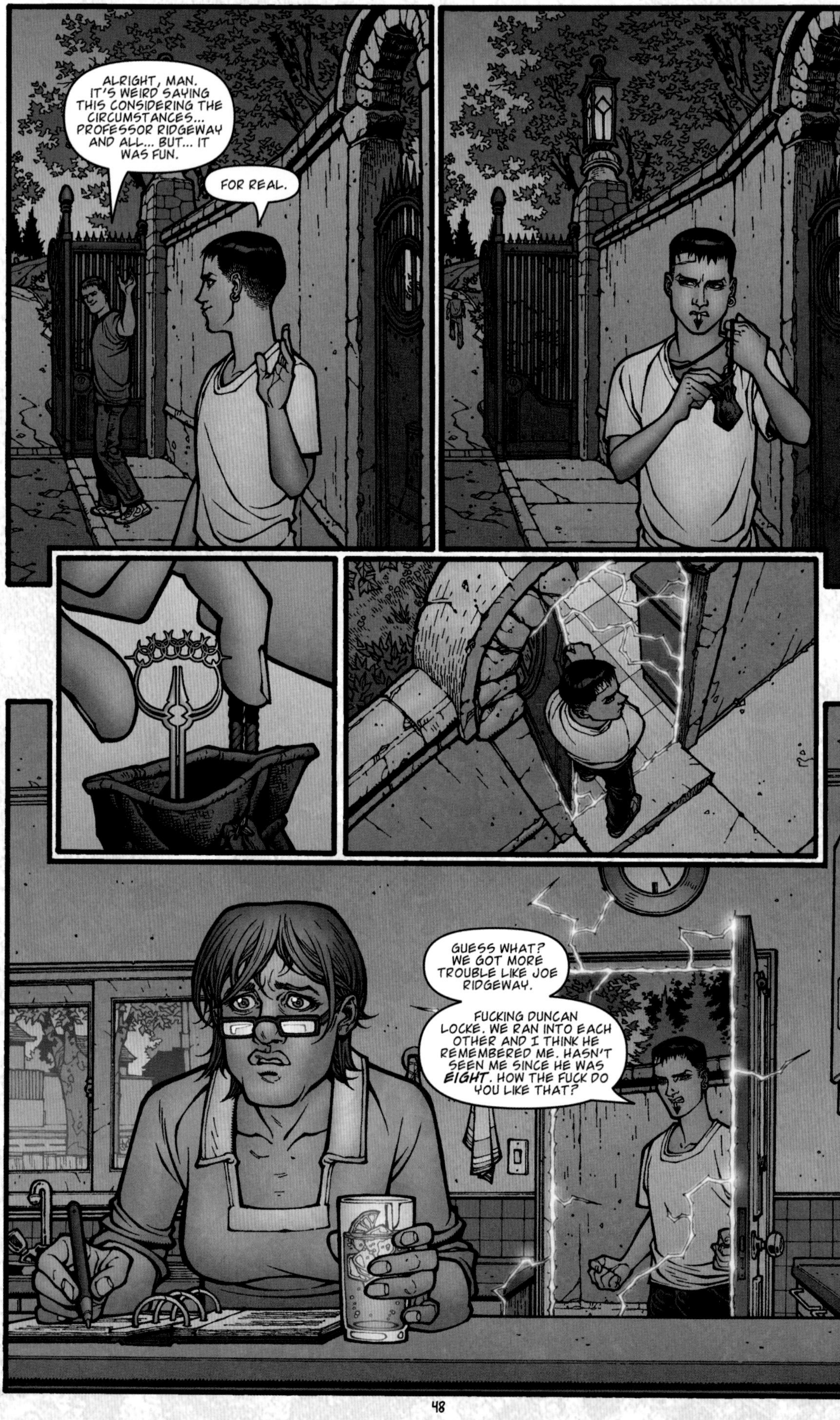
ALRIGHT, MAN. IT'S WEIRD SAYING THIS CONSIDERING THE CIRCUMSTANCES... PROFESSOR RIDGEWAY AND ALL... BUT... IT WAS FUN.
FOR REAL.
GUESS WHAT? WE GOT MORE TROUBLE LIKE JOE RIDGEWAY.
FUCKING DUNCAN LOCKE. WE RAN INTO EACH OTHER AND I THINK HE REMEMBERED ME. HASN'T SEEN ME SINCE HE WAS EIGHT. HOW THE FUCK DO YOU LIKE THAT?

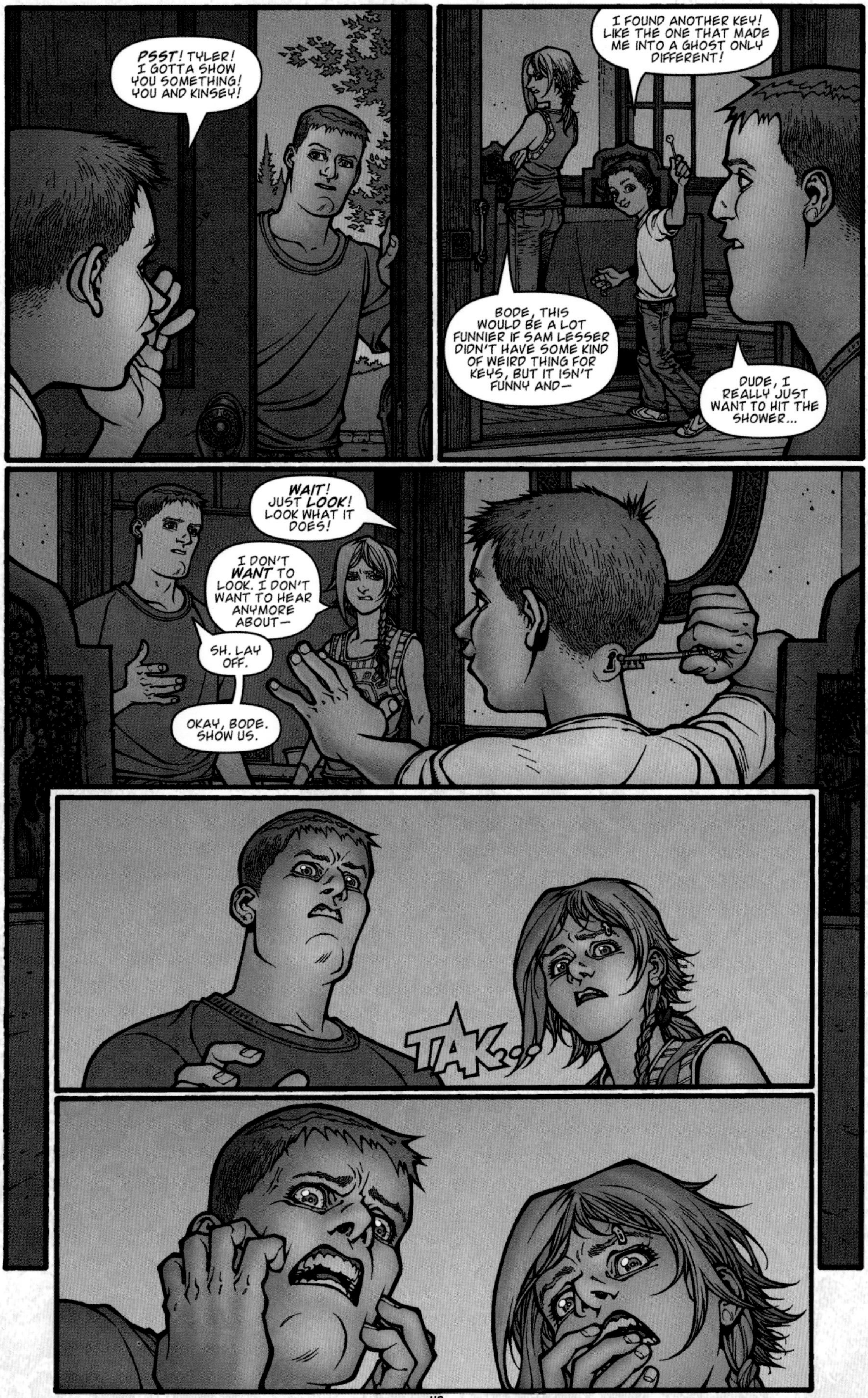
PSST! TYLER! I GOTTA SHOW YOU SOMETHING! YOU AND KINSEY!
I FOUND ANOTHER KEY! LIKE THE ONE THAT MADE ME INTO A GHOST ONLY DIFFERENT!
BODE, THIS WOULD BE A LOT FUNNIER IF SAM LESSER DIDN'T HAVE SOME KIND OF WEIRD THING FOR KEYS, BUT IT ISN'T FUNNY AND—
DUDE, I REALLY JUST WANT TO HIT THE SHOWER...
WAIT! JUST LOOK! LOOK WHAT IT DOES!
I DON'T WANT TO LOOK. I DON'T WANT TO HEAR ANYMORE ABOUT—
SH. LAY OFF.
OKAY, BODE. SHOW US.
TAK...

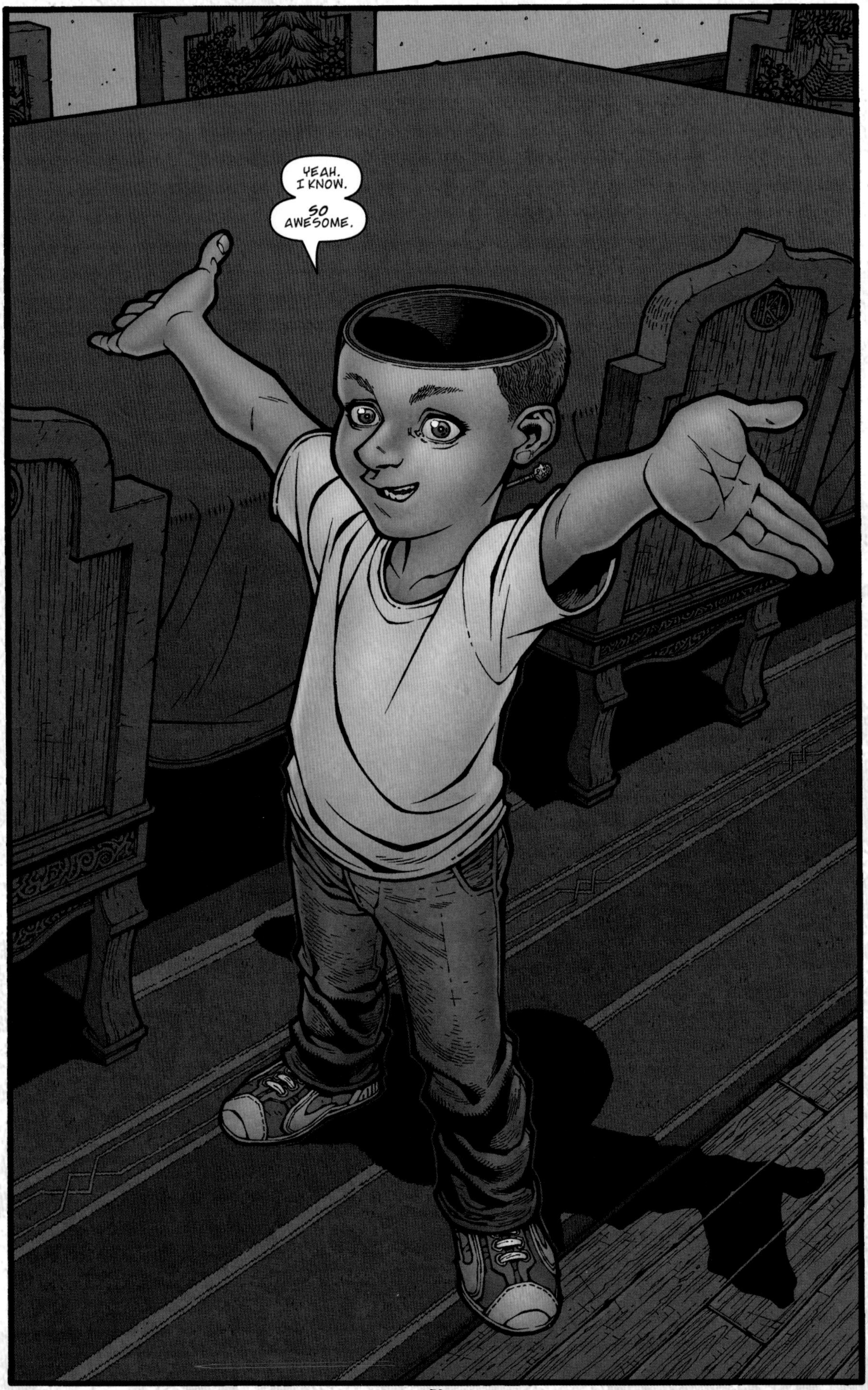
YEAH. I KNOW.
SO AWESOME.

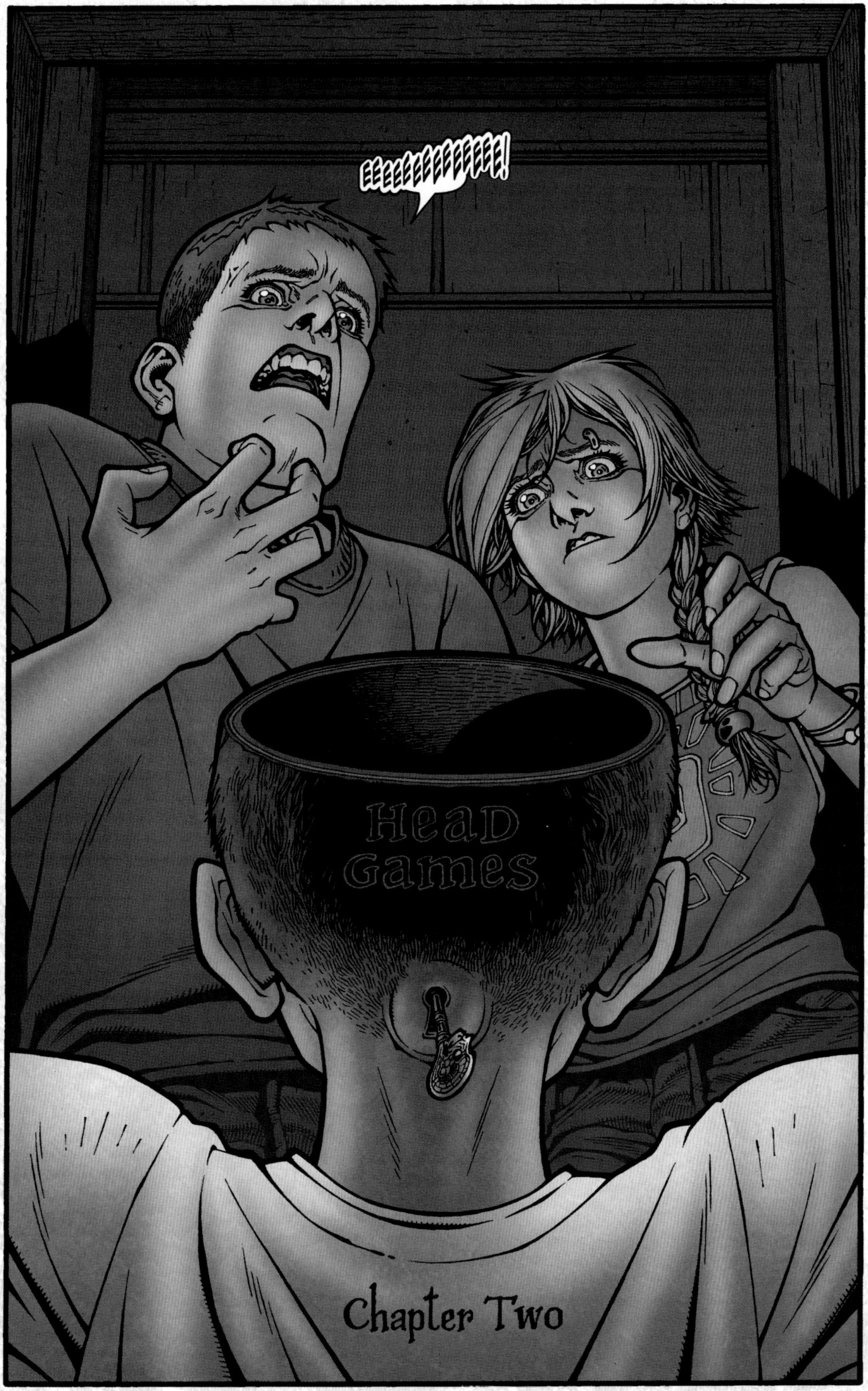
EEEEEEEEEEEEEEE!
Head
Games
Chapter Two

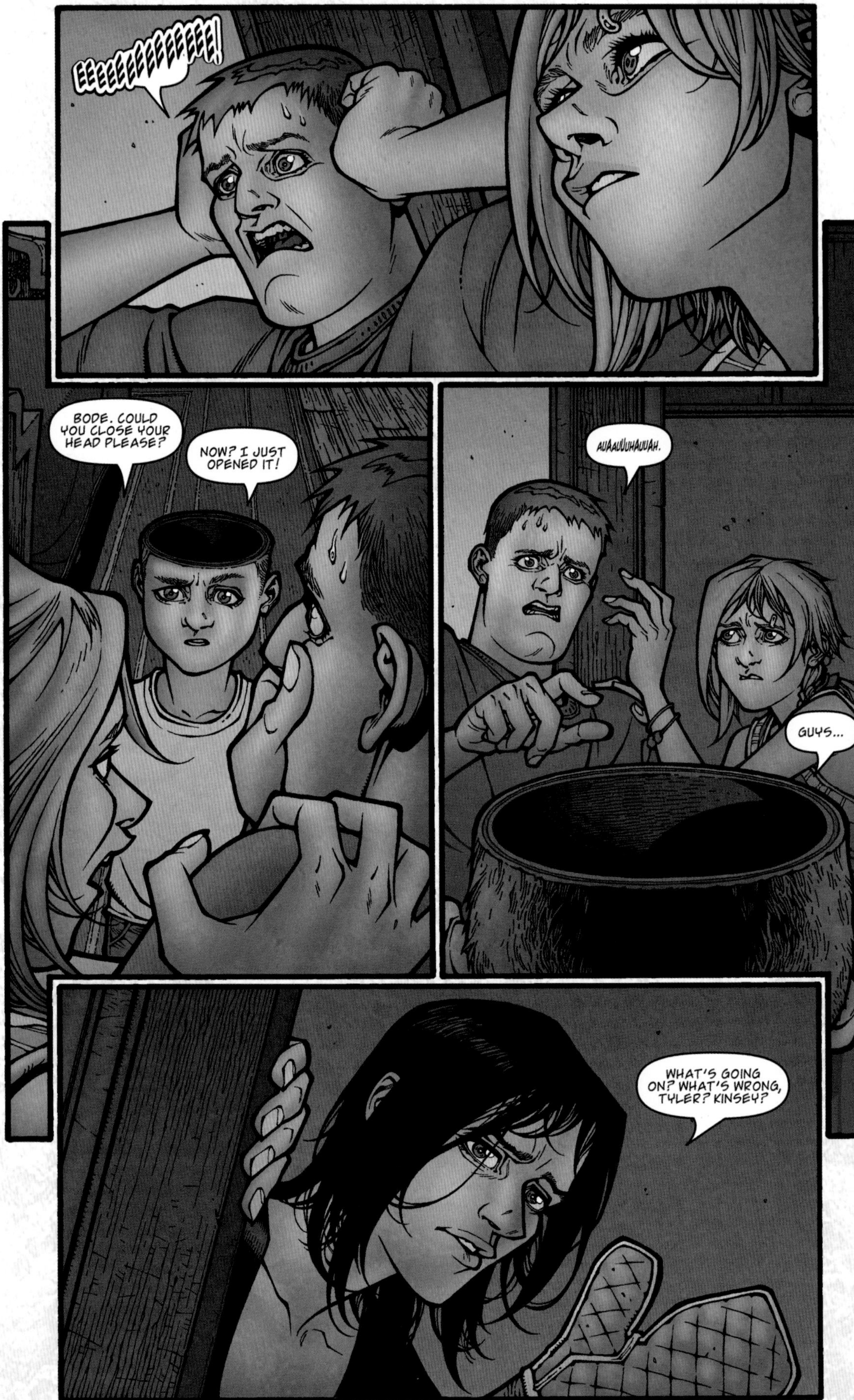
EEEEEEEEEEEEEE!
BODE. COULD YOU CLOSE YOUR HEAD PLEASE?
NOW? I JUST OPENED IT!
AUAAUUUHAUUAH.
GUYS...
WHAT'S GOING ON? WHAT'S WRONG, TYLER? KINSEY?

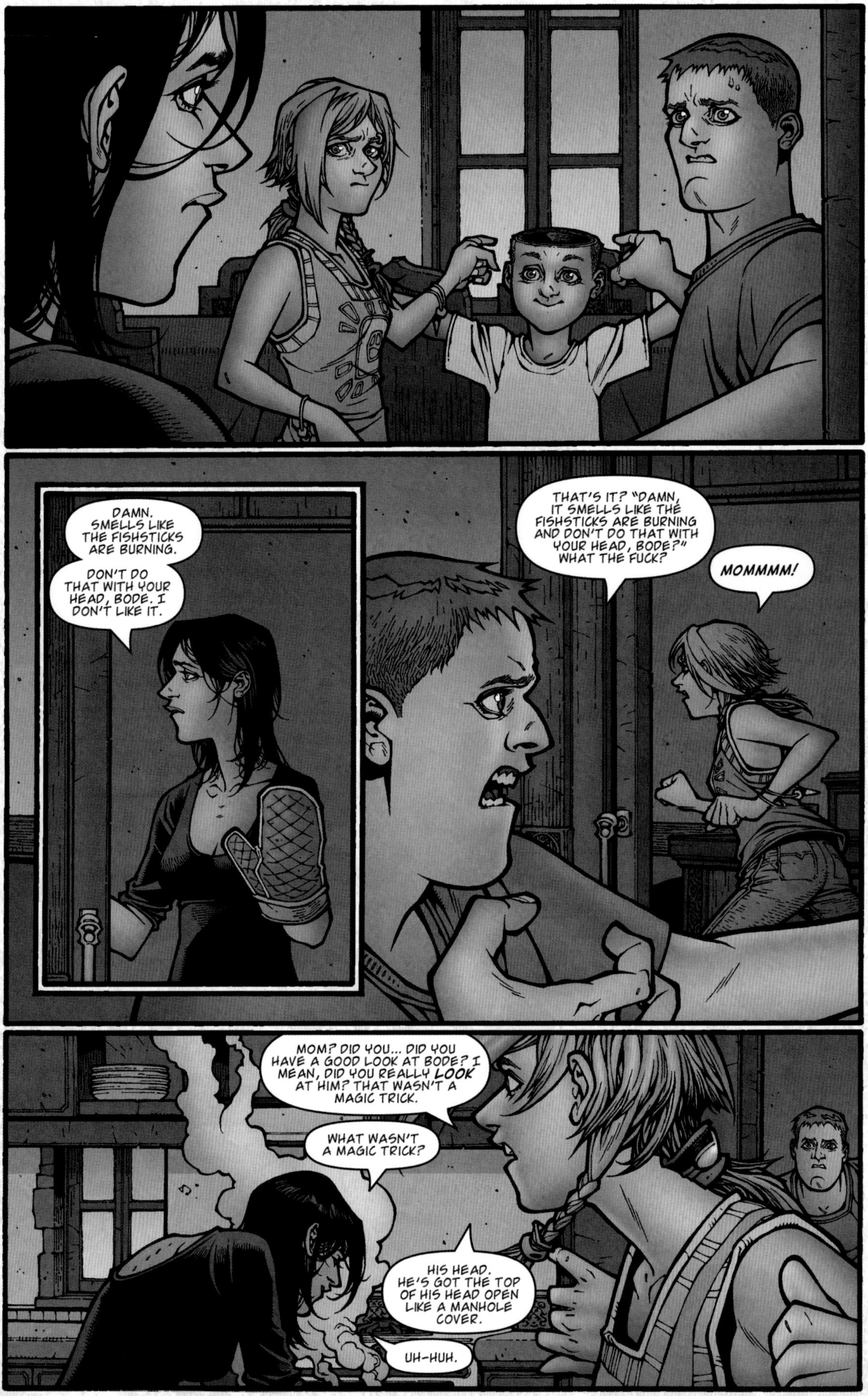

DAMN. SMELLS LIKE THE FISHSTICKS ARE BURNING.
DON'T DO THAT WITH YOUR HEAD, BODE. I DON'T LIKE IT.
THAT'S IT? "DAMN, IT SMELLS LIKE THE FISHSTICKS ARE BURNING AND DON'T DO THAT WITH YOUR HEAD, BODE?" WHAT THE FUCK?
MOMMMM!
MOM? DID YOU... DID YOU HAVE A GOOD LOOK AT BODE? I MEAN, DID YOU REALLY LOOK AT HIM? THAT WASN'T A MAGIC TRICK.
WHAT WASN'T A MAGIC TRICK?
HIS HEAD. HE'S GOT THE TOP OF HIS HEAD OPEN LIKE A MANHOLE COVER.
UH-HUH.

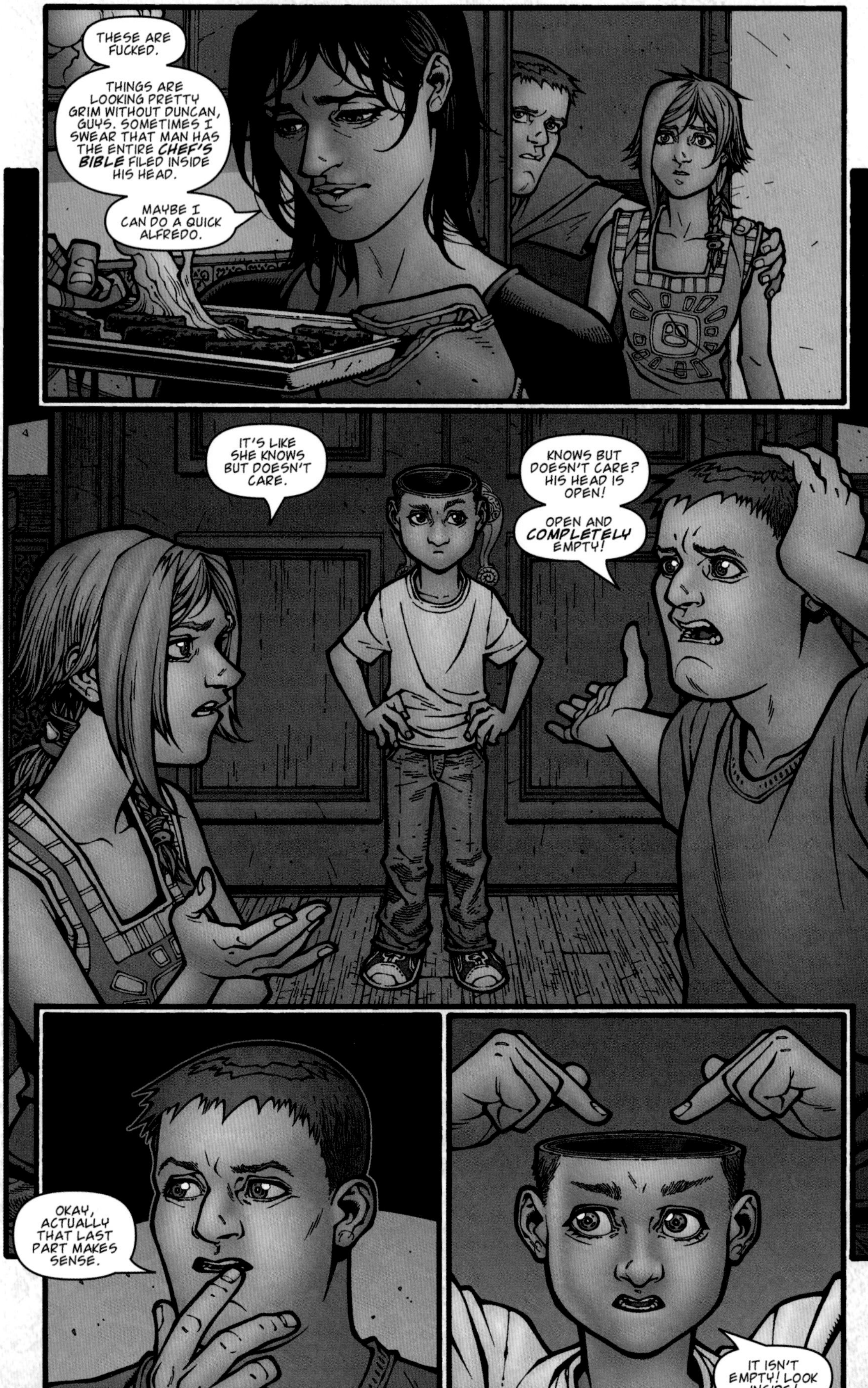
THESE ARE FUCKED.
THINGS ARE LOOKING PRETTY GRIM WITHOUT DUNCAN, GUYS. SOMETIMES I SWEAR THAT MAN HAS THE ENTIRE CHEF'S BIBLE FILED INSIDE HIS HEAD.
MAYBE I CAN DO A QUICK ALFREDO.
IT'S LIKE SHE KNOWS BUT DOESN'T CARE.
KNOWS BUT DOESN'T CARE? HIS HEAD IS OPEN!
OPEN AND COMPLETELY EMPTY!
OKAY, ACTUALLY THAT LAST PART MAKES SENSE.
IT ISN'T EMPTY! LOOK INSIDE!

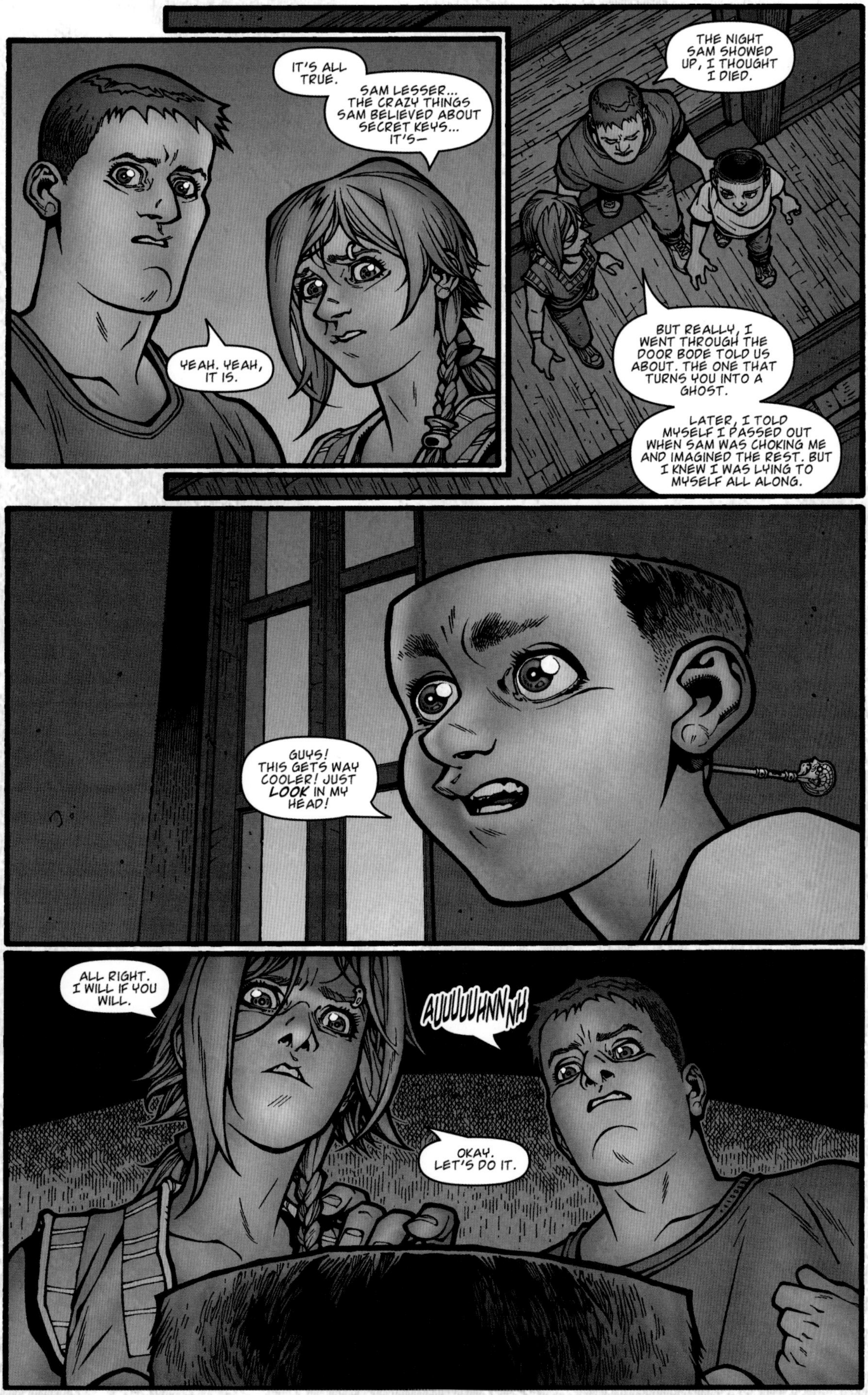
IT'S ALL TRUE.
SAM LESSER... THE CRAZY THINGS SAM BELIEVED ABOUT SECRET KEYS... IT'S—
YEAH. YEAH, IT IS.
THE NIGHT SAM SHOWED UP, I THOUGHT I DIED.
BUT REALLY, I WENT THROUGH THE DOOR BODE TOLD US ABOUT. THE ONE THAT TURNS YOU INTO A GHOST.
LATER, I TOLD MYSELF I PASSED OUT WHEN SAM WAS CHOKING ME AND IMAGINED THE REST. BUT I KNEW I WAS LYING TO MYSELF ALL ALONG.
GUYS! THIS GETS WAY COOLER! JUST LOOK IN MY HEAD!
ALL RIGHT. I WILL IF YOU WILL.
AUUUUHNNNH
OKAY. LET'S DO IT.

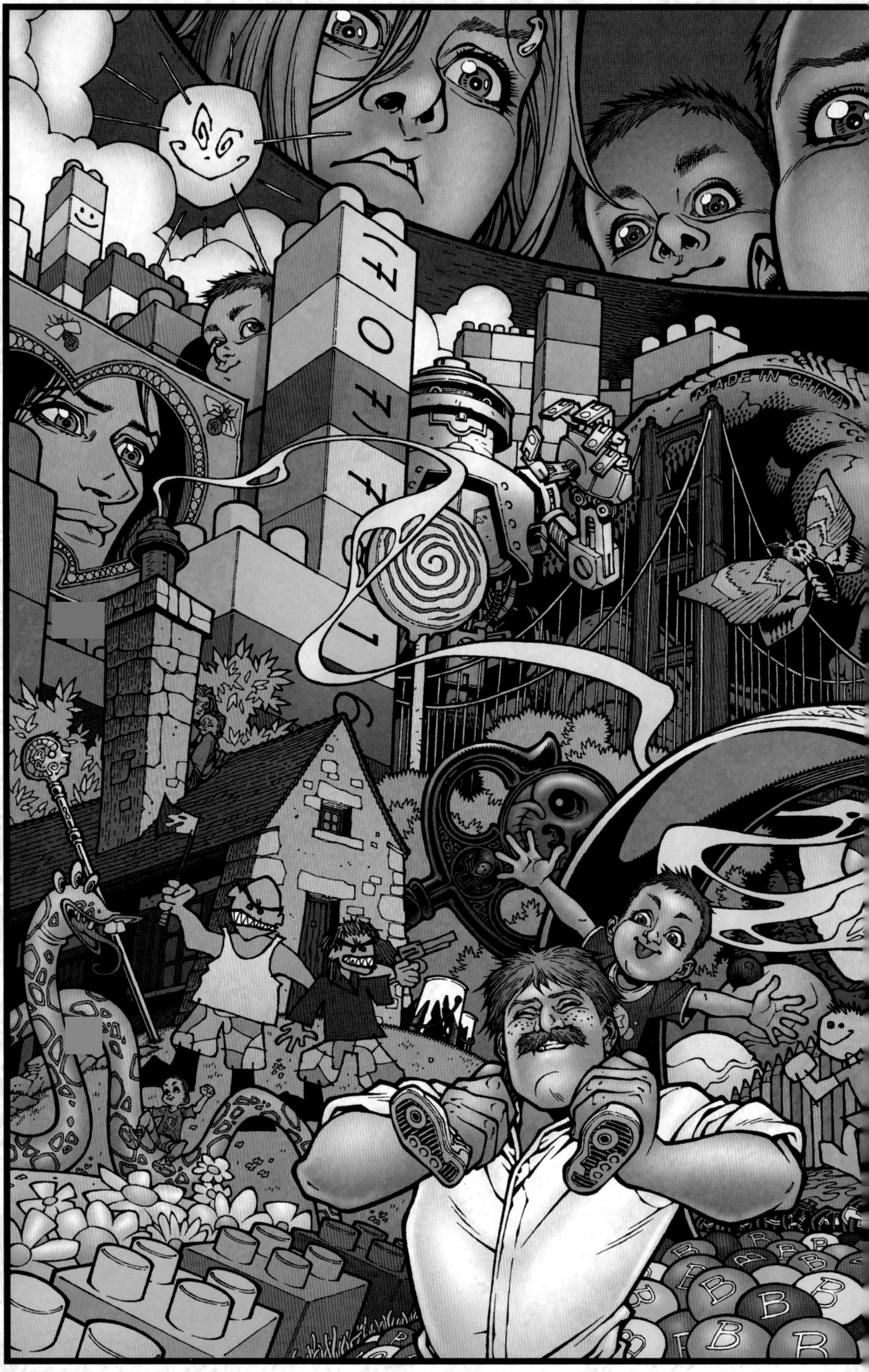
MADE IN CHINA

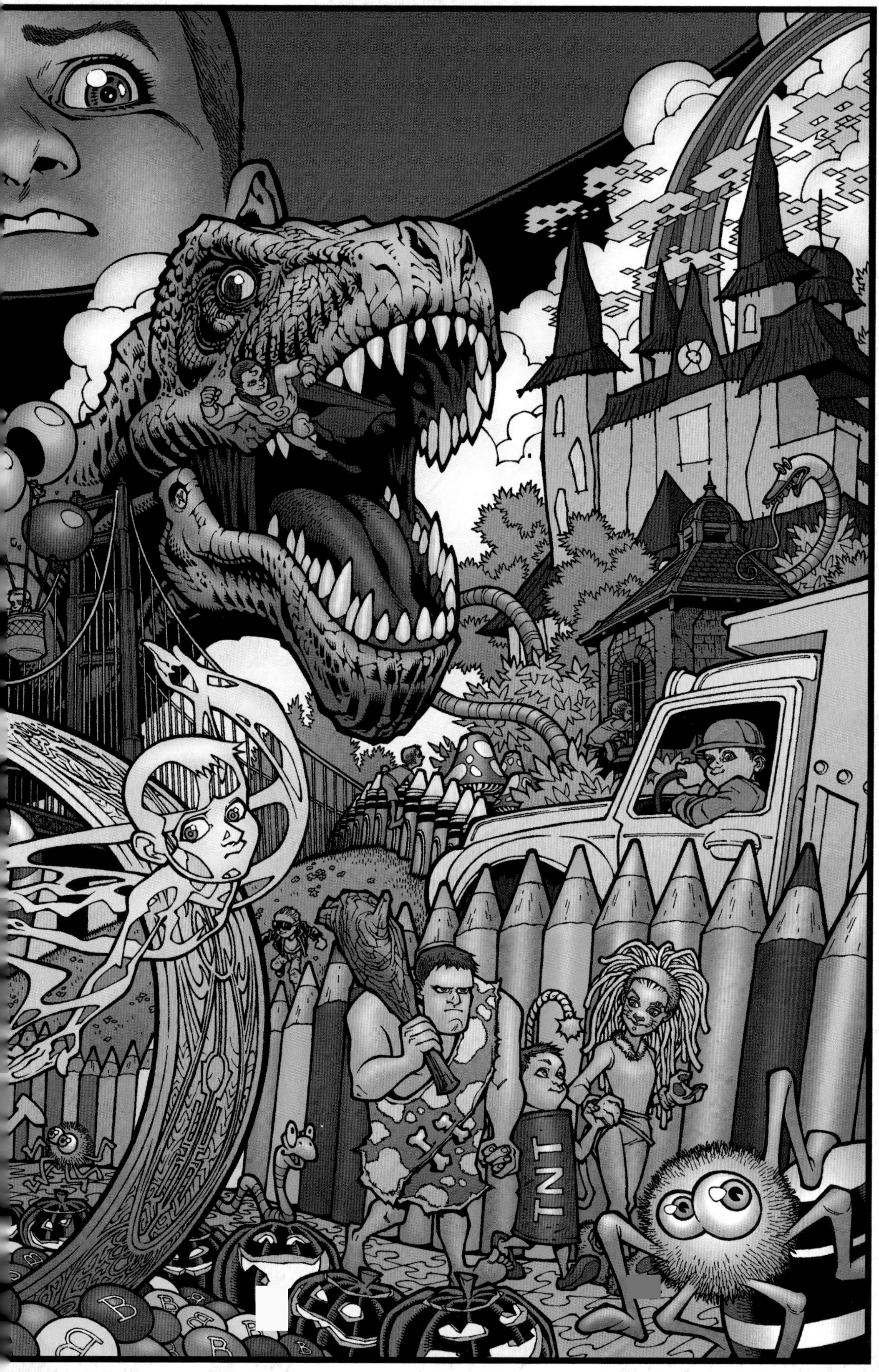
TNT

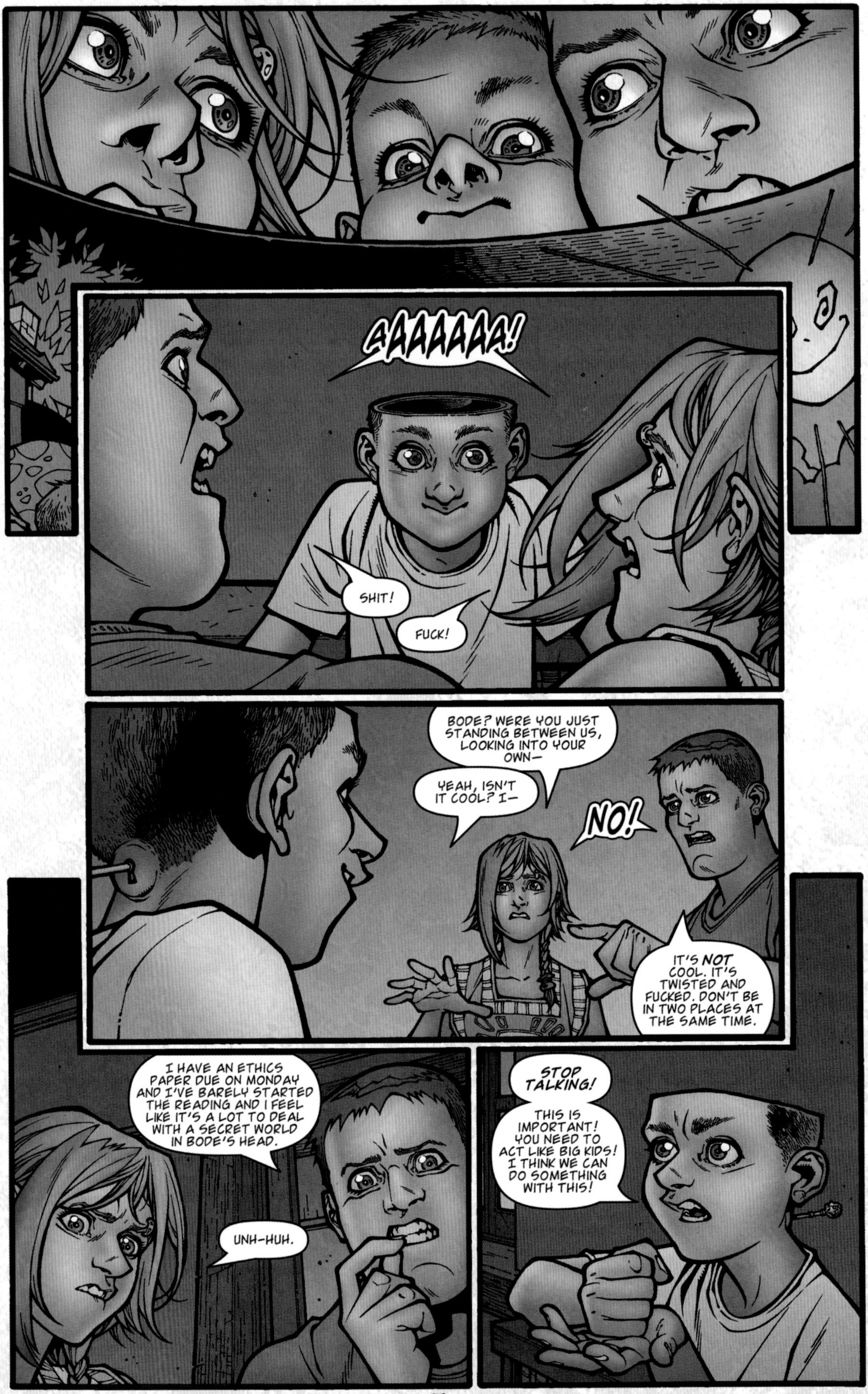
AAAAAAA!
SHIT!
FUCK!
BODE? WERE YOU JUST STANDING BETWEEN US, LOOKING INTO YOUR OWN—
YEAH, ISN'T IT COOL? I—
NO!
IT'S NOT COOL. IT'S TWISTED AND FUCKED. DON'T BE IN TWO PLACES AT THE SAME TIME.
I HAVE AN ETHICS PAPER DUE ON MONDAY AND I'VE BARELY STARTED THE READING AND I FEEL LIKE IT'S A LOT TO DEAL WITH A SECRET WORLD IN BODE'S HEAD.
UNH-HUH.
STOP TALKING!
THIS IS IMPORTANT! YOU NEED TO ACT LIKE BIG KIDS! I THINK WE CAN DO SOMETHING WITH THIS!

LIKE WHAT?

LIKE... PUT THINGS IN!

OH. EW. EW! NO! DUDE!

SO... SO... DO YOU KNOW STUFF ABOUT COOKING NOW?

THAT IS SO VERY WRONG-LOOKING.

SO EVERYTHING IN MY HEAD IS ALL THE STUFF I KNOW, RIGHT?

I WAS JUST THINKING, WHY CAN'T—UNFF—WE JUST—UNN—PUT MORE STUFF IN THERE?

GUNNH. THERE.

The Chef's BIBLE °°°
More than 320 recipes!

UH...

LIKE... HOW WOULD YOU MAKE FETTUCCINE ALFREDO?

1 CUP OF WHIPPING CREAM. 1 CUP LIGHT CREAM. 1 SLASH 4 CUPS BUTTER, SOFTENED...

...1 AND 1 SLASH 2 CUPS FRESHLY GRATED PARMESAN CHEESE...

OKAY. IT WORKED.

THAT'S FINE, BODE...

...1 SLASH 4 TISSPS OF FRESHLY GROUND PEPPER... SALT... NUTMEG...

ALL RIGHT ENOUGH! CUT IT OUT!

WHAT'S A TISSP?

...1 LIB FETTUCCINE...

59

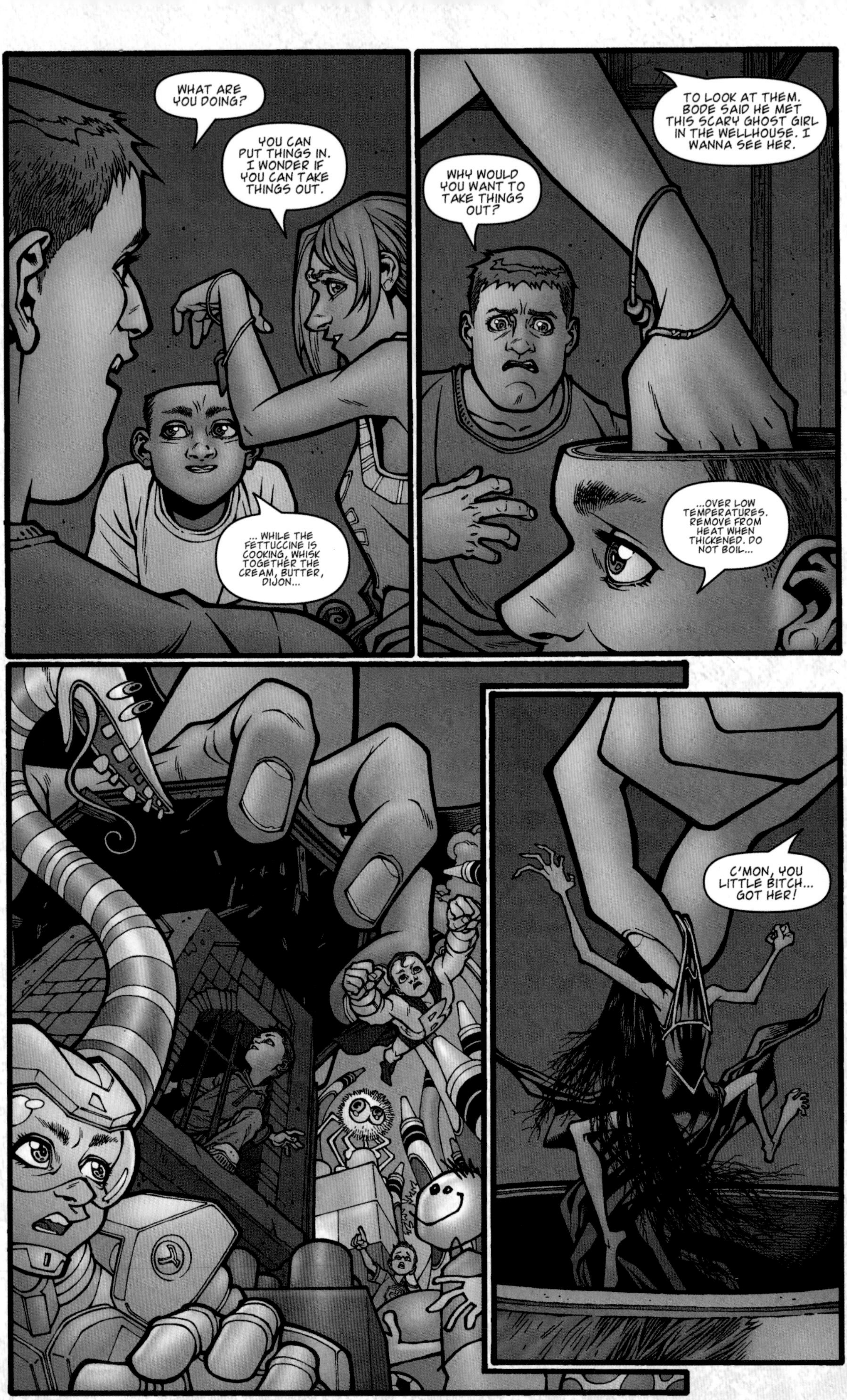
WHAT ARE YOU DOING?
YOU CAN PUT THINGS IN. I WONDER IF YOU CAN TAKE THINGS OUT.
... WHILE THE FETTUCCINE IS COOKING, WHISK TOGETHER THE CREAM, BUTTER, DIJON...
WHY WOULD YOU WANT TO TAKE THINGS OUT?
TO LOOK AT THEM. BODE SAID HE MET THIS SCARY GHOST GIRL IN THE WELLHOUSE. I WANNA SEE HER.
...OVER LOW TEMPERATURES. REMOVE FROM HEAT WHEN THICKENED. DO NOT BOIL...
C'MON, YOU LITTLE BITCH... GOT HER!

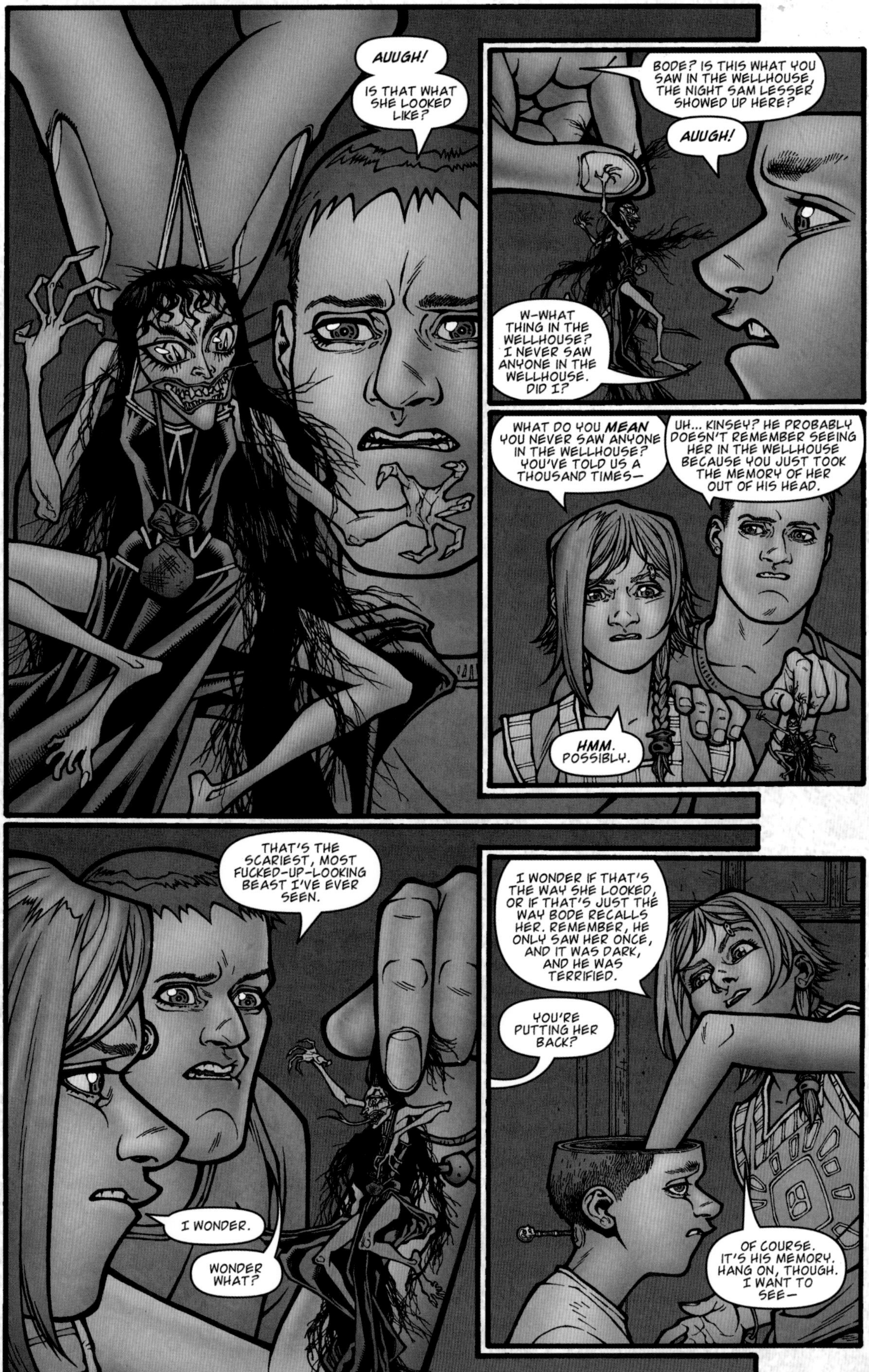
AUUGH!
IS THAT WHAT SHE LOOKED LIKE?
BODE? IS THIS WHAT YOU SAW IN THE WELLHOUSE, THE NIGHT SAM LESSER SHOWED UP HERE?
AUUGH!
W-WHAT THING IN THE WELLHOUSE? I NEVER SAW ANYONE IN THE WELLHOUSE. DID I?
WHAT DO YOU MEAN YOU NEVER SAW ANYONE IN THE WELLHOUSE? YOU'VE TOLD US A THOUSAND TIMES—
UH... KINSEY? HE PROBABLY DOESN'T REMEMBER SEEING HER IN THE WELLHOUSE BECAUSE YOU JUST TOOK THE MEMORY OF HER OUT OF HIS HEAD.
HMM. POSSIBLY.
THAT'S THE SCARIEST, MOST FUCKED-UP-LOOKING BEAST I'VE EVER SEEN.
I WONDER.
WONDER WHAT?
I WONDER IF THAT'S THE WAY SHE LOOKED, OR IF THAT'S JUST THE WAY BODE RECALLS HER. REMEMBER, HE ONLY SAW HER ONCE, AND IT WAS DARK, AND HE WAS TERRIFIED.
YOU'RE PUTTING HER BACK?
OF COURSE. IT'S HIS MEMORY. HANG ON, THOUGH. I WANT TO SEE—

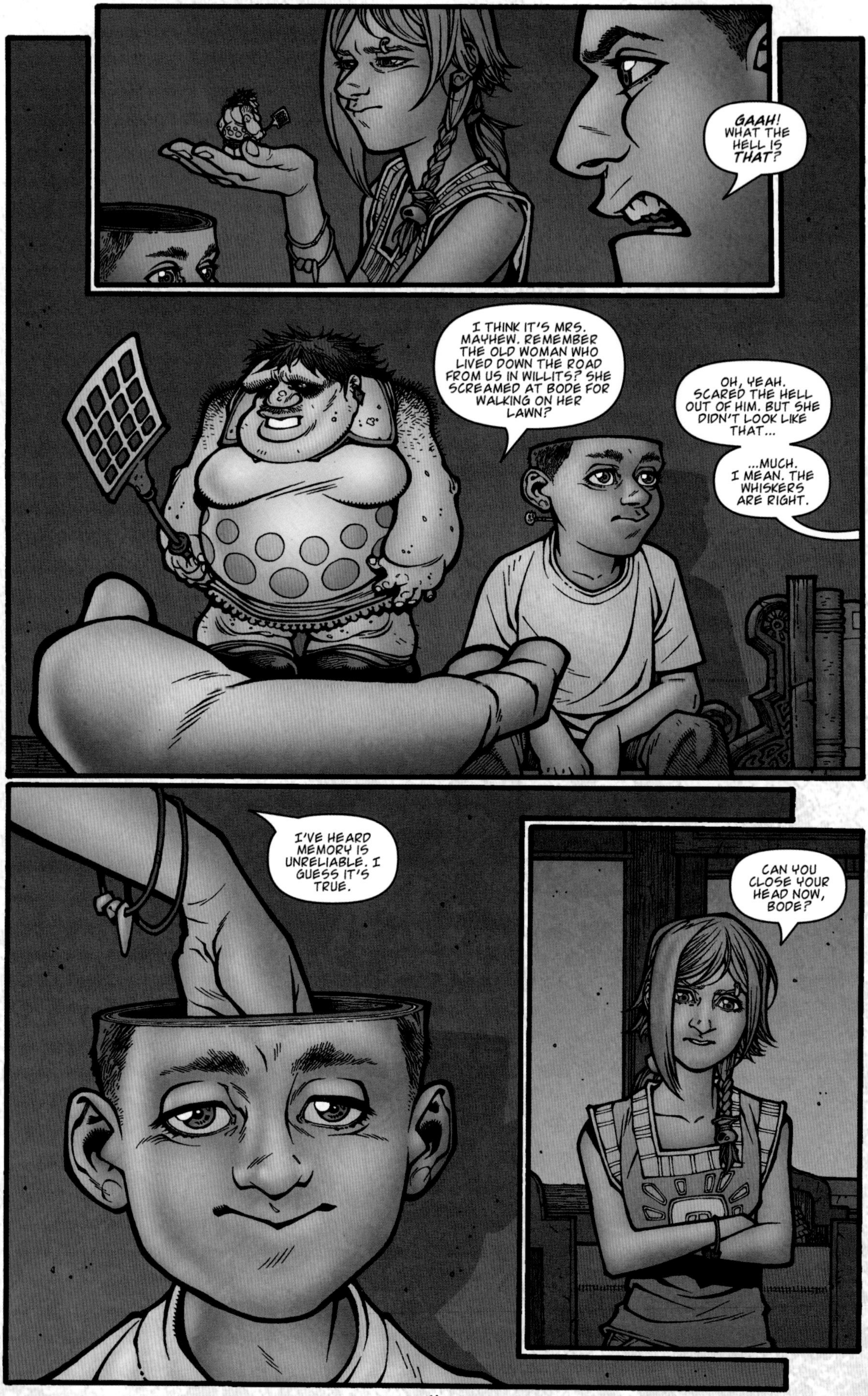
GAAH! WHAT THE HELL IS THAT?
I THINK IT'S MRS. MAYHEW. REMEMBER THE OLD WOMAN WHO LIVED DOWN THE ROAD FROM US IN WILLITS? SHE SCREAMED AT BODE FOR WALKING ON HER LAWN?
OH, YEAH. SCARED THE HELL OUT OF HIM. BUT SHE DIDN'T LOOK LIKE THAT...
...MUCH. I MEAN. THE WHISKERS ARE RIGHT.
I'VE HEARD MEMORY IS UNRELIABLE. I GUESS IT'S TRUE.
CAN YOU CLOSE YOUR HEAD NOW, BODE?

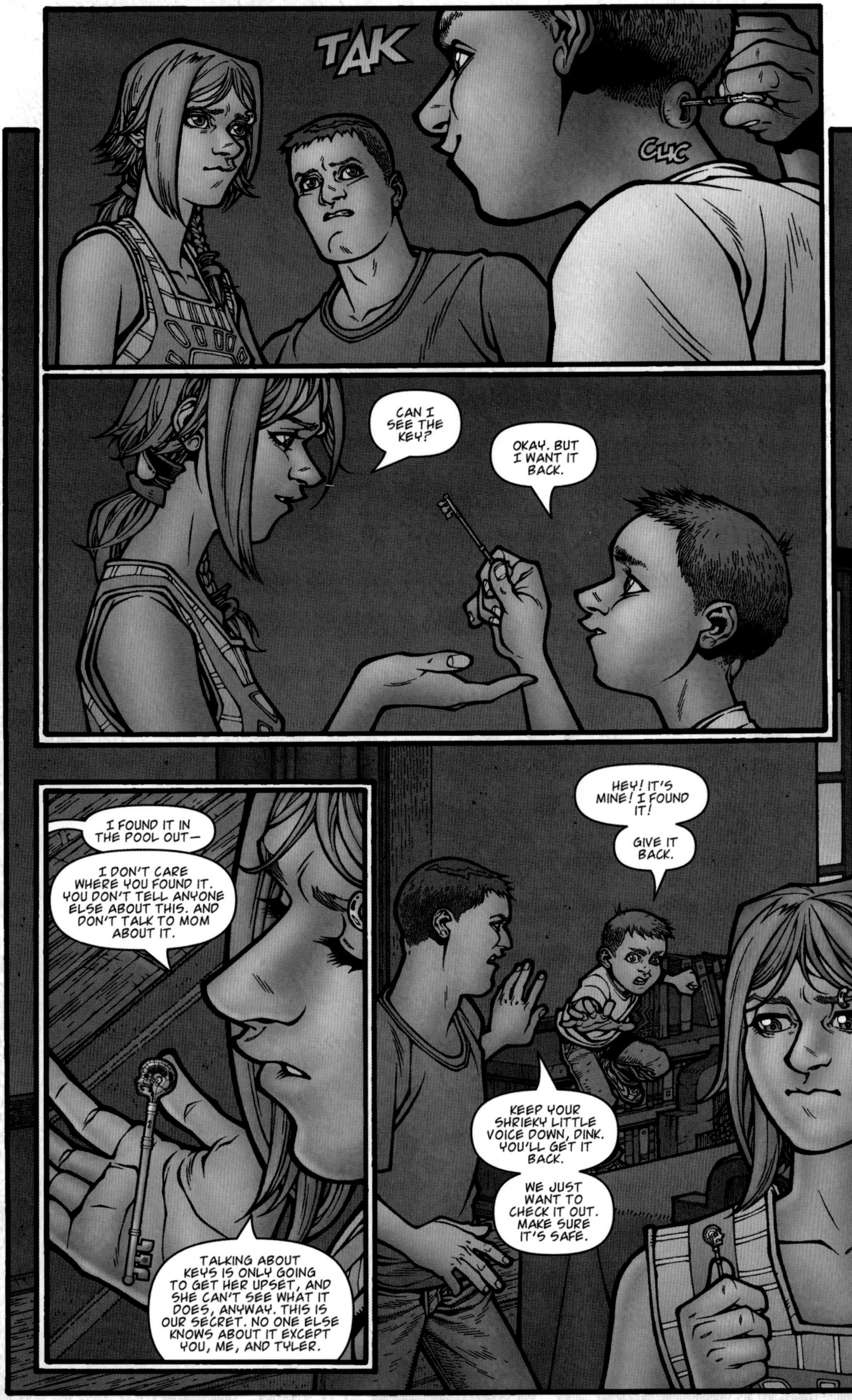

TAK
CLIC
CAN I SEE THE KEY?
OKAY. BUT I WANT IT BACK.
HEY! IT'S MINE! I FOUND IT!
GIVE IT BACK.
KEEP YOUR SHRIEKY LITTLE VOICE DOWN, DINK. YOU'LL GET IT BACK.
WE JUST WANT TO CHECK IT OUT. MAKE SURE IT'S SAFE.
I FOUND IT IN THE POOL OUT—
I DON'T CARE WHERE YOU FOUND IT. YOU DON'T TELL ANYONE ELSE ABOUT THIS. AND DON'T TALK TO MOM ABOUT IT.
TALKING ABOUT KEYS IS ONLY GOING TO GET HER UPSET, AND SHE CAN'T SEE WHAT IT DOES, ANYWAY. THIS IS OUR SECRET. NO ONE ELSE KNOWS ABOUT IT EXCEPT YOU, ME, AND TYLER.

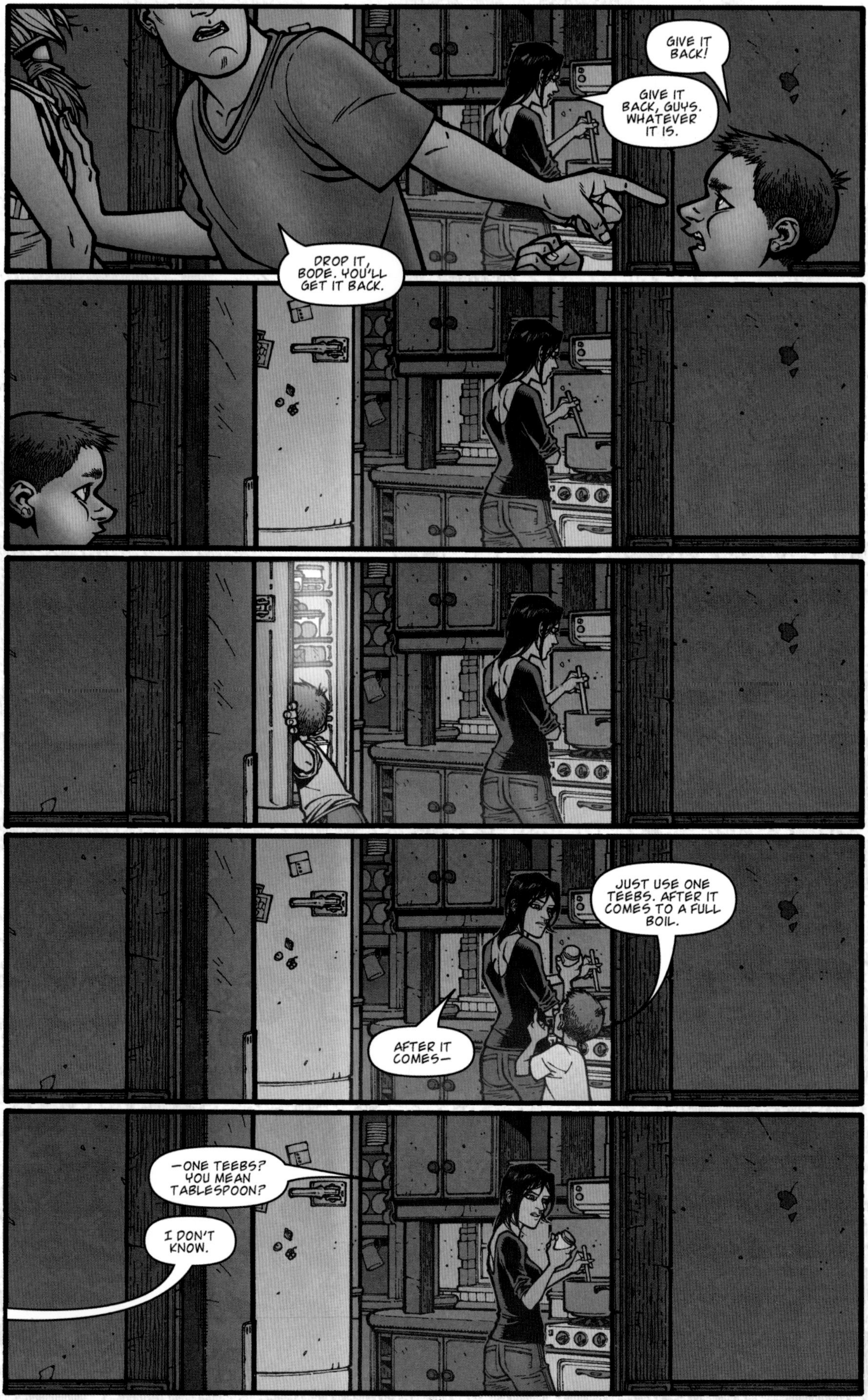
GIVE IT BACK!
GIVE IT BACK, GUYS. WHATEVER IT IS.
DROP IT, BODE. YOU'LL GET IT BACK.
JUST USE ONE TEEBS. AFTER IT COMES TO A FULL BOIL.
AFTER IT COMES—
—ONE TEEBS? YOU MEAN TABLESPOON?
I DON'T KNOW.

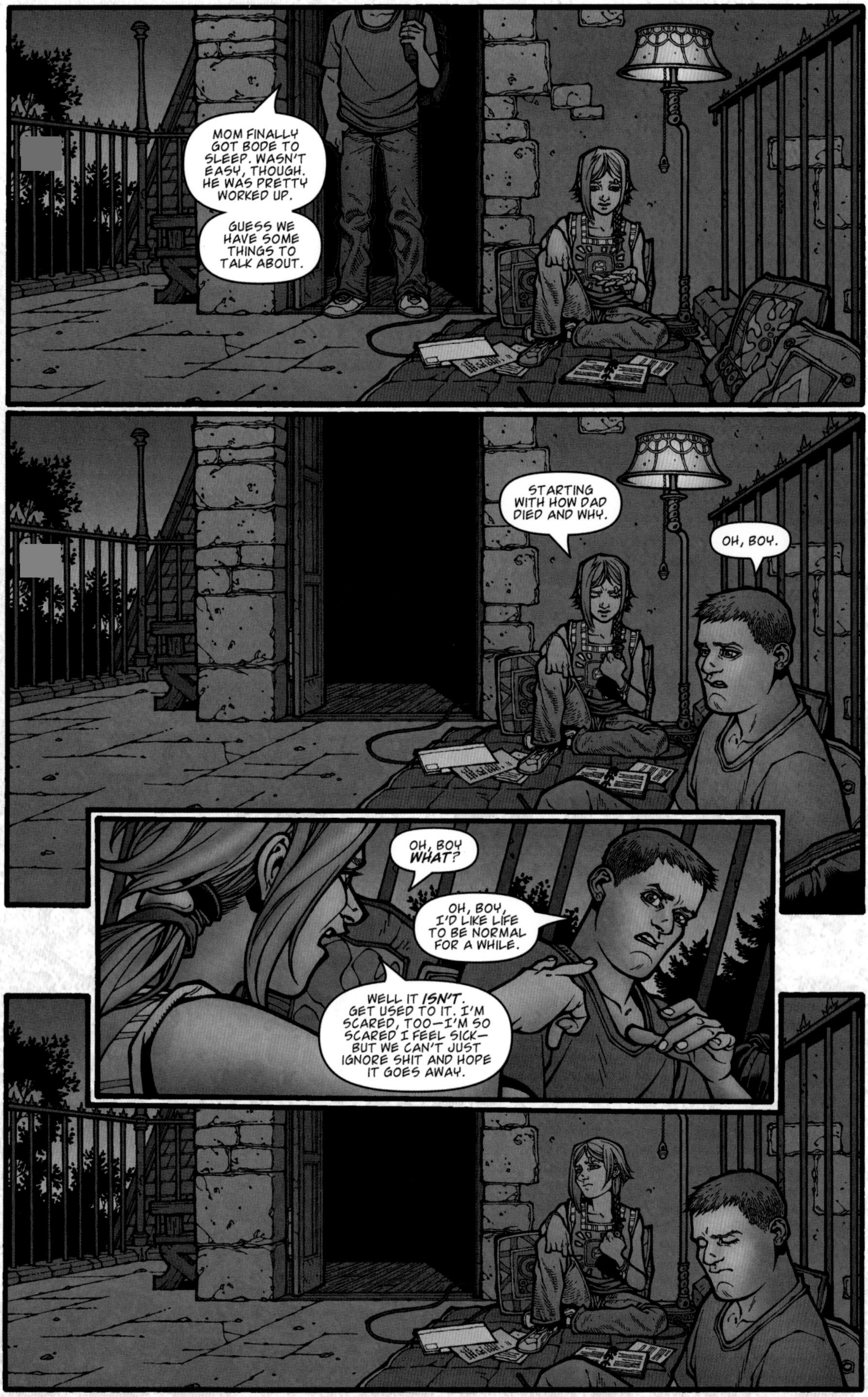
MOM FINALLY GOT BODE TO SLEEP. WASN'T EASY, THOUGH. HE WAS PRETTY WORKED UP.
GUESS WE HAVE SOME THINGS TO TALK ABOUT.
STARTING WITH HOW DAD DIED AND WHY.
OH, BOY.
OH, BOY ***WHAT***?
OH, BOY, I'D LIKE LIFE TO BE NORMAL FOR A WHILE.
WELL IT ***ISN'T***. GET USED TO IT. I'M SCARED, TOO—I'M SO SCARED I FEEL SICK—BUT WE CAN'T JUST IGNORE SHIT AND HOPE IT GOES AWAY.

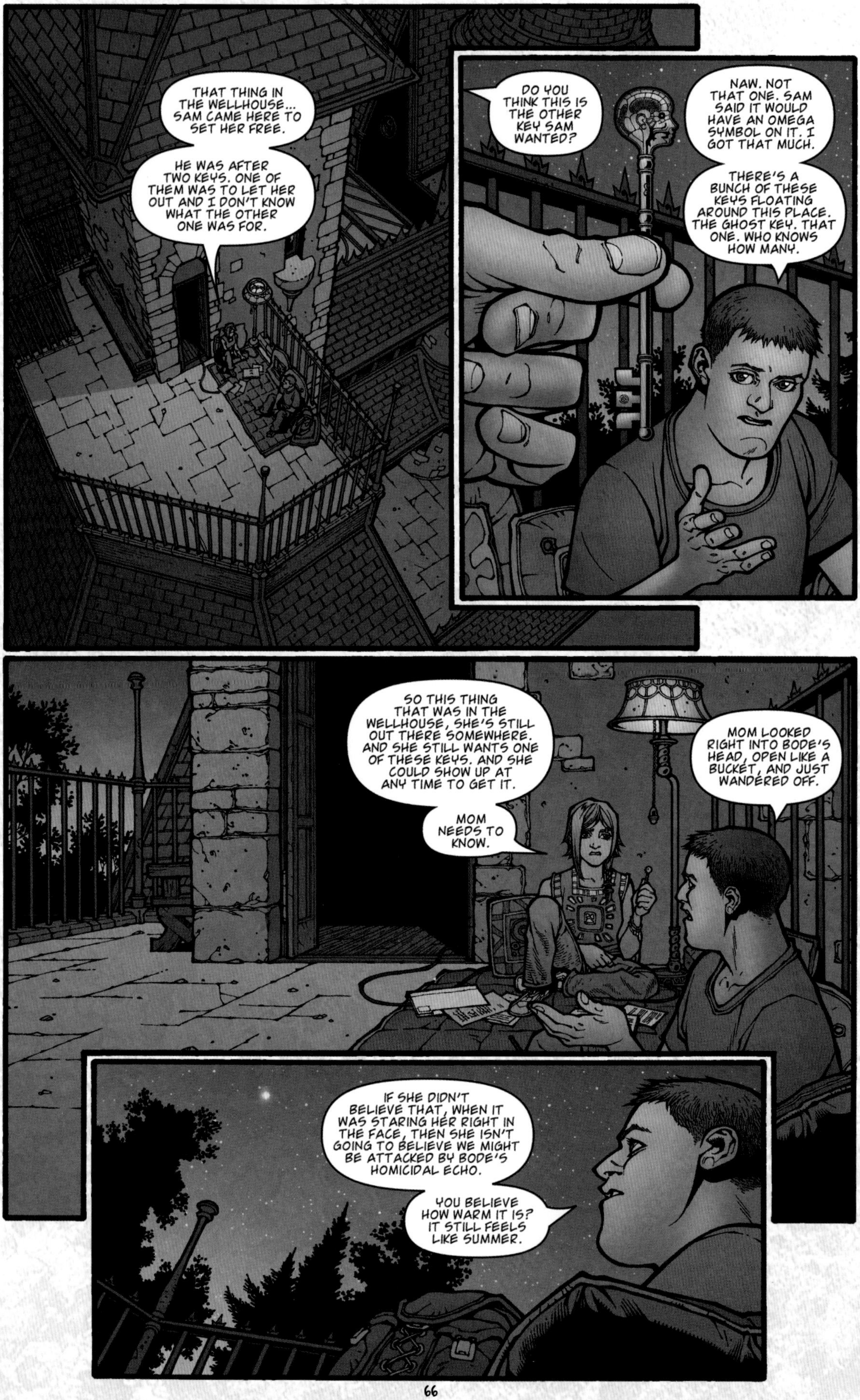
THAT THING IN THE WELLHOUSE... SAM CAME HERE TO SET HER FREE.
HE WAS AFTER TWO KEYS. ONE OF THEM WAS TO LET HER OUT AND I DON'T KNOW WHAT THE OTHER ONE WAS FOR.
DO YOU THINK THIS IS THE OTHER KEY SAM WANTED?
NAW. NOT THAT ONE. SAM SAID IT WOULD HAVE AN OMEGA SYMBOL ON IT. I GOT THAT MUCH.
THERE'S A BUNCH OF THESE KEYS FLOATING AROUND THIS PLACE. THE GHOST KEY. THAT ONE. WHO KNOWS HOW MANY.
SO THIS THING THAT WAS IN THE WELLHOUSE, SHE'S STILL OUT THERE SOMEWHERE. AND SHE STILL WANTS ONE OF THESE KEYS. AND SHE COULD SHOW UP AT ANY TIME TO GET IT.
MOM NEEDS TO KNOW.
MOM LOOKED RIGHT INTO BODE'S HEAD, OPEN LIKE A BUCKET, AND JUST WANDERED OFF.
IF SHE DIDN'T BELIEVE THAT, WHEN IT WAS STARING HER RIGHT IN THE FACE, THEN SHE ISN'T GOING TO BELIEVE WE MIGHT BE ATTACKED BY BODE'S HOMICIDAL ECHO.
YOU BELIEVE HOW WARM IT IS? IT STILL FEELS LIKE SUMMER.

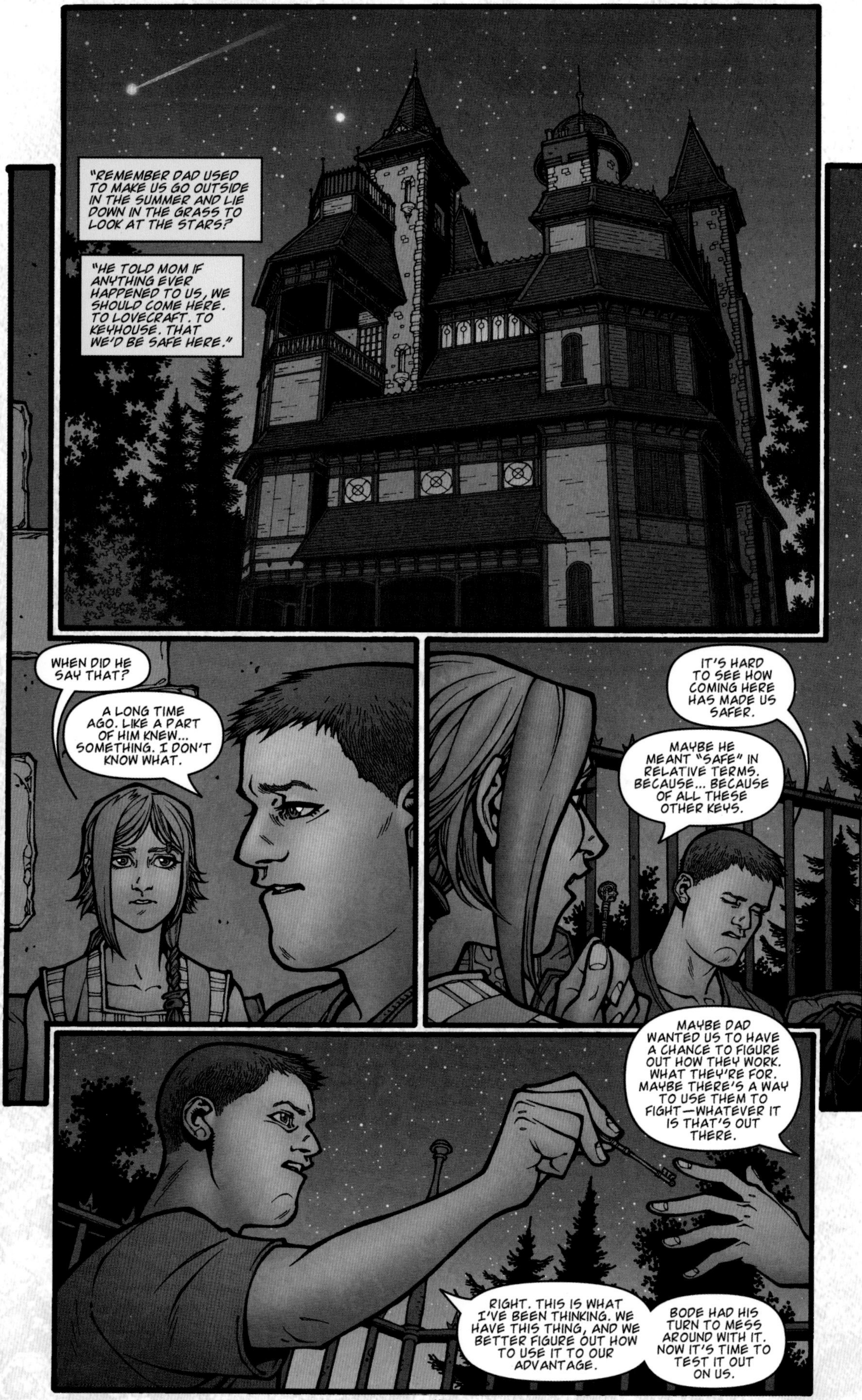
"REMEMBER DAD USED TO MAKE US GO OUTSIDE IN THE SUMMER AND LIE DOWN IN THE GRASS TO LOOK AT THE STARS?
"HE TOLD MOM IF ANYTHING EVER HAPPENED TO US, WE SHOULD COME HERE. TO LOVECRAFT. TO KEYHOUSE. THAT WE'D BE SAFE HERE."
WHEN DID HE SAY THAT?
A LONG TIME AGO. LIKE A PART OF HIM KNEW... SOMETHING. I DON'T KNOW WHAT.
IT'S HARD TO SEE HOW COMING HERE HAS MADE US SAFER.
MAYBE HE MEANT "SAFE" IN RELATIVE TERMS. BECAUSE... BECAUSE OF ALL THESE OTHER KEYS.
MAYBE DAD WANTED US TO HAVE A CHANCE TO FIGURE OUT HOW THEY WORK. WHAT THEY'RE FOR. MAYBE THERE'S A WAY TO USE THEM TO FIGHT—WHATEVER IT IS THAT'S OUT THERE.
RIGHT. THIS IS WHAT I'VE BEEN THINKING. WE HAVE THIS THING, AND WE BETTER FIGURE OUT HOW TO USE IT TO OUR ADVANTAGE.
BODE HAD HIS TURN TO MESS AROUND WITH IT. NOW IT'S TIME TO TEST IT OUT ON US.

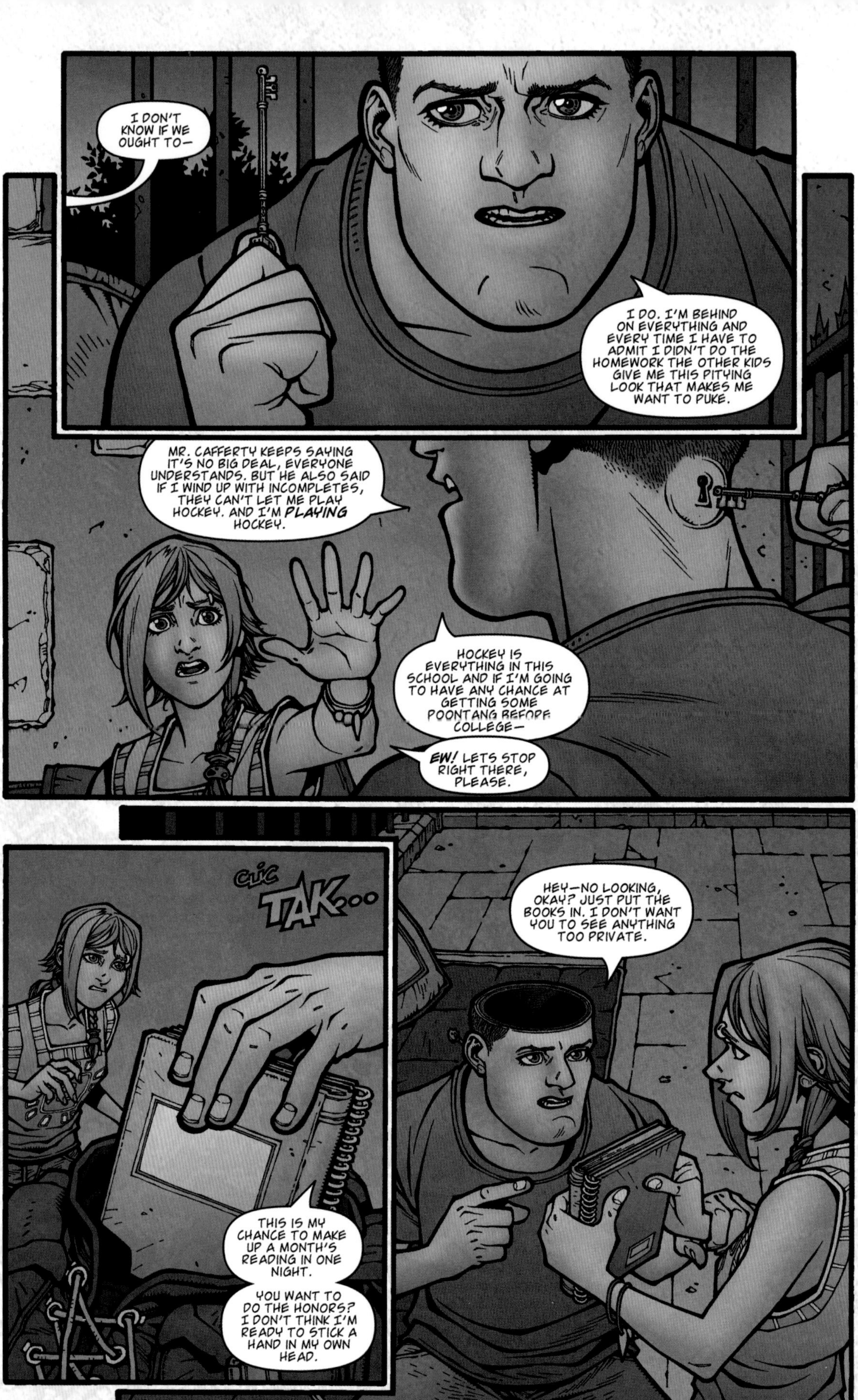
I DON'T KNOW IF WE OUGHT TO—
I DO. I'M BEHIND ON EVERYTHING AND EVERY TIME I HAVE TO ADMIT I DIDN'T DO THE HOMEWORK THE OTHER KIDS GIVE ME THIS PITYING LOOK THAT MAKES ME WANT TO PUKE.
MR. CAFFERTY KEEPS SAYING IT'S NO BIG DEAL, EVERYONE UNDERSTANDS. BUT HE ALSO SAID IF I WIND UP WITH INCOMPLETES, THEY CAN'T LET ME PLAY HOCKEY. AND I'M PLAYING HOCKEY.
HOCKEY IS EVERYTHING IN THIS SCHOOL AND IF I'M GOING TO HAVE ANY CHANCE AT GETTING SOME POONTANG BEFORE COLLEGE—
EW! LETS STOP RIGHT THERE, PLEASE.
CLIC
TAK...
THIS IS MY CHANCE TO MAKE UP A MONTH'S READING IN ONE NIGHT.
YOU WANT TO DO THE HONORS? I DON'T THINK I'M READY TO STICK A HAND IN MY OWN HEAD.
HEY—NO LOOKING, OKAY? JUST PUT THE BOOKS IN. I DON'T WANT YOU TO SEE ANYTHING TOO PRIVATE.

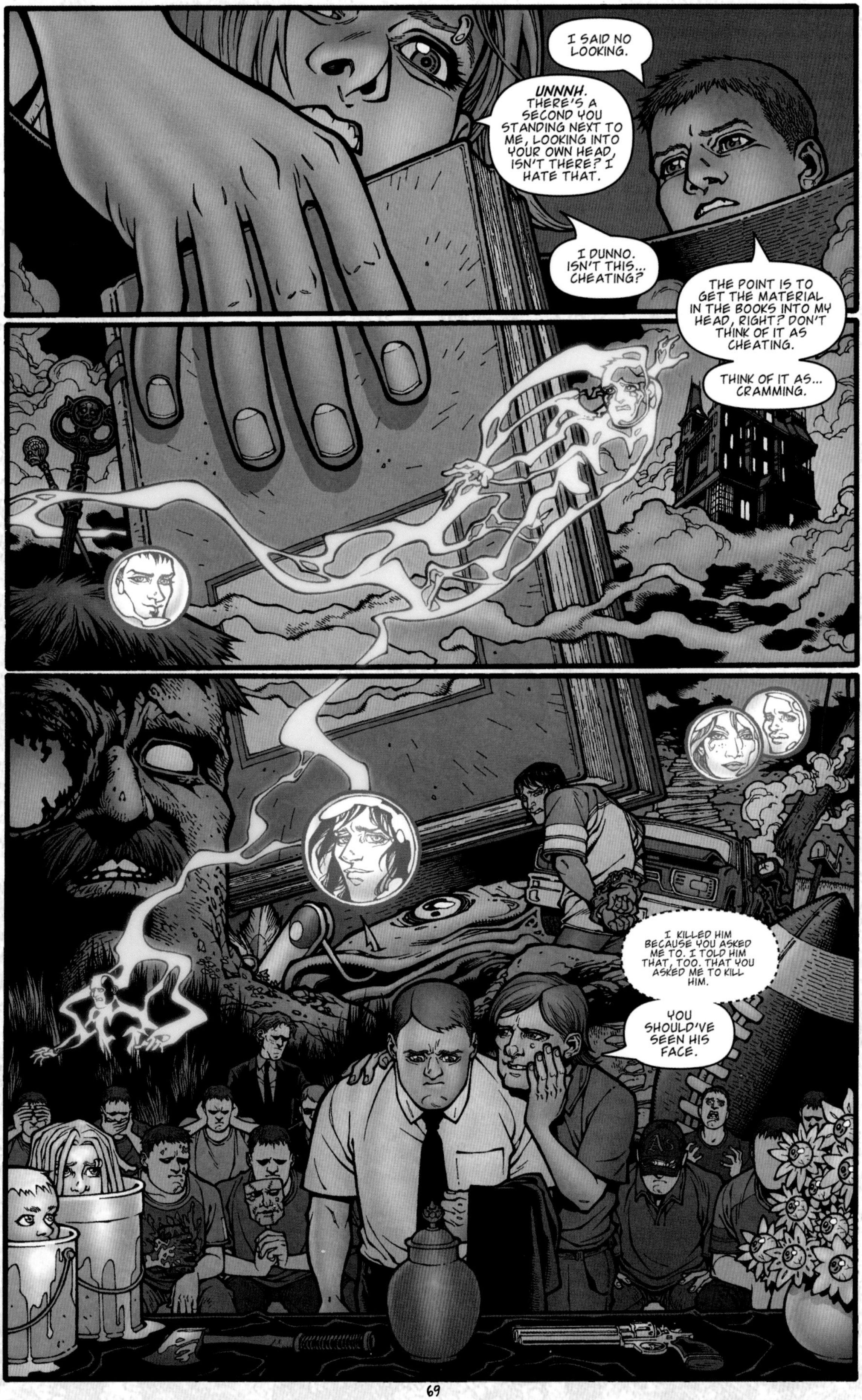
I SAID NO LOOKING.
UNNNH. THERE'S A SECOND YOU STANDING NEXT TO ME, LOOKING INTO YOUR OWN HEAD, ISN'T THERE? I HATE THAT.
I DUNNO. ISN'T THIS... CHEATING?
THE POINT IS TO GET THE MATERIAL IN THE BOOKS INTO MY HEAD, RIGHT? DON'T THINK OF IT AS CHEATING.
THINK OF IT AS... CRAMMING.
I KILLED HIM BECAUSE YOU ASKED ME TO. I TOLD HIM THAT, TOO. THAT YOU ASKED ME TO KILL HIM.
YOU SHOULD'VE SEEN HIS FACE.

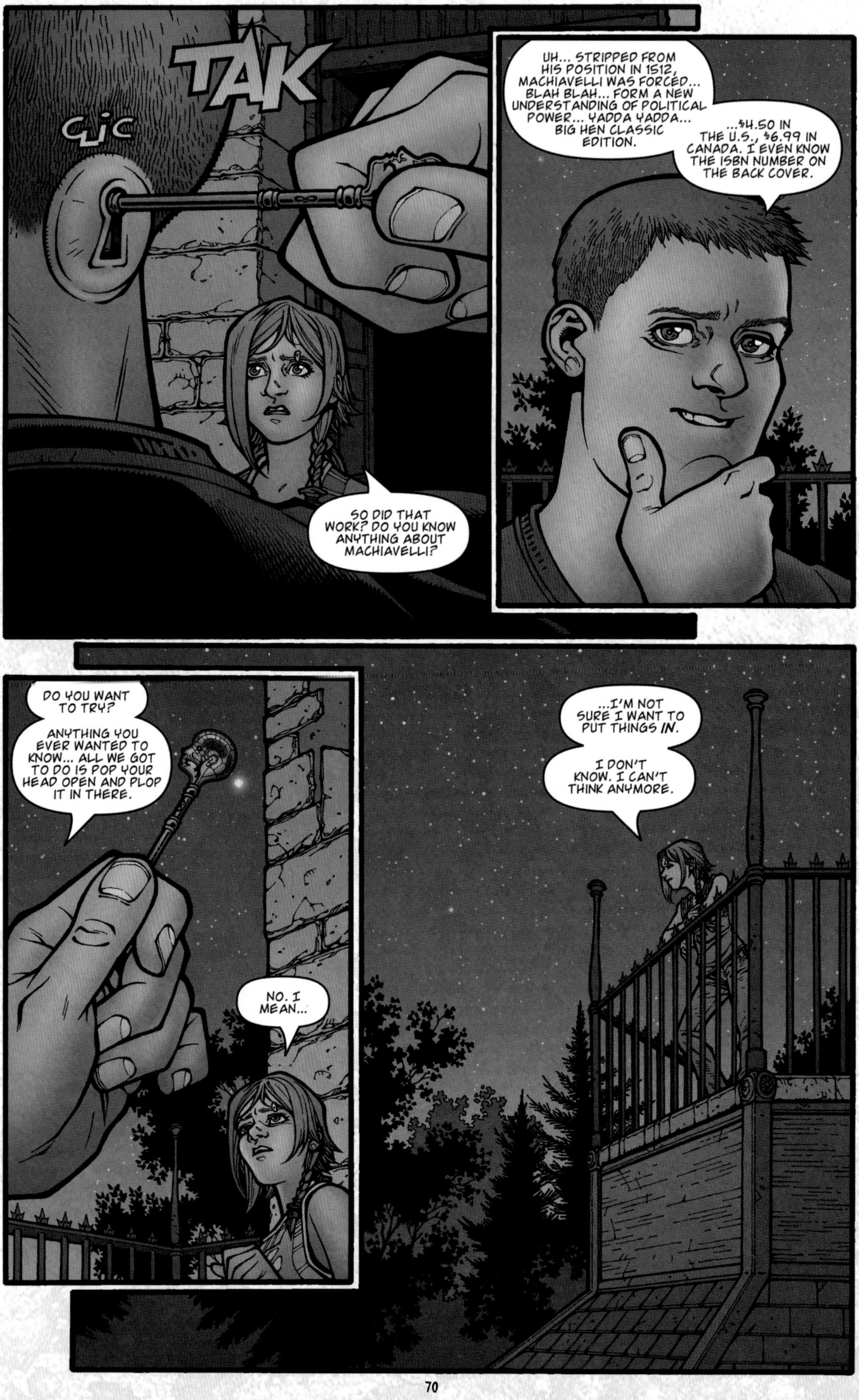
TAK
CLIC
SO DID THAT WORK? DO YOU KNOW ANYTHING ABOUT MACHIAVELLI?
UH... STRIPPED FROM HIS POSITION IN 1512, MACHIAVELLI WAS FORCED... BLAH BLAH... FORM A NEW UNDERSTANDING OF POLITICAL POWER... YADDA YADDA... BIG HEN CLASSIC EDITION.
...$4.50 IN THE U.S., $6.99 IN CANADA. I EVEN KNOW THE ISBN NUMBER ON THE BACK COVER.
DO YOU WANT TO TRY?
ANYTHING YOU EVER WANTED TO KNOW... ALL WE GOT TO DO IS POP YOUR HEAD OPEN AND PLOP IT IN THERE.
NO. I MEAN...
...I'M NOT SURE I WANT TO PUT THINGS *IN*.
I DON'T KNOW. I CAN'T THINK ANYMORE.

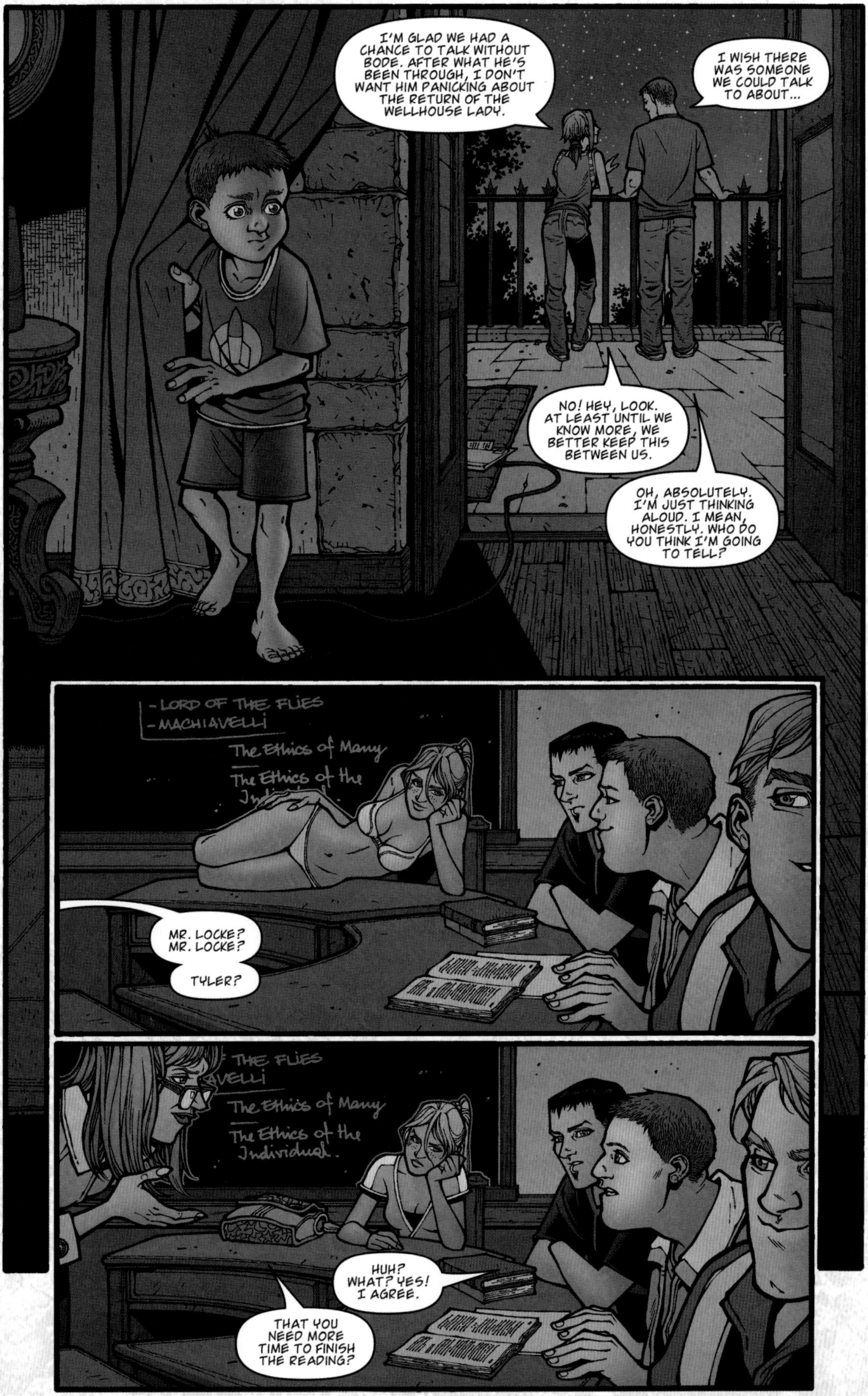
I'M GLAD WE HAD A CHANCE TO TALK WITHOUT BODE. AFTER WHAT HE'S BEEN THROUGH, I DON'T WANT HIM PANICKING ABOUT THE RETURN OF THE WELLHOUSE LADY.
I WISH THERE WAS SOMEONE WE COULD TALK TO ABOUT...
NO! HEY, LOOK. AT LEAST UNTIL WE KNOW MORE, WE BETTER KEEP THIS BETWEEN US.
OH, ABSOLUTELY. I'M JUST THINKING ALOUD. I MEAN, HONESTLY. WHO DO YOU THINK I'M GOING TO TELL?
- LORD OF THE FLIES
- MACHIAVELLI
The Ethics of Many
The Ethics of the
MR. LOCKE? MR. LOCKE?
TYLER?
THE FLIES
AVELLI
The Ethics of Many
The Ethics of the Individual.
HUH? WHAT? YES! I AGREE.
THAT YOU NEED MORE TIME TO FINISH THE READING?

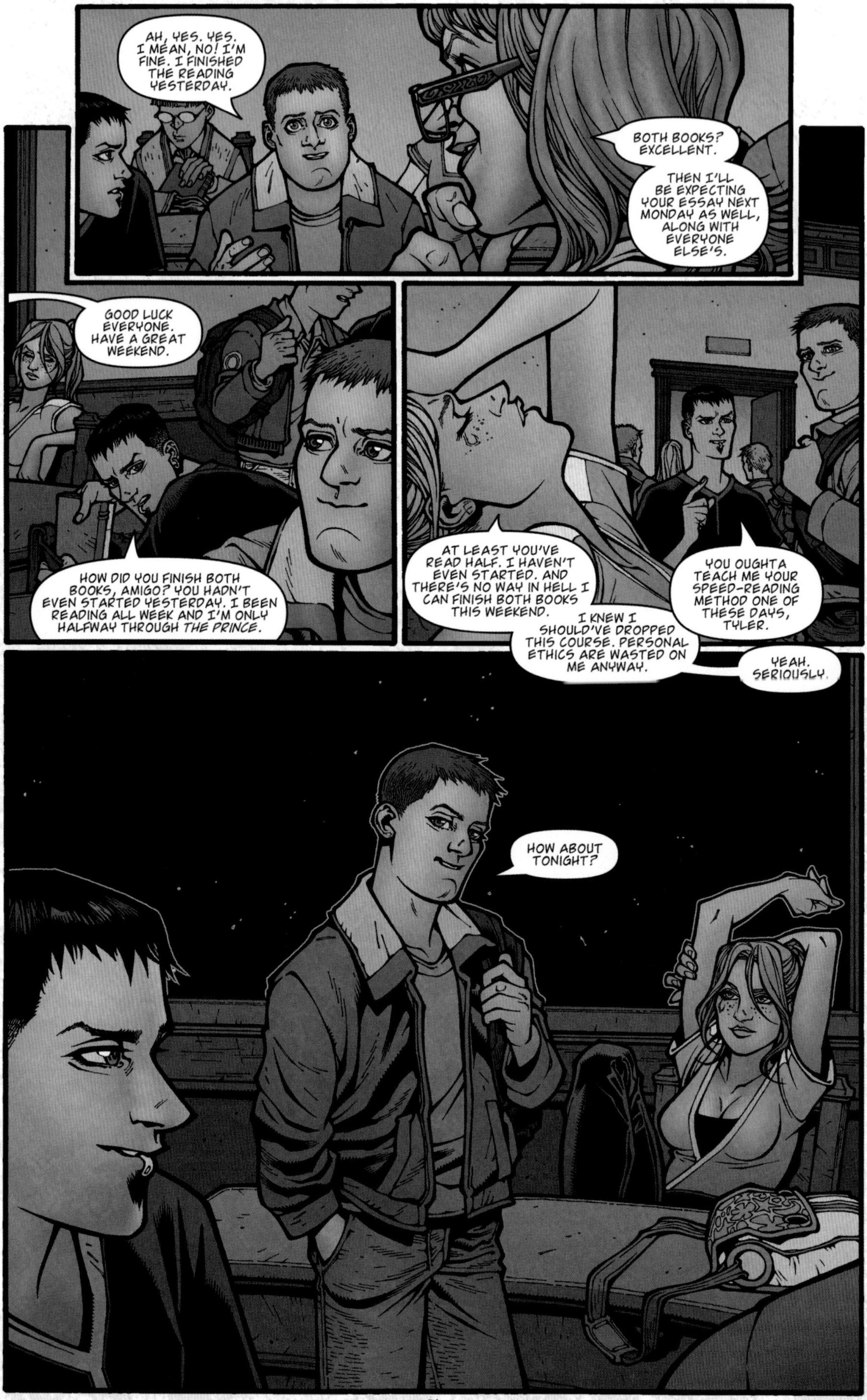
AH, YES. YES. I MEAN, NO! I'M FINE. I FINISHED THE READING YESTERDAY.
BOTH BOOKS? EXCELLENT.
THEN I'LL BE EXPECTING YOUR ESSAY NEXT MONDAY AS WELL, ALONG WITH EVERYONE ELSE'S.
GOOD LUCK EVERYONE. HAVE A GREAT WEEKEND.
HOW DID YOU FINISH BOTH BOOKS, AMIGO? YOU HADN'T EVEN STARTED YESTERDAY. I BEEN READING ALL WEEK AND I'M ONLY HALFWAY THROUGH *THE PRINCE*.
AT LEAST YOU'VE READ HALF. I HAVEN'T EVEN STARTED. AND THERE'S NO WAY IN HELL I CAN FINISH BOTH BOOKS THIS WEEKEND.
I KNEW I SHOULD'VE DROPPED THIS COURSE. PERSONAL ETHICS ARE WASTED ON ME ANYWAY.
YOU OUGHTA TEACH ME YOUR SPEED-READING METHOD ONE OF THESE DAYS, TYLER.
YEAH. SERIOUSLY.
HOW ABOUT TONIGHT?

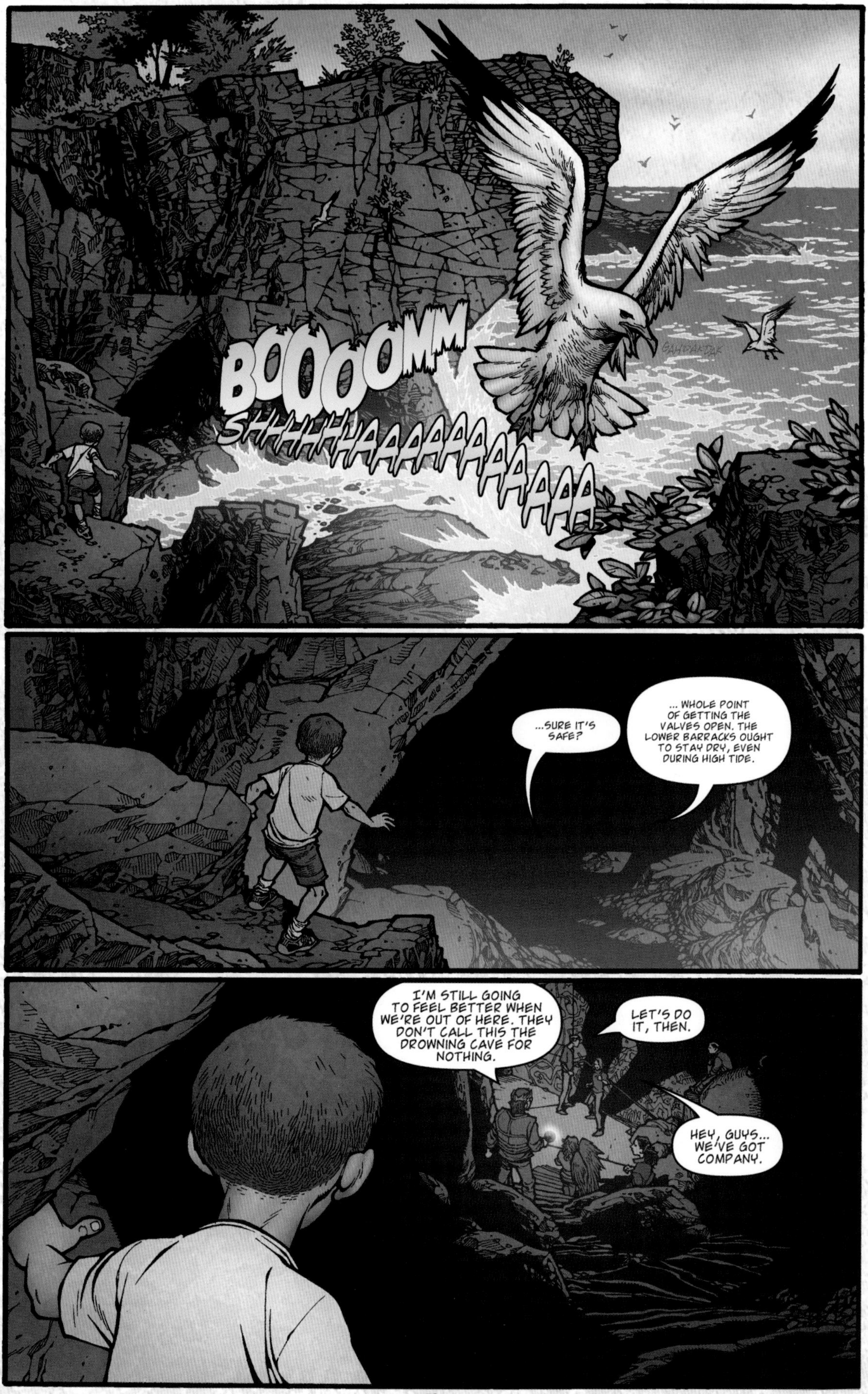
BOOOOMM
SHHHHAAAAAAAAAAAA
...SURE IT'S SAFE?
... WHOLE POINT OF GETTING THE VALVES OPEN. THE LOWER BARRACKS OUGHT TO STAY DRY, EVEN DURING HIGH TIDE.
I'M STILL GOING TO FEEL BETTER WHEN WE'RE OUT OF HERE. THEY DON'T CALL THIS THE DROWNING CAVE FOR NOTHING.
LET'S DO IT, THEN.
HEY, GUYS... WE'VE GOT COMPANY.

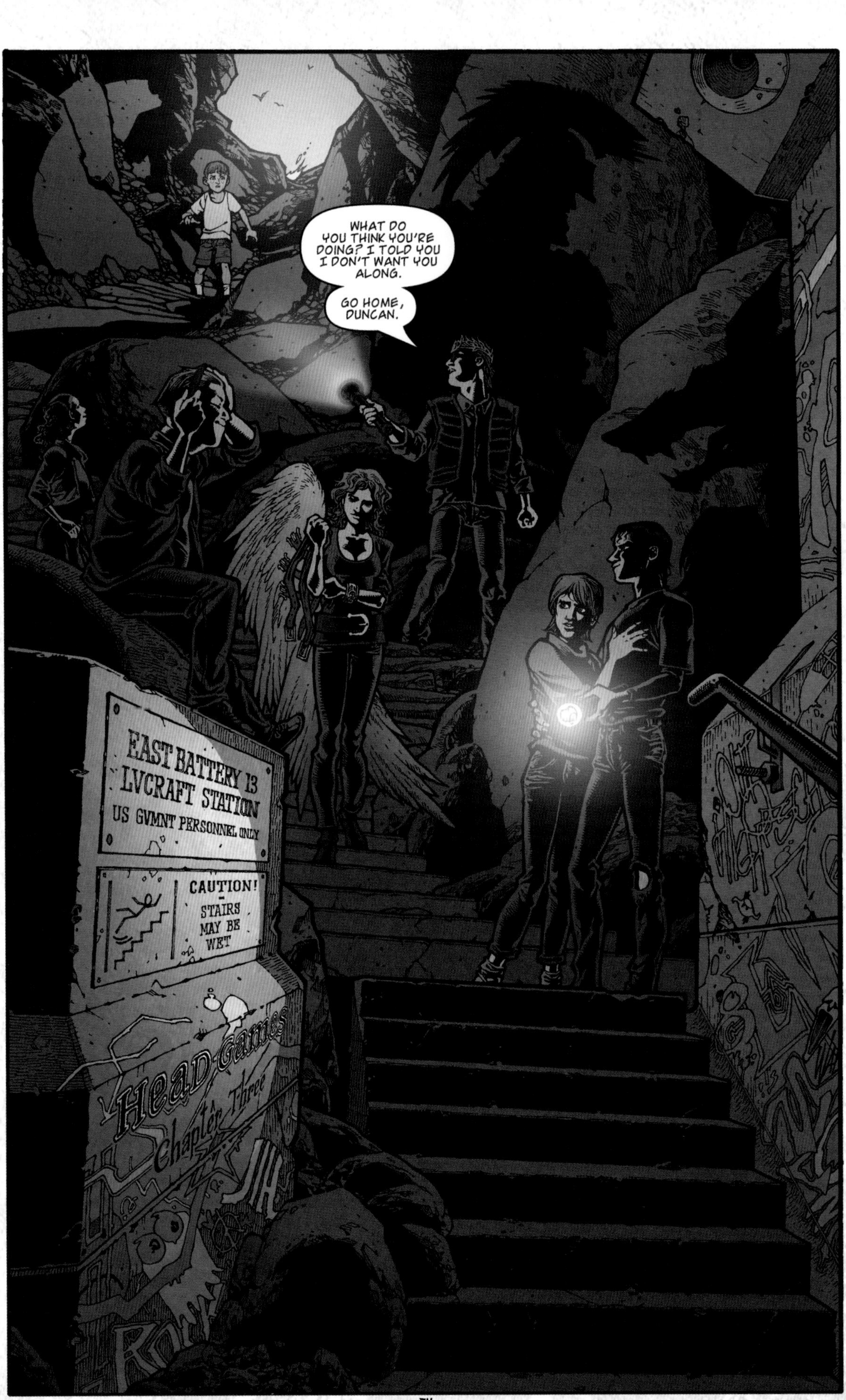
WHAT DO YOU THINK YOU'RE DOING? I TOLD YOU I DON'T WANT YOU ALONG.
GO HOME, DUNCAN.
EAST BATTERY 13
LVCRAFT STATION
US GVMNT PERSONNEL ONLY
CAUTION!
STAIRS MAY BE WET
Head Games
Chapter Three

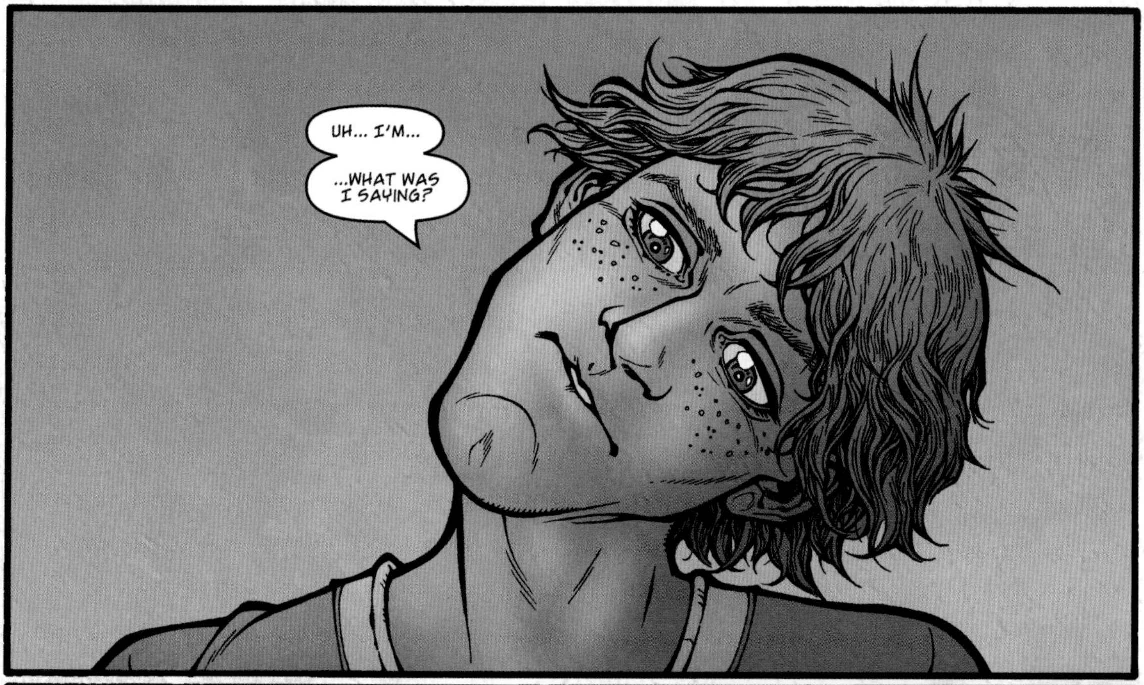
UH... I'M...
...WHAT WAS I SAYING?

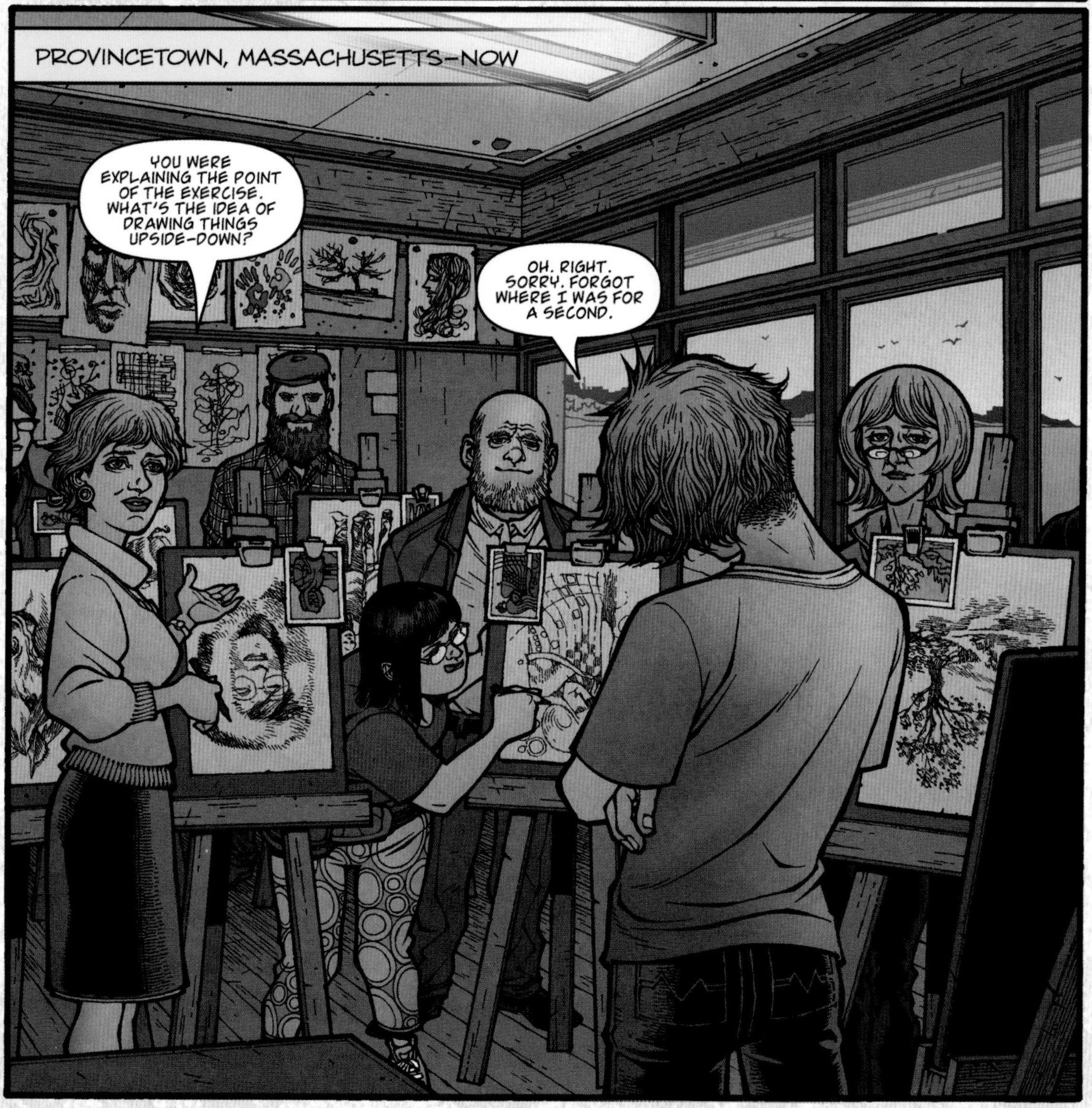
PROVINCETOWN, MASSACHUSETTS—NOW
YOU WERE EXPLAINING THE POINT OF THE EXERCISE. WHAT'S THE IDEA OF DRAWING THINGS UPSIDE-DOWN?
OH. RIGHT. SORRY. FORGOT WHERE I WAS FOR A SECOND.

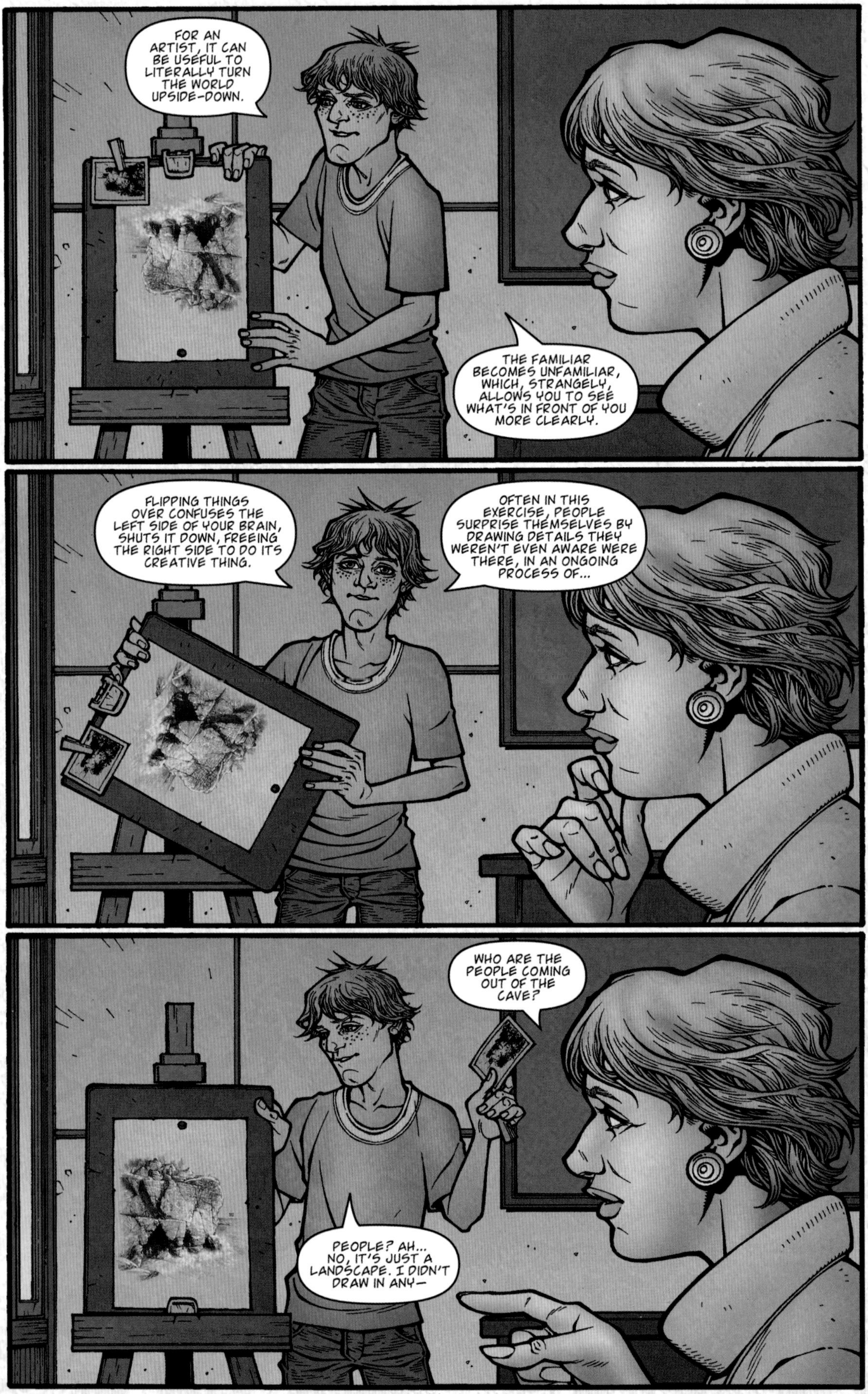
FOR AN ARTIST, IT CAN BE USEFUL TO LITERALLY TURN THE WORLD UPSIDE-DOWN.
THE FAMILIAR BECOMES UNFAMILIAR, WHICH, STRANGELY, ALLOWS YOU TO SEE WHAT'S IN FRONT OF YOU MORE CLEARLY.
FLIPPING THINGS OVER CONFUSES THE LEFT SIDE OF YOUR BRAIN, SHUTS IT DOWN, FREEING THE RIGHT SIDE TO DO ITS CREATIVE THING.
OFTEN IN THIS EXERCISE, PEOPLE SURPRISE THEMSELVES BY DRAWING DETAILS THEY WEREN'T EVEN AWARE WERE THERE, IN AN ONGOING PROCESS OF...
WHO ARE THE PEOPLE COMING OUT OF THE CAVE?
PEOPLE? AH... NO, IT'S JUST A LANDSCAPE. I DIDN'T DRAW IN ANY—

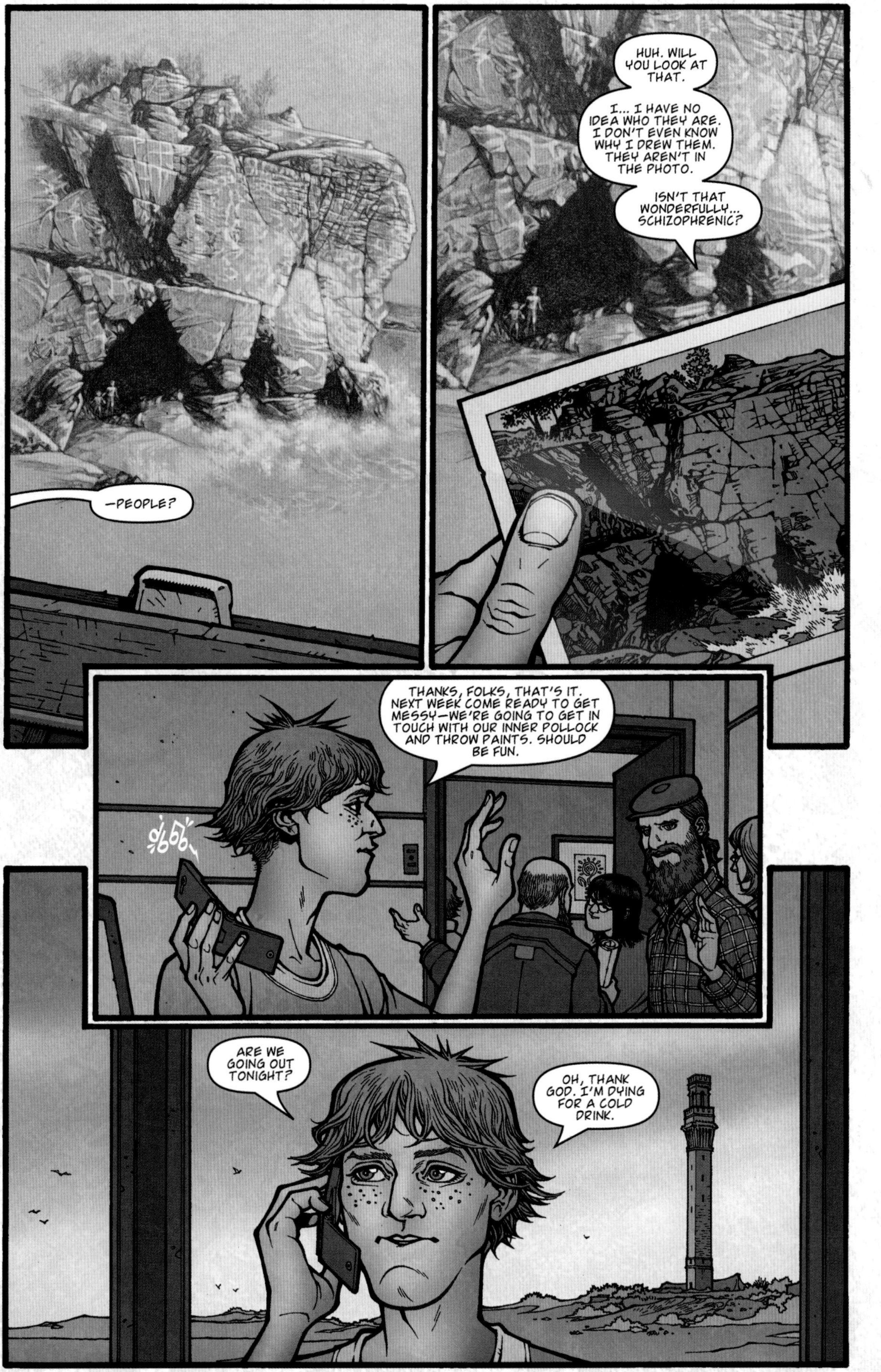
—PEOPLE?
HUH. WILL YOU LOOK AT THAT.
I... I HAVE NO IDEA WHO THEY ARE. I DON'T EVEN KNOW WHY I DREW THEM. THEY AREN'T IN THE PHOTO.
ISN'T THAT WONDERFULLY... SCHIZOPHRENIC?
THANKS, FOLKS, THAT'S IT. NEXT WEEK COME READY TO GET MESSY—WE'RE GOING TO GET IN TOUCH WITH OUR INNER POLLOCK AND THROW PAINTS. SHOULD BE FUN.
ARE WE GOING OUT TONIGHT?
OH, THANK GOD. I'M DYING FOR A COLD DRINK.

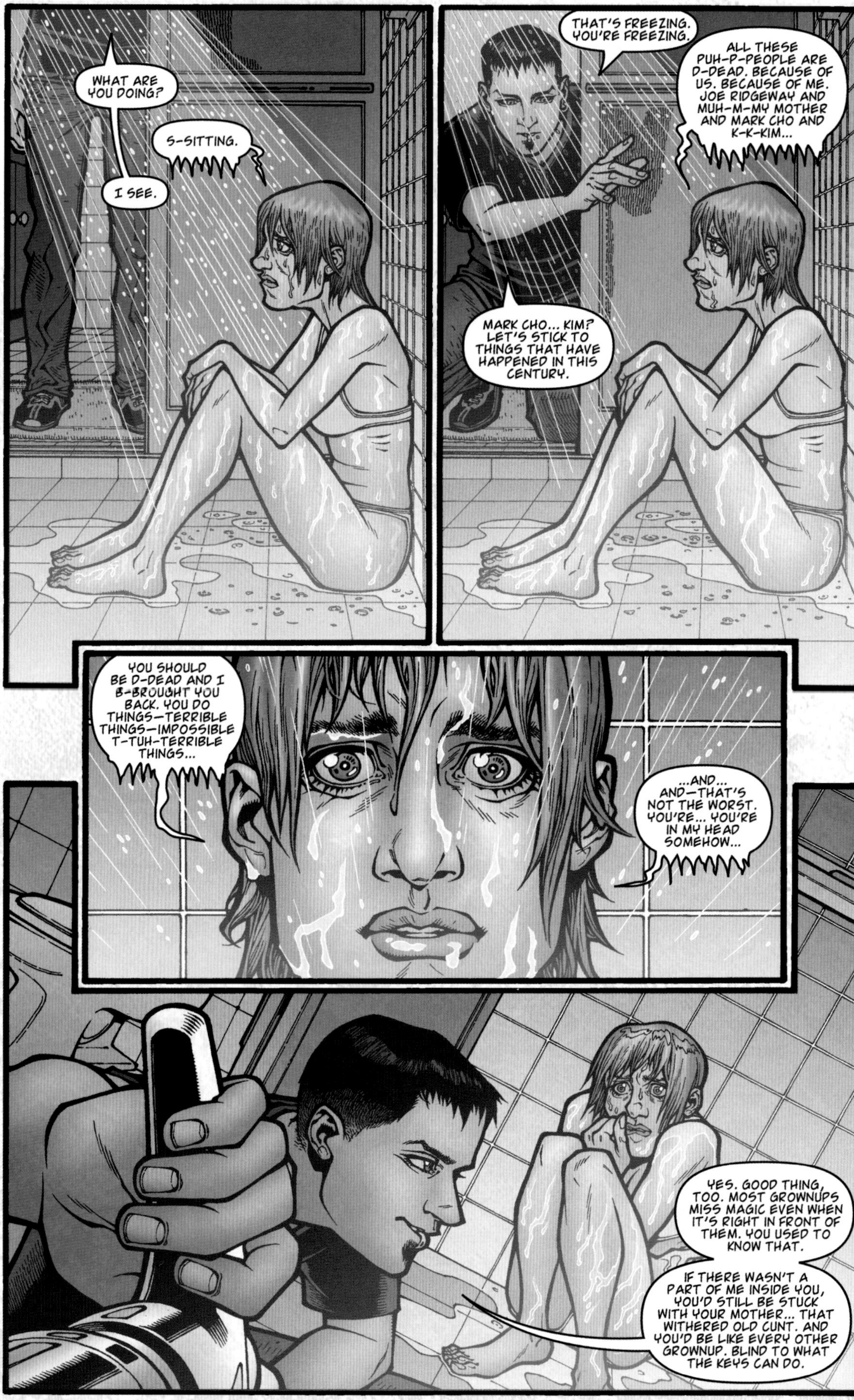

WHAT ARE YOU DOING?
S-SITTING.
I SEE.
THAT'S FREEZING. YOU'RE FREEZING.
ALL THESE PUH-P-PEOPLE ARE D-DEAD. BECAUSE OF US. BECAUSE OF ME. JOE RIDGEWAY AND MUH-M-MY MOTHER AND MARK CHO AND K-K-KIM...
MARK CHO... KIM? LET'S STICK TO THINGS THAT HAVE HAPPENED IN THIS CENTURY.
YOU SHOULD BE D-DEAD AND I B-BROUGHT YOU BACK. YOU DO THINGS—TERRIBLE THINGS—IMPOSSIBLE T-TUH-TERRIBLE THINGS...
...AND... AND—THAT'S NOT THE WORST. YOU'RE... YOU'RE IN MY HEAD SOMEHOW...
YES. GOOD THING, TOO. MOST GROWNUPS MISS MAGIC EVEN WHEN IT'S RIGHT IN FRONT OF THEM. YOU USED TO KNOW THAT.
IF THERE WASN'T A PART OF ME INSIDE YOU, YOU'D STILL BE STUCK WITH YOUR MOTHER... THAT WITHERED OLD CUNT. AND YOU'D BE LIKE EVERY OTHER GROWNUP. BLIND TO WHAT THE KEYS CAN DO.

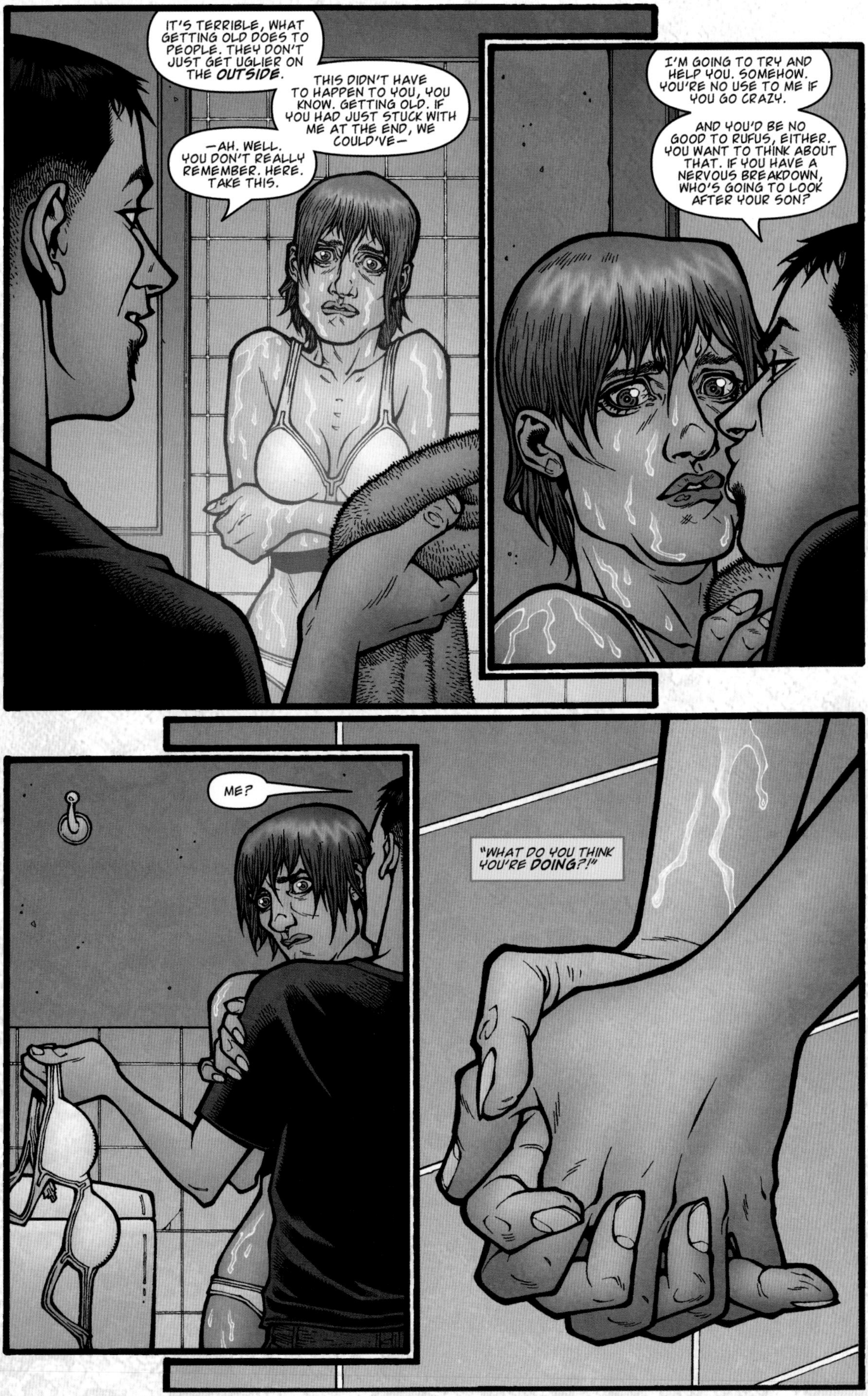
IT'S TERRIBLE, WHAT GETTING OLD DOES TO PEOPLE. THEY DON'T JUST GET UGLIER ON THE OUTSIDE.
THIS DIDN'T HAVE TO HAPPEN TO YOU, YOU KNOW. GETTING OLD. IF YOU HAD JUST STUCK WITH ME AT THE END, WE COULD'VE—
—AH. WELL. YOU DON'T REALLY REMEMBER. HERE. TAKE THIS.
I'M GOING TO TRY AND HELP YOU. SOMEHOW. YOU'RE NO USE TO ME IF YOU GO CRAZY.
AND YOU'D BE NO GOOD TO RUFUS, EITHER. YOU WANT TO THINK ABOUT THAT. IF YOU HAVE A NERVOUS BREAKDOWN, WHO'S GOING TO LOOK AFTER YOUR SON?
ME?
"WHAT DO YOU THINK YOU'RE DOING?!"

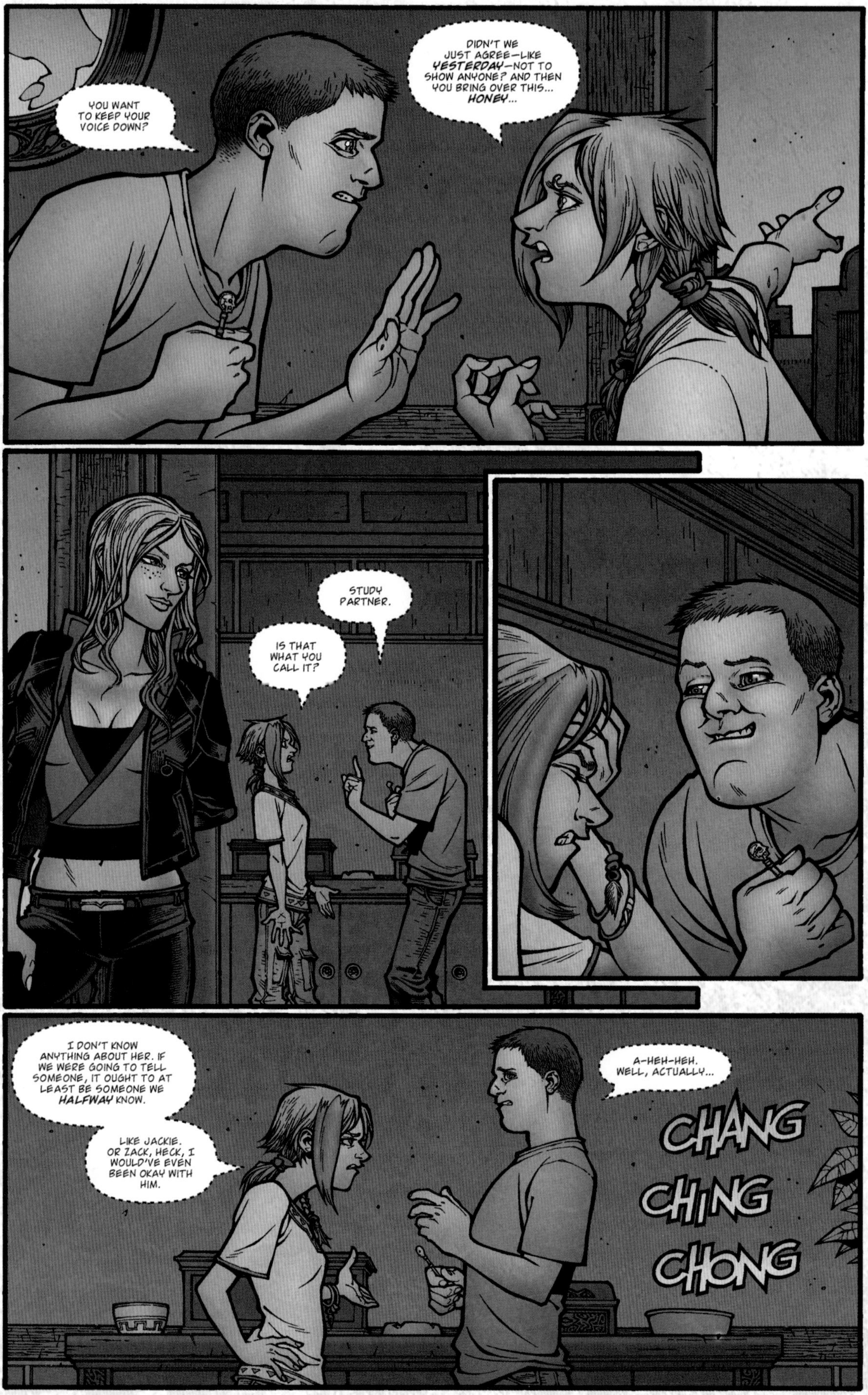
YOU WANT TO KEEP YOUR VOICE DOWN?
DIDN'T WE JUST AGREE—LIKE YESTERDAY—NOT TO SHOW ANYONE? AND THEN YOU BRING OVER THIS... HONEY...
STUDY PARTNER.
IS THAT WHAT YOU CALL IT?
I DON'T KNOW ANYTHING ABOUT HER. IF WE WERE GOING TO TELL SOMEONE, IT OUGHT TO AT LEAST BE SOMEONE WE HALFWAY KNOW.
LIKE JACKIE. OR ZACK, HECK, I WOULD'VE EVEN BEEN OKAY WITH HIM.
A-HEH-HEH. WELL, ACTUALLY...
CHANG
CHING
CHONG

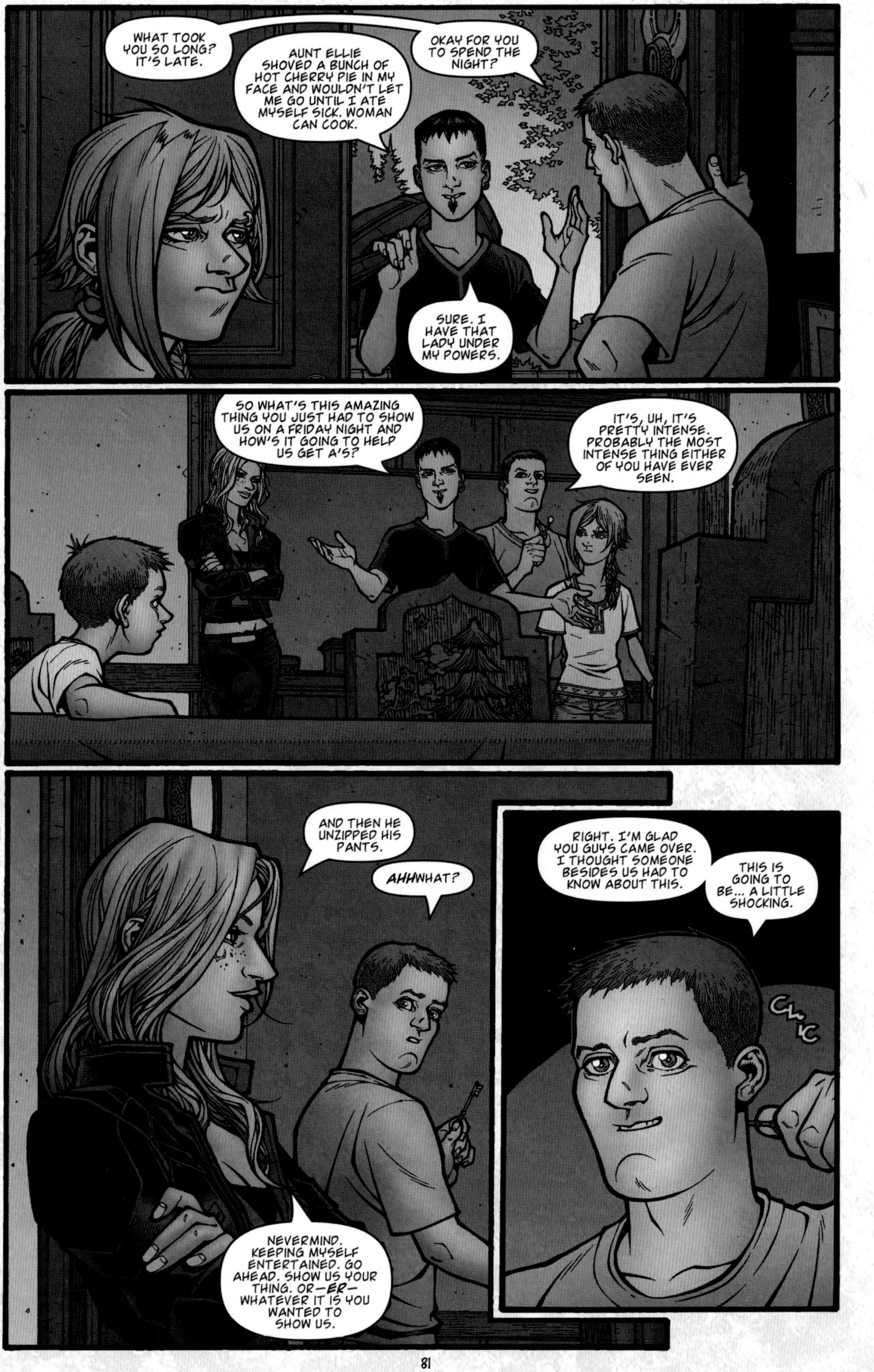
WHAT TOOK YOU SO LONG? IT'S LATE.
AUNT ELLIE SHOVED A BUNCH OF HOT CHERRY PIE IN MY FACE AND WOULDN'T LET ME GO UNTIL I ATE MYSELF SICK. WOMAN CAN COOK.
OKAY FOR YOU TO SPEND THE NIGHT?
SURE. I HAVE THAT LADY UNDER MY POWERS.
SO WHAT'S THIS AMAZING THING YOU JUST HAD TO SHOW US ON A FRIDAY NIGHT AND HOW'S IT GOING TO HELP US GET A'S?
IT'S, UH, IT'S PRETTY INTENSE. PROBABLY THE MOST INTENSE THING EITHER OF YOU HAVE EVER SEEN.
AND THEN HE UNZIPPED HIS PANTS.
AHHWHAT?
NEVERMIND. KEEPING MYSELF ENTERTAINED. GO AHEAD. SHOW US YOUR THING. OR—ER—WHATEVER IT IS YOU WANTED TO SHOW US.
RIGHT. I'M GLAD YOU GUYS CAME OVER. I THOUGHT SOMEONE BESIDES US HAD TO KNOW ABOUT THIS.
THIS IS GOING TO BE... A LITTLE SHOCKING.
CLIC

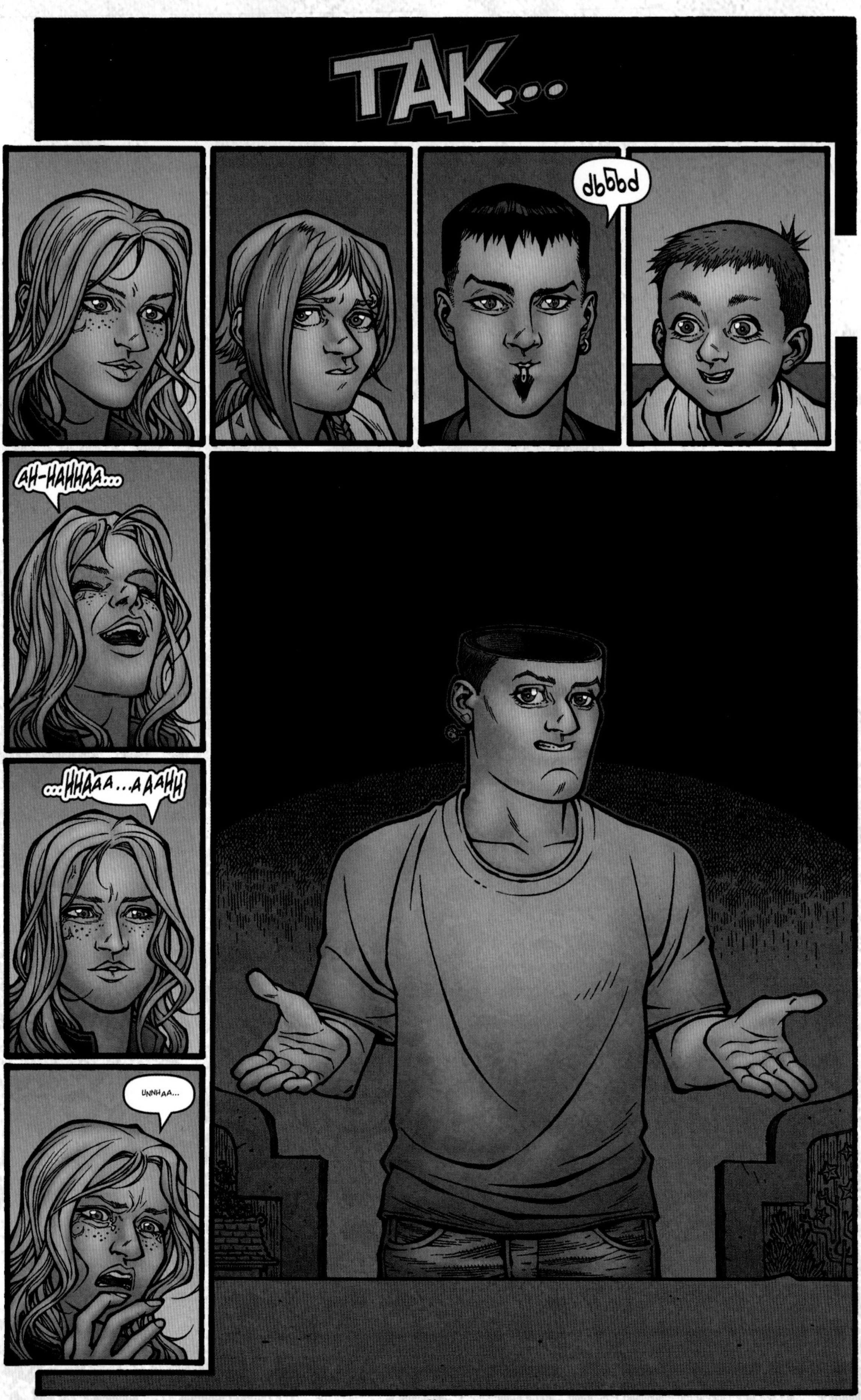
TAK...
dbbbd
AH-HAHHAA...
...HHAAA...AAAHH
UNNHAA...

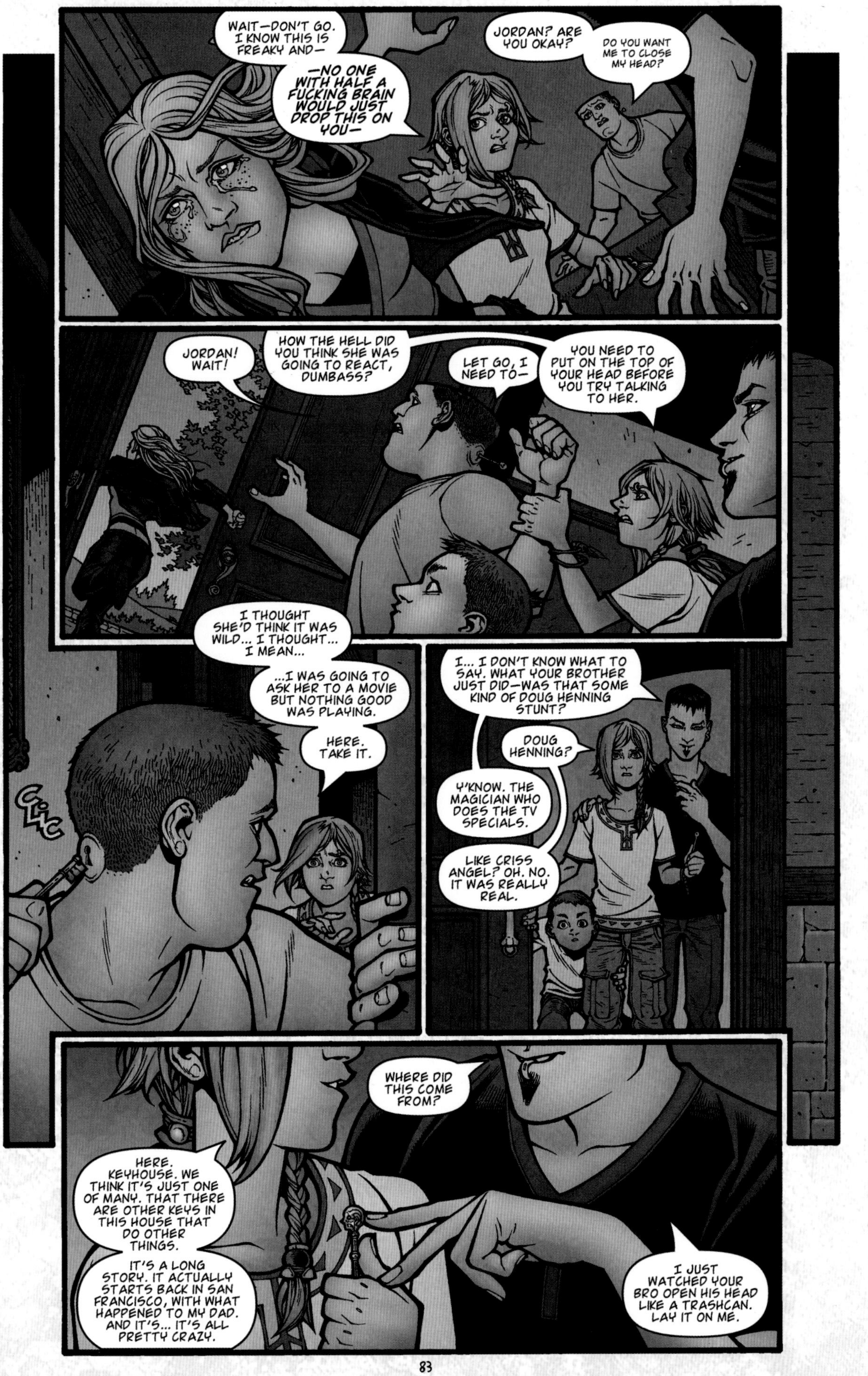
WAIT—DON'T GO. I KNOW THIS IS FREAKY AND—
—NO ONE WITH HALF A FUCKING BRAIN WOULD JUST DROP THIS ON YOU—
JORDAN? ARE YOU OKAY?
DO YOU WANT ME TO CLOSE MY HEAD?
JORDAN! WAIT!
HOW THE HELL DID YOU THINK SHE WAS GOING TO REACT, DUMBASS?
LET GO, I NEED TO—
YOU NEED TO PUT ON THE TOP OF YOUR HEAD BEFORE YOU TRY TALKING TO HER.
I THOUGHT SHE'D THINK IT WAS WILD... I THOUGHT... I MEAN...
...I WAS GOING TO ASK HER TO A MOVIE BUT NOTHING GOOD WAS PLAYING.
HERE. TAKE IT.
CLIC
I... I DON'T KNOW WHAT TO SAY. WHAT YOUR BROTHER JUST DID—WAS THAT SOME KIND OF DOUG HENNING STUNT?
DOUG HENNING?
Y'KNOW. THE MAGICIAN WHO DOES THE TV SPECIALS.
LIKE CRISS ANGEL? OH. NO. IT WAS REALLY REAL.
WHERE DID THIS COME FROM?
HERE. KEYHOUSE. WE THINK IT'S JUST ONE OF MANY. THAT THERE ARE OTHER KEYS IN THIS HOUSE THAT DO OTHER THINGS.
IT'S A LONG STORY. IT ACTUALLY STARTS BACK IN SAN FRANCISCO, WITH WHAT HAPPENED TO MY DAD. AND IT'S... IT'S ALL PRETTY CRAZY.
I JUST WATCHED YOUR BRO OPEN HIS HEAD LIKE A TRASHCAN. LAY IT ON ME.

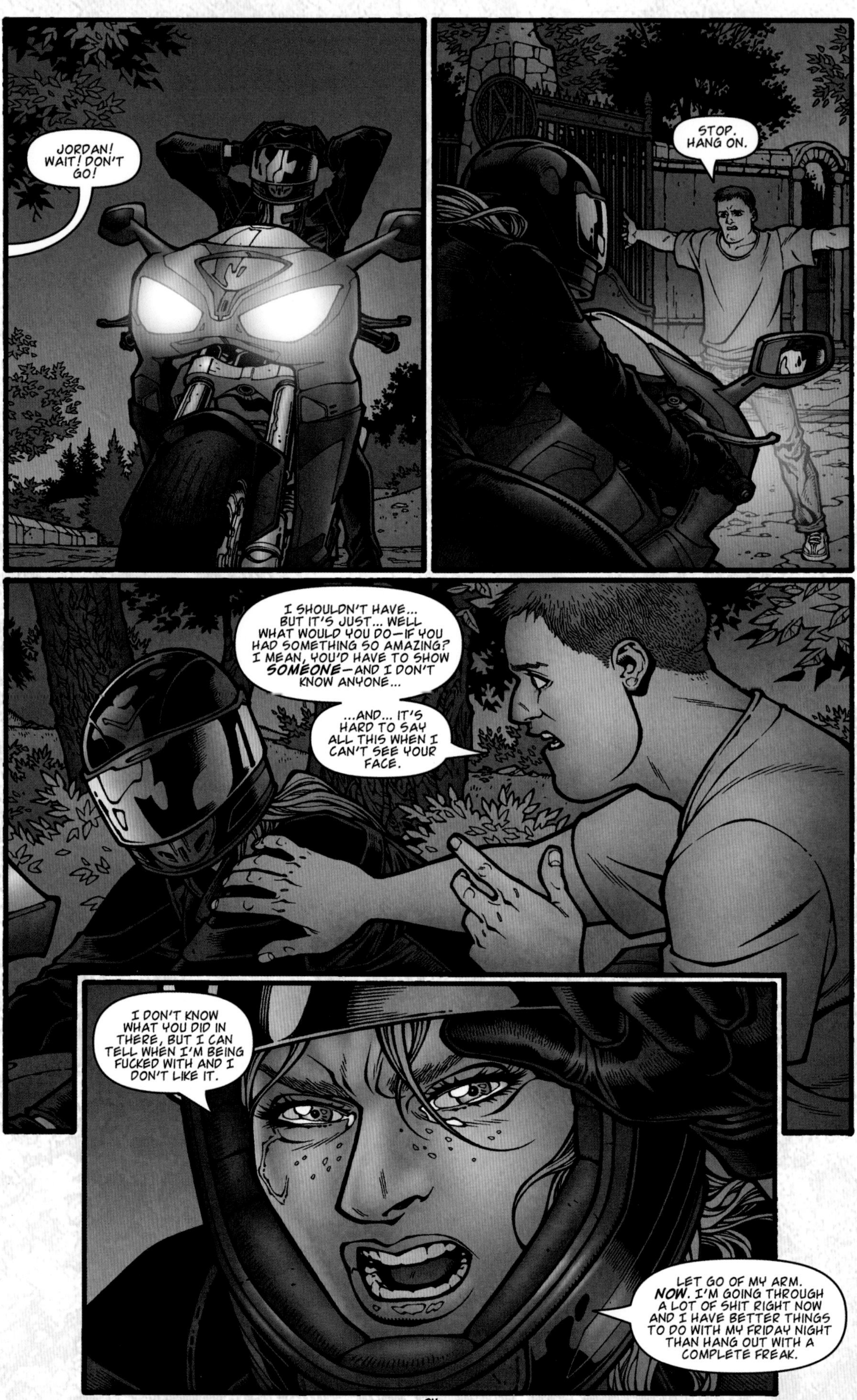
JORDAN! WAIT! DON'T GO!
STOP. HANG ON.
I SHOULDN'T HAVE... BUT IT'S JUST... WELL WHAT WOULD YOU DO—IF YOU HAD SOMETHING SO AMAZING? I MEAN, YOU'D HAVE TO SHOW SOMEONE—AND I DON'T KNOW ANYONE...
...AND... IT'S HARD TO SAY ALL THIS WHEN I CAN'T SEE YOUR FACE.
I DON'T KNOW WHAT YOU DID IN THERE, BUT I CAN TELL WHEN I'M BEING FUCKED WITH AND I DON'T LIKE IT.
LET GO OF MY ARM. NOW. I'M GOING THROUGH A LOT OF SHIT RIGHT NOW AND I HAVE BETTER THINGS TO DO WITH MY FRIDAY NIGHT THAN HANG OUT WITH A COMPLETE FREAK.

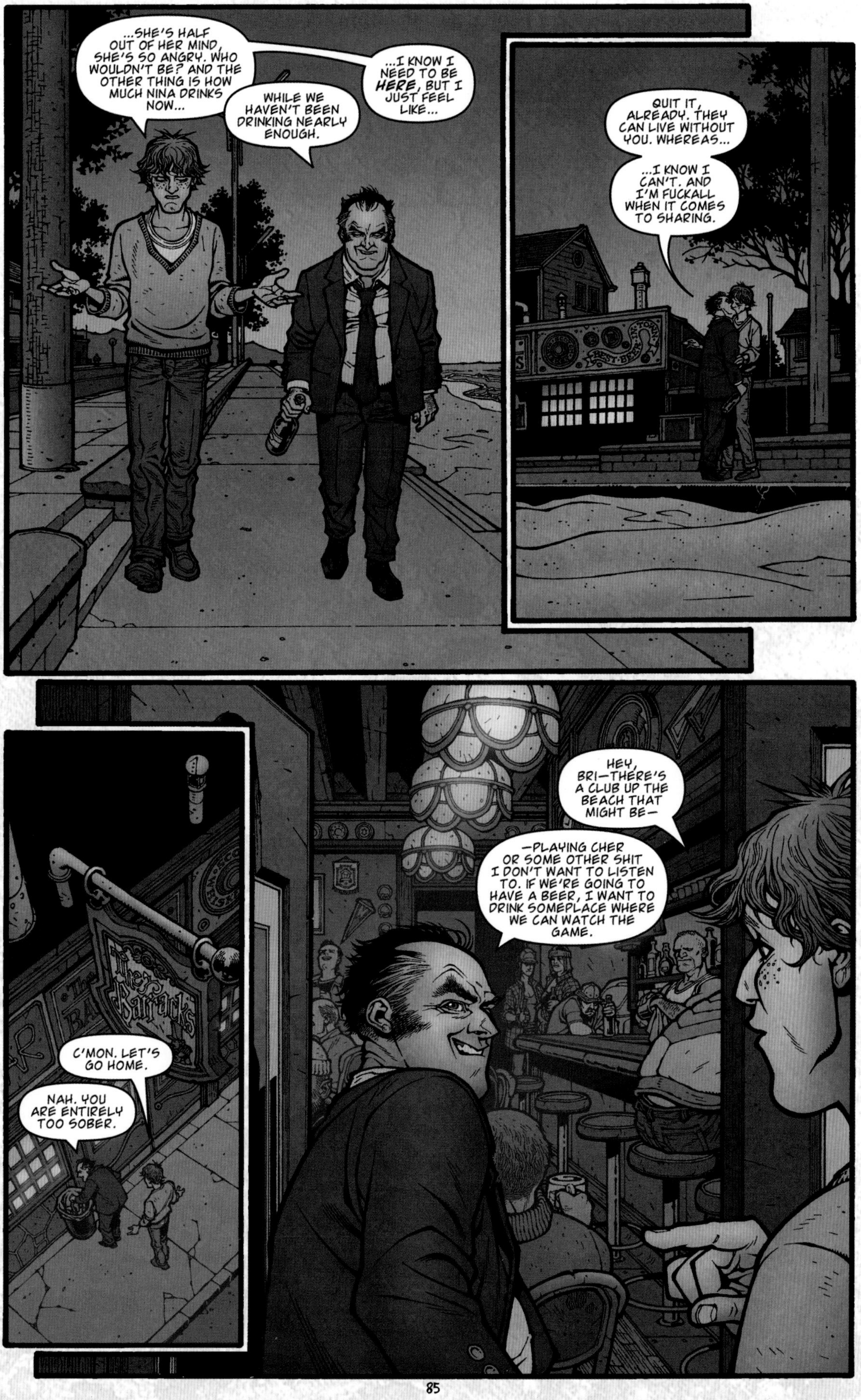

...SHE'S HALF OUT OF HER MIND, SHE'S SO ANGRY. WHO WOULDN'T BE? AND THE OTHER THING IS HOW MUCH NINA DRINKS NOW...
...I KNOW I NEED TO BE HERE, BUT I JUST FEEL LIKE...
WHILE WE HAVEN'T BEEN DRINKING NEARLY ENOUGH.
QUIT IT, ALREADY. THEY CAN LIVE WITHOUT YOU. WHEREAS...
...I KNOW I CAN'T. AND I'M FUCKALL WHEN IT COMES TO SHARING.
BEST BEER IN TOWN
The Barracks
C'MON. LET'S GO HOME.
NAH. YOU ARE ENTIRELY TOO SOBER.
HEY, BRI—THERE'S A CLUB UP THE BEACH THAT MIGHT BE—
—PLAYING CHER OR SOME OTHER SHIT I DON'T WANT TO LISTEN TO. IF WE'RE GOING TO HAVE A BEER, I WANT TO DRINK SOMEPLACE WHERE WE CAN WATCH THE GAME.

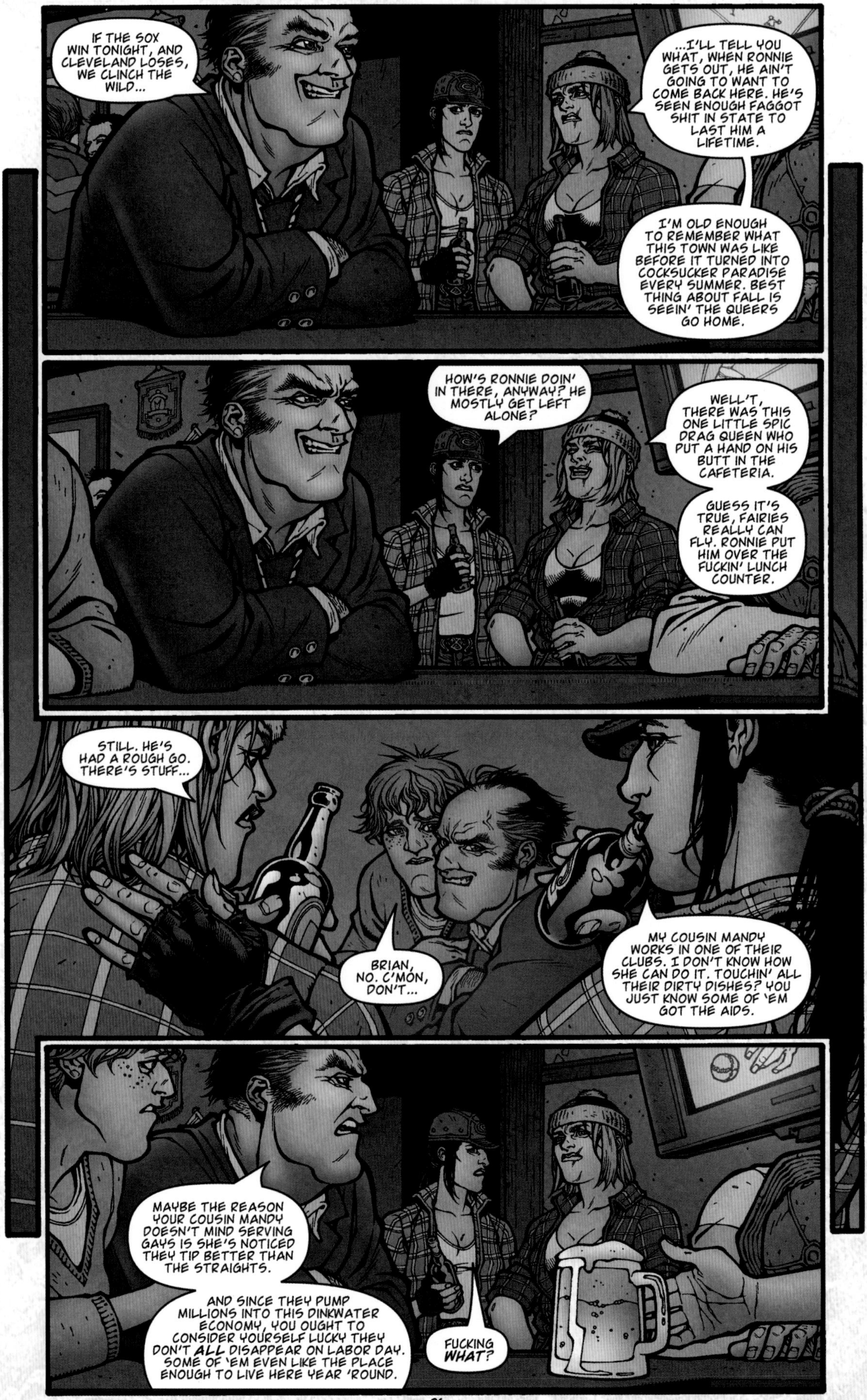
IF THE SOX WIN TONIGHT, AND CLEVELAND LOSES, WE CLINCH THE WILD...
...I'LL TELL YOU WHAT, WHEN RONNIE GETS OUT, HE AIN'T GOING TO WANT TO COME BACK HERE. HE'S SEEN ENOUGH FAGGOT SHIT IN STATE TO LAST HIM A LIFETIME.
I'M OLD ENOUGH TO REMEMBER WHAT THIS TOWN WAS LIKE BEFORE IT TURNED INTO COCKSUCKER PARADISE EVERY SUMMER. BEST THING ABOUT FALL IS SEEIN' THE QUEERS GO HOME.
HOW'S RONNIE DOIN' IN THERE, ANYWAY? HE MOSTLY GET LEFT ALONE?
WELL'T, THERE WAS THIS ONE LITTLE SPIC DRAG QUEEN WHO PUT A HAND ON HIS BUTT IN THE CAFETERIA.
GUESS IT'S TRUE, FAIRIES REALLY CAN FLY. RONNIE PUT HIM OVER THE FUCKIN' LUNCH COUNTER.
STILL. HE'S HAD A ROUGH GO. THERE'S STUFF...
BRIAN, NO. C'MON, DON'T...
MY COUSIN MANDY WORKS IN ONE OF THEIR CLUBS. I DON'T KNOW HOW SHE CAN DO IT. TOUCHIN' ALL THEIR DIRTY DISHES? YOU JUST KNOW SOME OF 'EM GOT THE AIDS.
MAYBE THE REASON YOUR COUSIN MANDY DOESN'T MIND SERVING GAYS IS SHE'S NOTICED THEY TIP BETTER THAN THE STRAIGHTS.
AND SINCE THEY PUMP MILLIONS INTO THIS DINKWATER ECONOMY, YOU OUGHT TO CONSIDER YOURSELF LUCKY THEY DON'T ALL DISAPPEAR ON LABOR DAY. SOME OF 'EM EVEN LIKE THE PLACE ENOUGH TO LIVE HERE YEAR 'ROUND.
FUCKING WHAT?

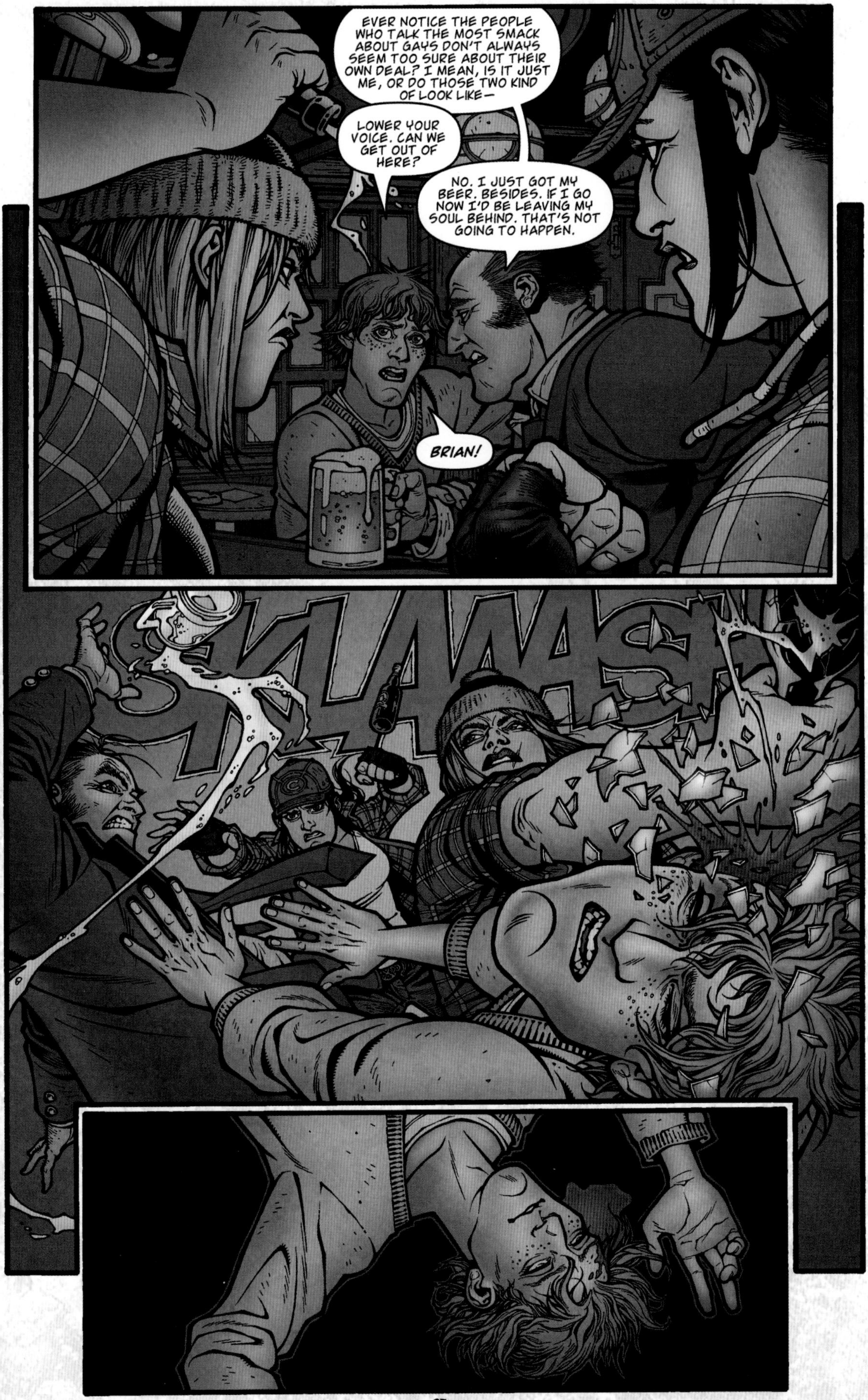
EVER NOTICE THE PEOPLE WHO TALK THE MOST SMACK ABOUT GAYS DON'T ALWAYS SEEM TOO SURE ABOUT THEIR OWN DEAL? I MEAN, IS IT JUST ME, OR DO THOSE TWO KIND OF LOOK LIKE—
LOWER YOUR VOICE. CAN WE GET OUT OF HERE?
NO. I JUST GOT MY BEER. BESIDES. IF I GO NOW I'D BE LEAVING MY SOUL BEHIND. THAT'S NOT GOING TO HAPPEN.
BRIAN!
KLAASH!

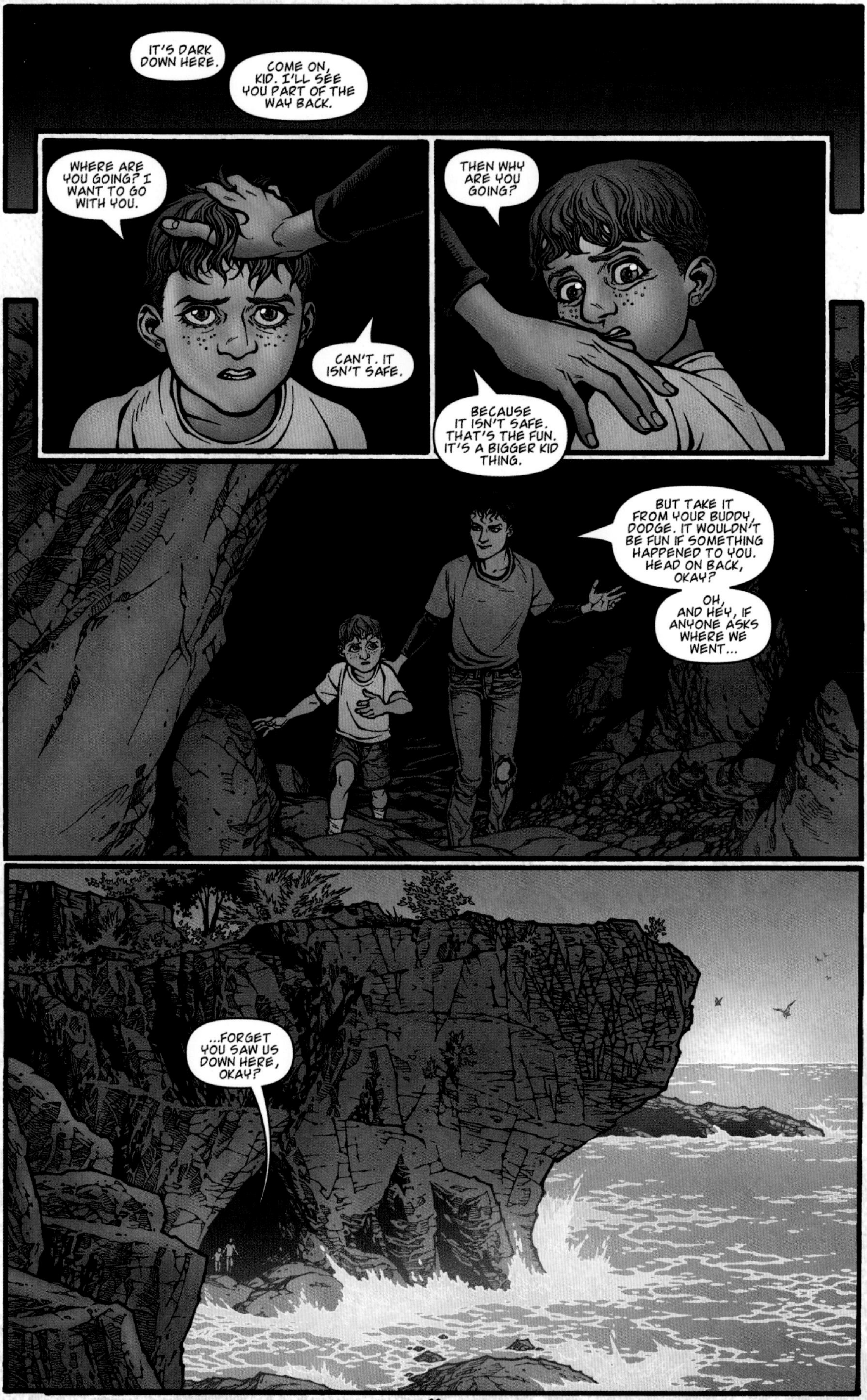
IT'S DARK DOWN HERE.
COME ON, KID. I'LL SEE YOU PART OF THE WAY BACK.
WHERE ARE YOU GOING? I WANT TO GO WITH YOU.
CAN'T. IT ISN'T SAFE.
THEN WHY ARE YOU GOING?
BECAUSE IT ISN'T SAFE. THAT'S THE FUN. IT'S A BIGGER KID THING.
BUT TAKE IT FROM YOUR BUDDY, DODGE. IT WOULDN'T BE FUN IF SOMETHING HAPPENED TO YOU. HEAD ON BACK, OKAY?
OH, AND HEY, IF ANYONE ASKS WHERE WE WENT...
...FORGET YOU SAW US DOWN HERE, OKAY?

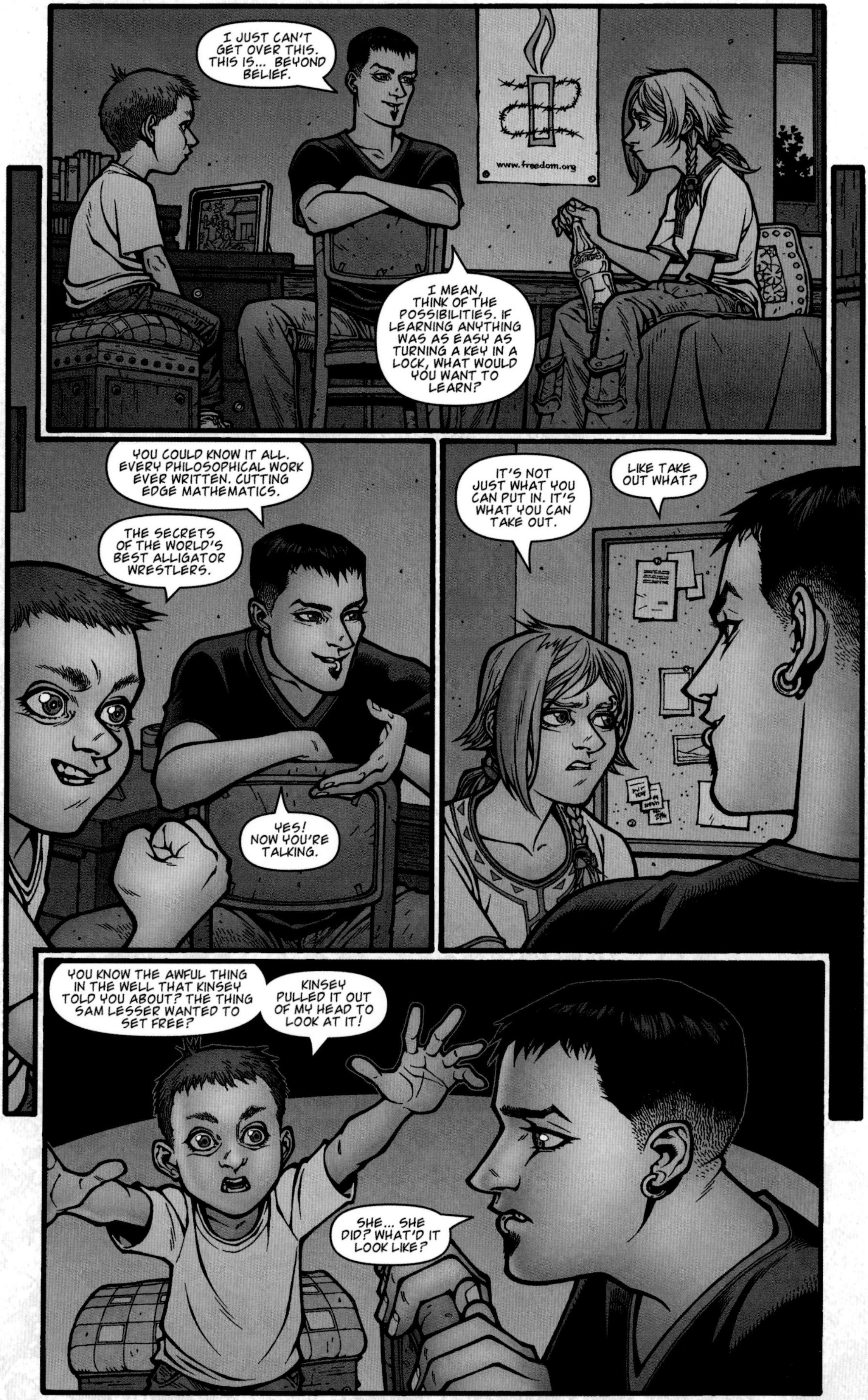
I JUST CAN'T GET OVER THIS. THIS IS... BEYOND BELIEF.
www.freedom.org
I MEAN, THINK OF THE POSSIBILITIES. IF LEARNING ANYTHING WAS AS EASY AS TURNING A KEY IN A LOCK, WHAT WOULD YOU WANT TO LEARN?
YOU COULD KNOW IT ALL. EVERY PHILOSOPHICAL WORK EVER WRITTEN. CUTTING EDGE MATHEMATICS.
THE SECRETS OF THE WORLD'S BEST ALLIGATOR WRESTLERS.
YES! NOW YOU'RE TALKING.
IT'S NOT JUST WHAT YOU CAN PUT IN. IT'S WHAT YOU CAN TAKE OUT.
LIKE TAKE OUT WHAT?
YOU KNOW THE AWFUL THING IN THE WELL THAT KINSEY TOLD YOU ABOUT? THE THING SAM LESSER WANTED TO SET FREE?
KINSEY PULLED IT OUT OF MY HEAD TO LOOK AT IT!
SHE... SHE DID? WHAT'D IT LOOK LIKE?

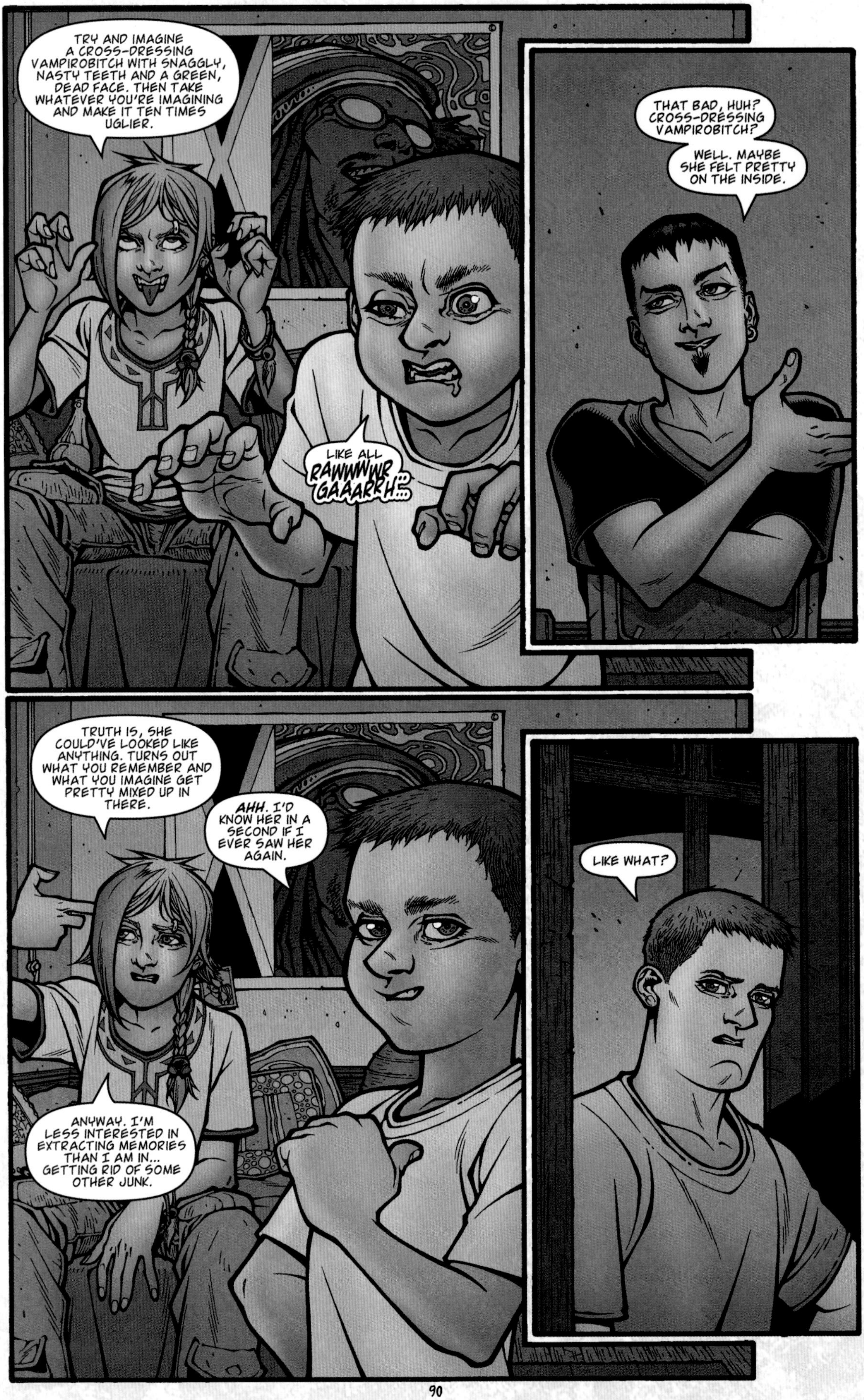
TRY AND IMAGINE A CROSS-DRESSING VAMPIROBITCH WITH SNAGGLY, NASTY TEETH AND A GREEN, DEAD FACE. THEN TAKE WHATEVER YOU'RE IMAGINING AND MAKE IT TEN TIMES UGLIER.
LIKE ALL RAWWWWR GAAARRH...
THAT BAD, HUH? CROSS-DRESSING VAMPIROBITCH?
WELL. MAYBE SHE FELT PRETTY ON THE INSIDE.
TRUTH IS, SHE COULD'VE LOOKED LIKE ANYTHING. TURNS OUT WHAT YOU REMEMBER AND WHAT YOU IMAGINE GET PRETTY MIXED UP IN THERE.
AHH. I'D KNOW HER IN A SECOND IF I EVER SAW HER AGAIN.
LIKE WHAT?
ANYWAY. I'M LESS INTERESTED IN EXTRACTING MEMORIES THAN I AM IN... GETTING RID OF SOME OTHER JUNK.

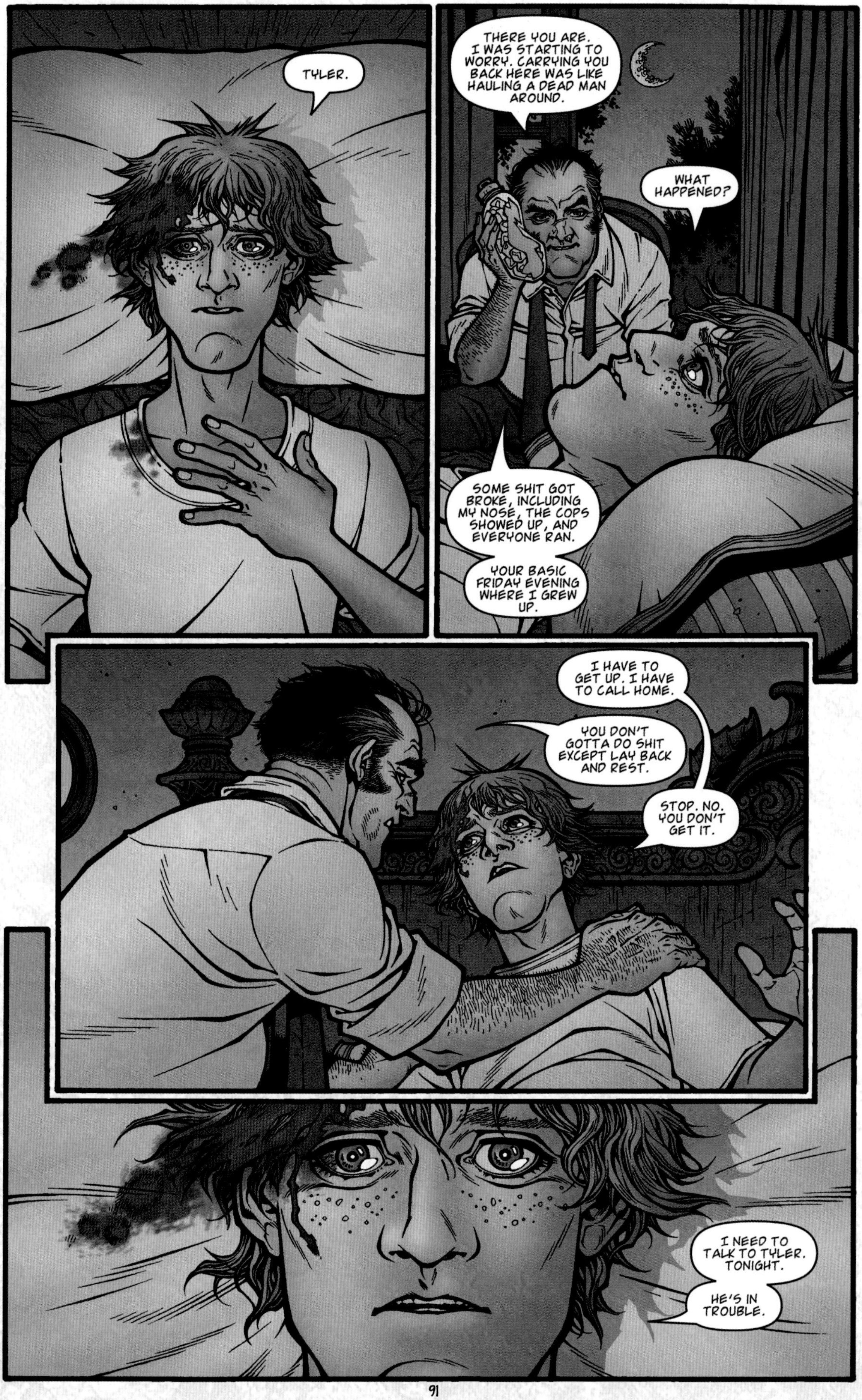
TYLER.
THERE YOU ARE. I WAS STARTING TO WORRY. CARRYING YOU BACK HERE WAS LIKE HAULING A DEAD MAN AROUND.
WHAT HAPPENED?
SOME SHIT GOT BROKE, INCLUDING MY NOSE, THE COPS SHOWED UP, AND EVERYONE RAN.
YOUR BASIC FRIDAY EVENING WHERE I GREW UP.
I HAVE TO GET UP. I HAVE TO CALL HOME.
YOU DON'T GOTTA DO SHIT EXCEPT LAY BACK AND REST.
STOP. NO. YOU DON'T GET IT.
I NEED TO TALK TO TYLER. TONIGHT.
HE'S IN TROUBLE.

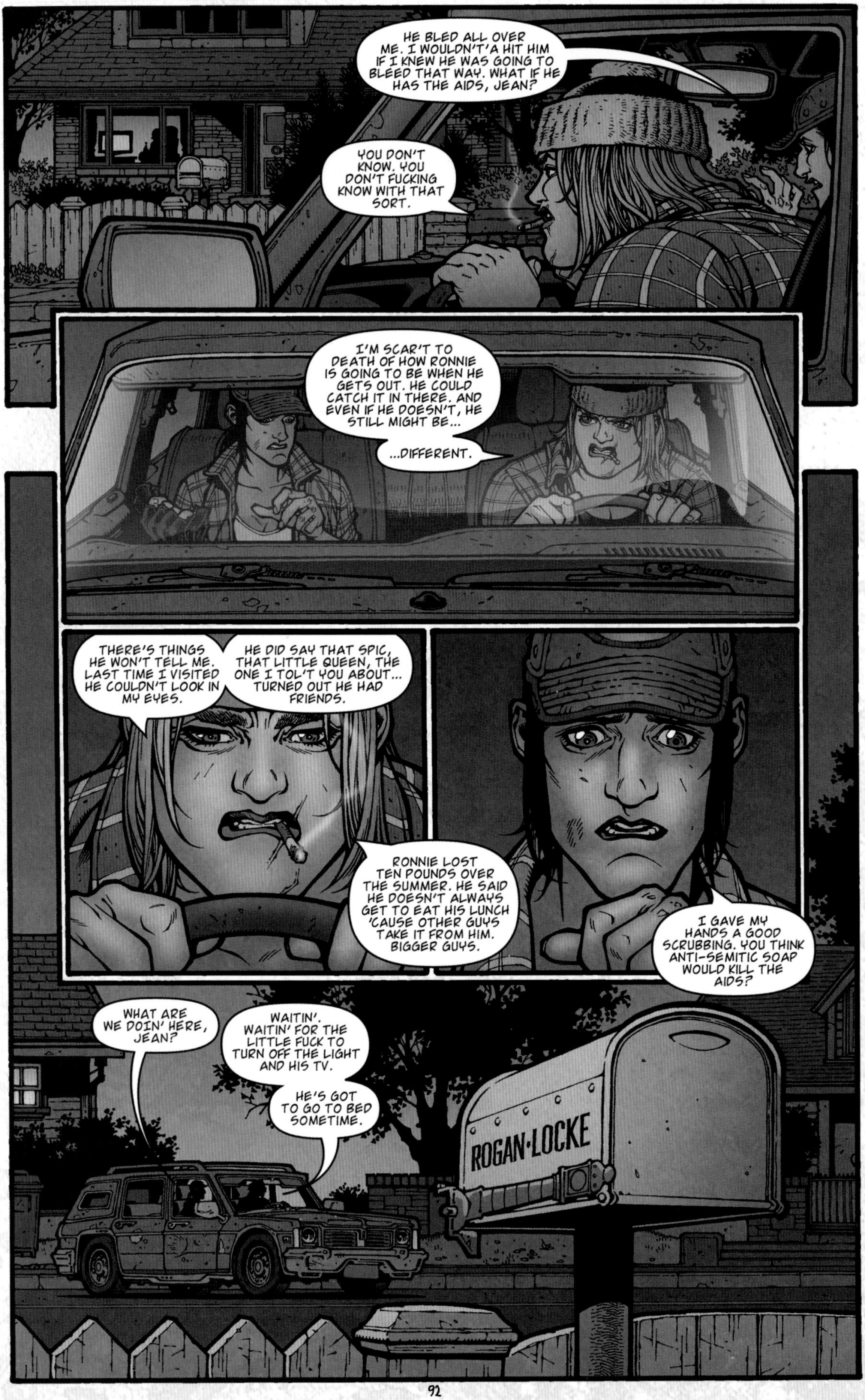
HE BLED ALL OVER ME. I WOULDN'T'A HIT HIM IF I KNEW HE WAS GOING TO BLEED THAT WAY. WHAT IF HE HAS THE AIDS, JEAN?
YOU DON'T KNOW. YOU DON'T FUCKING KNOW WITH THAT SORT.
I'M SCAR'T TO DEATH OF HOW RONNIE IS GOING TO BE WHEN HE GETS OUT. HE COULD CATCH IT IN THERE. AND EVEN IF HE DOESN'T, HE STILL MIGHT BE...
...DIFFERENT.
THERE'S THINGS HE WON'T TELL ME. LAST TIME I VISITED HE COULDN'T LOOK IN MY EYES.
HE DID SAY THAT SPIC, THAT LITTLE QUEEN, THE ONE I TOL'T YOU ABOUT... TURNED OUT HE HAD FRIENDS.
RONNIE LOST TEN POUNDS OVER THE SUMMER. HE SAID HE DOESN'T ALWAYS GET TO EAT HIS LUNCH 'CAUSE OTHER GUYS TAKE IT FROM HIM. BIGGER GUYS.
I GAVE MY HANDS A GOOD SCRUBBING. YOU THINK ANTI-SEMITIC SOAP WOULD KILL THE AIDS?
WHAT ARE WE DOIN' HERE, JEAN?
WAITIN'. WAITIN' FOR THE LITTLE FUCK TO TURN OFF THE LIGHT AND HIS TV.
HE'S GOT TO GO TO BED SOMETIME.
ROGAN·LOCKE

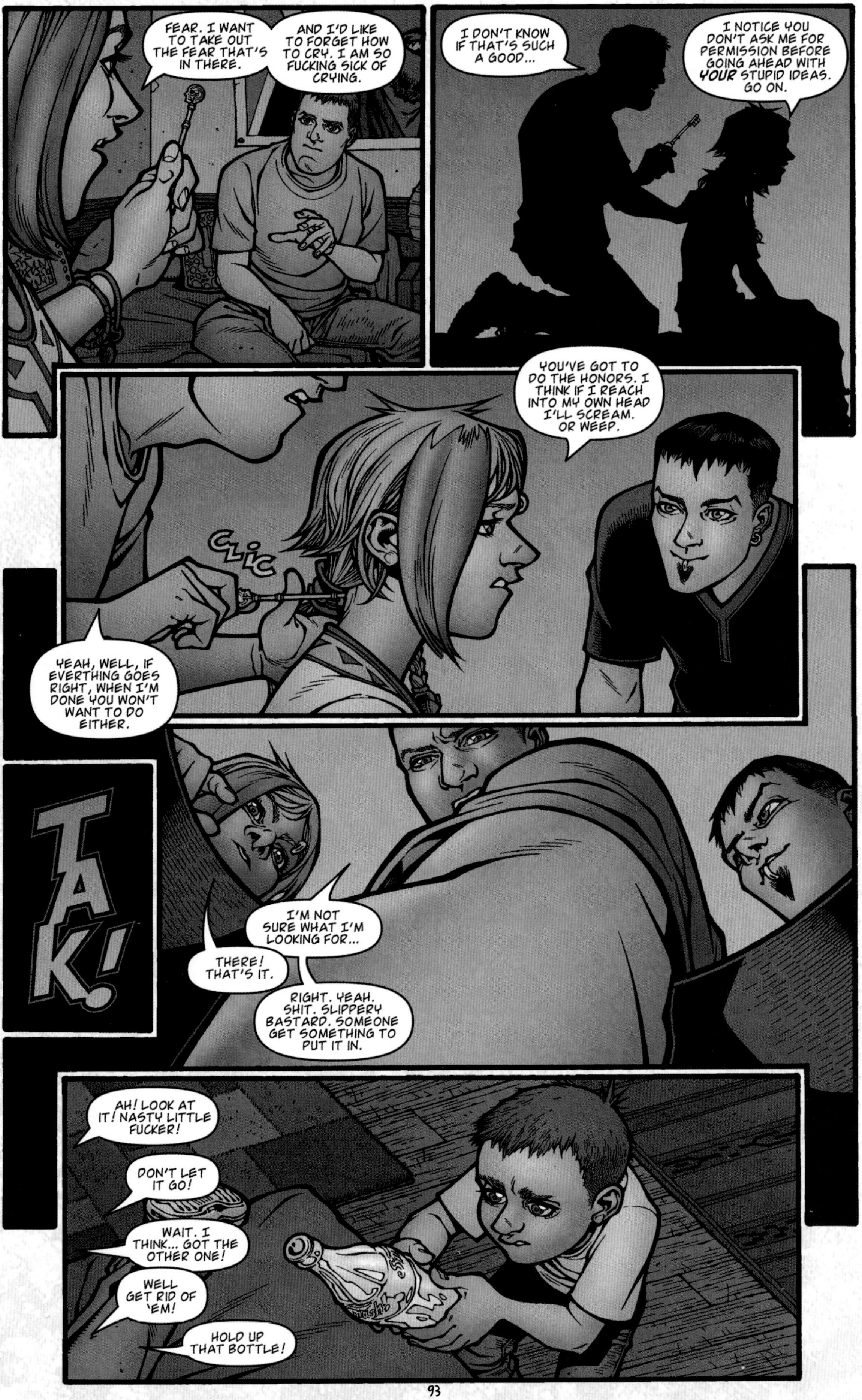
FEAR. I WANT TO TAKE OUT THE FEAR THAT'S IN THERE.
AND I'D LIKE TO FORGET HOW TO CRY. I AM SO FUCKING SICK OF CRYING.
I DON'T KNOW IF THAT'S SUCH A GOOD...
I NOTICE YOU DON'T ASK ME FOR PERMISSION BEFORE GOING AHEAD WITH YOUR STUPID IDEAS. GO ON.
YOU'VE GOT TO DO THE HONORS. I THINK IF I REACH INTO MY OWN HEAD I'LL SCREAM. OR WEEP.
CLIC
YEAH, WELL, IF EVERTHING GOES RIGHT, WHEN I'M DONE YOU WON'T WANT TO DO EITHER.
TAK!
I'M NOT SURE WHAT I'M LOOKING FOR...
THERE! THAT'S IT.
RIGHT. YEAH. SHIT. SLIPPERY BASTARD. SOMEONE GET SOMETHING TO PUT IT IN.
AH! LOOK AT IT! NASTY LITTLE FUCKER!
DON'T LET IT GO!
WAIT. I THINK... GOT THE OTHER ONE!
WELL GET RID OF 'EM!
HOLD UP THAT BOTTLE!

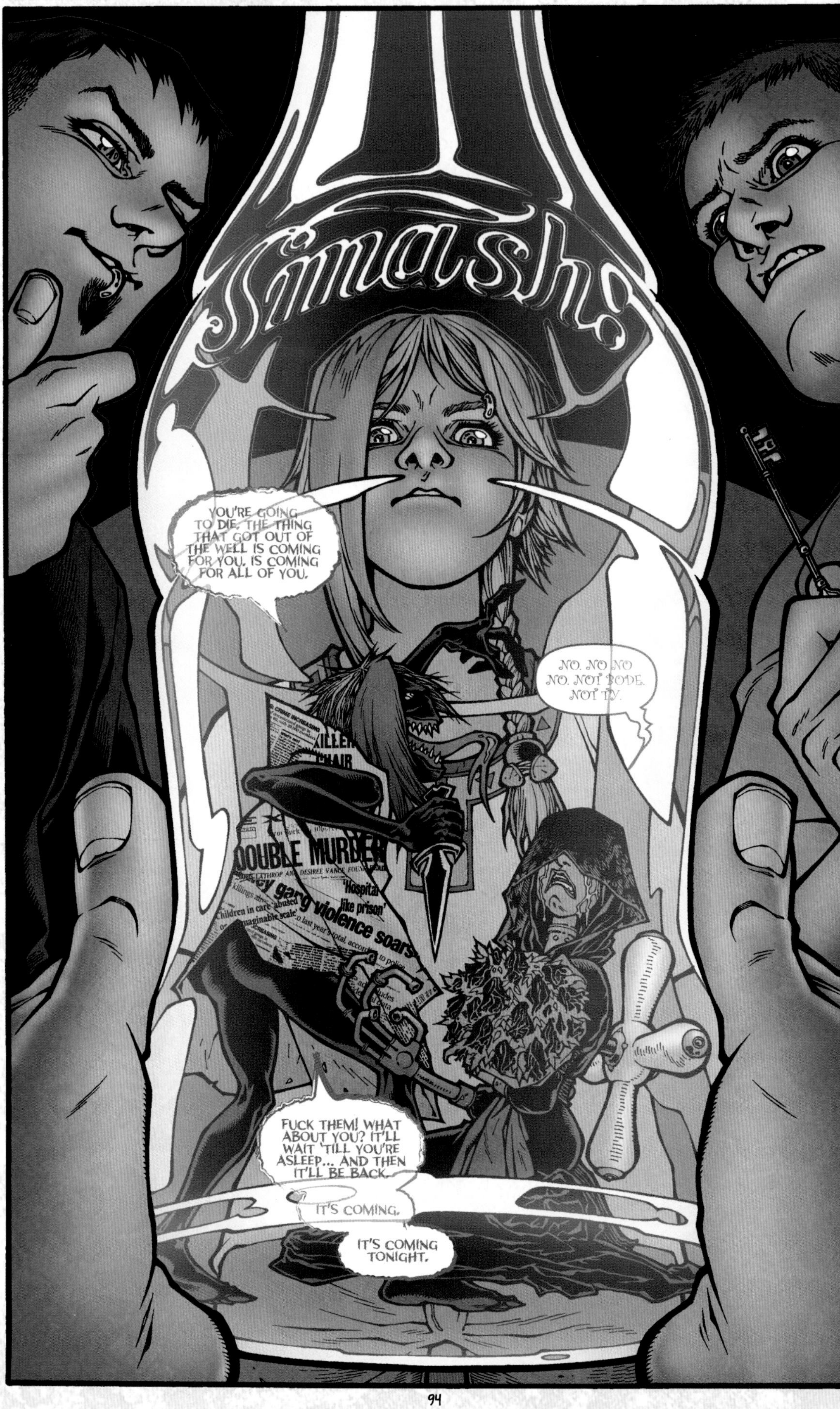

YOU'RE GOING TO DIE. THE THING THAT GOT OUT OF THE WELL IS COMING FOR YOU. IS COMING FOR ALL OF YOU.
NO. NO NO NO. NOT BODE. NOT TY.
CRIME INCREASING
DOUBLE MURDER
'Hospital like prison'
Children in care 'abused on unimaginable scale'
gang violence soars
FUCK THEM! WHAT ABOUT YOU? IT'LL WAIT 'TILL YOU'RE ASLEEP... AND THEN IT'LL BE BACK.
IT'S COMING.
IT'S COMING TONIGHT.

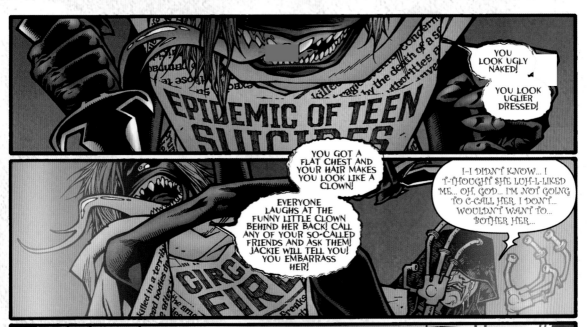

EPIDEMIC OF TEEN
YOU LOOK UGLY NAKED!
YOU LOOK UGLIER DRESSED!
YOU GOT A FLAT CHEST AND YOUR HAIR MAKES YOU LOOK LIKE A CLOWN!
EVERYONE LAUGHS AT THE FUNNY LITTLE CLOWN BEHIND HER BACK! CALL ANY OF YOUR SO-CALLED FRIENDS AND ASK THEM! JACKIE WILL TELL YOU! YOU EMBARRASS HER!
I-I DIDN'T KNOW... I T-THOUGHT SHE LUH-L-LIKED ME... OH, GOD... I'M NOT GOING TO C-CALL HER. I DON'T... WOULDN'T WANT TO... BOTHER HER...
YOUR CELL PHONE IS GOING TO GIVE YOU CANCER! CANCER IN THE BRAIN!
CANCER RATES RISE
I KNOW! I KNOW I TALK ON IT TOO MUCH. IT'S JUST... I'M SO LONELY...
JUST LIKE TAMMY FELLWORTH IN 3RD GRADE. SHE WAS ONLY EIGHT! BRAIN CANCER!
LITTLE TUH-TAMMY WAS SO NICE... SHE BROUGHT A M-M-MR. POTATO HEAD TO HER LUH-LAST SHOW-AND-TELL... SHE L-LET ME PLAY WITH IT...
NOW SHE'S DEAD! LIKE YOU'RE GOING TO DIE! YOU'RE GOING TO DIE A FLAT-CHESTED VIRGIN WITH NO FRIENDS AND BRAIN CANCER AND A WHOPPING CASE OF UGLY
YEEE-AAAAAAAHHH!
BOTTLED UNDER THE AUTHORITY OF IDW; SAN DIEGO, CA.
INGREDIENTS: Graphite & Ink - GABRIEL RODRÍGUEZ; Powdered Nonsense - JOE HILL; Caramel & Other Natural Colorings - JAY FOTOS; Benzoate (Preserves Freshness) - CHRIS RYALL; Carbonated Water; Natural & Artificial Lettering - ROBBIE ROBBINS; Caffeine.
Locke & Key created by J.Hill & G. Rodriguez Beverages Ltd.

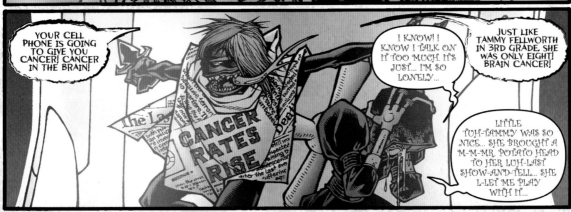

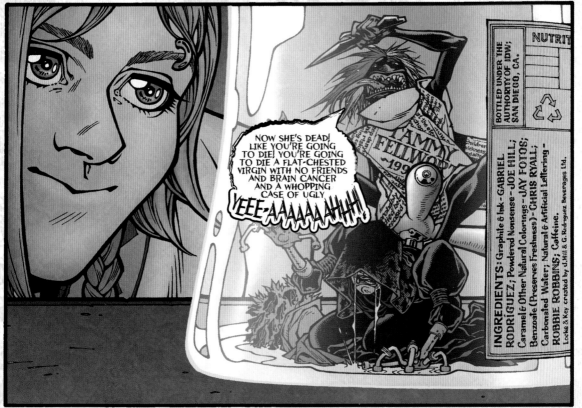

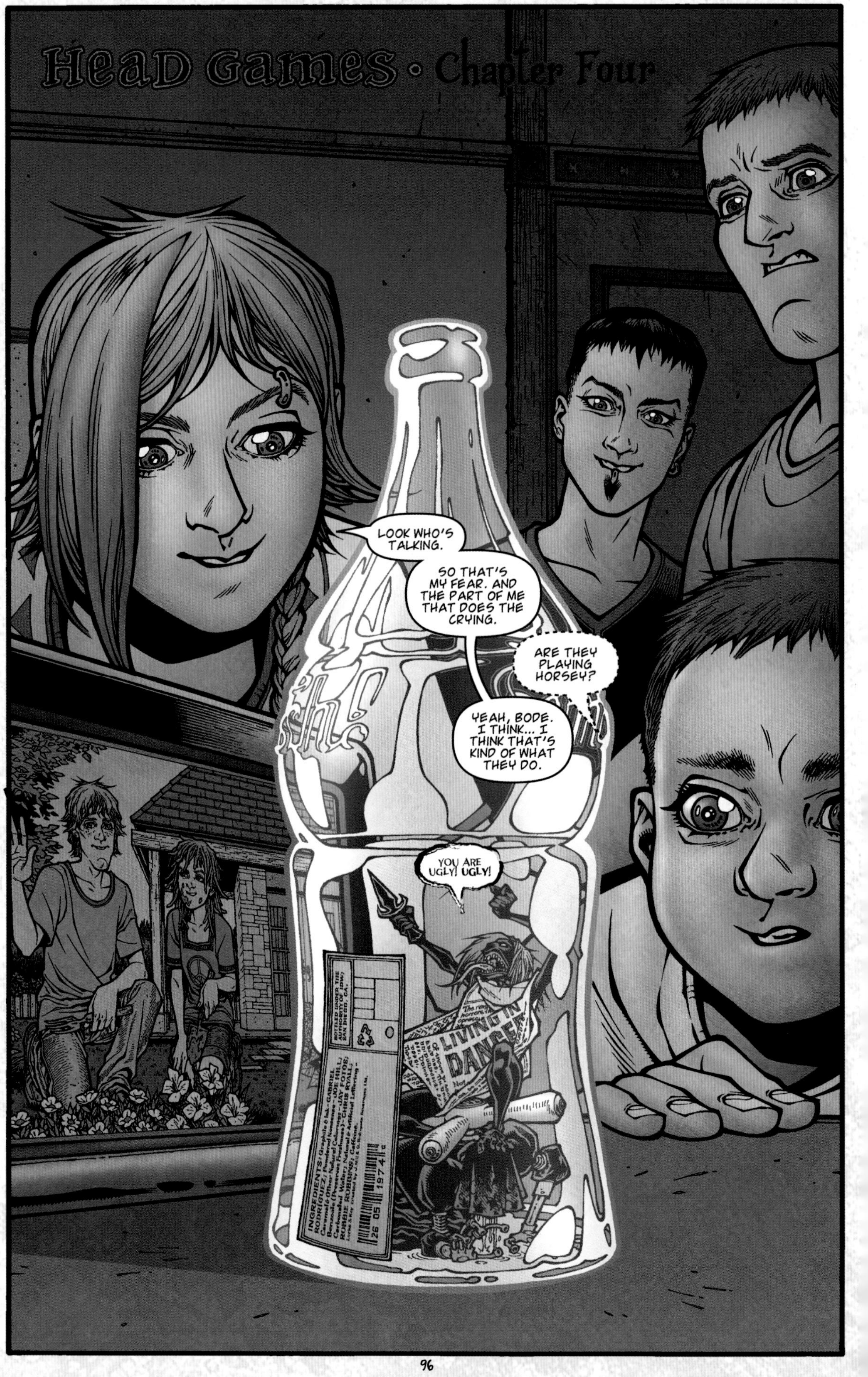
Head Games • Chapter Four
LOOK WHO'S TALKING.
SO THAT'S MY FEAR. AND THE PART OF ME THAT DOES THE CRYING.
ARE THEY PLAYING HORSEY?
YEAH, BODE. I THINK... I THINK THAT'S KIND OF WHAT THEY DO.
YOU ARE UGLY! UGLY!
LIVING IN DANGER
BOTTLED UNDER THE AUTHORITY OF IDW; SAN DIEGO, CA.

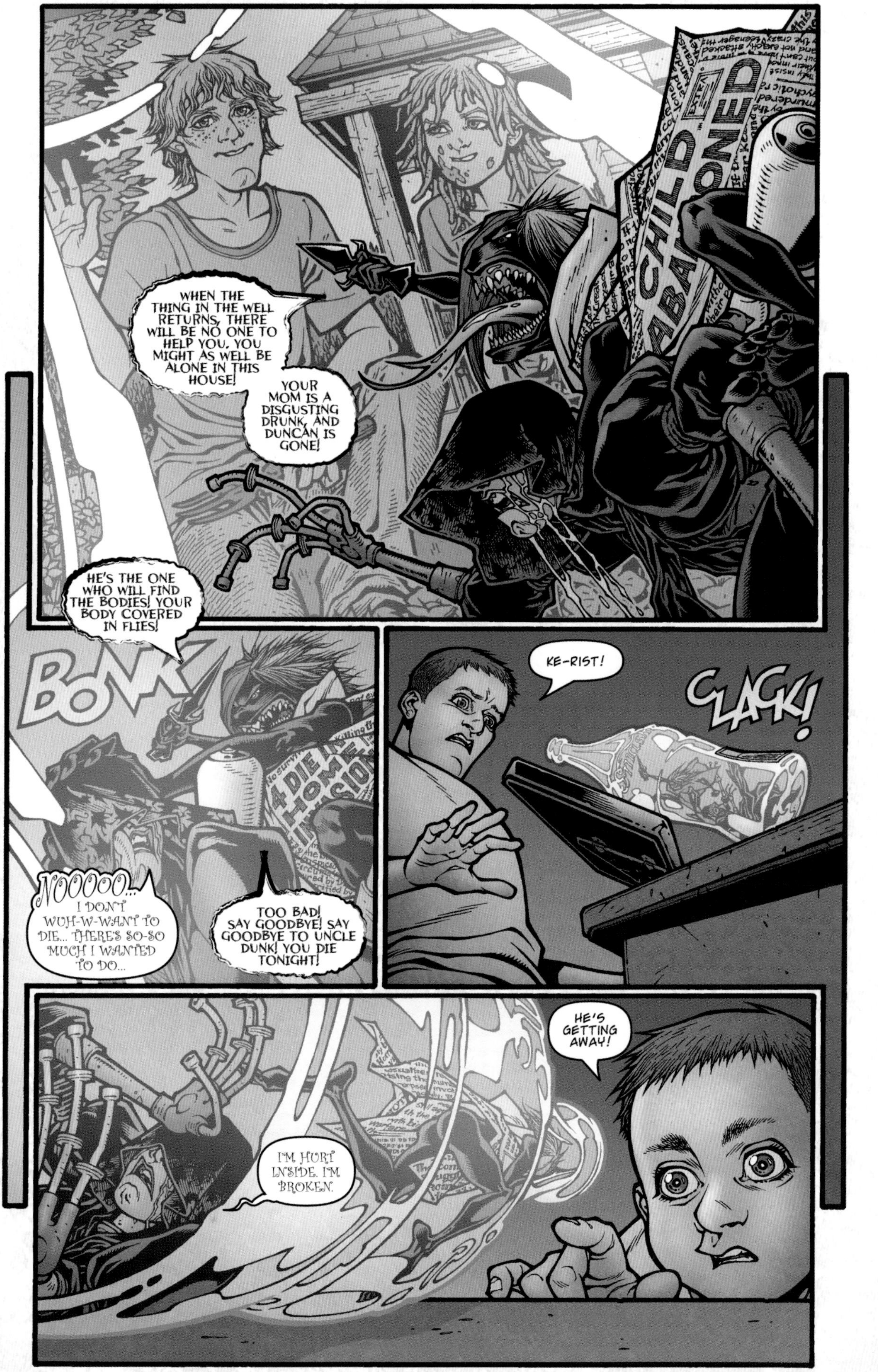
WHEN THE THING IN THE WELL RETURNS, THERE WILL BE NO ONE TO HELP YOU. YOU MIGHT AS WELL BE ALONE IN THIS HOUSE!
YOUR MOM IS A DISGUSTING DRUNK, AND DUNCAN IS GONE!
HE'S THE ONE WHO WILL FIND THE BODIES! YOUR BODY COVERED IN FLIES!
CHILD ABANDONED
BONK
4 DIE IN HOME INVASION
NOOOOO... I DON'T WUH-W-WANT TO DIE... THERE'S SO-SO MUCH I WANTED TO DO...
TOO BAD! SAY GOODBYE! SAY GOODBYE TO UNCLE DUNK! YOU DIE TONIGHT!
KE-RIST!
CLACK!
HE'S GETTING AWAY!
I'M HURT INSIDE. I'M BROKEN.

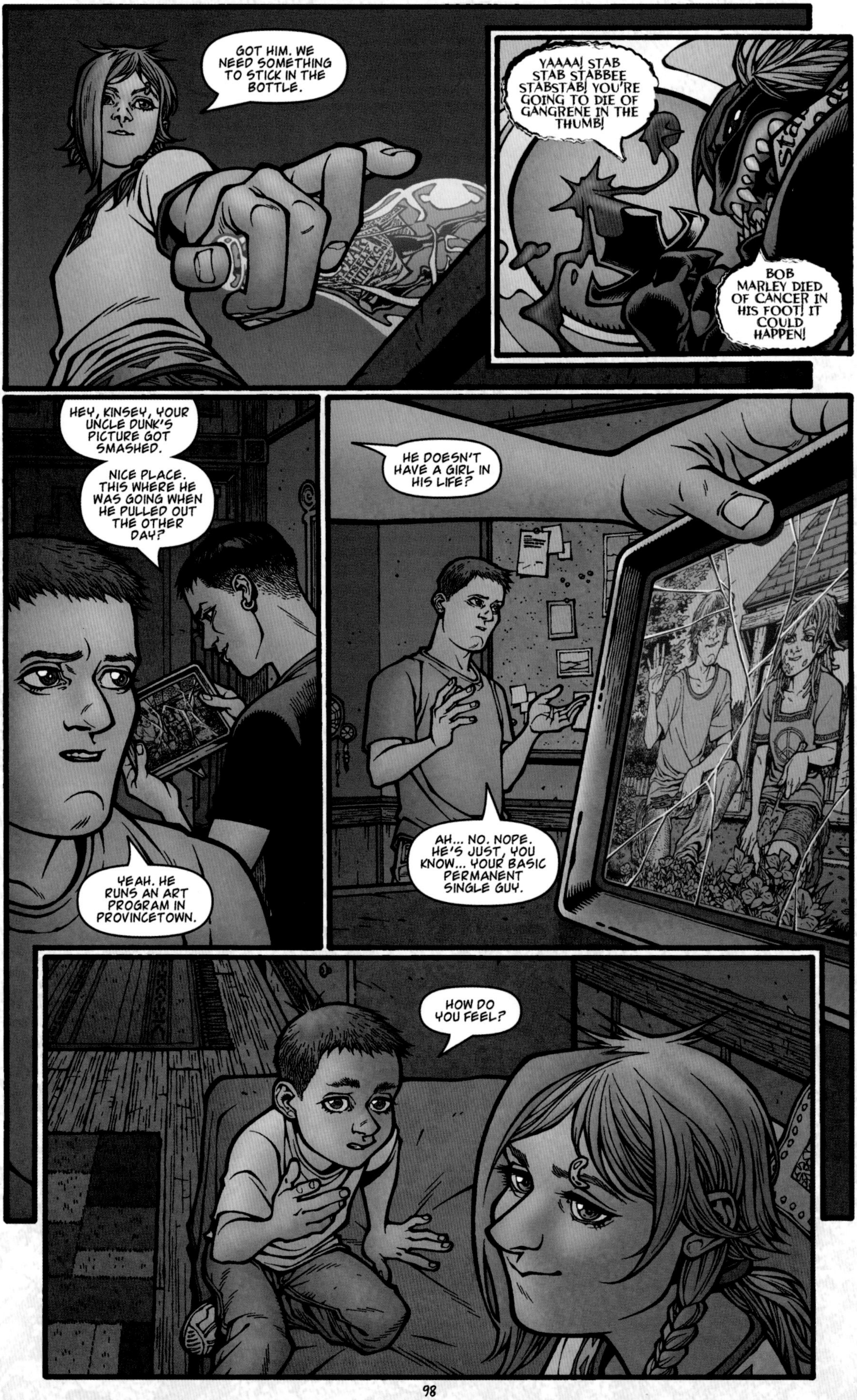
GOT HIM. WE NEED SOMETHING TO STICK IN THE BOTTLE.
YAAAA! STAB STAB STABBEE STABSTAB! YOU'RE GOING TO DIE OF GANGRENE IN THE THUMB!
BOB MARLEY DIED OF CANCER IN HIS FOOT! IT COULD HAPPEN!
HEY, KINSEY, YOUR UNCLE DUNK'S PICTURE GOT SMASHED.
NICE PLACE. THIS WHERE HE WAS GOING WHEN HE PULLED OUT THE OTHER DAY?
YEAH. HE RUNS AN ART PROGRAM IN PROVINCETOWN.
HE DOESN'T HAVE A GIRL IN HIS LIFE?
AH... NO. NOPE. HE'S JUST, YOU KNOW... YOUR BASIC PERMANENT SINGLE GUY.
HOW DO YOU FEEL?

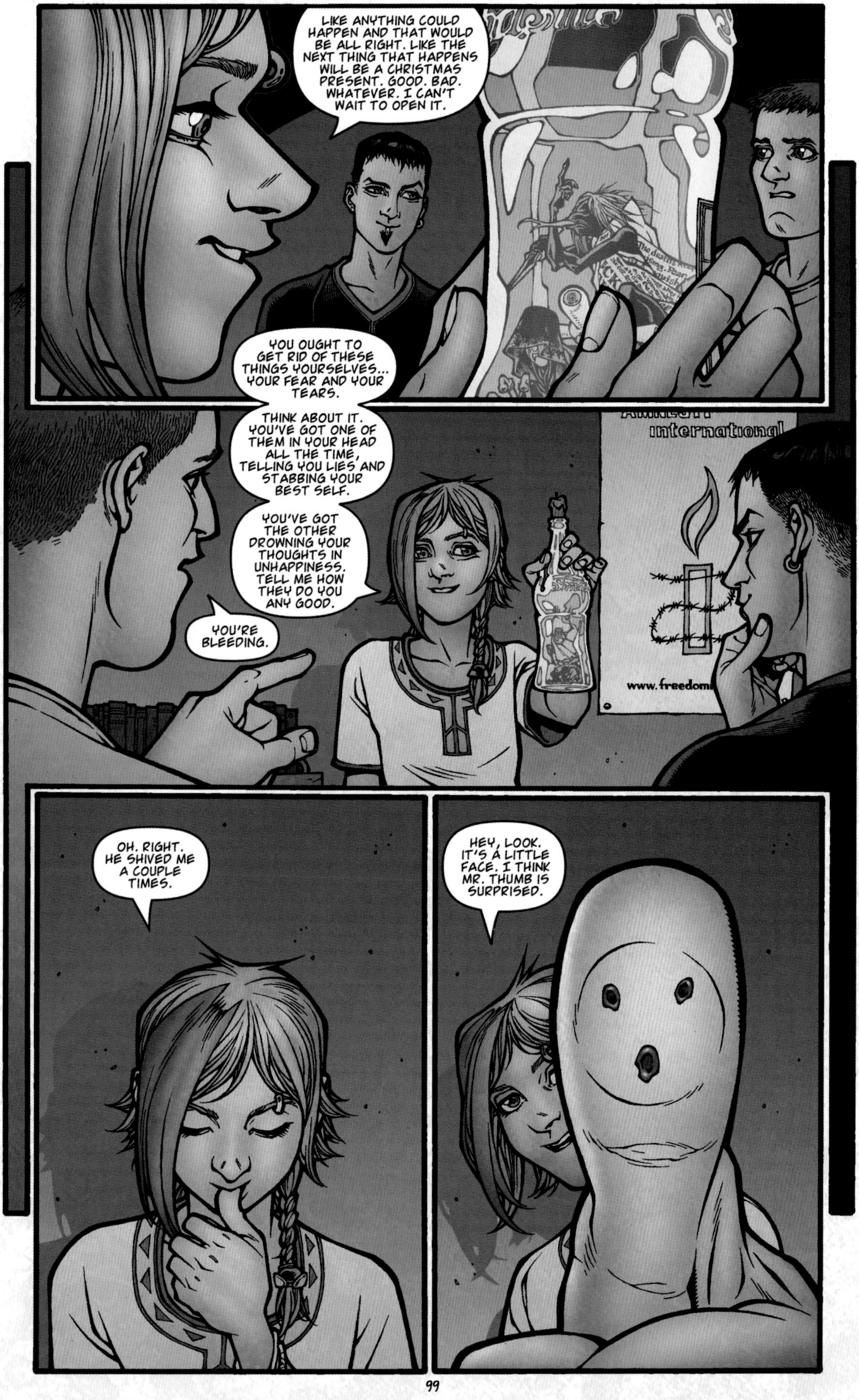
LIKE ANYTHING COULD HAPPEN AND THAT WOULD BE ALL RIGHT. LIKE THE NEXT THING THAT HAPPENS WILL BE A CHRISTMAS PRESENT. GOOD. BAD. WHATEVER. I CAN'T WAIT TO OPEN IT.
YOU OUGHT TO GET RID OF THESE THINGS YOURSELVES... YOUR FEAR AND YOUR TEARS.
THINK ABOUT IT. YOU'VE GOT ONE OF THEM IN YOUR HEAD ALL THE TIME, TELLING YOU LIES AND STABBING YOUR BEST SELF.
YOU'VE GOT THE OTHER DROWNING YOUR THOUGHTS IN UNHAPPINESS. TELL ME HOW THEY DO YOU ANY GOOD.
YOU'RE BLEEDING.
international
www.freedom
OH. RIGHT. HE SHIVED ME A COUPLE TIMES.
HEY, LOOK. IT'S A LITTLE FACE. I THINK MR. THUMB IS SURPRISED.

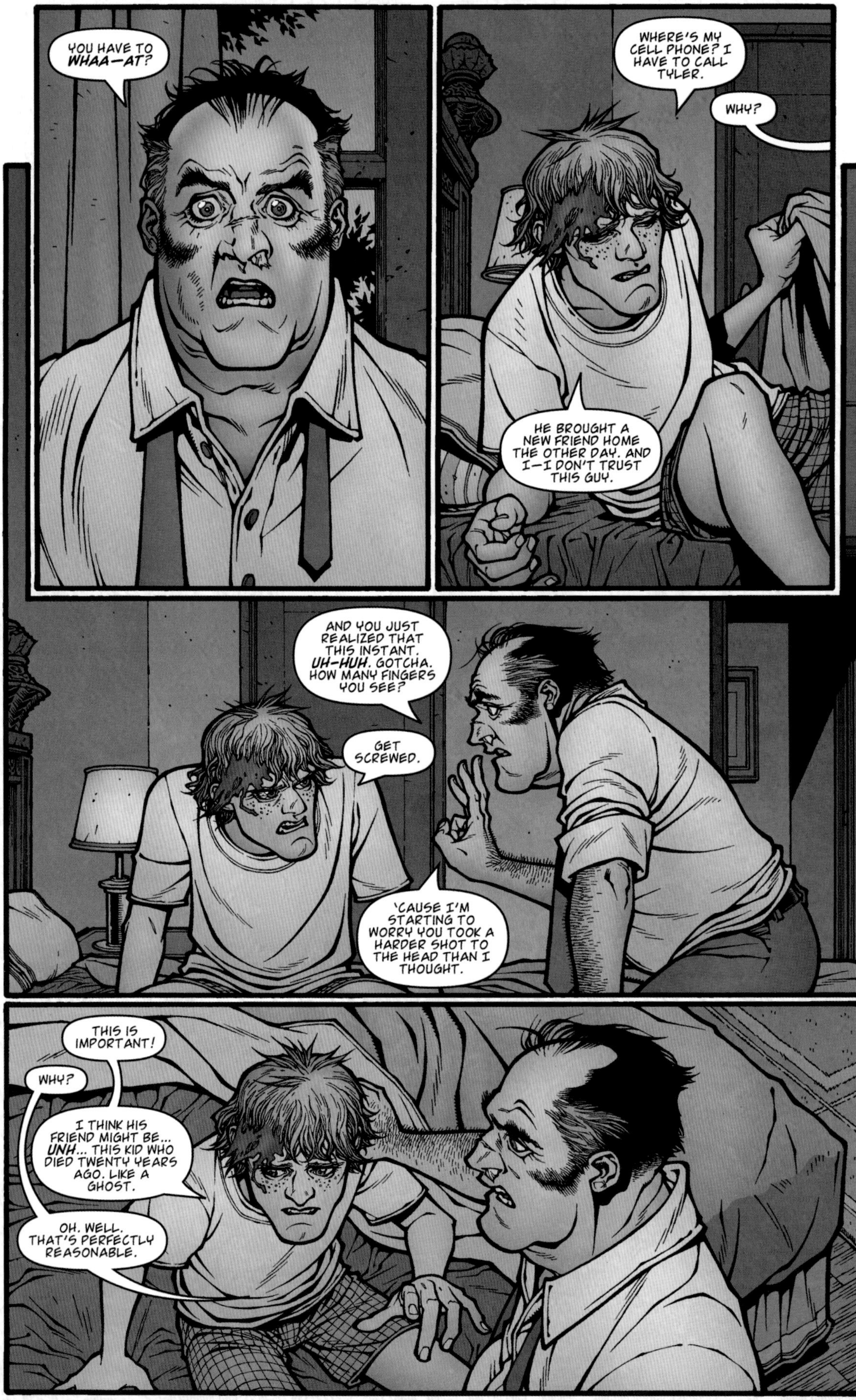
YOU HAVE TO WHAA—AT?
WHERE'S MY CELL PHONE? I HAVE TO CALL TYLER.
WHY?
HE BROUGHT A NEW FRIEND HOME THE OTHER DAY. AND I—I DON'T TRUST THIS GUY.
AND YOU JUST REALIZED THAT THIS INSTANT. UH-HUH. GOTCHA. HOW MANY FINGERS YOU SEE?
GET SCREWED.
'CAUSE I'M STARTING TO WORRY YOU TOOK A HARDER SHOT TO THE HEAD THAN I THOUGHT.
THIS IS IMPORTANT!
WHY?
I THINK HIS FRIEND MIGHT BE... UNH... THIS KID WHO DIED TWENTY YEARS AGO. LIKE A GHOST.
OH. WELL. THAT'S PERFECTLY REASONABLE.

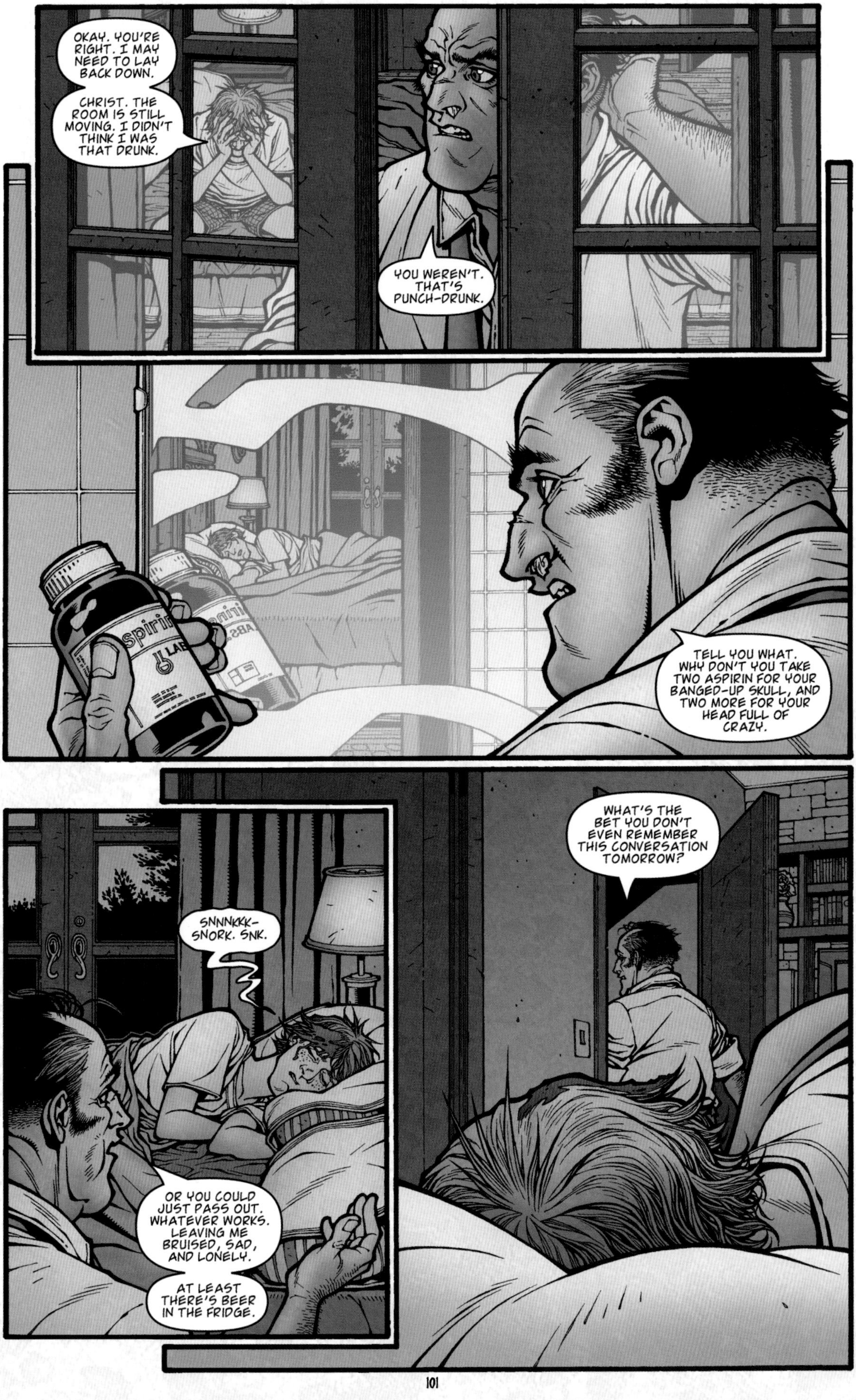
OKAY. YOU'RE RIGHT. I MAY NEED TO LAY BACK DOWN.
CHRIST. THE ROOM IS STILL MOVING. I DIDN'T THINK I WAS THAT DRUNK.
YOU WEREN'T. THAT'S PUNCH-DRUNK.
TELL YOU WHAT. WHY DON'T YOU TAKE TWO ASPIRIN FOR YOUR BANGED-UP SKULL, AND TWO MORE FOR YOUR HEAD FULL OF CRAZY.
WHAT'S THE BET YOU DON'T EVEN REMEMBER THIS CONVERSATION TOMORROW?
SNNNKKK-SNORK. SNK.
OR YOU COULD JUST PASS OUT. WHATEVER WORKS. LEAVING ME BRUISED, SAD, AND LONELY.
AT LEAST THERE'S BEER IN THE FRIDGE.

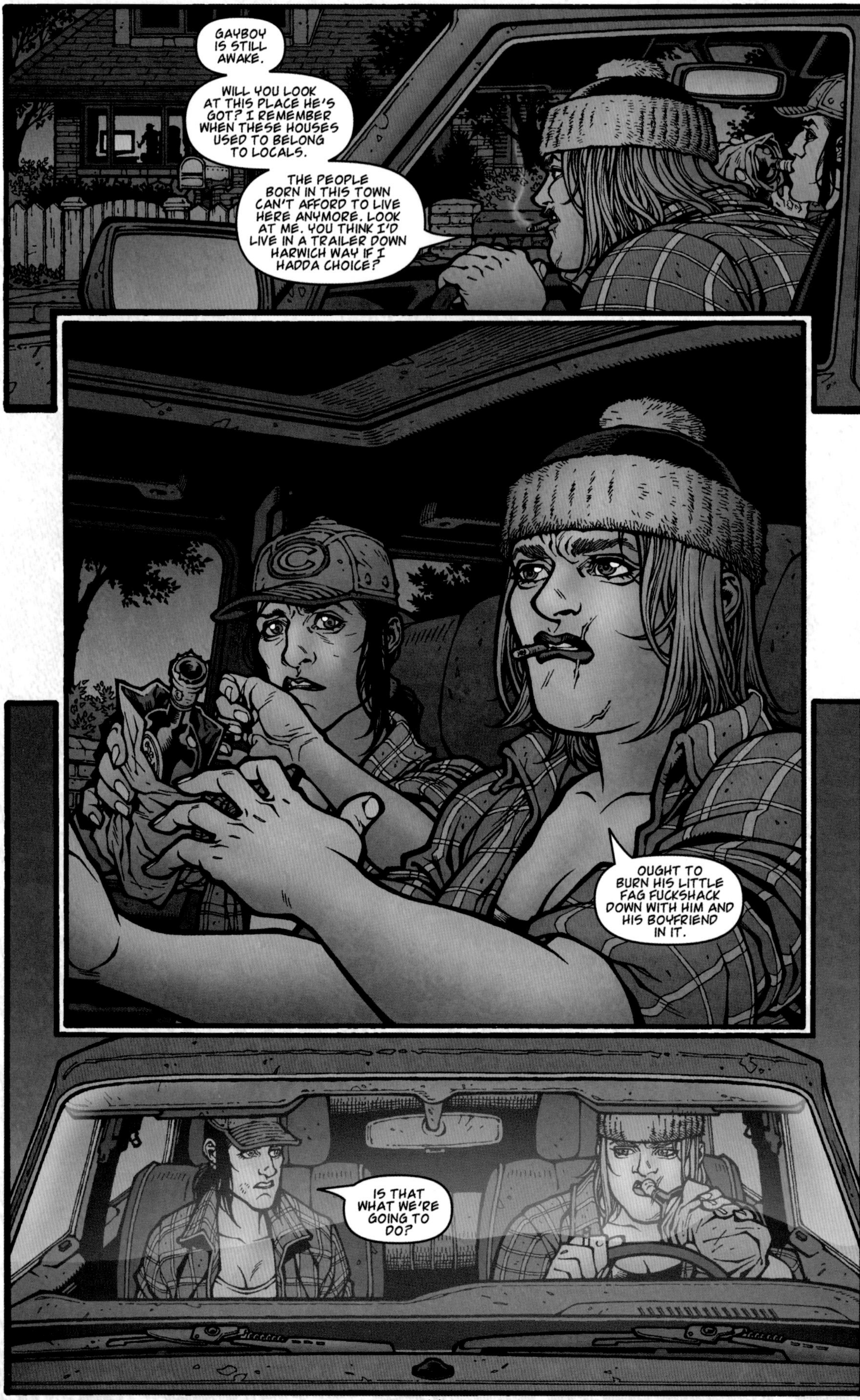
GAYBOY IS STILL AWAKE.
WILL YOU LOOK AT THIS PLACE HE'S GOT? I REMEMBER WHEN THESE HOUSES USED TO BELONG TO LOCALS.
THE PEOPLE BORN IN THIS TOWN CAN'T AFFORD TO LIVE HERE ANYMORE. LOOK AT ME. YOU THINK I'D LIVE IN A TRAILER DOWN HARWICH WAY IF I HADDA CHOICE?
OUGHT TO BURN HIS LITTLE FAG FUCKSHACK DOWN WITH HIM AND HIS BOYFRIEND IN IT.
IS THAT WHAT WE'RE GOING TO DO?

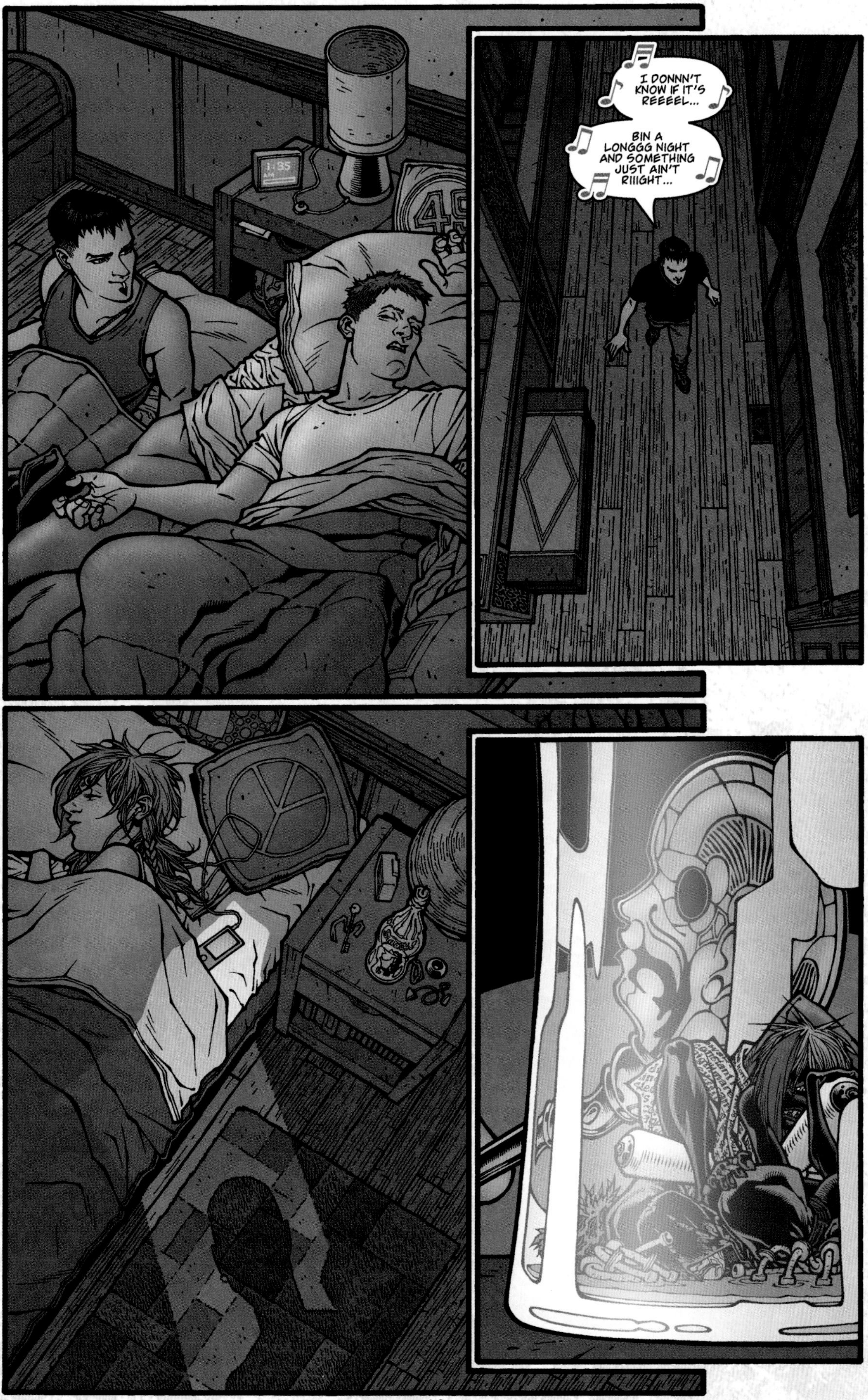
1:35 AM
49
I DONNN'T KNOW IF IT'S REEEEL...
BIN A LONGGG NIGHT AND SOMETHING JUST AIN'T RIIIGHT...

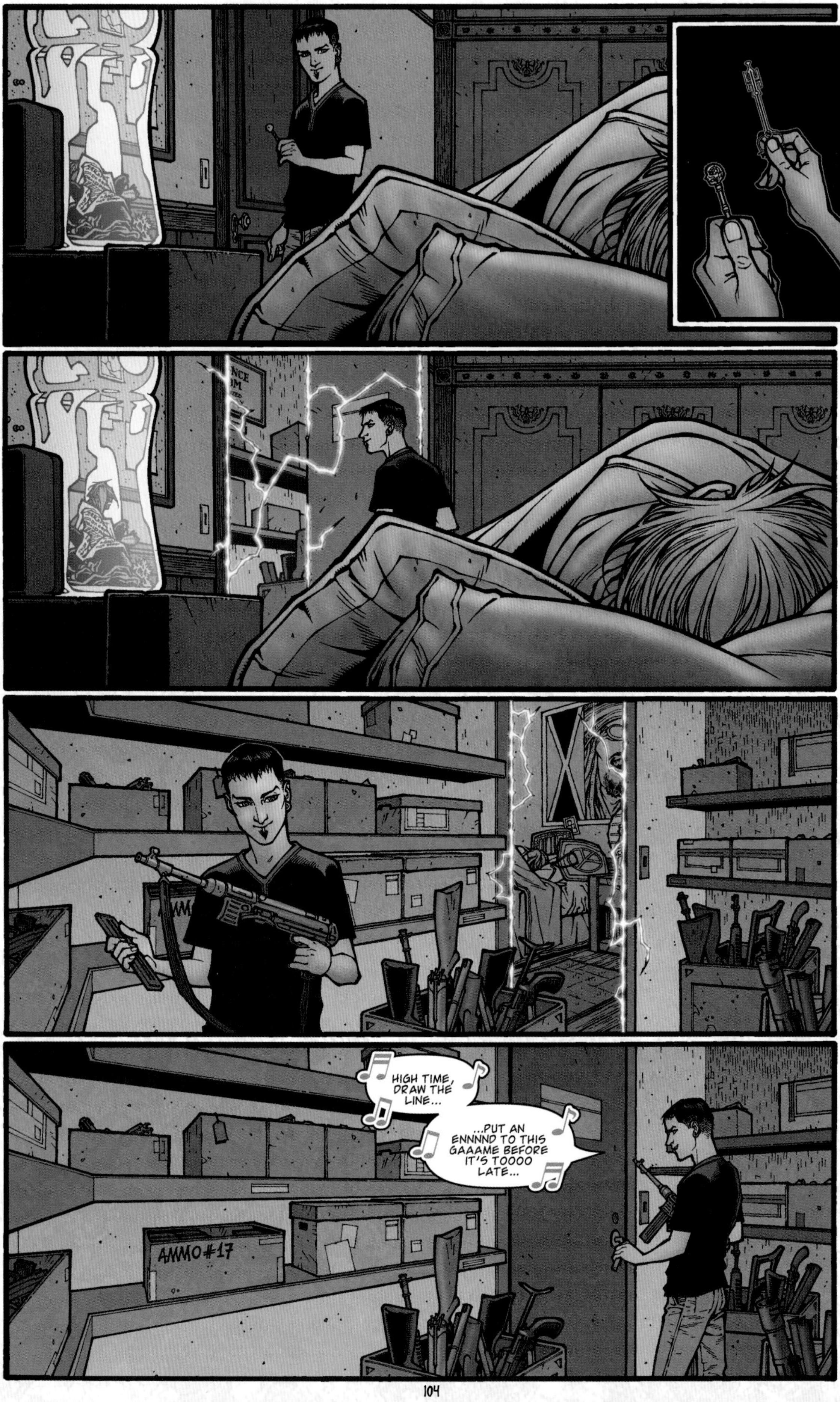
HIGH TIME, DRAW THE LINE...
...PUT AN ENNNND TO THIS GAAAME BEFORE IT'S TOOOO LATE...
AMMO #17

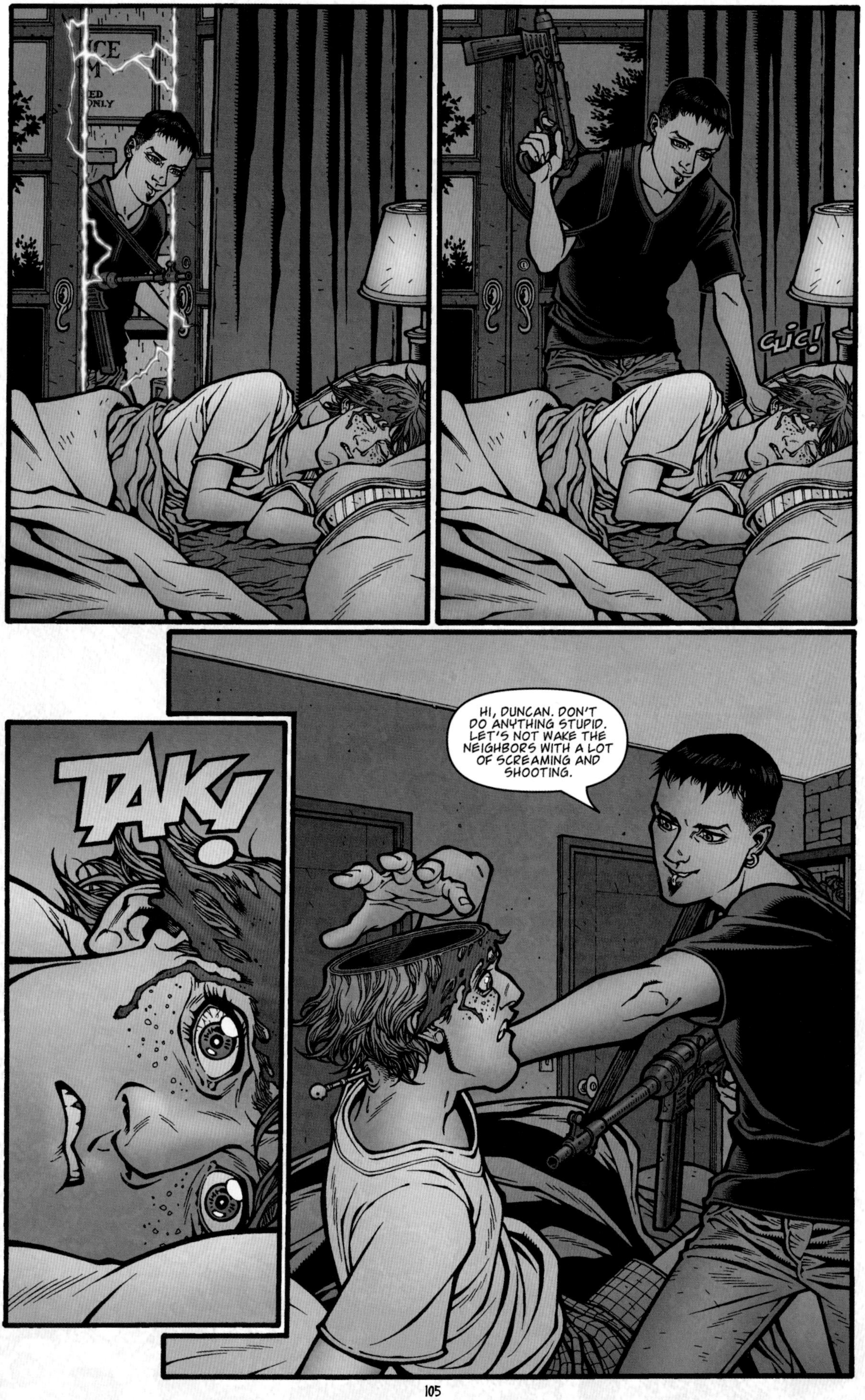
CLIC!
TAK!
HI, DUNCAN. DON'T DO ANYTHING STUPID. LET'S NOT WAKE THE NEIGHBORS WITH A LOT OF SCREAMING AND SHOOTING.

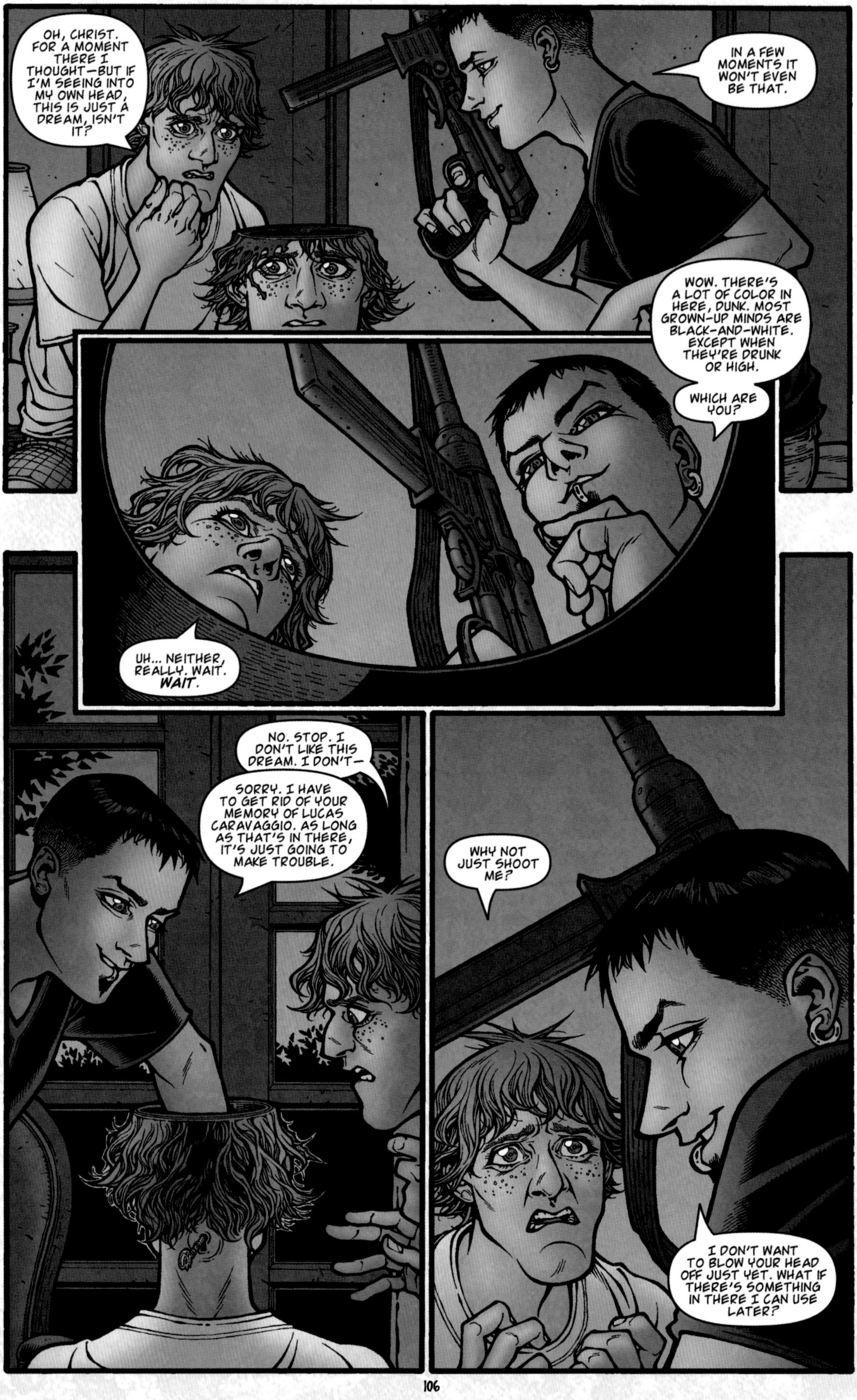
OH, CHRIST. FOR A MOMENT THERE I THOUGHT—BUT IF I'M SEEING INTO MY OWN HEAD, THIS IS JUST A DREAM, ISN'T IT?
IN A FEW MOMENTS IT WON'T EVEN BE THAT.
WOW. THERE'S A LOT OF COLOR IN HERE, DUNK. MOST GROWN-UP MINDS ARE BLACK-AND-WHITE. EXCEPT WHEN THEY'RE DRUNK OR HIGH.
WHICH ARE YOU?
UH... NEITHER, REALLY. WAIT. *WAIT*.
NO. STOP. I DON'T LIKE THIS DREAM. I DON'T—
SORRY. I HAVE TO GET RID OF YOUR MEMORY OF LUCAS CARAVAGGIO. AS LONG AS THAT'S IN THERE, IT'S JUST GOING TO MAKE TROUBLE.
WHY NOT JUST SHOOT ME?
I DON'T WANT TO BLOW YOUR HEAD OFF JUST YET. WHAT IF THERE'S SOMETHING IN THERE I CAN USE LATER?

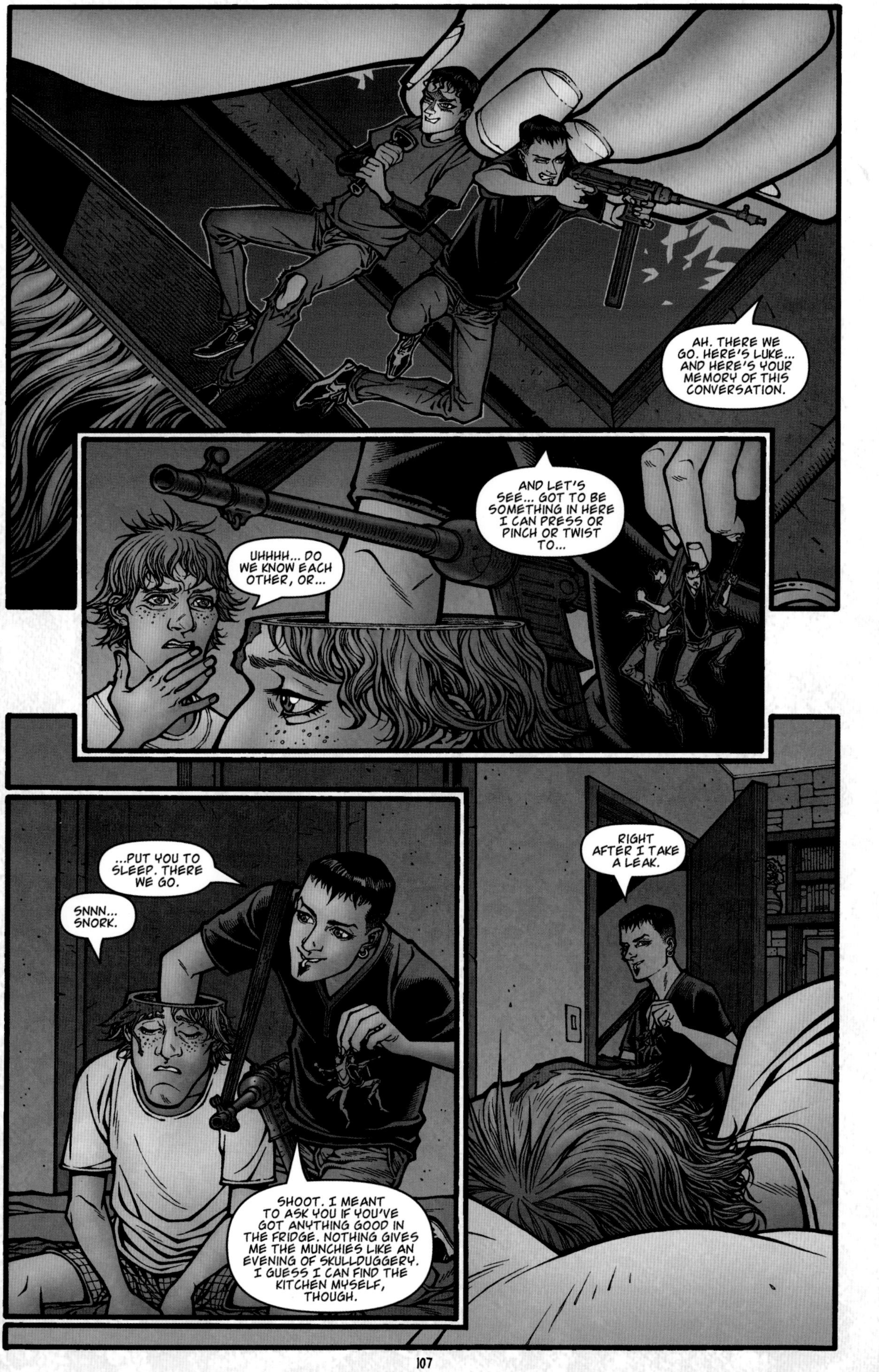
AH. THERE WE GO. HERE'S LUKE... AND HERE'S YOUR MEMORY OF THIS CONVERSATION.
UHHHH... DO WE KNOW EACH OTHER, OR...
AND LET'S SEE... GOT TO BE SOMETHING IN HERE I CAN PRESS OR PINCH OR TWIST TO...
...PUT YOU TO SLEEP. THERE WE GO.
SNNN... SNORK.
SHOOT. I MEANT TO ASK YOU IF YOU'VE GOT ANYTHING GOOD IN THE FRIDGE. NOTHING GIVES ME THE MUNCHIES LIKE AN EVENING OF SKULLDUGGERY. I GUESS I CAN FIND THE KITCHEN MYSELF, THOUGH.
RIGHT AFTER I TAKE A LEAK.

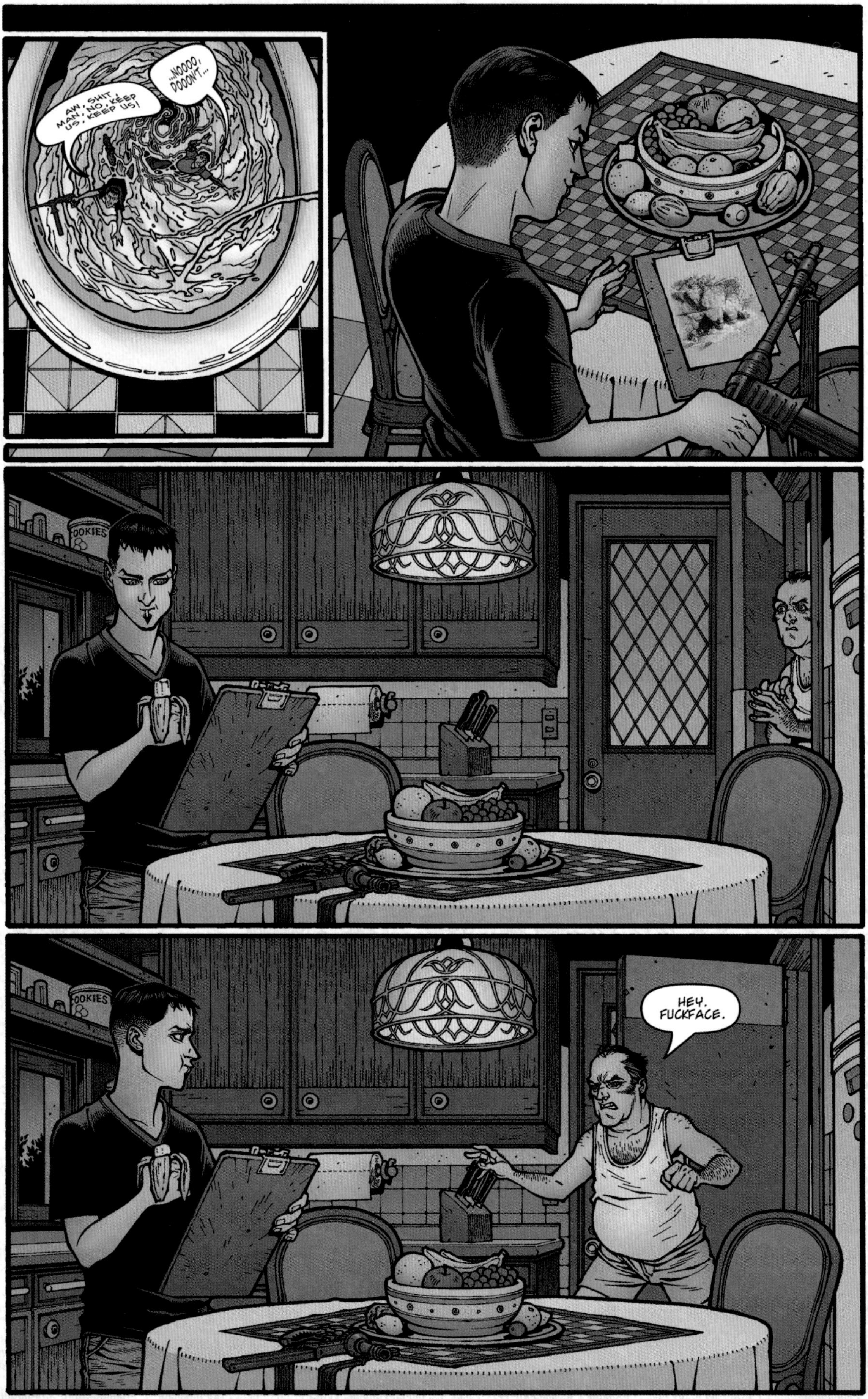
AW, SHIT, MAN, NO, KEEP US, KEEP US!
...NOOOO, DOOON'T...
COOKIES
COOKIES
HEY. FUCKFACE.

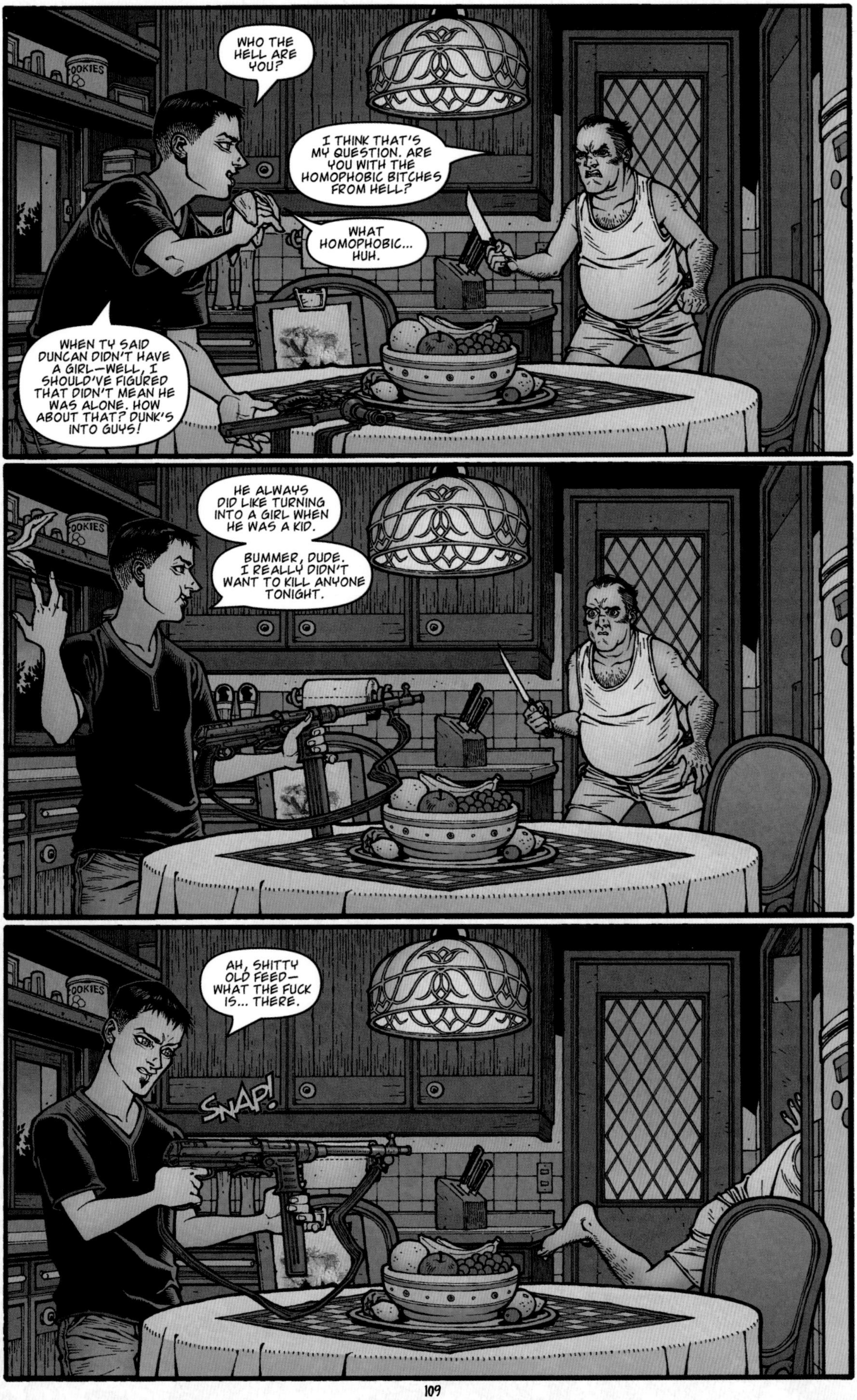
WHO THE HELL ARE YOU?
I THINK THAT'S MY QUESTION. ARE YOU WITH THE HOMOPHOBIC BITCHES FROM HELL?
WHAT HOMOPHOBIC... HUH.
WHEN TY SAID DUNCAN DIDN'T HAVE A GIRL—WELL, I SHOULD'VE FIGURED THAT DIDN'T MEAN HE WAS ALONE. HOW ABOUT THAT? DUNK'S INTO GUYS!
COOKIES
HE ALWAYS DID LIKE TURNING INTO A GIRL WHEN HE WAS A KID.
BUMMER, DUDE. I REALLY DIDN'T WANT TO KILL ANYONE TONIGHT.
AH, SHITTY OLD FEED—WHAT THE FUCK IS... THERE.
SNAP!

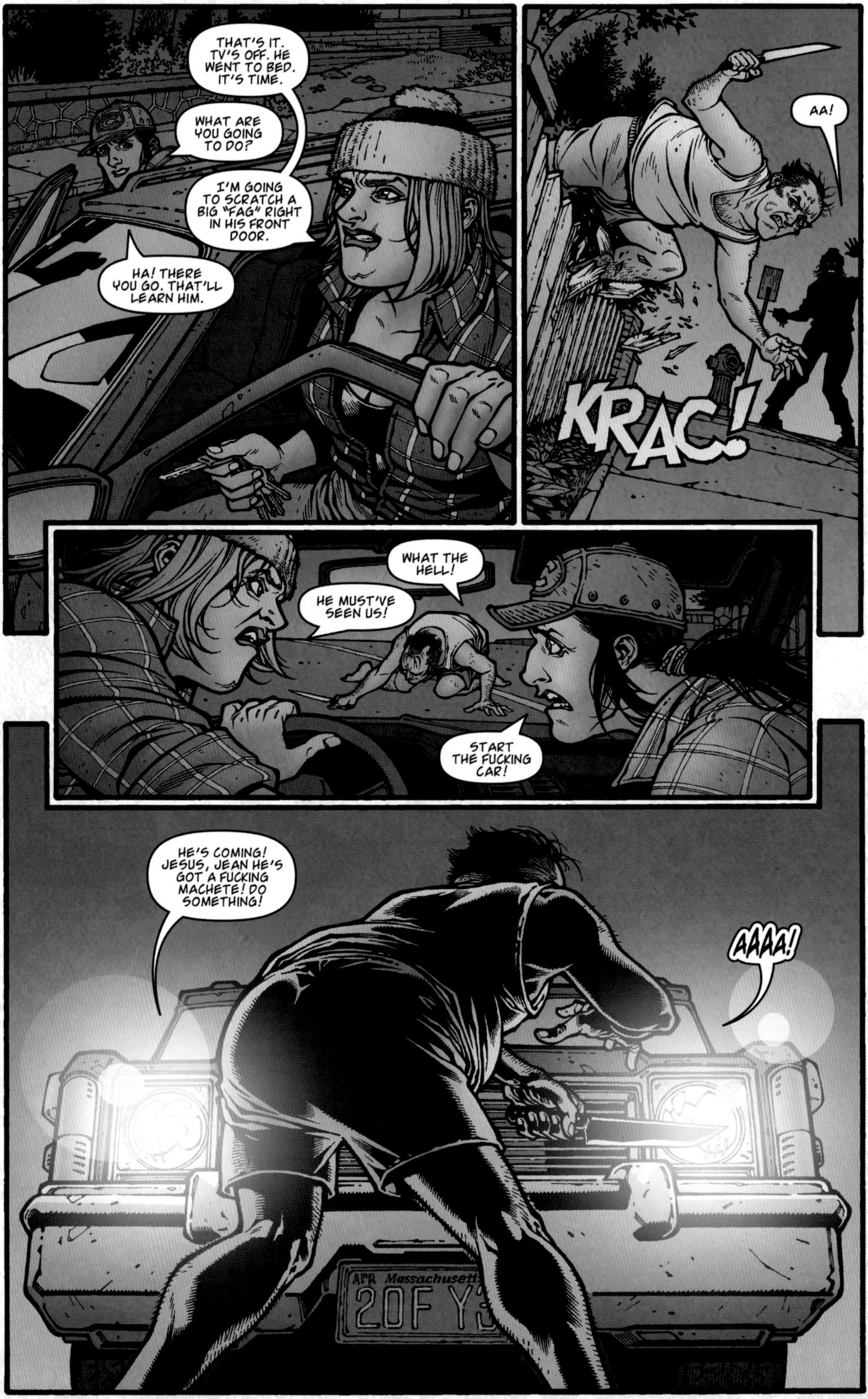
THAT'S IT. TV'S OFF. HE WENT TO BED. IT'S TIME.
WHAT ARE YOU GOING TO DO?
I'M GOING TO SCRATCH A BIG "FAG" RIGHT IN HIS FRONT DOOR.
HA! THERE YOU GO. THAT'LL LEARN HIM.
AA!
KRAC!
WHAT THE HELL!
HE MUST'VE SEEN US!
START THE FUCKING CAR!
HE'S COMING! JESUS, JEAN HE'S GOT A FUCKING MACHETE! DO SOMETHING!
AAAA!
APR Massachusetts
20F Y3

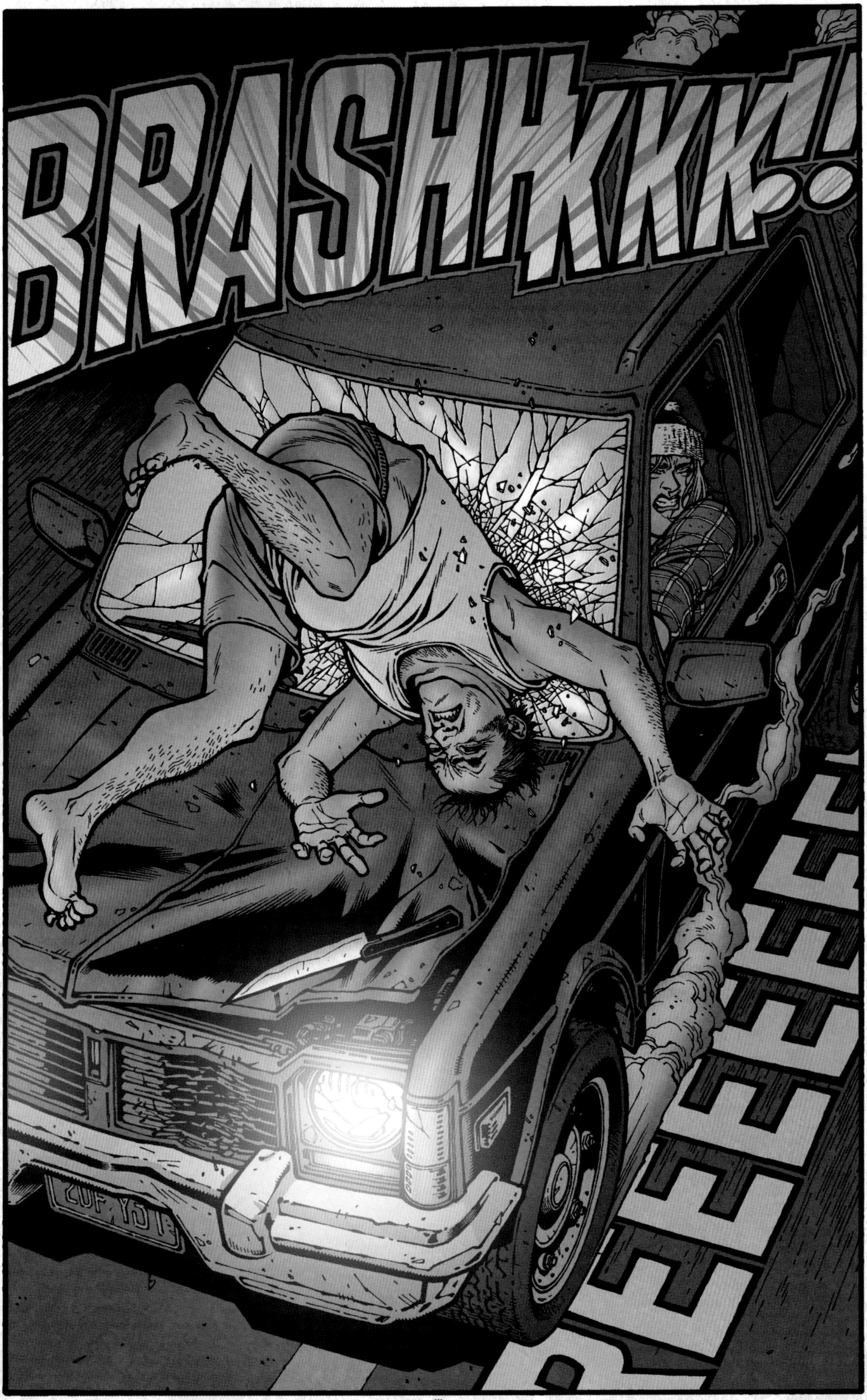
BRASHKKK!!
REEEEEEE

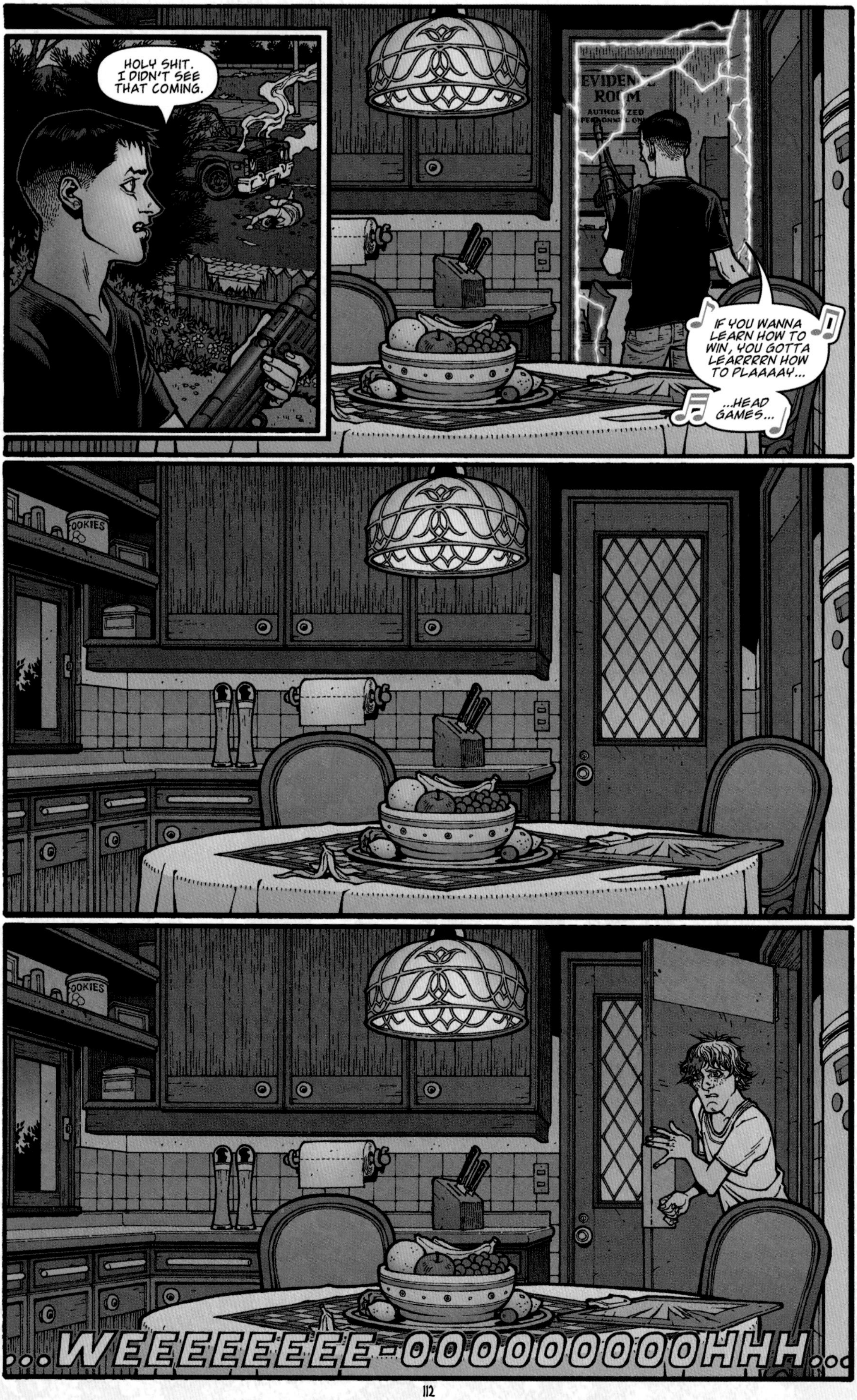
HOLY SHIT. I DIDN'T SEE THAT COMING.
EVIDENCE ROOM
AUTHORIZED PERSONNEL ONLY
IF YOU WANNA LEARN HOW TO WIN, YOU GOTTA LEARRRRN HOW TO PLAAAAY...
...HEAD GAMES...
COOKIES
...WEEEEEEEEE-OOOOOOOOOOHHH...

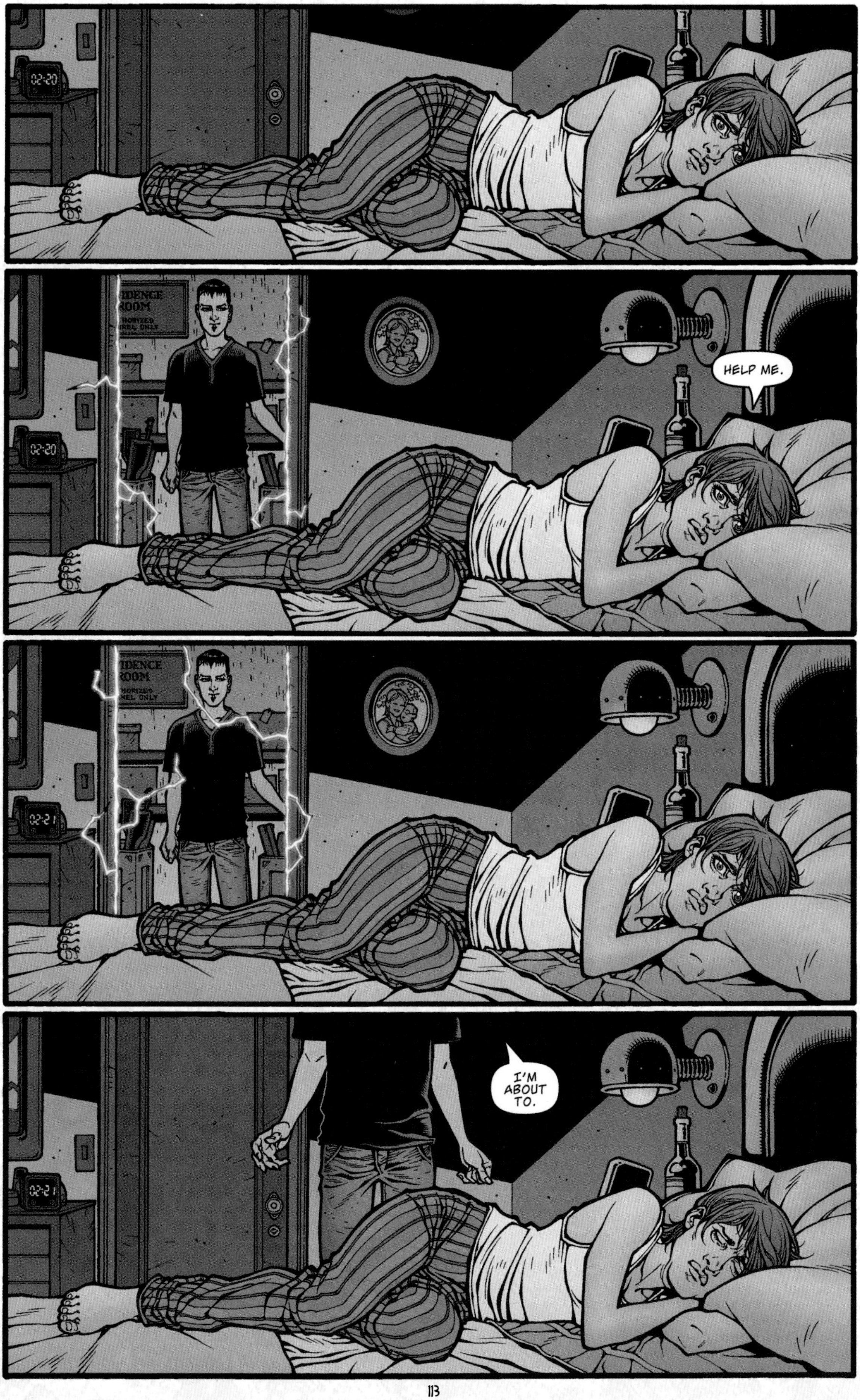
HELP ME.
I'M ABOUT TO.

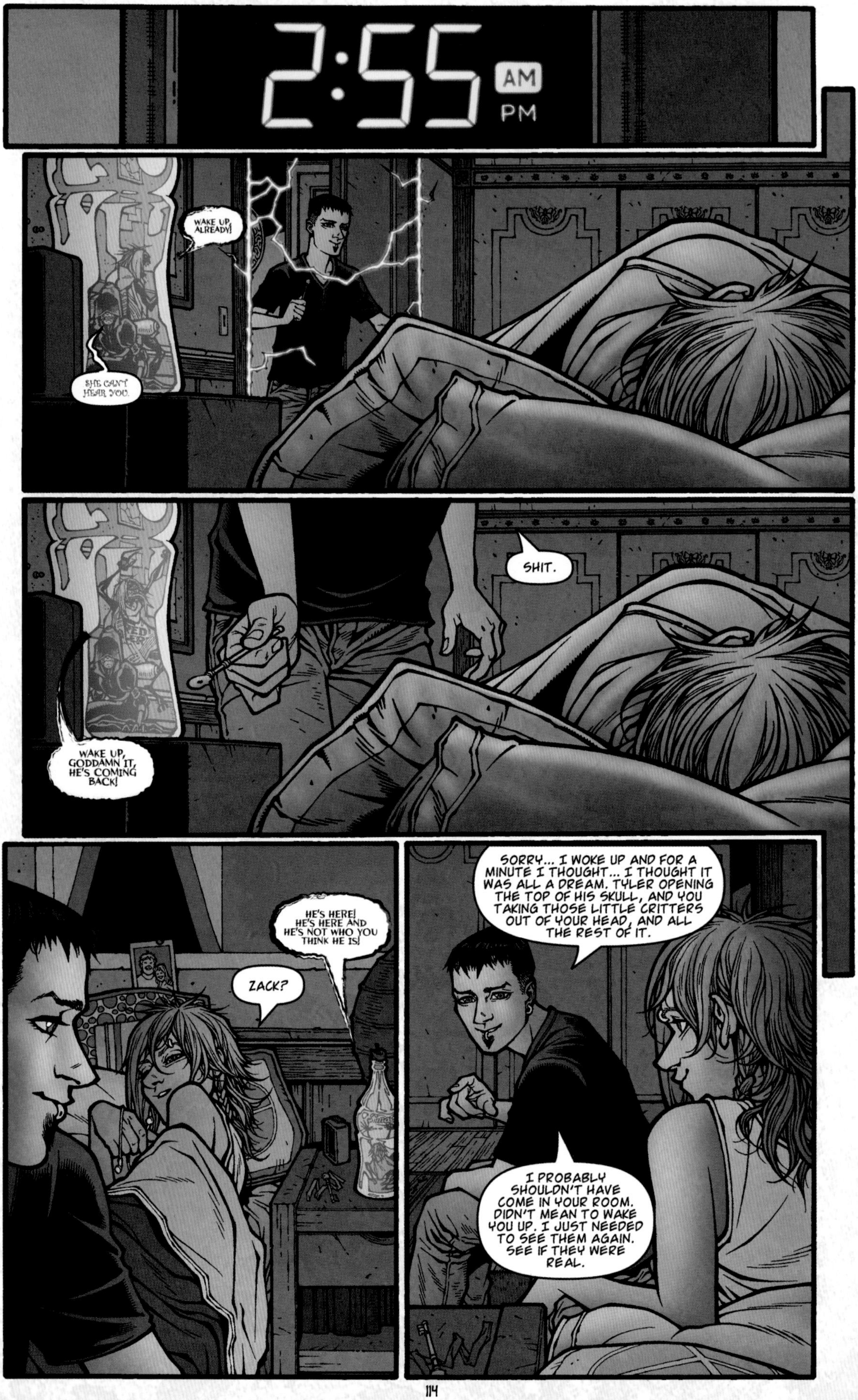

2:55 AM PM
WAKE UP, ALREADY!
SHE CAN'T HEAR YOU.
SHIT.
WAKE UP, GODDAMN IT, HE'S COMING BACK!
ZACK?
HE'S HERE! HE'S HERE AND HE'S NOT WHO YOU THINK HE IS!
SORRY... I WOKE UP AND FOR A MINUTE I THOUGHT... I THOUGHT IT WAS ALL A DREAM. TYLER OPENING THE TOP OF HIS SKULL, AND YOU TAKING THOSE LITTLE CRITTERS OUT OF YOUR HEAD, AND ALL THE REST OF IT.
I PROBABLY SHOULDN'T HAVE COME IN YOUR ROOM. DIDN'T MEAN TO WAKE YOU UP. I JUST NEEDED TO SEE THEM AGAIN. SEE IF THEY WERE REAL.

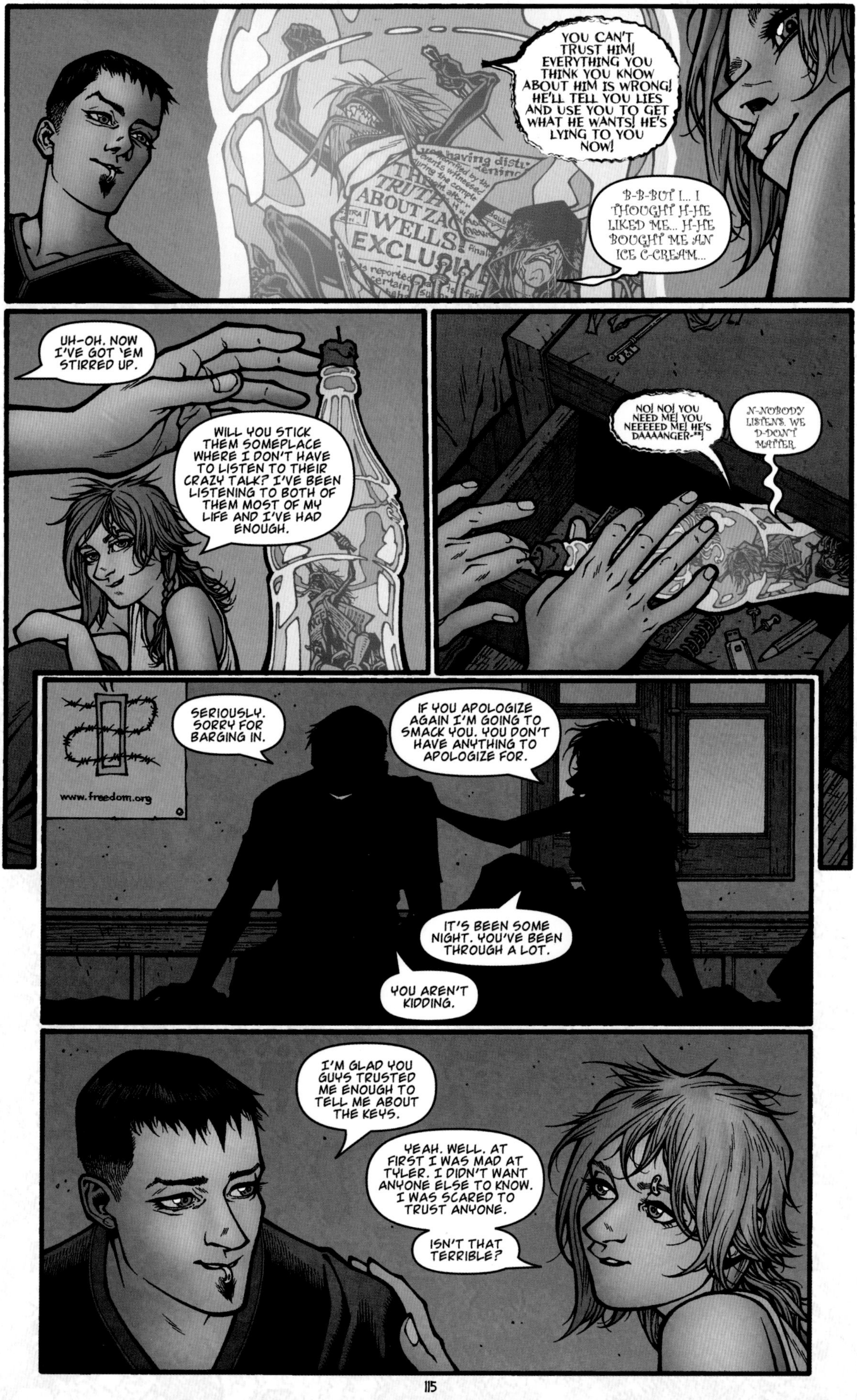
YOU CAN'T TRUST HIM! EVERYTHING YOU THINK YOU KNOW ABOUT HIM IS WRONG! HE'LL TELL YOU LIES AND USE YOU TO GET WHAT HE WANTS! HE'S LYING TO YOU NOW!
B-B-BUT I... I THOUGHT H-HE LIKED ME... H-HE BOUGHT ME AN ICE C-CREAM...
UH-OH. NOW I'VE GOT 'EM STIRRED UP.
WILL YOU STICK THEM SOMEPLACE WHERE I DON'T HAVE TO LISTEN TO THEIR CRAZY TALK? I'VE BEEN LISTENING TO BOTH OF THEM MOST OF MY LIFE AND I'VE HAD ENOUGH.
NO! NO! YOU NEED ME! YOU NEEEEED ME! HE'S DAAAANGER-**!
N-NOBODY LISTENS. WE D-DON'T MATTER.
www.freedom.org
SERIOUSLY. SORRY FOR BARGING IN.
IF YOU APOLOGIZE AGAIN I'M GOING TO SMACK YOU. YOU DON'T HAVE ANYTHING TO APOLOGIZE FOR.
IT'S BEEN SOME NIGHT. YOU'VE BEEN THROUGH A LOT.
YOU AREN'T KIDDING.
I'M GLAD YOU GUYS TRUSTED ME ENOUGH TO TELL ME ABOUT THE KEYS.
YEAH. WELL. AT FIRST I WAS MAD AT TYLER. I DIDN'T WANT ANYONE ELSE TO KNOW. I WAS SCARED TO TRUST ANYONE.
ISN'T THAT TERRIBLE?

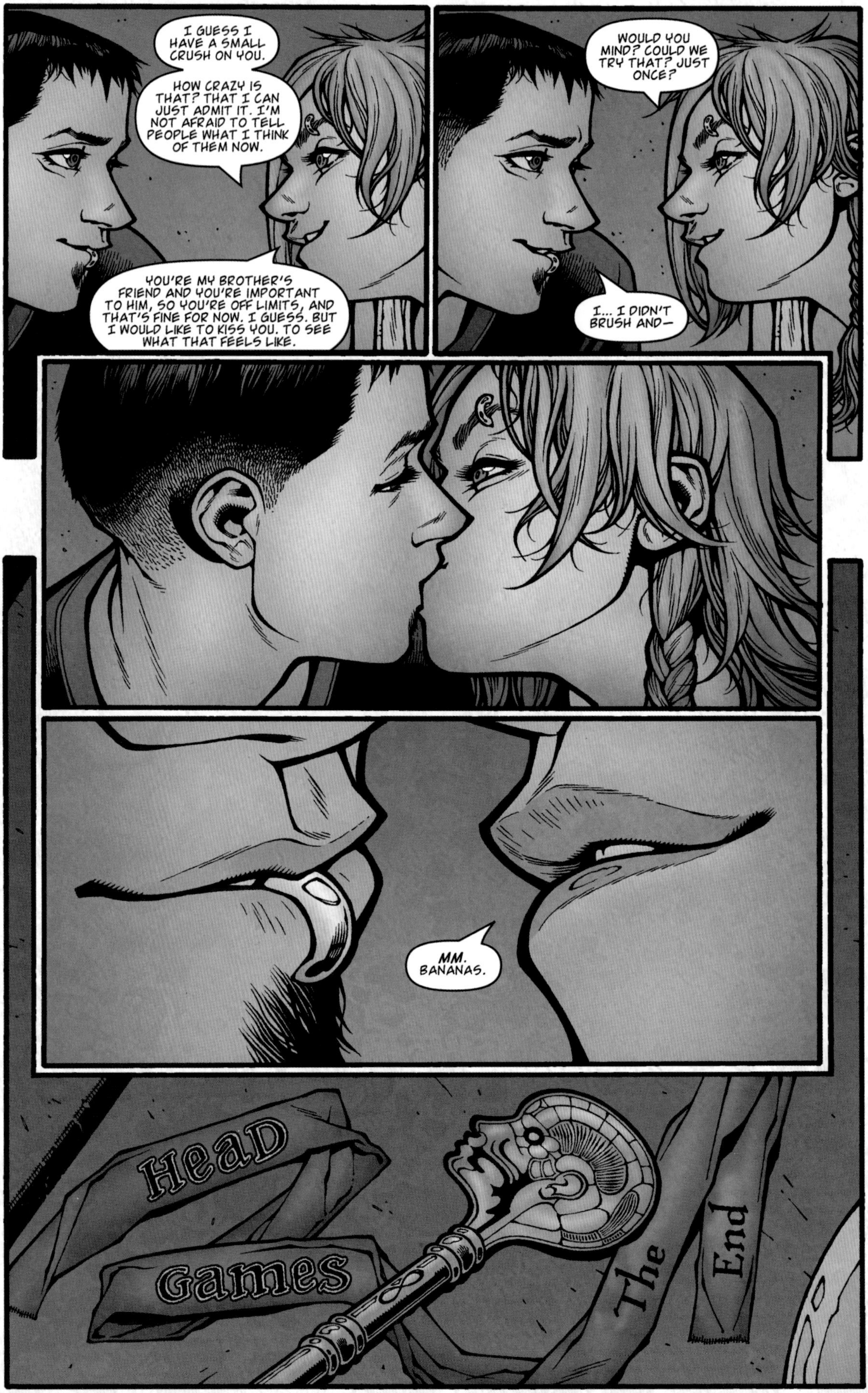
I GUESS I HAVE A SMALL CRUSH ON YOU.
HOW CRAZY IS THAT? THAT I CAN JUST ADMIT IT. I'M NOT AFRAID TO TELL PEOPLE WHAT I THINK OF THEM NOW.
YOU'RE MY BROTHER'S FRIEND AND YOU'RE IMPORTANT TO HIM, SO YOU'RE OFF LIMITS, AND THAT'S FINE FOR NOW. I GUESS. BUT I WOULD LIKE TO KISS YOU. TO SEE WHAT THAT FEELS LIKE.
WOULD YOU MIND? COULD WE TRY THAT? JUST ONCE?
I... I DIDN'T BRUSH AND—
MM. BANANAS.
Head Games
The End

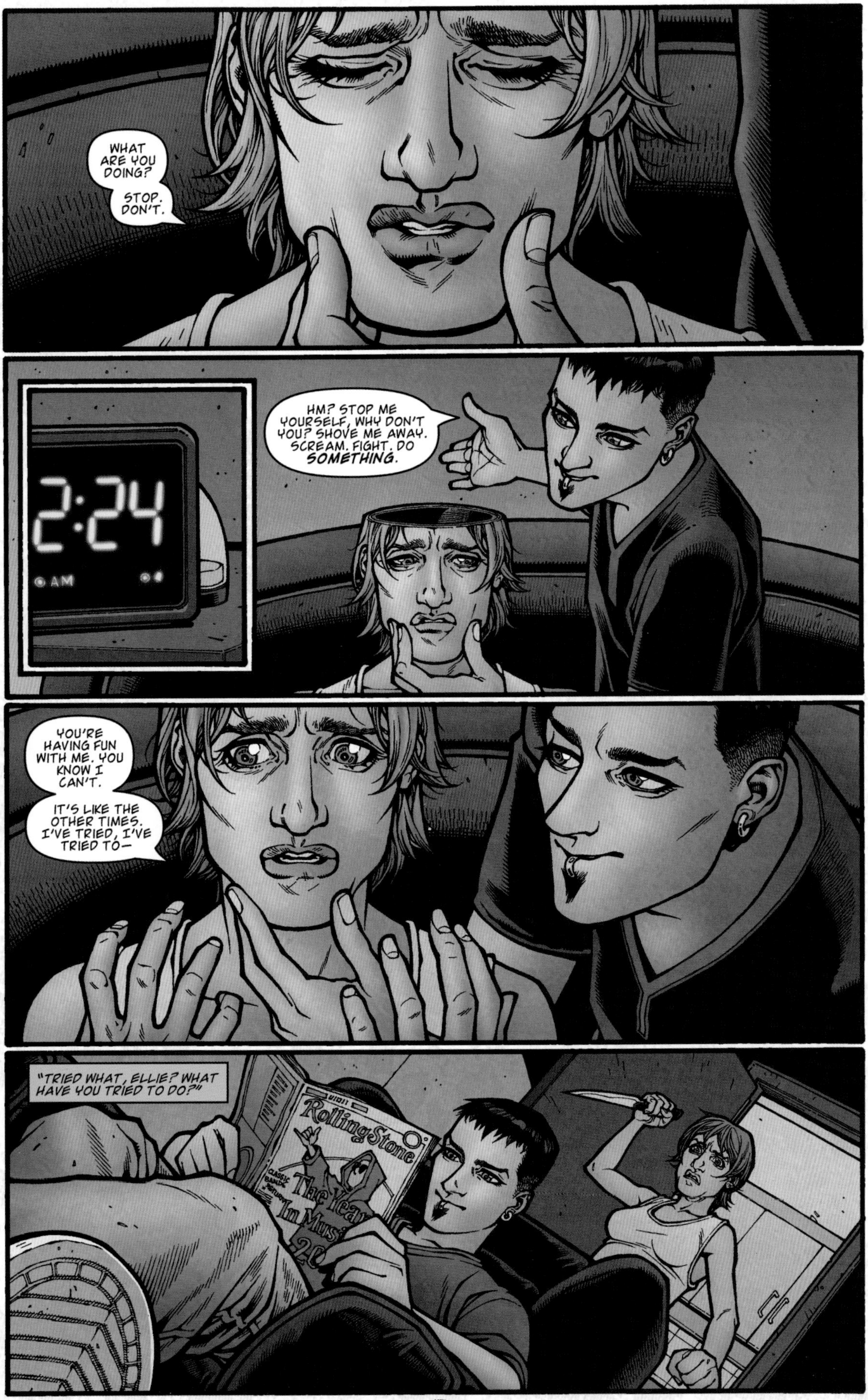
WHAT ARE YOU DOING?
STOP. DON'T.
HM? STOP ME YOURSELF, WHY DON'T YOU? SHOVE ME AWAY. SCREAM. FIGHT. DO SOMETHING.
2:24
AM
YOU'RE HAVING FUN WITH ME. YOU KNOW I CAN'T.
IT'S LIKE THE OTHER TIMES. I'VE TRIED, I'VE TRIED TO—
"TRIED WHAT, ELLIE? WHAT HAVE YOU TRIED TO DO?"
RollingStone
The Year In Music

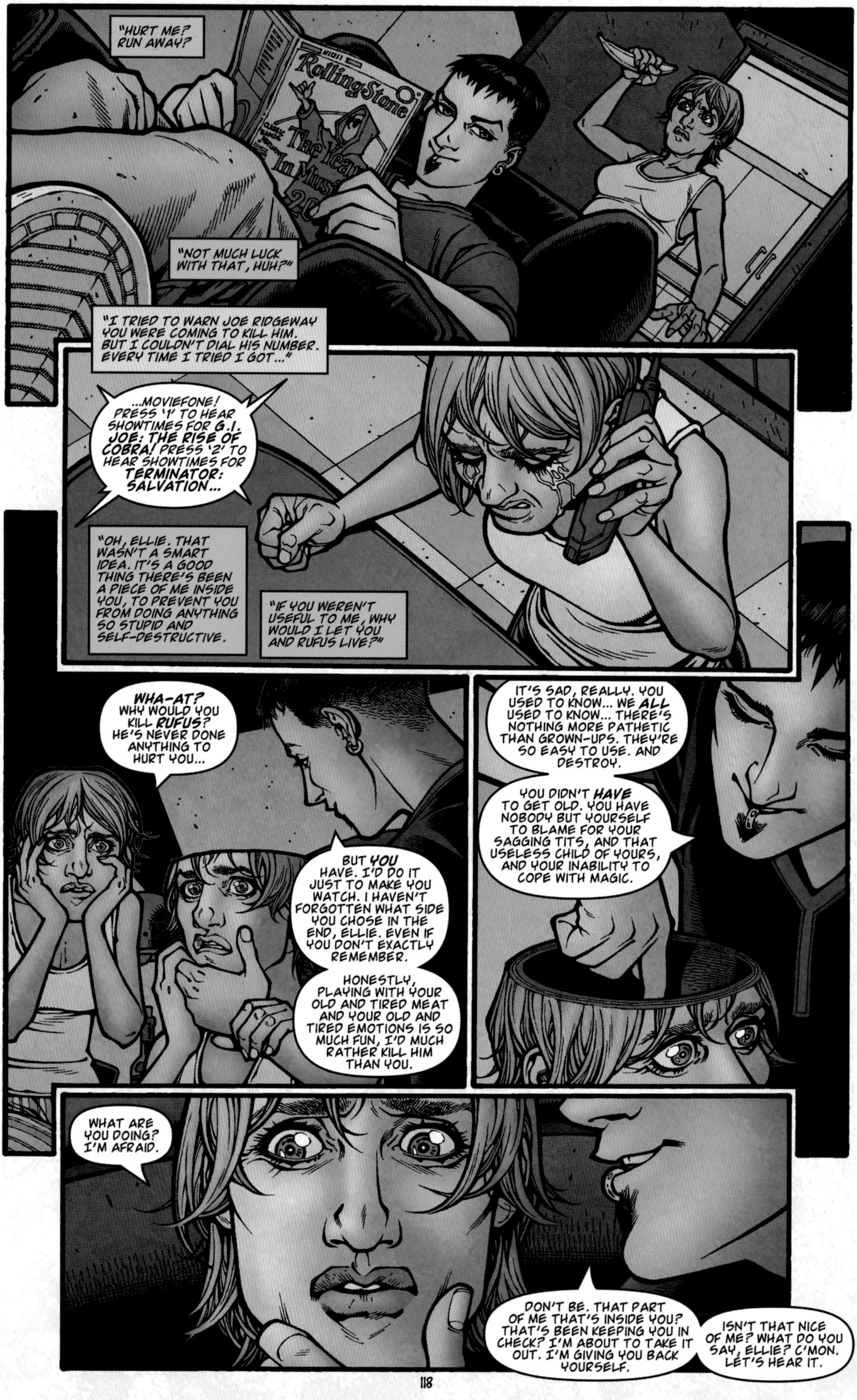

"HURT ME? RUN AWAY?
"NOT MUCH LUCK WITH THAT, HUH?"
"I TRIED TO WARN JOE RIDGEWAY YOU WERE COMING TO KILL HIM. BUT I COULDN'T DIAL HIS NUMBER. EVERY TIME I TRIED I GOT..."
...MOVIEFONE! PRESS '1' TO HEAR SHOWTIMES FOR G.I. JOE: THE RISE OF COBRA! PRESS '2' TO HEAR SHOWTIMES FOR TERMINATOR: SALVATION...
"OH, ELLIE. THAT WASN'T A SMART IDEA. IT'S A GOOD THING THERE'S BEEN A PIECE OF ME INSIDE YOU, TO PREVENT YOU FROM DOING ANYTHING SO STUPID AND SELF-DESTRUCTIVE.
"IF YOU WEREN'T USEFUL TO ME, WHY WOULD I LET YOU AND RUFUS LIVE?"
WHA-AT? WHY WOULD YOU KILL RUFUS? HE'S NEVER DONE ANYTHING TO HURT YOU...
BUT YOU HAVE. I'D DO IT JUST TO MAKE YOU WATCH. I HAVEN'T FORGOTTEN WHAT SIDE YOU CHOSE IN THE END, ELLIE. EVEN IF YOU DON'T EXACTLY REMEMBER.
HONESTLY, PLAYING WITH YOUR OLD AND TIRED MEAT AND YOUR OLD AND TIRED EMOTIONS IS SO MUCH FUN, I'D MUCH RATHER KILL HIM THAN YOU.
IT'S SAD, REALLY. YOU USED TO KNOW... WE ALL USED TO KNOW... THERE'S NOTHING MORE PATHETIC THAN GROWN-UPS. THEY'RE SO EASY TO USE. AND DESTROY.
YOU DIDN'T HAVE TO GET OLD. YOU HAVE NOBODY BUT YOURSELF TO BLAME FOR YOUR SAGGING TITS, AND THAT USELESS CHILD OF YOURS, AND YOUR INABILITY TO COPE WITH MAGIC.
WHAT ARE YOU DOING? I'M AFRAID.
DON'T BE. THAT PART OF ME THAT'S INSIDE YOU? THAT'S BEEN KEEPING YOU IN CHECK? I'M ABOUT TO TAKE IT OUT. I'M GIVING YOU BACK YOURSELF.
ISN'T THAT NICE OF ME? WHAT DO YOU SAY, ELLIE? C'MON. LET'S HEAR IT.

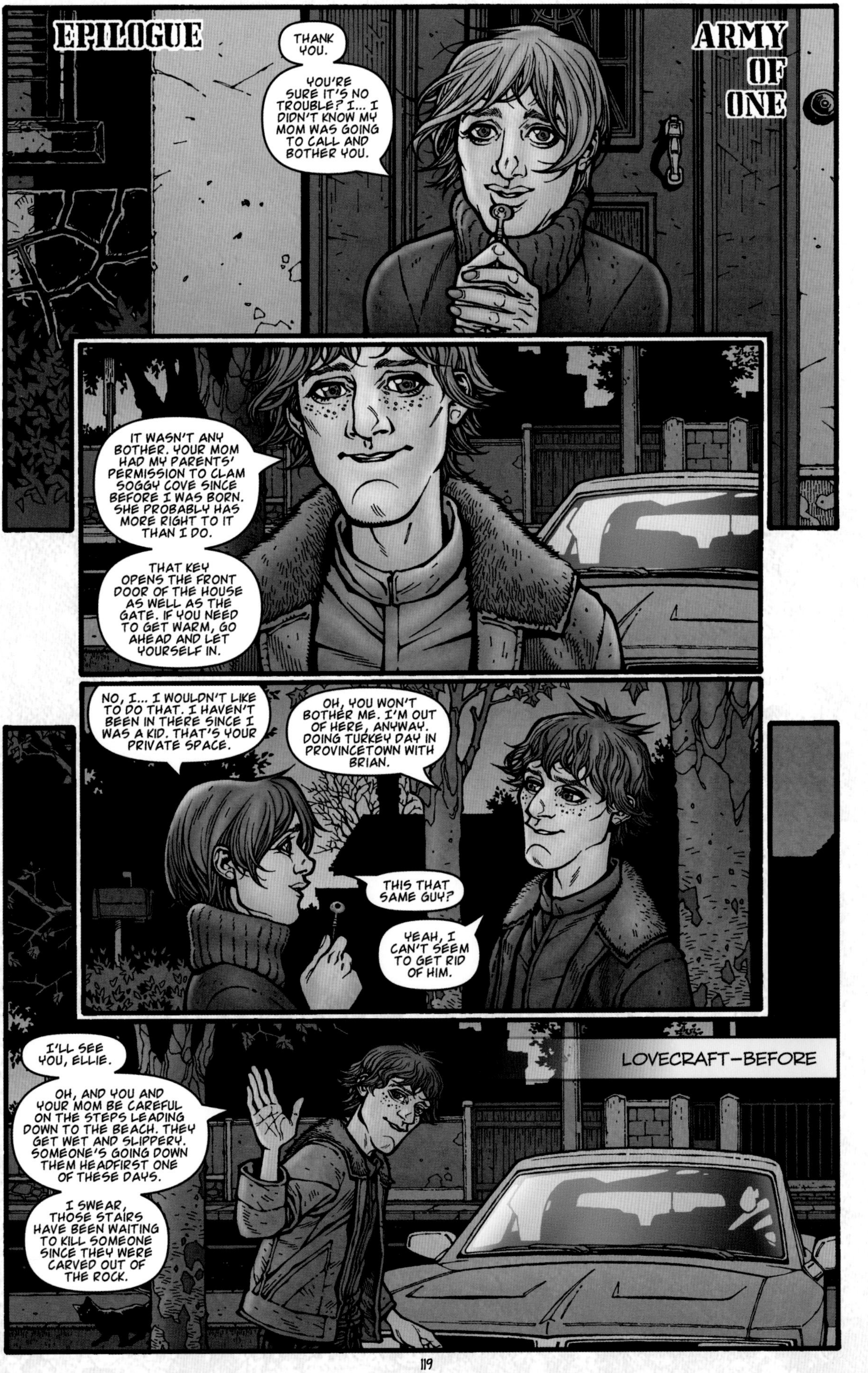
EPILOGUE
ARMY OF ONE
THANK YOU.
YOU'RE SURE IT'S NO TROUBLE? I... I DIDN'T KNOW MY MOM WAS GOING TO CALL AND BOTHER YOU.
IT WASN'T ANY BOTHER. YOUR MOM HAD MY PARENTS' PERMISSION TO CLAM SOGGY COVE SINCE BEFORE I WAS BORN. SHE PROBABLY HAS MORE RIGHT TO IT THAN I DO.
THAT KEY OPENS THE FRONT DOOR OF THE HOUSE AS WELL AS THE GATE. IF YOU NEED TO GET WARM, GO AHEAD AND LET YOURSELF IN.
NO, I... I WOULDN'T LIKE TO DO THAT. I HAVEN'T BEEN IN THERE SINCE I WAS A KID. THAT'S YOUR PRIVATE SPACE.
OH, YOU WON'T BOTHER ME. I'M OUT OF HERE, ANYWAY. DOING TURKEY DAY IN PROVINCETOWN WITH BRIAN.
THIS THAT SAME GUY?
YEAH, I CAN'T SEEM TO GET RID OF HIM.
I'LL SEE YOU, ELLIE.
LOVECRAFT—BEFORE
OH, AND YOU AND YOUR MOM BE CAREFUL ON THE STEPS LEADING DOWN TO THE BEACH. THEY GET WET AND SLIPPERY. SOMEONE'S GOING DOWN THEM HEADFIRST ONE OF THESE DAYS.
I SWEAR, THOSE STAIRS HAVE BEEN WAITING TO KILL SOMEONE SINCE THEY WERE CARVED OUT OF THE ROCK.

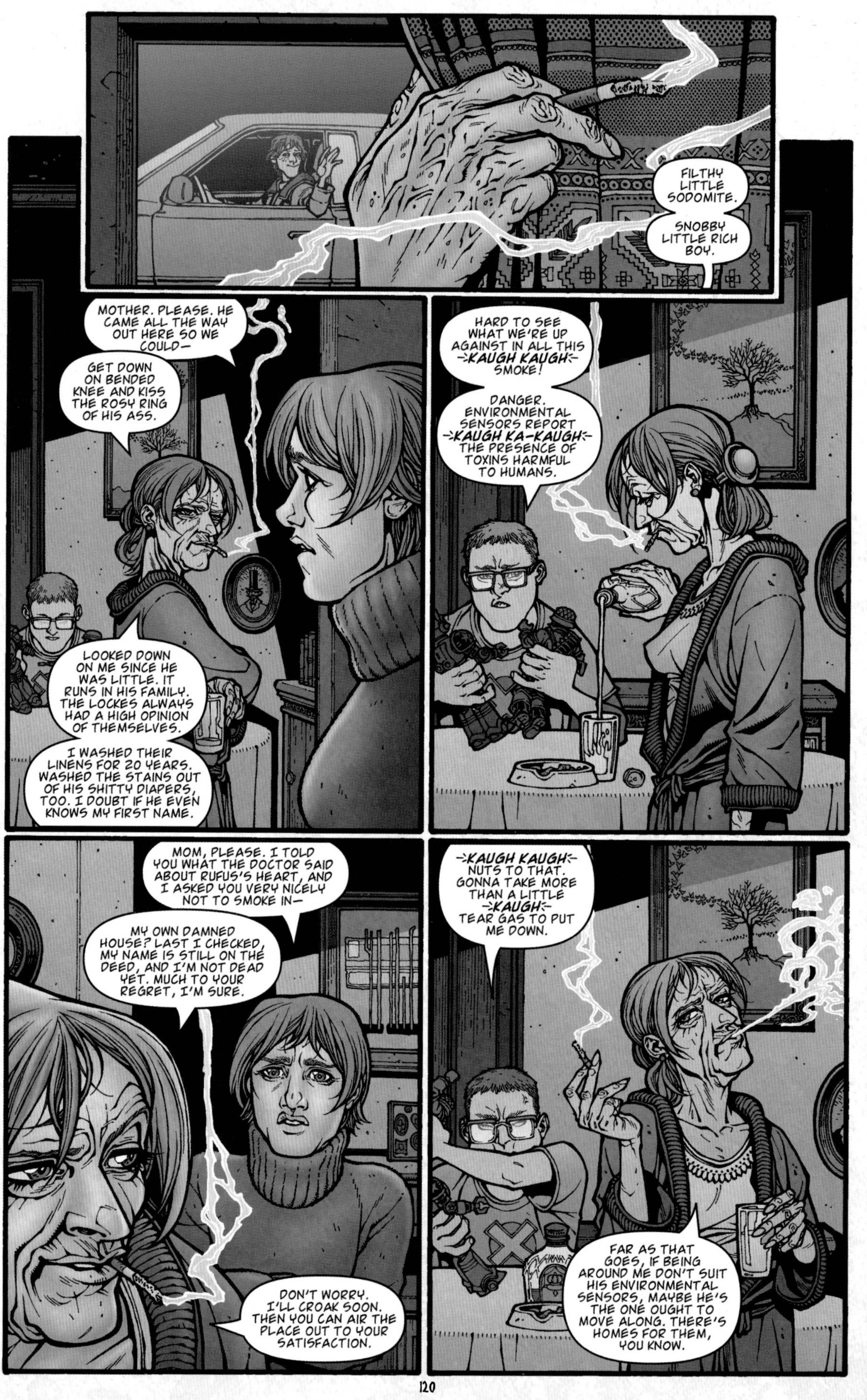
FILTHY LITTLE SODOMITE.
SNOBBY LITTLE RICH BOY.
MOTHER. PLEASE. HE CAME ALL THE WAY OUT HERE SO WE COULD—
GET DOWN ON BENDED KNEE AND KISS THE ROSY RING OF HIS ASS.
LOOKED DOWN ON ME SINCE HE WAS LITTLE. IT RUNS IN HIS FAMILY. THE LOCKES ALWAYS HAD A HIGH OPINION OF THEMSELVES.
I WASHED THEIR LINENS FOR 20 YEARS. WASHED THE STAINS OUT OF HIS SHITTY DIAPERS, TOO. I DOUBT IF HE EVEN KNOWS MY FIRST NAME.
HARD TO SEE WHAT WE'RE UP AGAINST IN ALL THIS -KAUGH KAUGH- SMOKE!
DANGER. ENVIRONMENTAL SENSORS REPORT -KAUGH KA-KAUGH- THE PRESENCE OF TOXINS HARMFUL TO HUMANS.
MOM, PLEASE. I TOLD YOU WHAT THE DOCTOR SAID ABOUT RUFUS'S HEART, AND I ASKED YOU VERY NICELY NOT TO SMOKE IN—
MY OWN DAMNED HOUSE? LAST I CHECKED, MY NAME IS STILL ON THE DEED, AND I'M NOT DEAD YET. MUCH TO YOUR REGRET, I'M SURE.
DON'T WORRY. I'LL CROAK SOON. THEN YOU CAN AIR THE PLACE OUT TO YOUR SATISFACTION.
-KAUGH KAUGH- NUTS TO THAT. GONNA TAKE MORE THAN A LITTLE -KAUGH- TEAR GAS TO PUT ME DOWN.
FAR AS THAT GOES, IF BEING AROUND ME DON'T SUIT HIS ENVIRONMENTAL SENSORS, MAYBE HE'S THE ONE OUGHT TO MOVE ALONG. THERE'S HOMES FOR THEM, YOU KNOW.

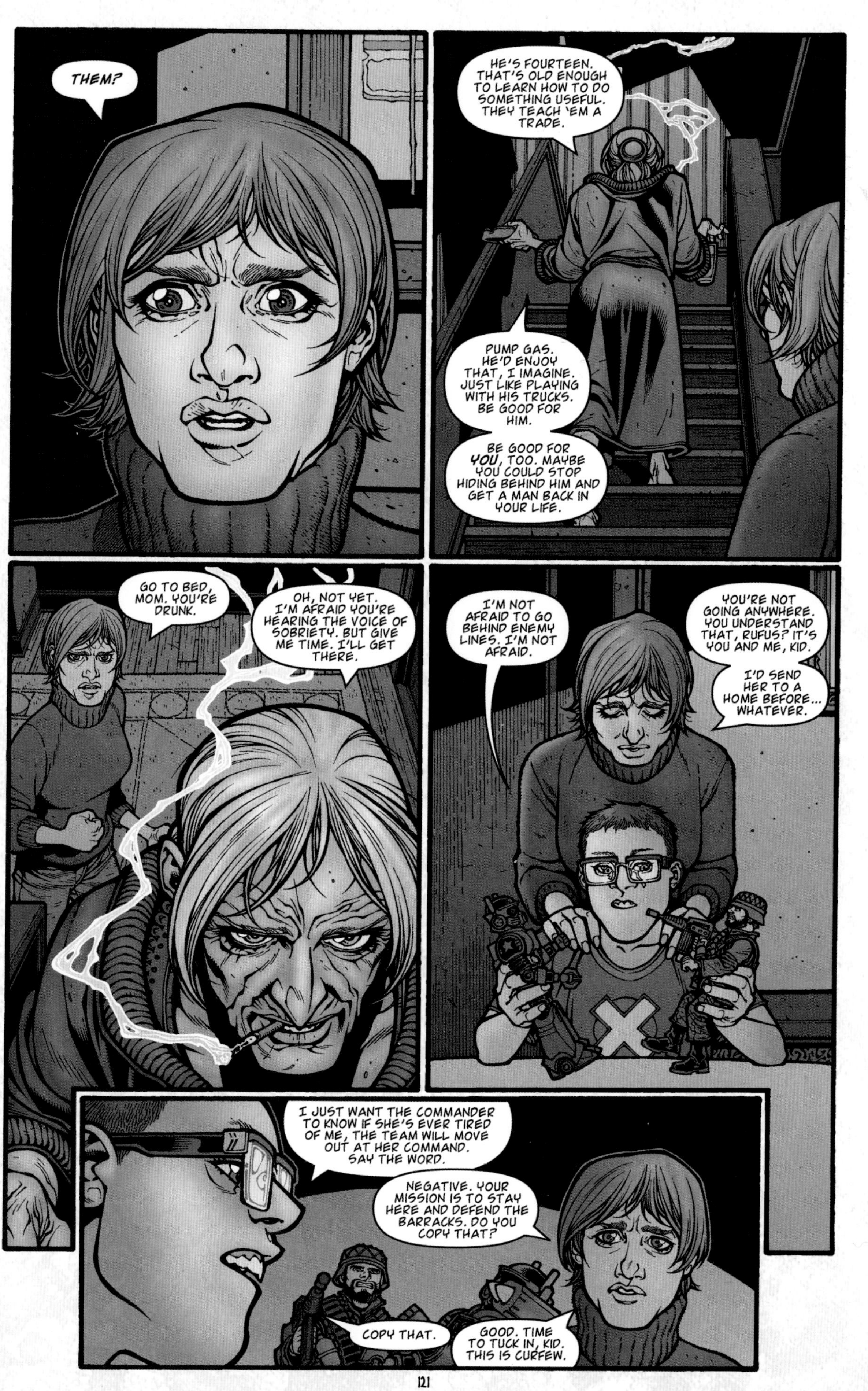
THEM?
HE'S FOURTEEN. THAT'S OLD ENOUGH TO LEARN HOW TO DO SOMETHING USEFUL. THEY TEACH 'EM A TRADE.
PUMP GAS. HE'D ENJOY THAT, I IMAGINE. JUST LIKE PLAYING WITH HIS TRUCKS. BE GOOD FOR HIM.
BE GOOD FOR YOU, TOO. MAYBE YOU COULD STOP HIDING BEHIND HIM AND GET A MAN BACK IN YOUR LIFE.
GO TO BED, MOM. YOU'RE DRUNK.
OH, NOT YET. I'M AFRAID YOU'RE HEARING THE VOICE OF SOBRIETY. BUT GIVE ME TIME. I'LL GET THERE.
I'M NOT AFRAID TO GO BEHIND ENEMY LINES. I'M NOT AFRAID.
YOU'RE NOT GOING ANYWHERE. YOU UNDERSTAND THAT, RUFUS? IT'S YOU AND ME, KID.
I'D SEND HER TO A HOME BEFORE... WHATEVER.
I JUST WANT THE COMMANDER TO KNOW IF SHE'S EVER TIRED OF ME, THE TEAM WILL MOVE OUT AT HER COMMAND. SAY THE WORD.
NEGATIVE. YOUR MISSION IS TO STAY HERE AND DEFEND THE BARRACKS. DO YOU COPY THAT?
COPY THAT.
GOOD. TIME TO TUCK IN, KID. THIS IS CURFEW.

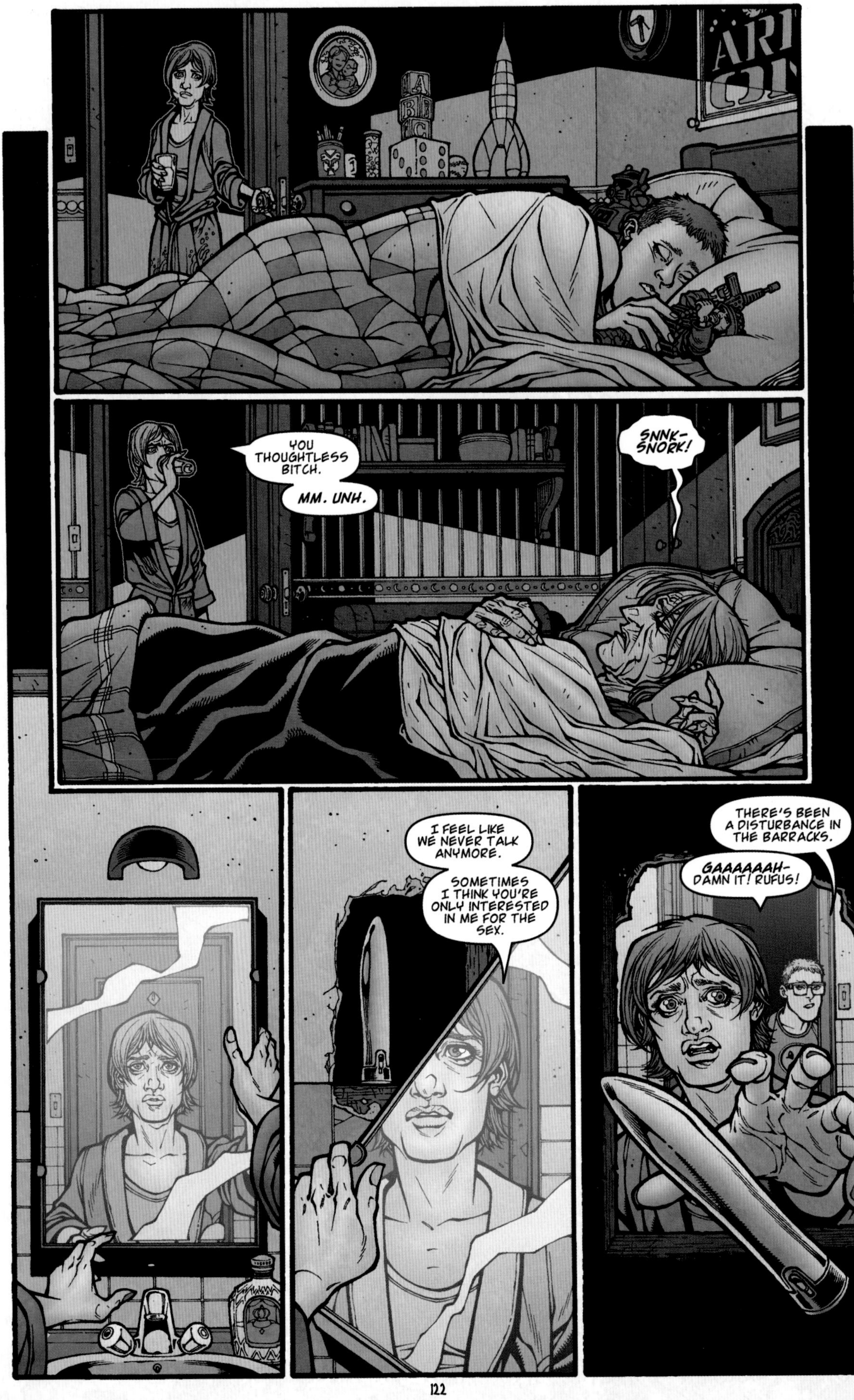

YOU THOUGHTLESS BITCH.
MM. UNH.
SNNK-SNORK!
I FEEL LIKE WE NEVER TALK ANYMORE.
SOMETIMES I THINK YOU'RE ONLY INTERESTED IN ME FOR THE SEX.
THERE'S BEEN A DISTURBANCE IN THE BARRACKS.
GAAAAAAH-DAMN IT! RUFUS!

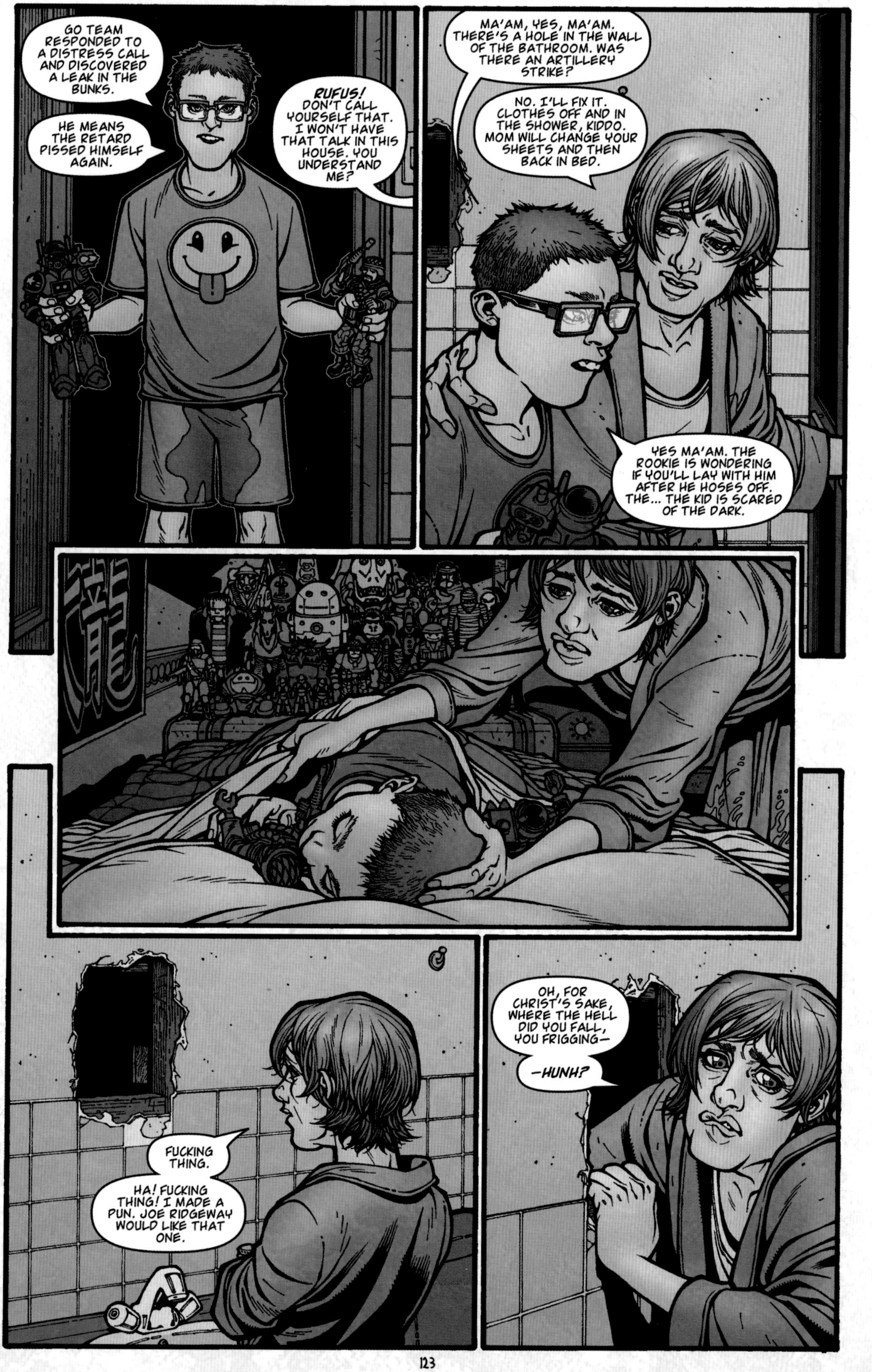

GO TEAM RESPONDED TO A DISTRESS CALL AND DISCOVERED A LEAK IN THE BUNKS.
HE MEANS THE RETARD PISSED HIMSELF AGAIN.
RUFUS! DON'T CALL YOURSELF THAT. I WON'T HAVE THAT TALK IN THIS HOUSE. YOU UNDERSTAND ME?
MA'AM, YES, MA'AM. THERE'S A HOLE IN THE WALL OF THE BATHROOM. WAS THERE AN ARTILLERY STRIKE?
NO. I'LL FIX IT. CLOTHES OFF AND IN THE SHOWER, KIDDO. MOM WILL CHANGE YOUR SHEETS AND THEN BACK IN BED.
YES MA'AM. THE ROOKIE IS WONDERING IF YOU'LL LAY WITH HIM AFTER HE HOSES OFF. THE... THE KID IS SCARED OF THE DARK.
FUCKING THING.
HA! FUCKING THING! I MADE A PUN. JOE RIDGEWAY WOULD LIKE THAT ONE.
OH, FOR CHRIST'S SAKE, WHERE THE HELL DID YOU FALL, YOU FRIGGING—
—HUNH?

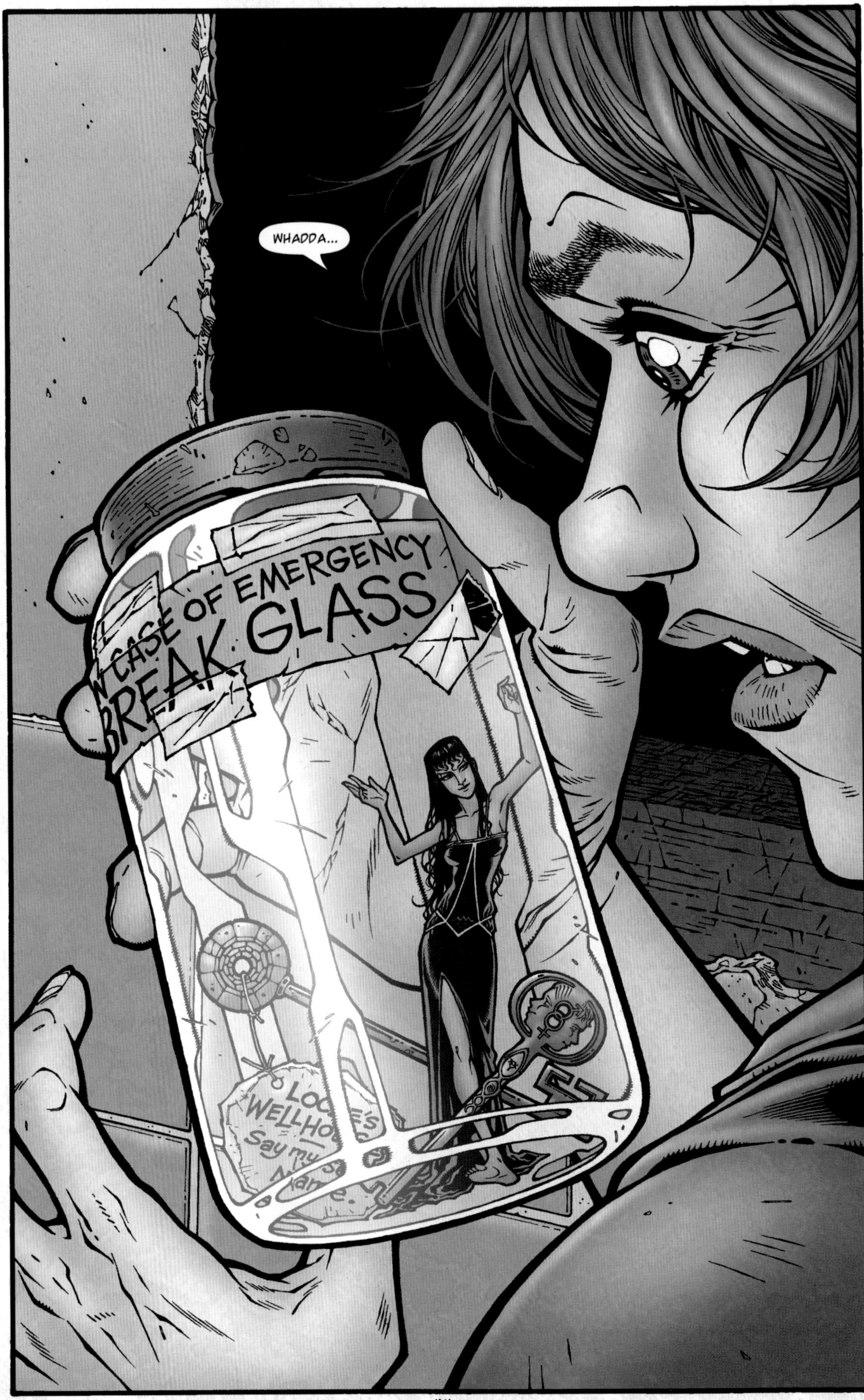
WHADDA...
CASE OF EMERGENCY
BREAK GLASS

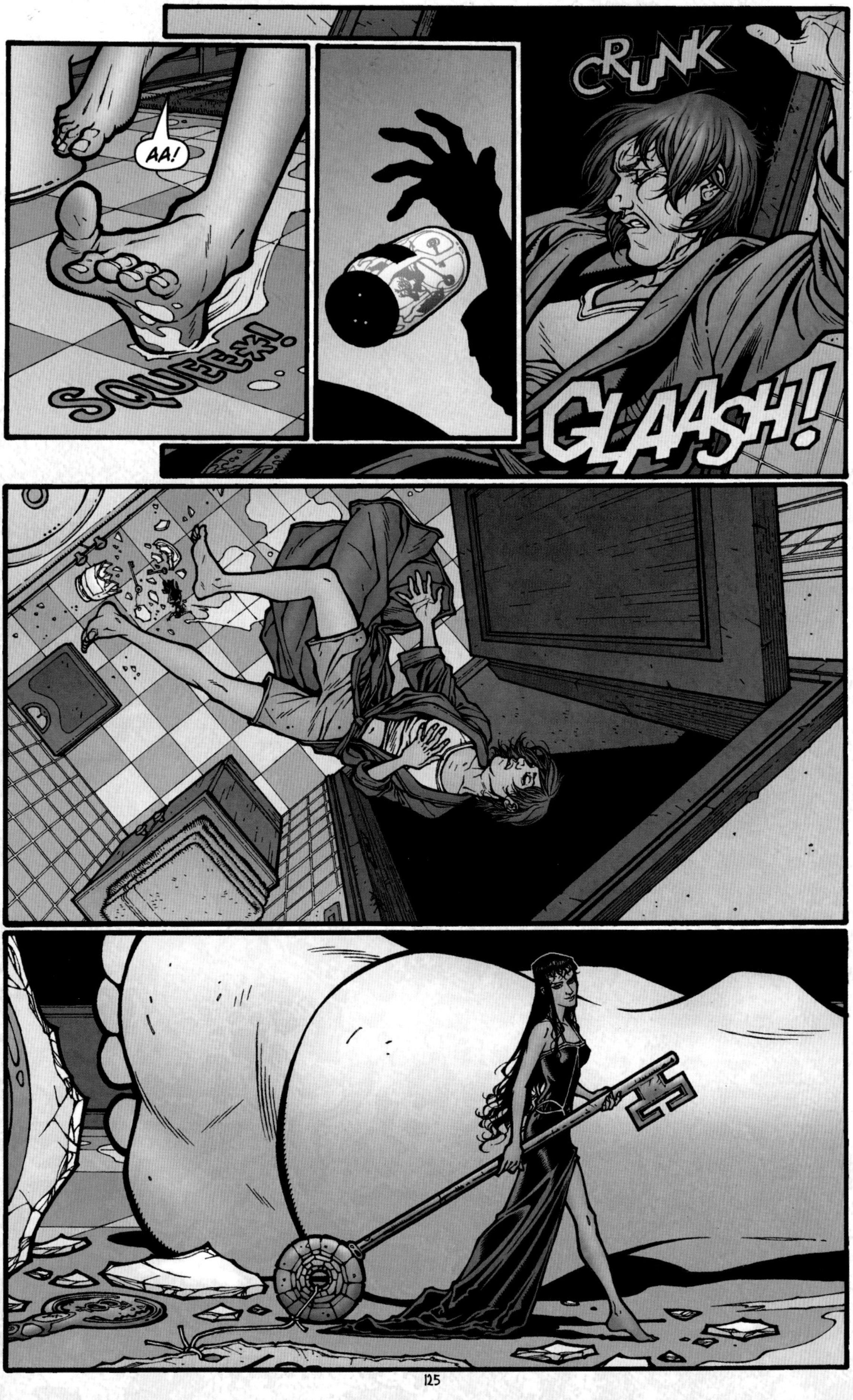
AA!
SQUEE*!
CRUNK
GLAASH!

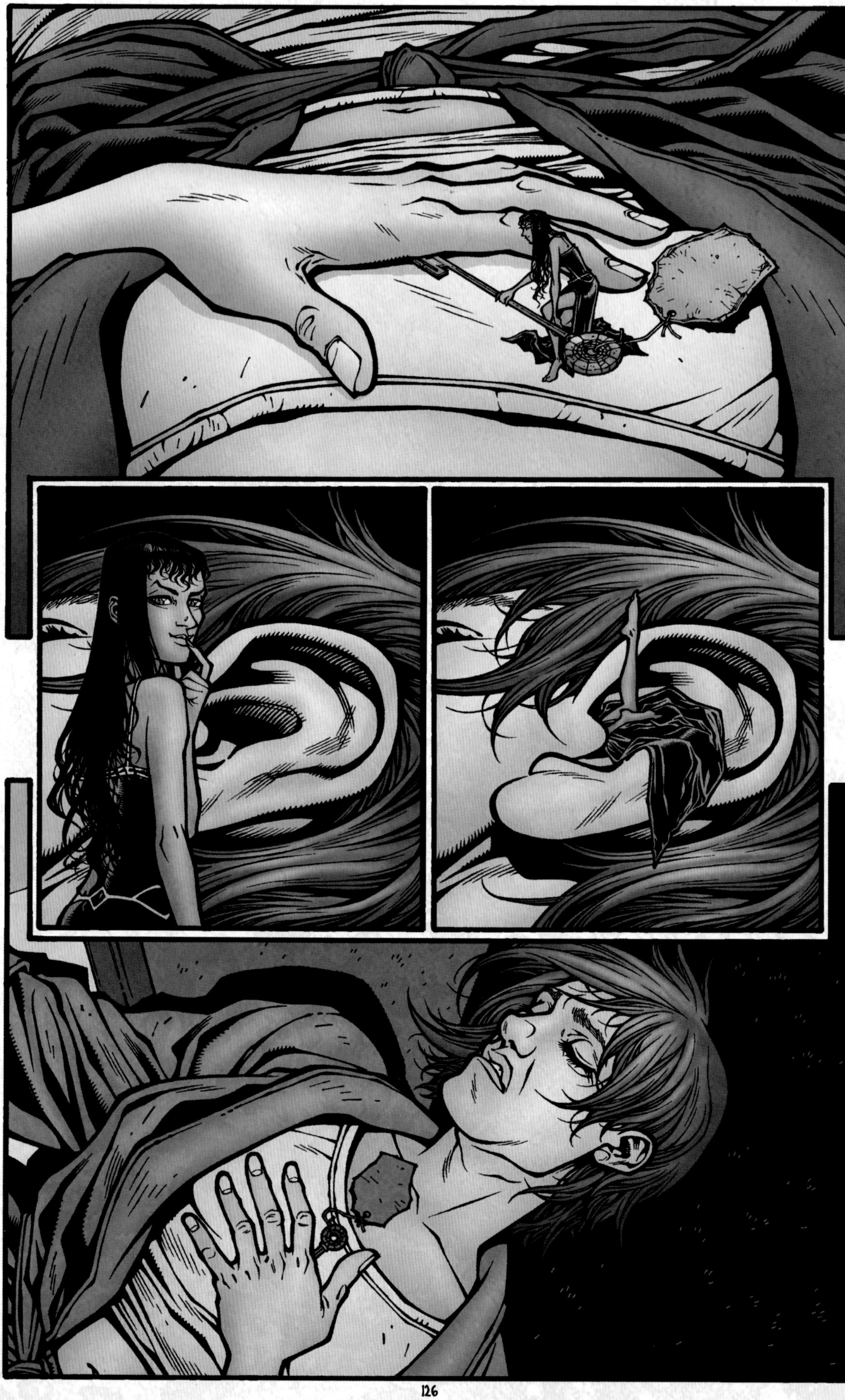

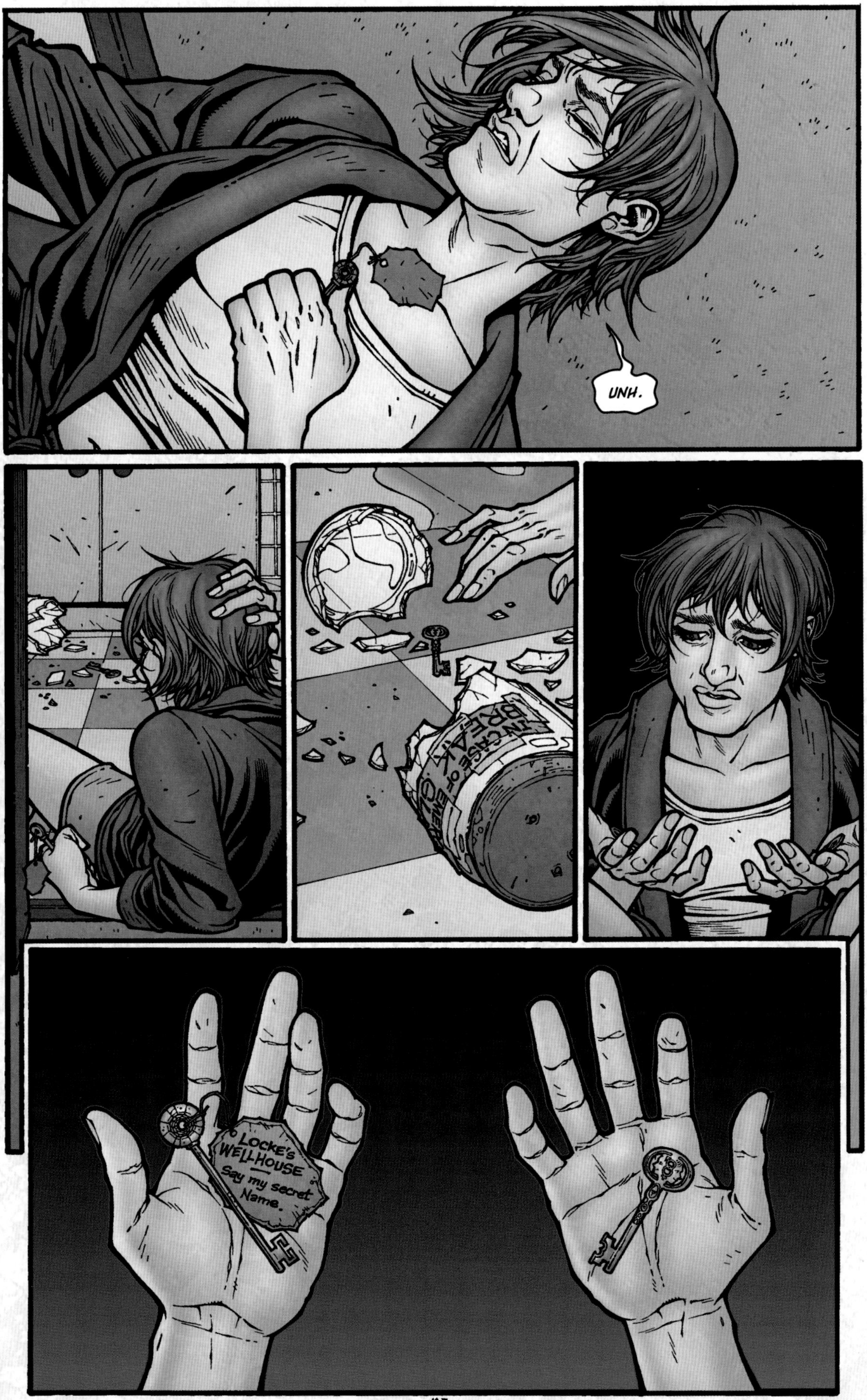
UNH.
Locke's WELLHOUSE
Say my secret Name.

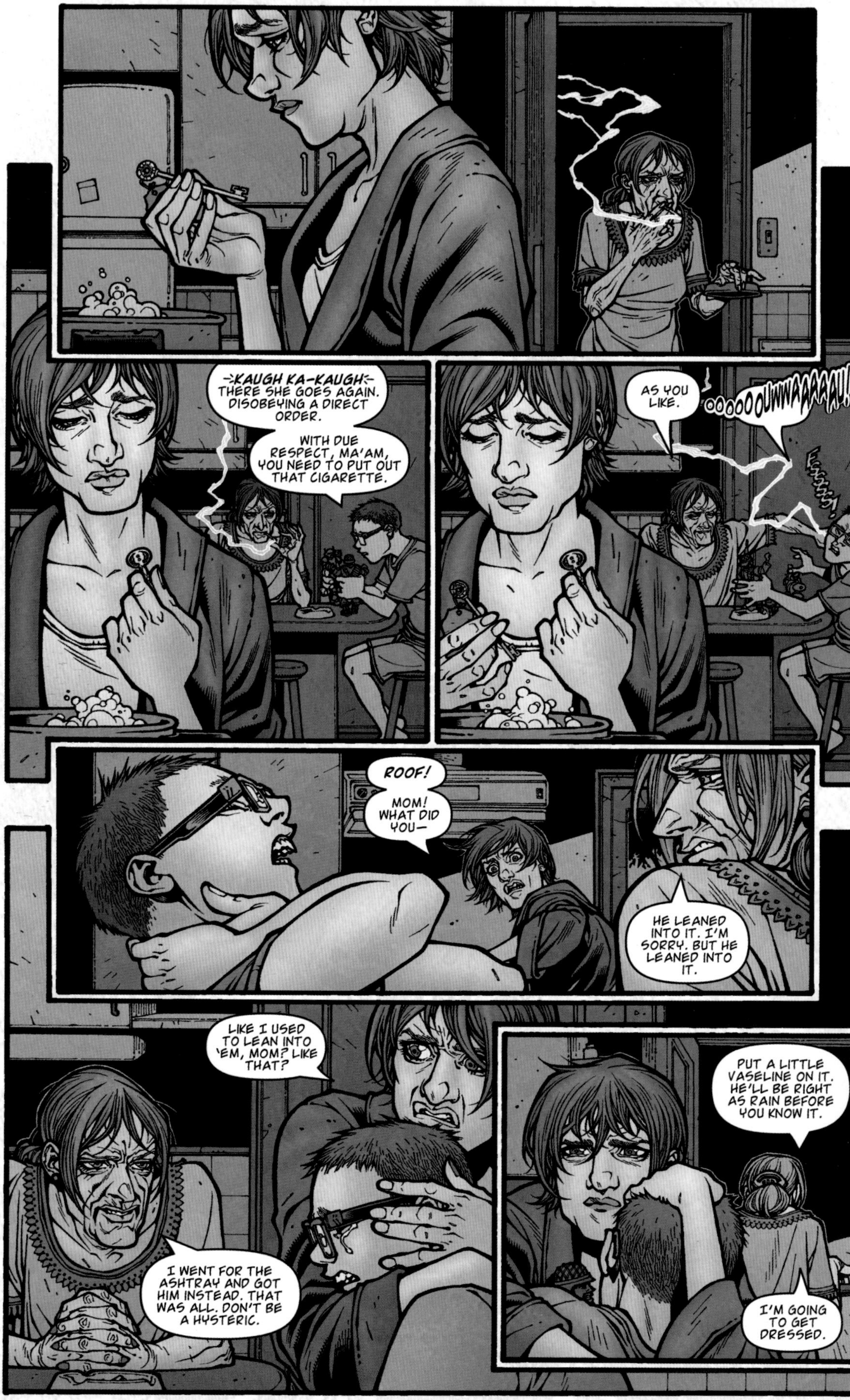
-KAUGH KA-KAUGH- THERE SHE GOES AGAIN. DISOBEYING A DIRECT ORDER.
WITH DUE RESPECT, MA'AM, YOU NEED TO PUT OUT THAT CIGARETTE.
AS YOU LIKE.
OOOOOOUWWAAAAAU!!
ESSSSSS!
ROOF!
MOM! WHAT DID YOU—
HE LEANED INTO IT. I'M SORRY. BUT HE LEANED INTO IT.
LIKE I USED TO LEAN INTO 'EM, MOM? LIKE THAT?
I WENT FOR THE ASHTRAY AND GOT HIM INSTEAD. THAT WAS ALL. DON'T BE A HYSTERIC.
PUT A LITTLE VASELINE ON IT. HE'LL BE RIGHT AS RAIN BEFORE YOU KNOW IT.
I'M GOING TO GET DRESSED.

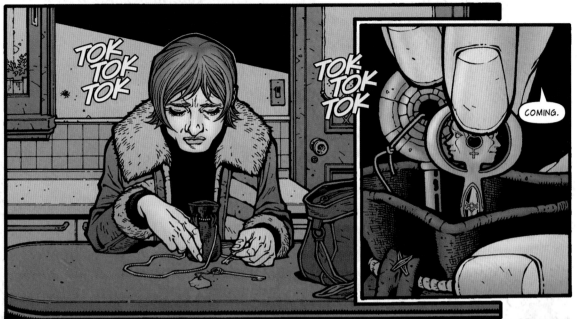

TOK TOK TOK

TOK TOK TOK

COMING.

JACKIE. THANKS FOR GIVING ME ONE OF YOUR SUNDAY MORNINGS. I KNOW RUFUS WILL BE EXCITED TO SEE YOU.

I'M READY FOR HIM. LITTLE LANEY DOES LOVE A MAN IN A UNIFORM.

YOU HAVE FUN. SO YOU AND YOUR MOM ARE GOING CLAMMING?

FOR THE THANKSGIVING STUFFING. IT'S AN... OLD YANKEE THING.

ARE WE GOING?

I THOUGHT YOU WERE MAD.

RUFUS SAID IT WAS AN ACCIDENT.

WELL. TRUE ENOUGH.

COME ON, MOTHER. IT MIGHT SNOW LATER. I WANT TO GET THIS OVER WITH.

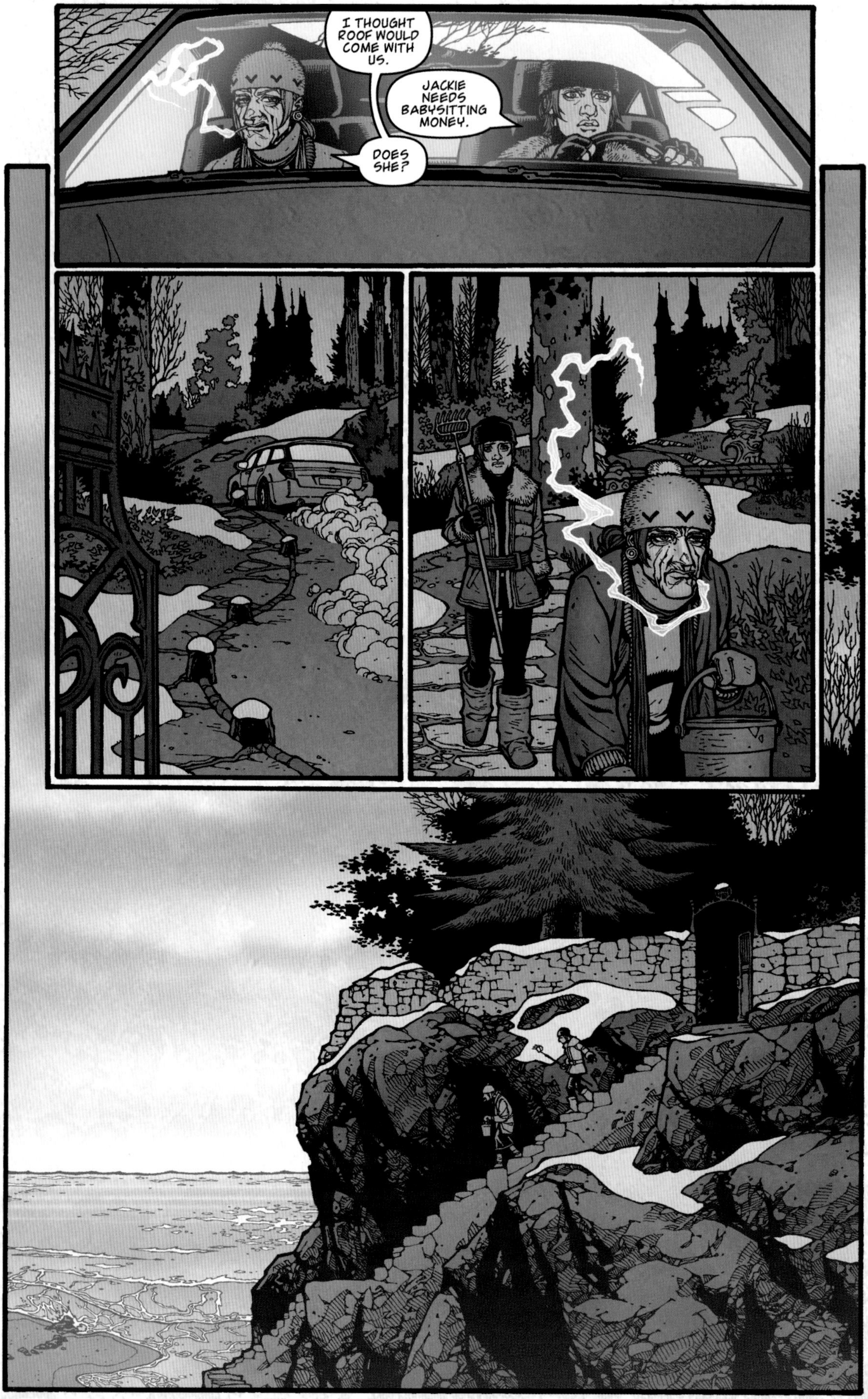
I THOUGHT ROOF WOULD COME WITH US.
JACKIE NEEDS BABYSITTING MONEY.
DOES SHE?

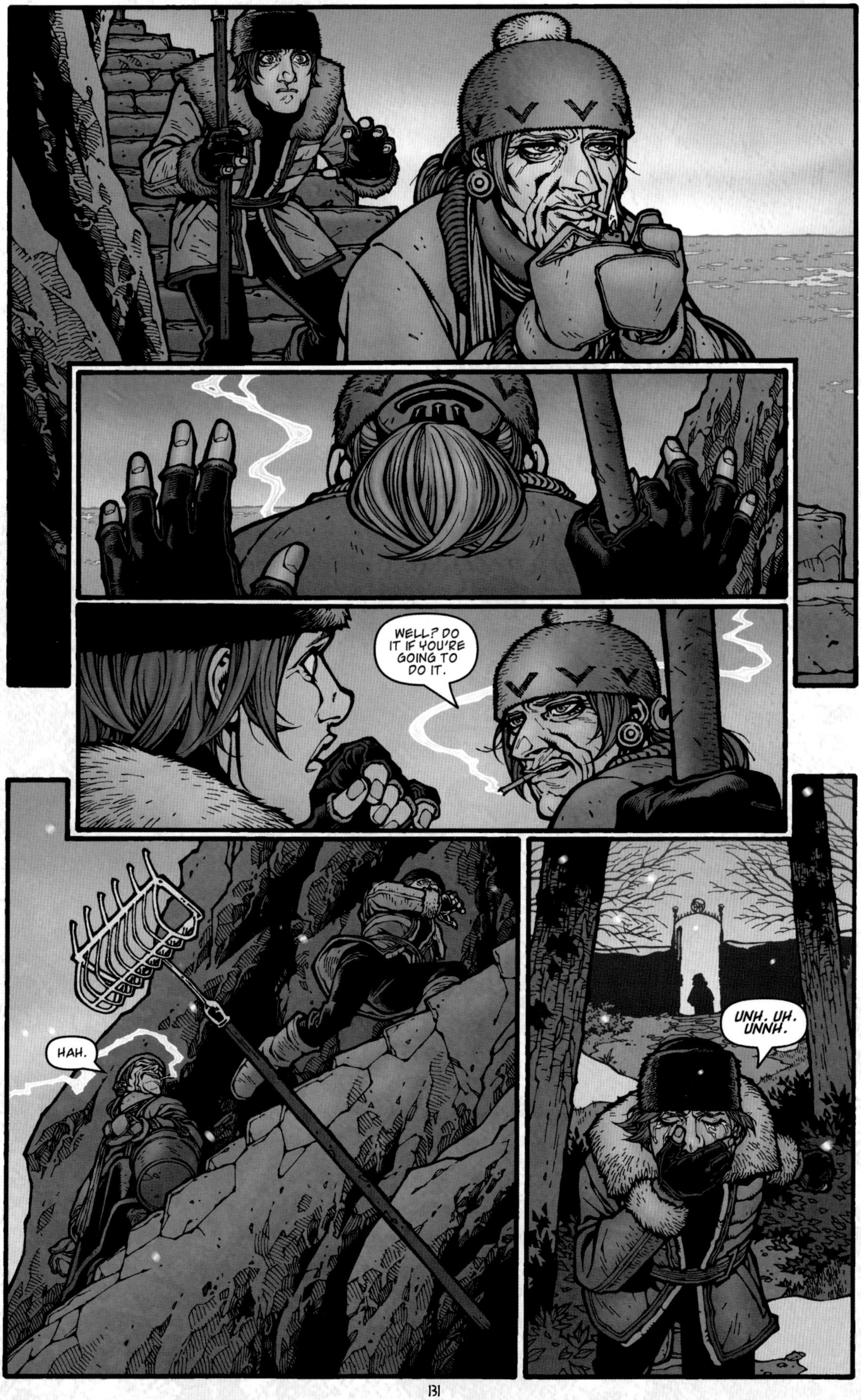
WELL? DO IT IF YOU'RE GOING TO DO IT.
HAH.
UNH. UH. UNNH.

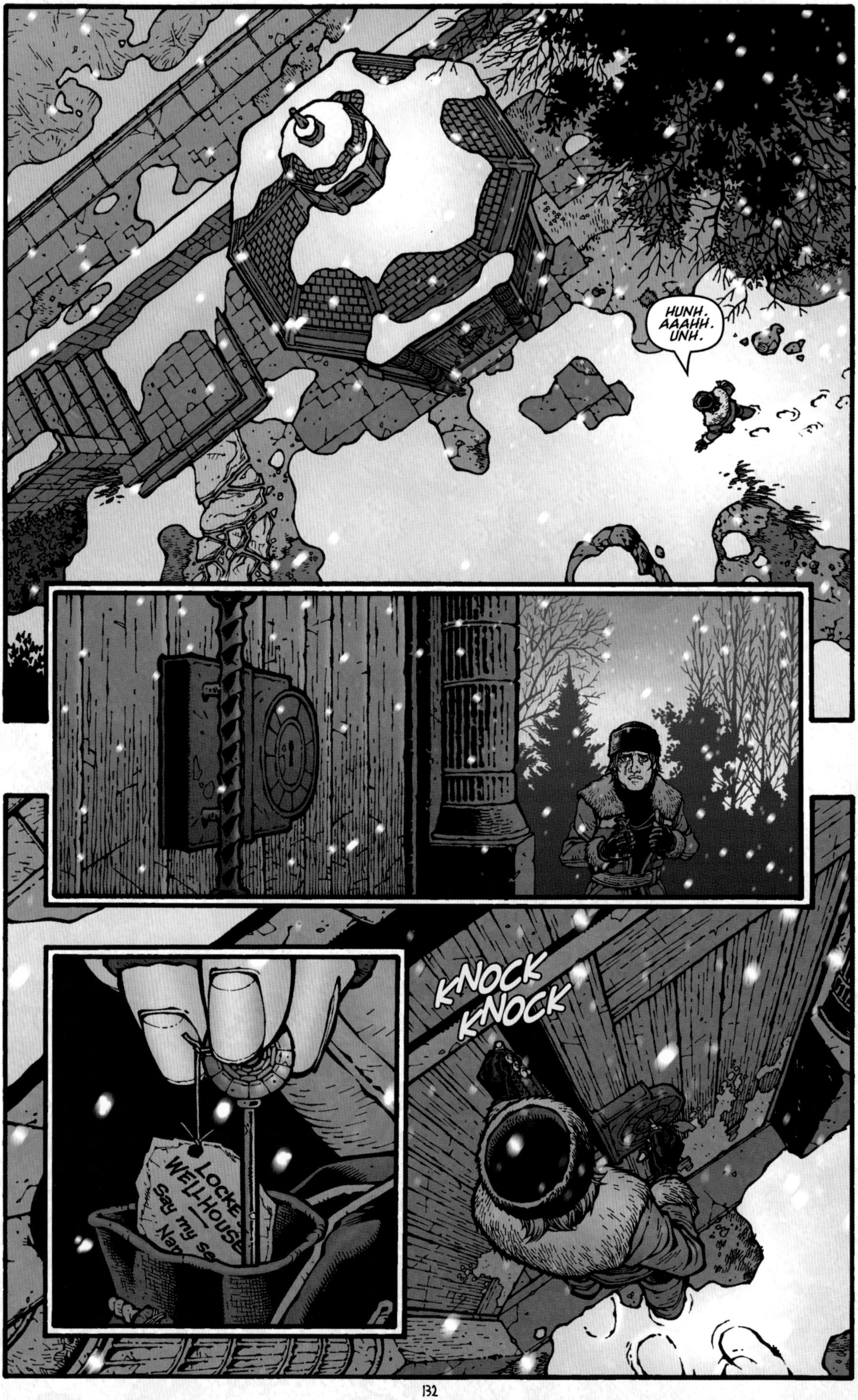
HUNH. AAAHH. UNH.
LOCKE
WELL-HOUSE
KNOCK KNOCK

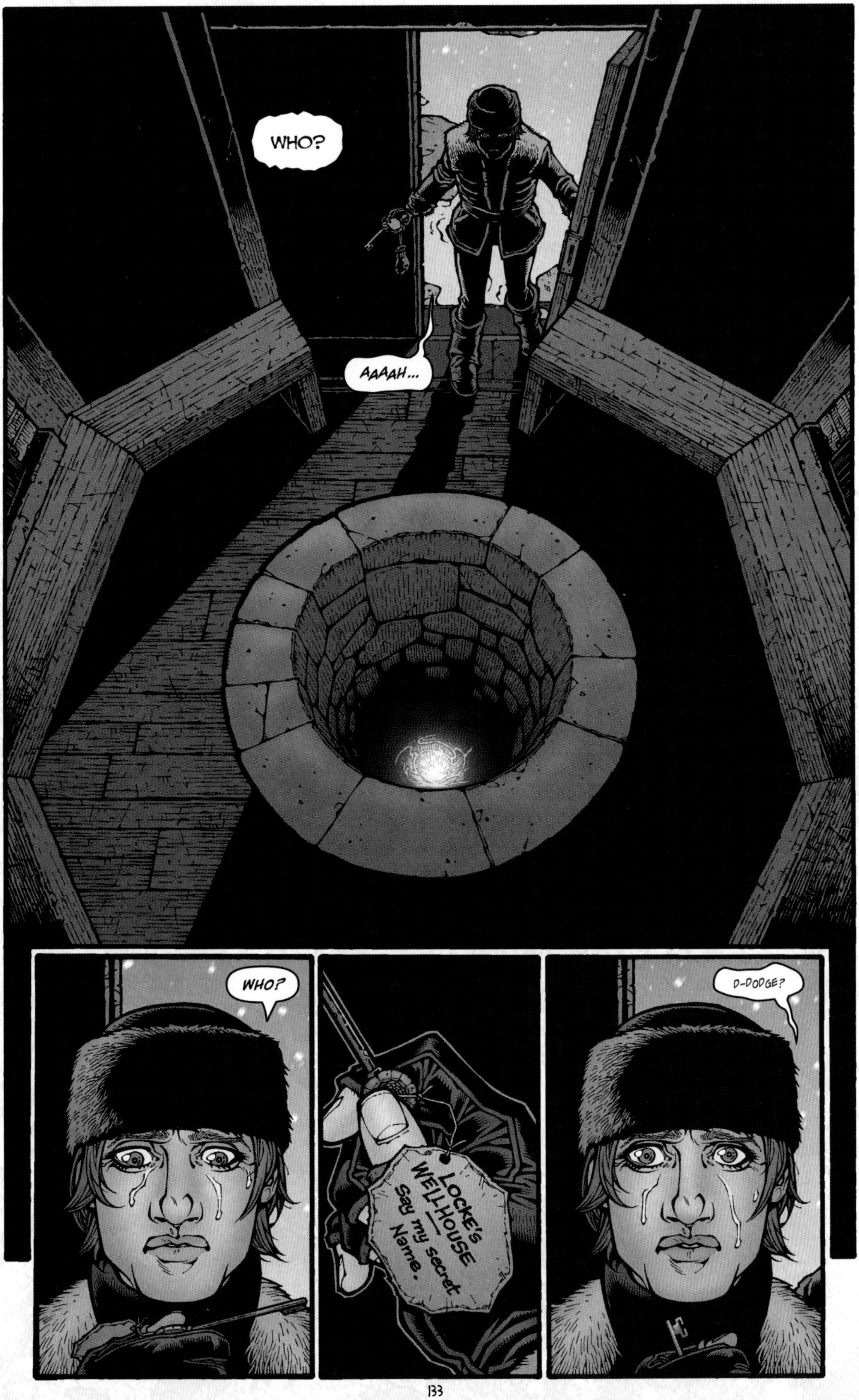
WHO?
AAAAH...
WHO?
LOCKE'S WELLHOUSE
Say my secret Name.
D-DODGE?

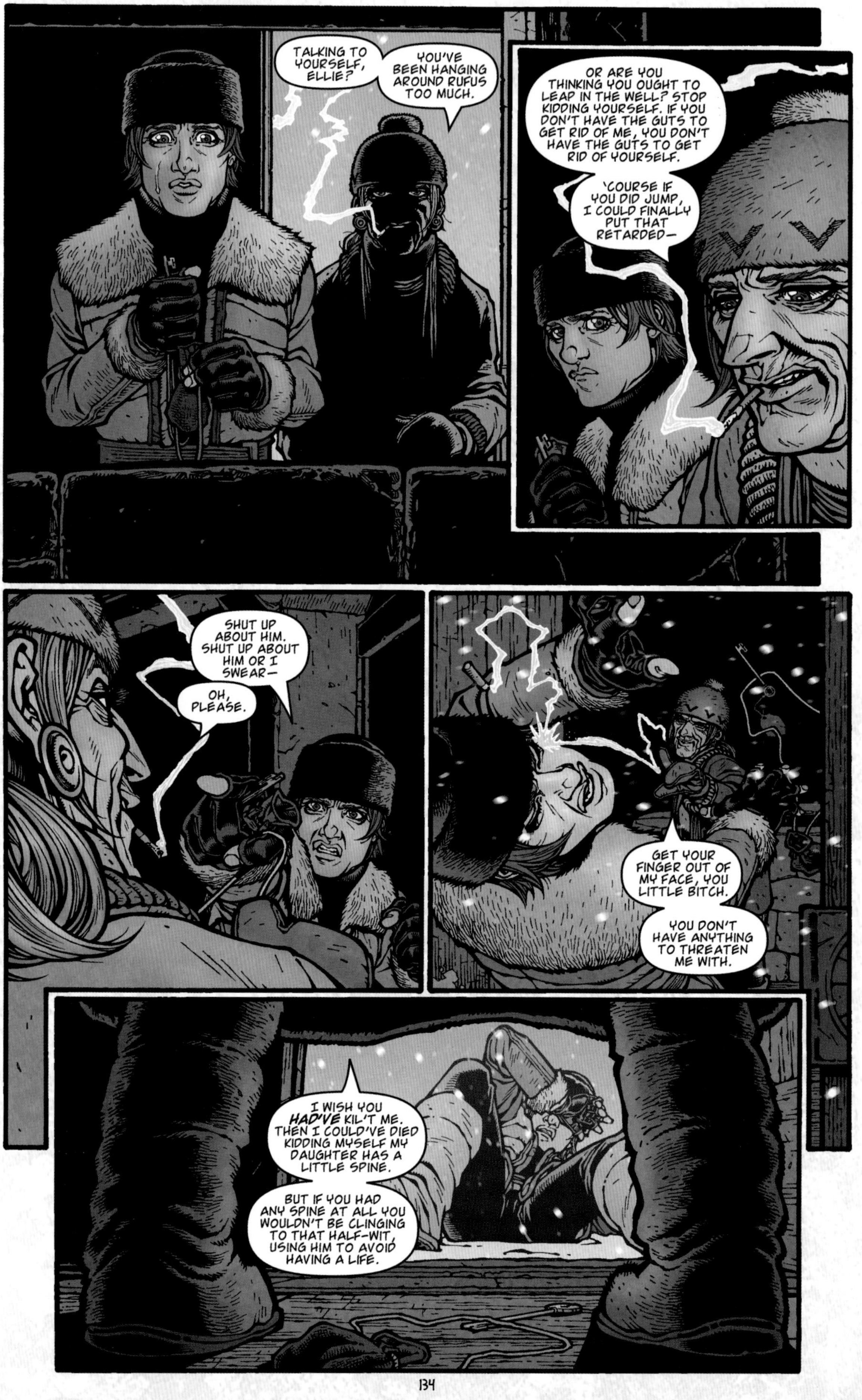
TALKING TO YOURSELF, ELLIE?
YOU'VE BEEN HANGING AROUND RUFUS TOO MUCH.
OR ARE YOU THINKING YOU OUGHT TO LEAP IN THE WELL? STOP KIDDING YOURSELF. IF YOU DON'T HAVE THE GUTS TO GET RID OF ME, YOU DON'T HAVE THE GUTS TO GET RID OF YOURSELF.
'COURSE IF YOU DID JUMP, I COULD FINALLY PUT THAT RETARDED—
SHUT UP ABOUT HIM. SHUT UP ABOUT HIM OR I SWEAR—
OH, PLEASE.
GET YOUR FINGER OUT OF MY FACE, YOU LITTLE BITCH.
YOU DON'T HAVE ANYTHING TO THREATEN ME WITH.
I WISH YOU **HAD'VE** KIL'T ME. THEN I COULD'VE DIED KIDDING MYSELF MY DAUGHTER HAS A LITTLE SPINE.
BUT IF YOU HAD ANY SPINE AT ALL YOU WOULDN'T BE CLINGING TO THAT HALF-WIT, USING HIM TO AVOID HAVING A LIFE.

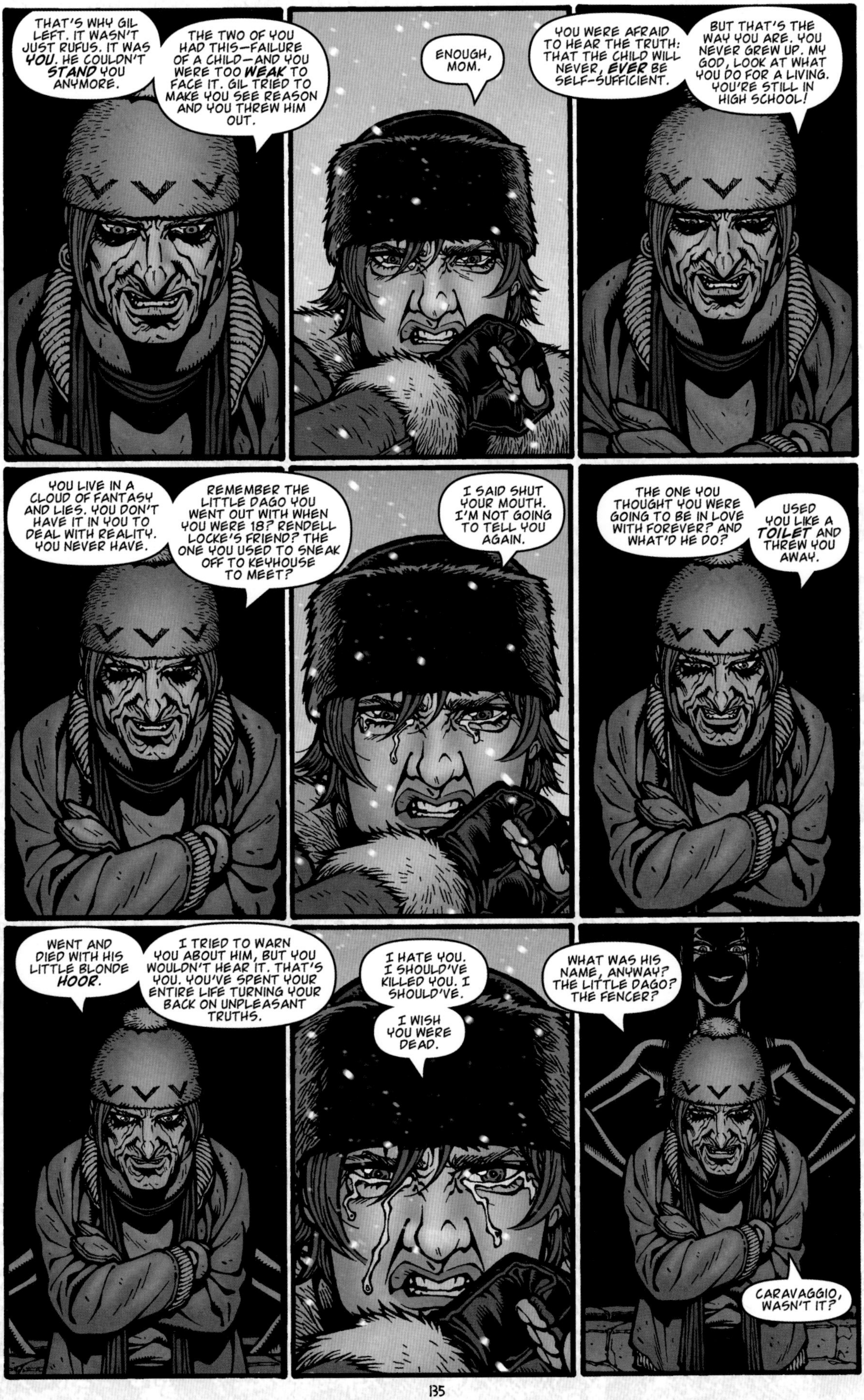

THAT'S WHY GIL LEFT. IT WASN'T JUST RUFUS. IT WAS YOU. HE COULDN'T STAND YOU ANYMORE.
THE TWO OF YOU HAD THIS—FAILURE OF A CHILD—AND YOU WERE TOO WEAK TO FACE IT. GIL TRIED TO MAKE YOU SEE REASON AND YOU THREW HIM OUT.
ENOUGH, MOM.
YOU WERE AFRAID TO HEAR THE TRUTH: THAT THE CHILD WILL NEVER, EVER BE SELF-SUFFICIENT.
BUT THAT'S THE WAY YOU ARE. YOU NEVER GREW UP. MY GOD, LOOK AT WHAT YOU DO FOR A LIVING. YOU'RE STILL IN HIGH SCHOOL!
YOU LIVE IN A CLOUD OF FANTASY AND LIES. YOU DON'T HAVE IT IN YOU TO DEAL WITH REALITY. YOU NEVER HAVE.
REMEMBER THE LITTLE DAGO YOU WENT OUT WITH WHEN YOU WERE 18? RENDELL LOCKE'S FRIEND? THE ONE YOU USED TO SNEAK OFF TO KEYHOUSE TO MEET?
I SAID SHUT YOUR MOUTH. I'M NOT GOING TO TELL YOU AGAIN.
THE ONE YOU THOUGHT YOU WERE GOING TO BE IN LOVE WITH FOREVER? AND WHAT'D HE DO?
USED YOU LIKE A TOILET AND THREW YOU AWAY.
WENT AND DIED WITH HIS LITTLE BLONDE HOOR.
I TRIED TO WARN YOU ABOUT HIM, BUT YOU WOULDN'T HEAR IT. THAT'S YOU. YOU'VE SPENT YOUR ENTIRE LIFE TURNING YOUR BACK ON UNPLEASANT TRUTHS.
I HATE YOU. I SHOULD'VE KILLED YOU. I SHOULD'VE.
I WISH YOU WERE DEAD.
WHAT WAS HIS NAME, ANYWAY? THE LITTLE DAGO? THE FENCER?
CARAVAGGIO, WASN'T IT?

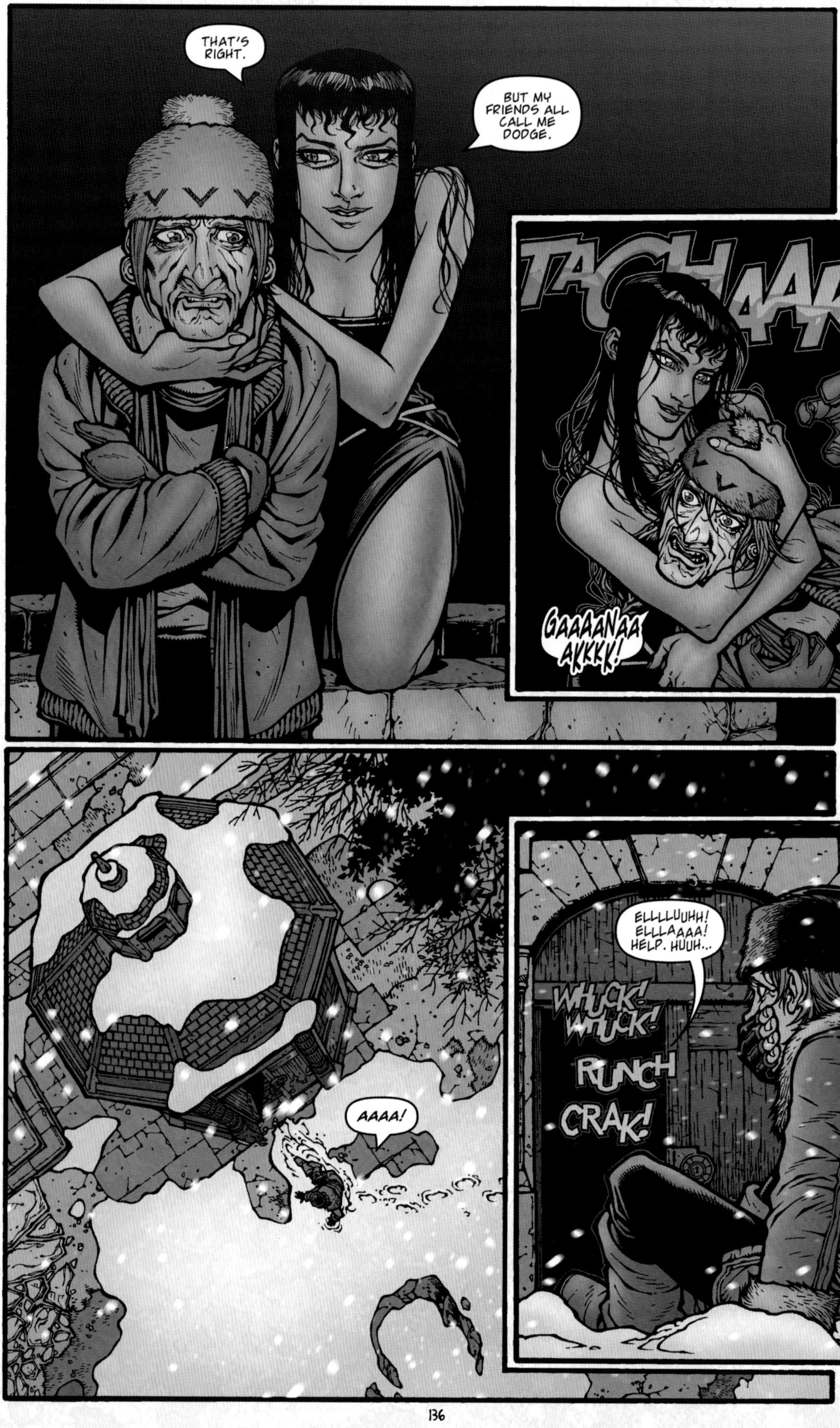
THAT'S RIGHT.
BUT MY FRIENDS ALL CALL ME DODGE.
TACHAAK
GAAAANAA AKKKK!
AAAA!
ELLLLUUHH! ELLLAAAA! HELP. HUUH...
WHUCK! WHUCK!
RUNCH
CRAK!

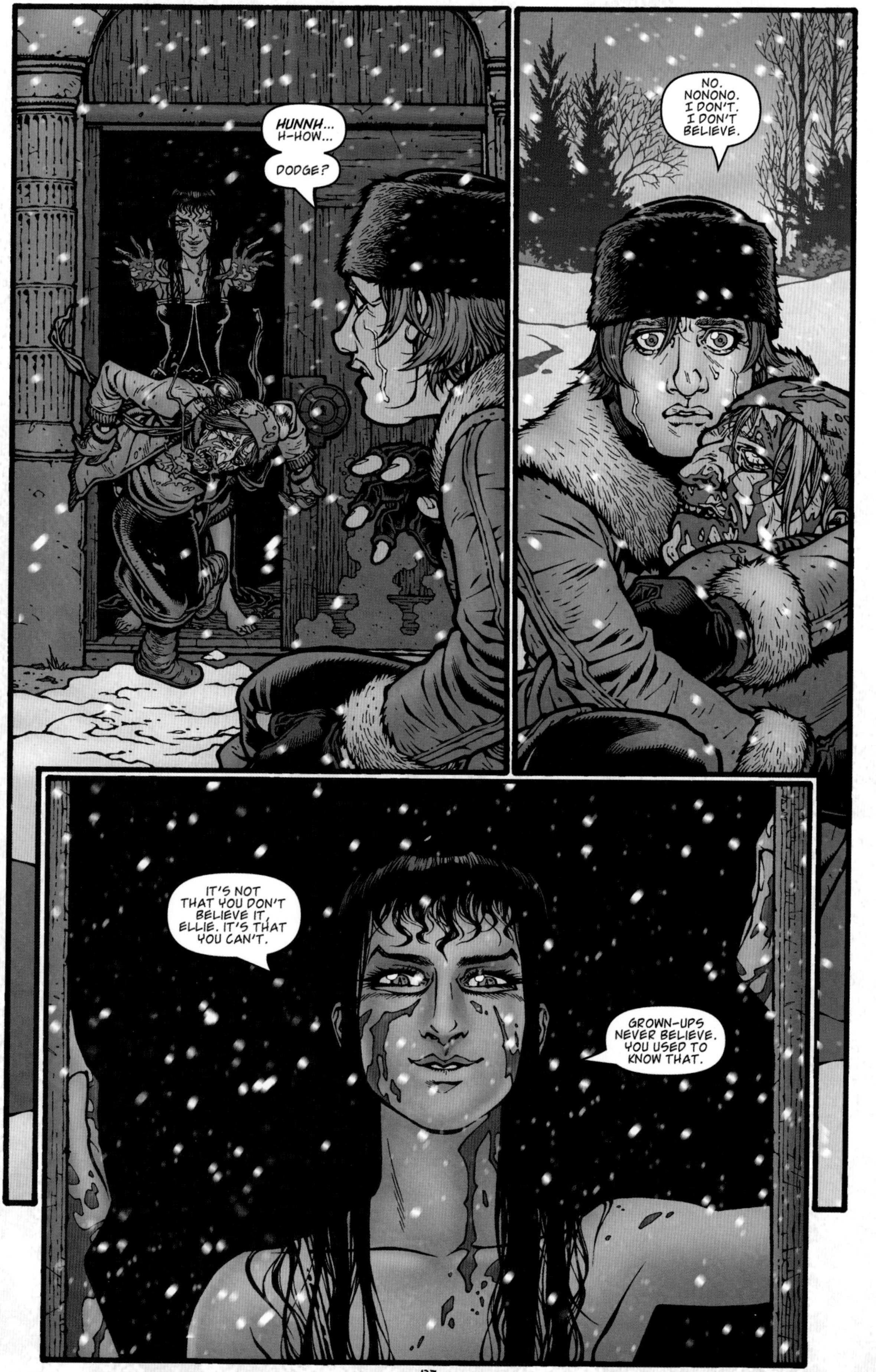
HUNNH... H-HOW...
DODGE?
NO. NONONO. I DON'T. I DON'T BELIEVE.
IT'S NOT THAT YOU DON'T BELIEVE IT, ELLIE. IT'S THAT YOU CAN'T.
GROWN-UPS NEVER BELIEVE. YOU USED TO KNOW THAT.

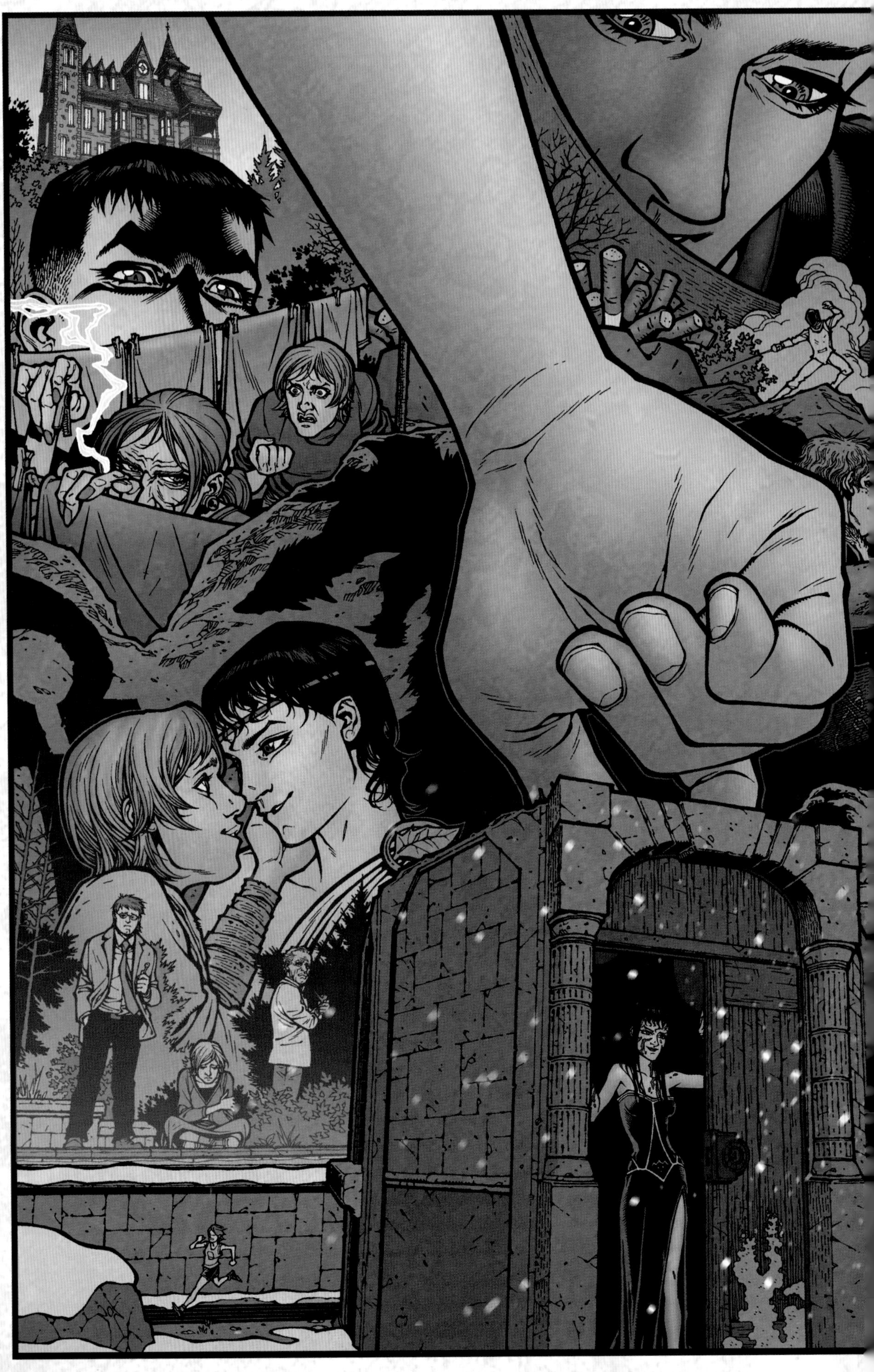

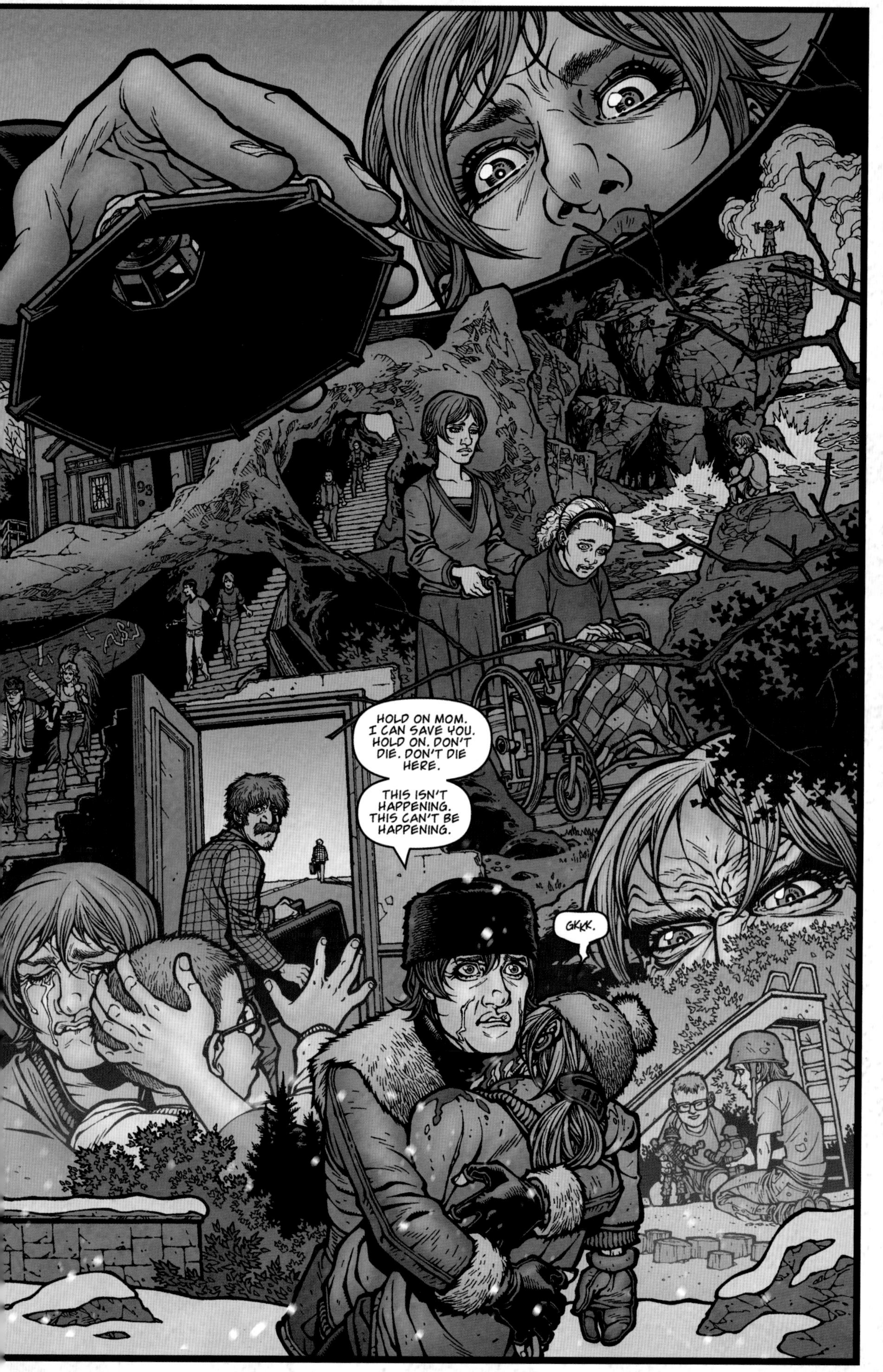
HOLD ON MOM. I CAN SAVE YOU. HOLD ON. DON'T DIE. DON'T DIE HERE.
THIS ISN'T HAPPENING. THIS CAN'T BE HAPPENING.
GKKK.

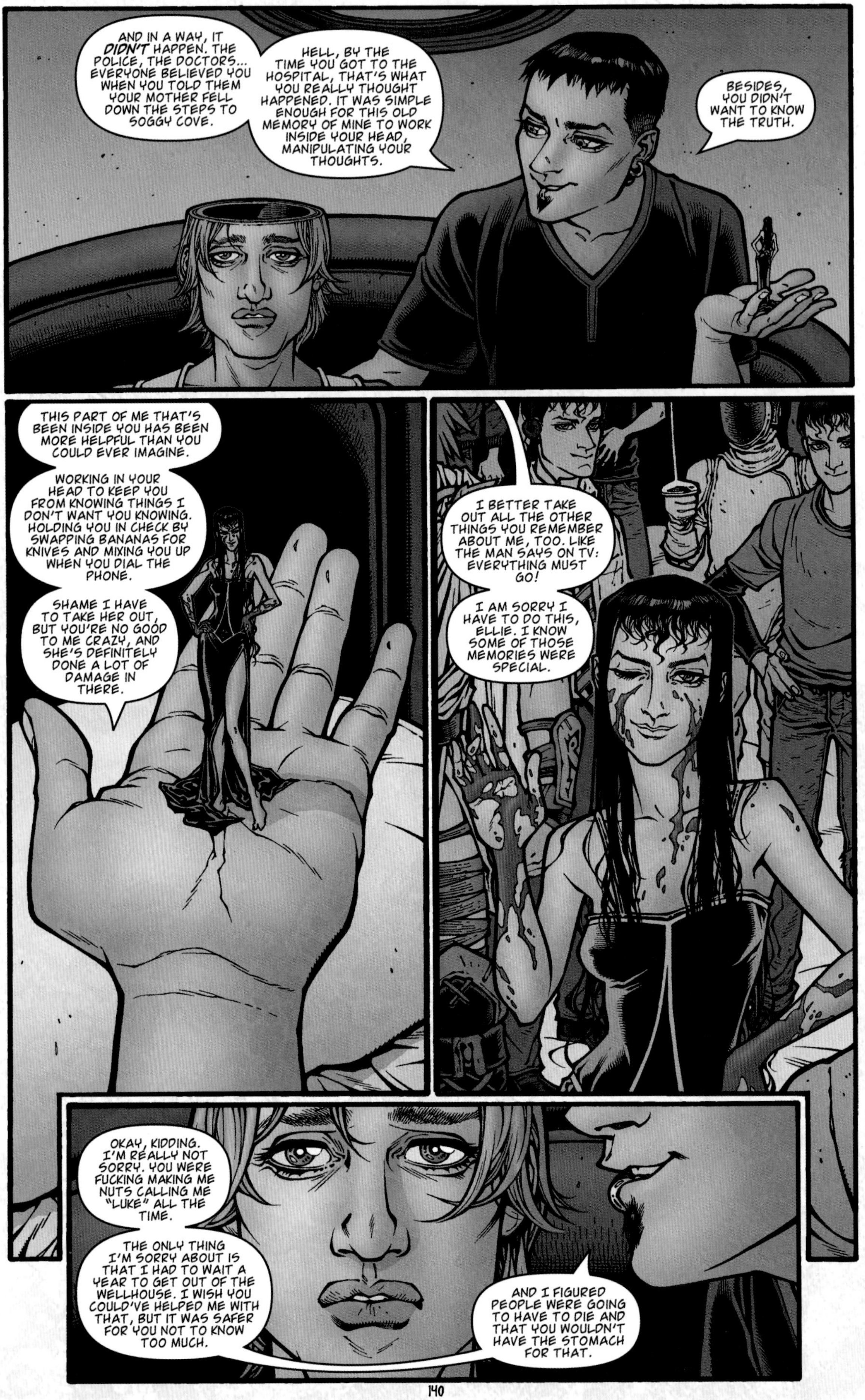
AND IN A WAY, IT DIDN'T HAPPEN. THE POLICE, THE DOCTORS... EVERYONE BELIEVED YOU WHEN YOU TOLD THEM YOUR MOTHER FELL DOWN THE STEPS TO SOGGY COVE.
HELL, BY THE TIME YOU GOT TO THE HOSPITAL, THAT'S WHAT YOU REALLY THOUGHT HAPPENED. IT WAS SIMPLE ENOUGH FOR THIS OLD MEMORY OF MINE TO WORK INSIDE YOUR HEAD, MANIPULATING YOUR THOUGHTS.
BESIDES, YOU DIDN'T WANT TO KNOW THE TRUTH.
THIS PART OF ME THAT'S BEEN INSIDE YOU HAS BEEN MORE HELPFUL THAN YOU COULD EVER IMAGINE.
WORKING IN YOUR HEAD TO KEEP YOU FROM KNOWING THINGS I DON'T WANT YOU KNOWING. HOLDING YOU IN CHECK BY SWAPPING BANANAS FOR KNIVES AND MIXING YOU UP WHEN YOU DIAL THE PHONE.
SHAME I HAVE TO TAKE HER OUT, BUT YOU'RE NO GOOD TO ME CRAZY, AND SHE'S DEFINITELY DONE A LOT OF DAMAGE IN THERE.
I BETTER TAKE OUT ALL THE OTHER THINGS YOU REMEMBER ABOUT ME, TOO. LIKE THE MAN SAYS ON TV: EVERYTHING MUST GO!
I AM SORRY I HAVE TO DO THIS, ELLIE. I KNOW SOME OF THOSE MEMORIES WERE SPECIAL.
OKAY, KIDDING. I'M REALLY NOT SORRY. YOU WERE FUCKING MAKING ME NUTS CALLING ME "LUKE" ALL THE TIME.
THE ONLY THING I'M SORRY ABOUT IS THAT I HAD TO WAIT A YEAR TO GET OUT OF THE WELLHOUSE. I WISH YOU COULD'VE HELPED ME WITH THAT, BUT IT WAS SAFER FOR YOU NOT TO KNOW TOO MUCH.
AND I FIGURED PEOPLE WERE GOING TO HAVE TO DIE AND THAT YOU WOULDN'T HAVE THE STOMACH FOR THAT.

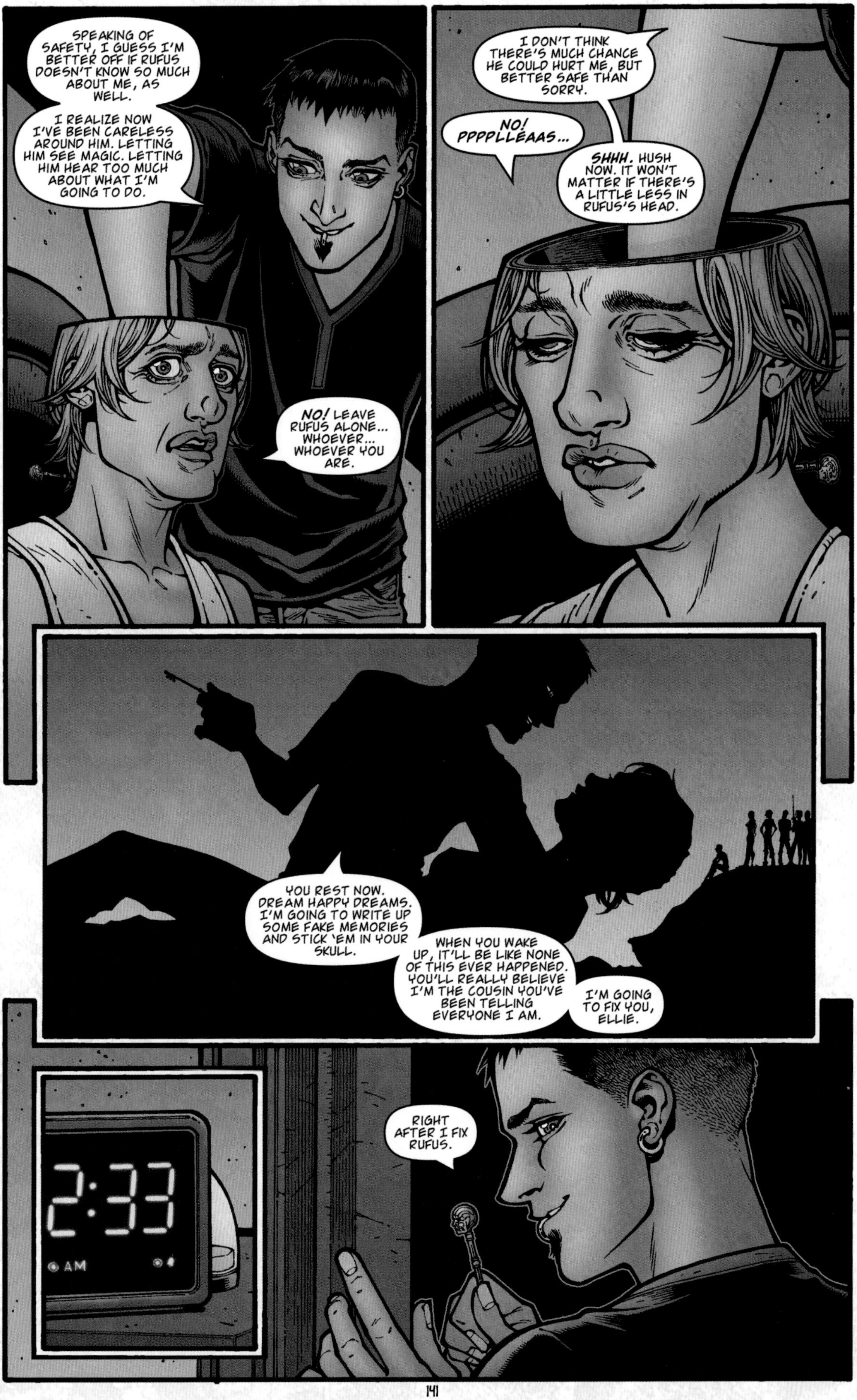
SPEAKING OF SAFETY, I GUESS I'M BETTER OFF IF RUFUS DOESN'T KNOW SO MUCH ABOUT ME, AS WELL.
I REALIZE NOW I'VE BEEN CARELESS AROUND HIM. LETTING HIM SEE MAGIC. LETTING HIM HEAR TOO MUCH ABOUT WHAT I'M GOING TO DO.
NO! LEAVE RUFUS ALONE... WHOEVER... WHOEVER YOU ARE.
I DON'T THINK THERE'S MUCH CHANCE HE COULD HURT ME, BUT BETTER SAFE THAN SORRY.
NO! PPPPLLEAAS...
SHHH. HUSH NOW. IT WON'T MATTER IF THERE'S A LITTLE LESS IN RUFUS'S HEAD.
YOU REST NOW. DREAM HAPPY DREAMS. I'M GOING TO WRITE UP SOME FAKE MEMORIES AND STICK 'EM IN YOUR SKULL.
WHEN YOU WAKE UP, IT'LL BE LIKE NONE OF THIS EVER HAPPENED. YOU'LL REALLY BELIEVE I'M THE COUSIN YOU'VE BEEN TELLING EVERYONE I AM.
I'M GOING TO FIX YOU, ELLIE.
2:33
AM
RIGHT AFTER I FIX RUFUS.

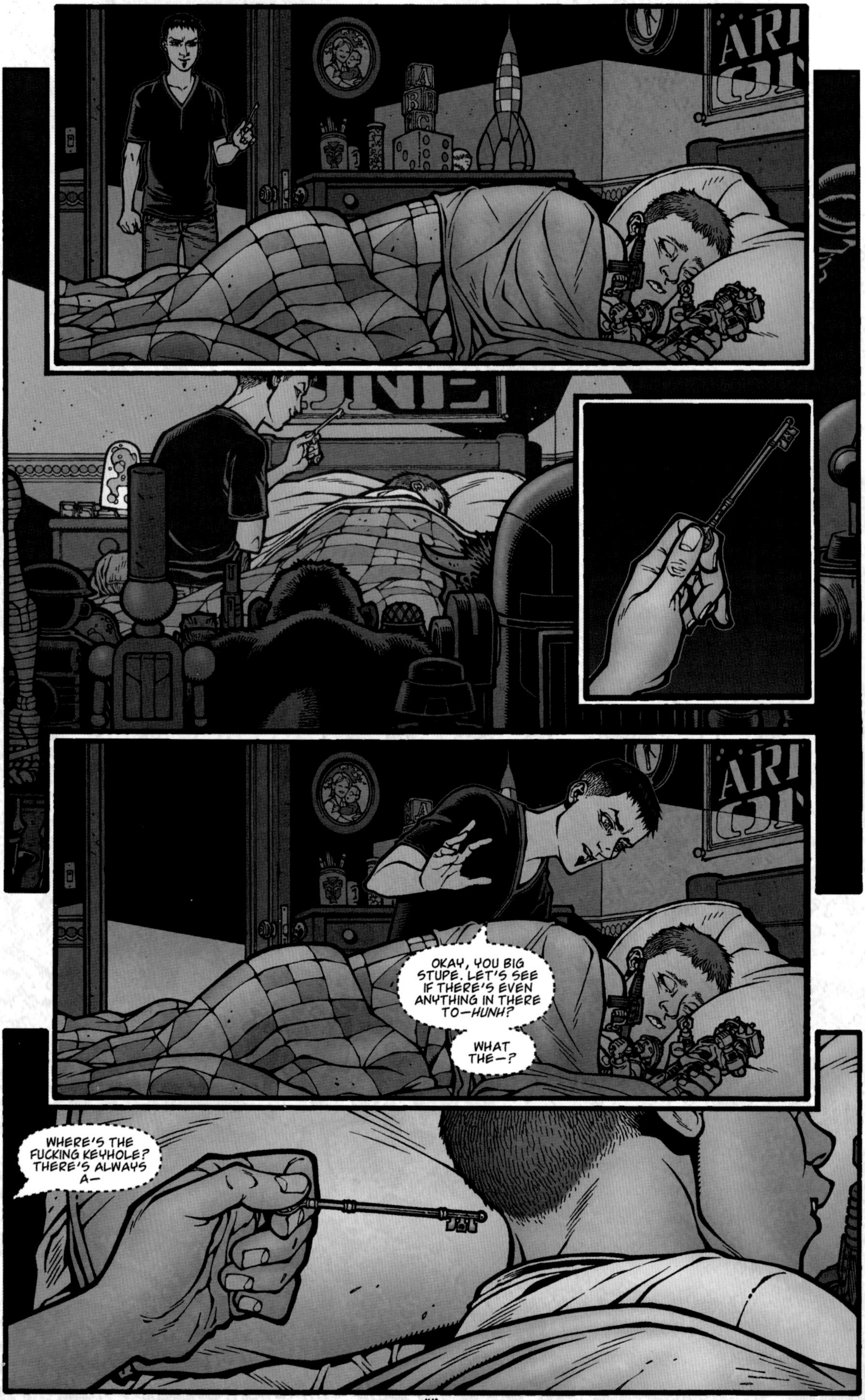
ONE
OKAY, YOU BIG STUPE. LET'S SEE IF THERE'S EVEN ANYTHING IN THERE TO—*HUNH?*
WHAT THE—?
WHERE'S THE FUCKING KEYHOLE? THERE'S ALWAYS A—

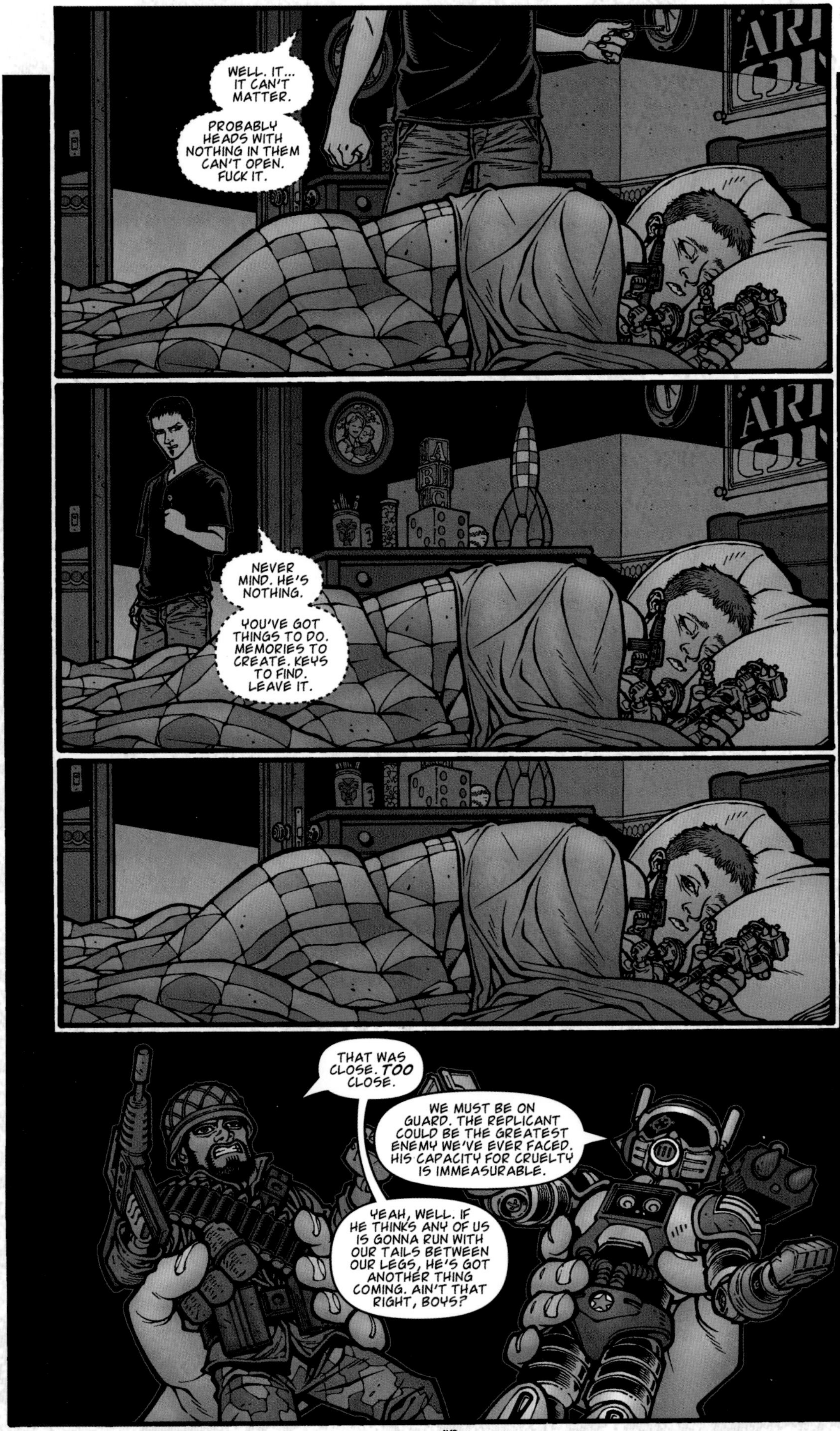
WELL. IT... IT CAN'T MATTER.
PROBABLY HEADS WITH NOTHING IN THEM CAN'T OPEN. FUCK IT.
NEVER MIND. HE'S NOTHING.
YOU'VE GOT THINGS TO DO. MEMORIES TO CREATE. KEYS TO FIND. LEAVE IT.
THAT WAS CLOSE. TOO CLOSE.
WE MUST BE ON GUARD. THE REPLICANT COULD BE THE GREATEST ENEMY WE'VE EVER FACED. HIS CAPACITY FOR CRUELTY IS IMMEASURABLE.
YEAH, WELL. IF HE THINKS ANY OF US IS GONNA RUN WITH OUR TAILS BETWEEN OUR LEGS, HE'S GOT ANOTHER THING COMING. AIN'T THAT RIGHT, BOYS?

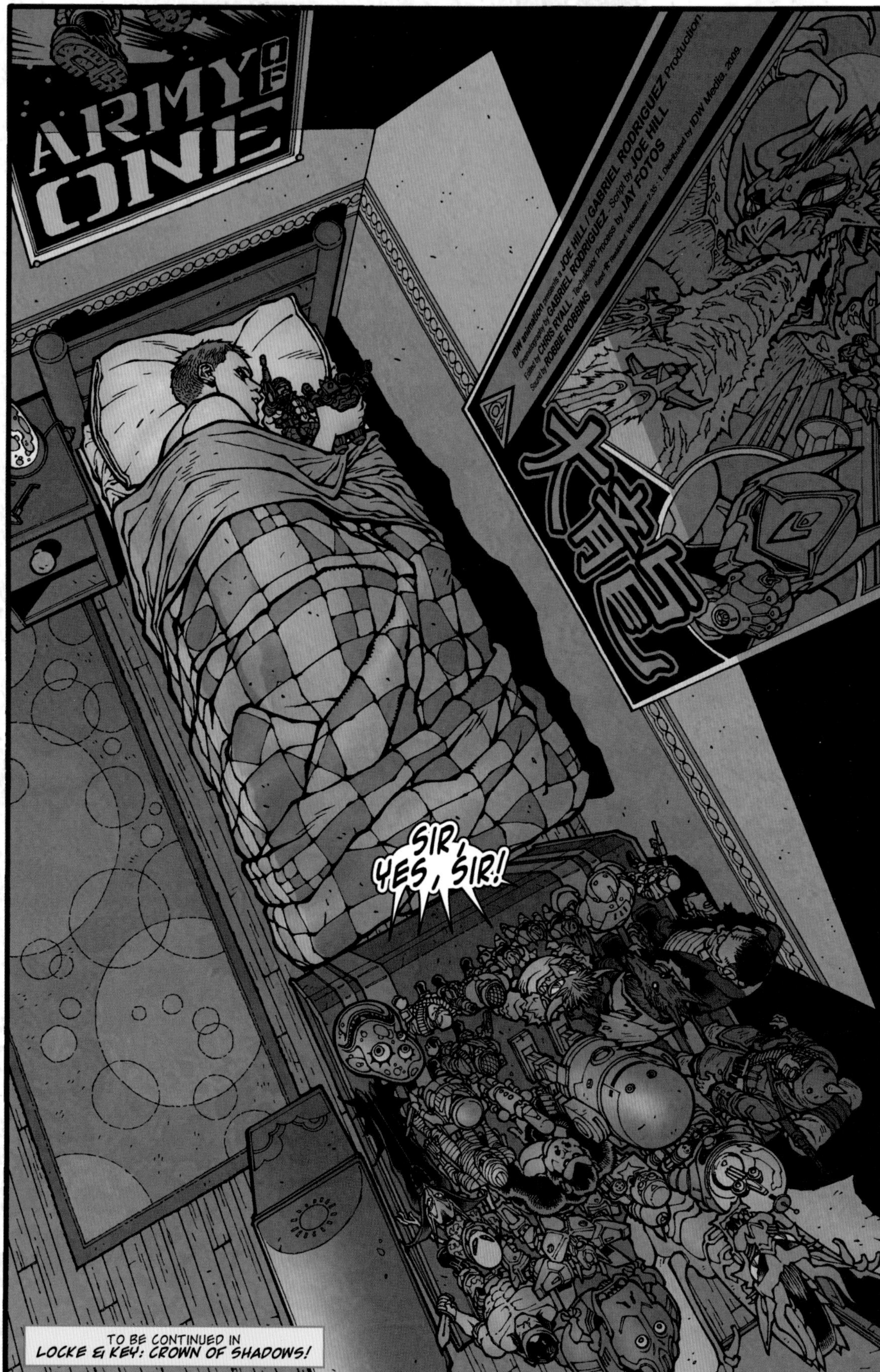
ARMY OF ONE
IDW animation presents a JOE HILL / GABRIEL RODRIGUEZ Production.
Distributed by IDW Media, 2009.
SIR, YES, SIR!
TO BE CONTINUED IN LOCKE & KEY: CROWN OF SHADOWS!

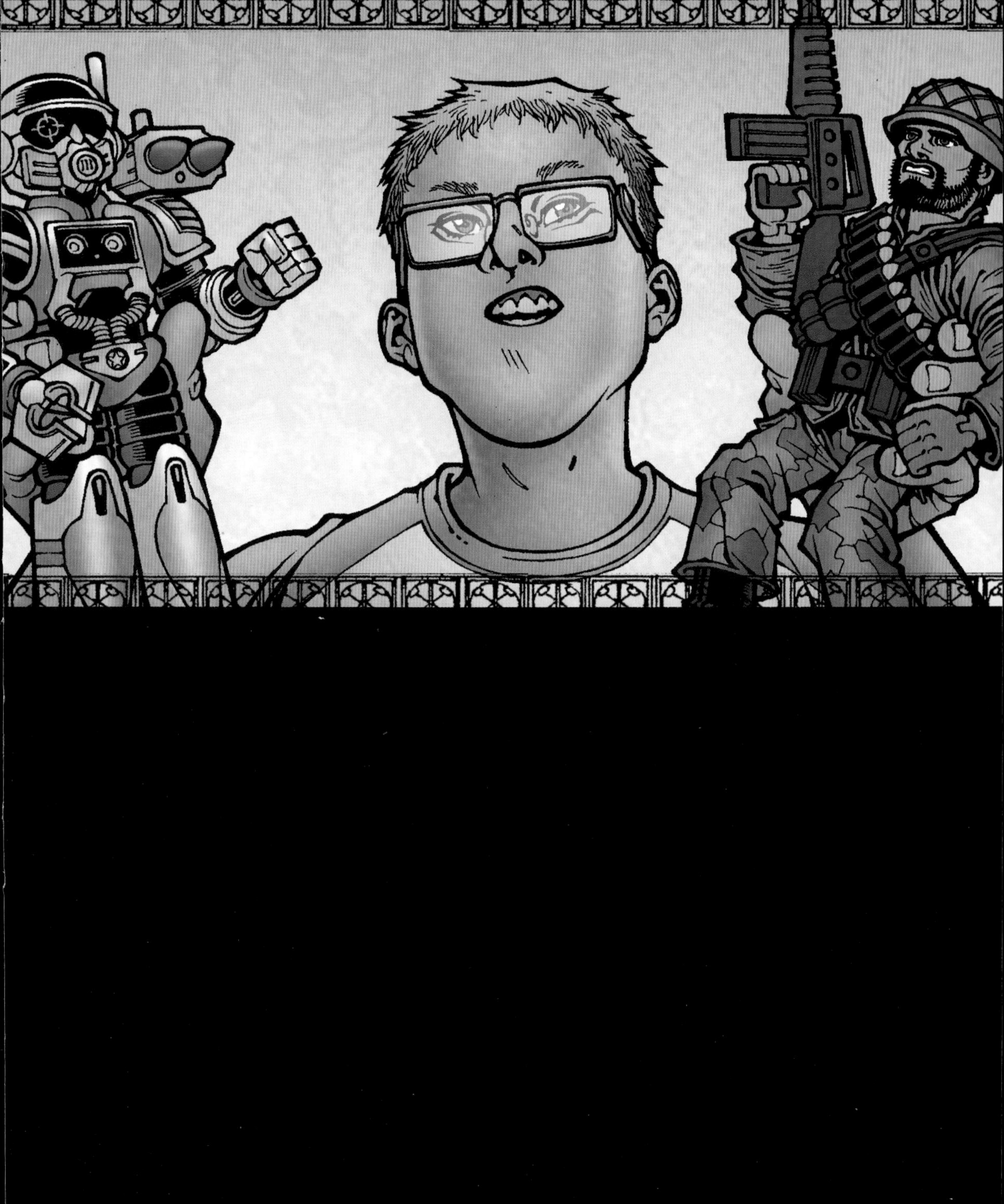

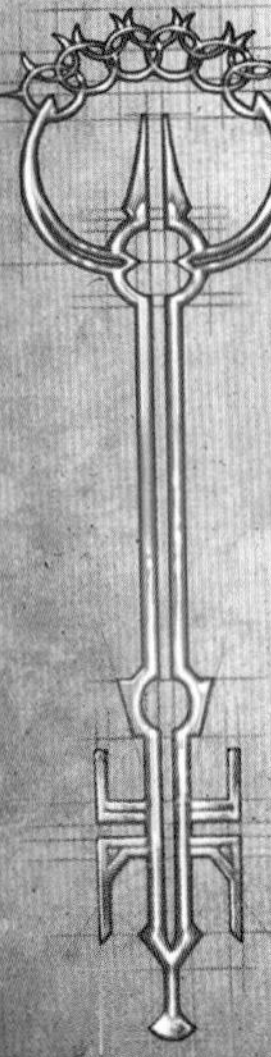

aNYWHeRe KEY

us'd the key to anyplaice againe, to return to Boston, & gaither intelaigents for Crais. Tis an act of terryble wychcraift, but better I do it, than my sister, who is obssaissed with REVENGING herself upon the RED-COATS, for thair violence agin our faither & brother & belov'd maither. Aye, my dredd of beeing called to account someday by SATAN HIMSELF is a trifling concern when maiched with my desyre to rid the worlde of the devylls who taik the King's Coyne to do raip & murdur...

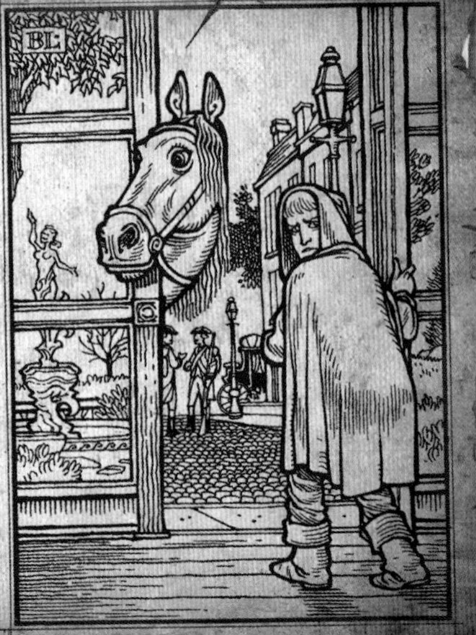

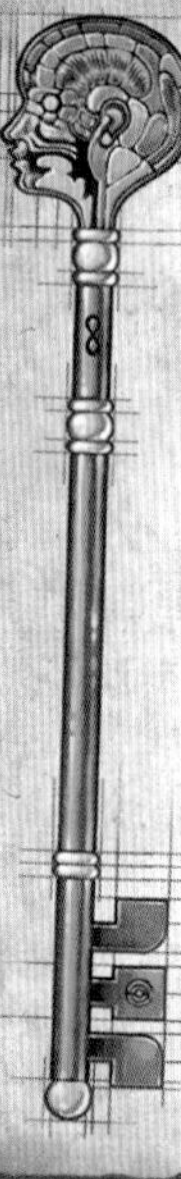

HeaD KEY

of alle the keys I have forged from the WHISP'RING IRON, 'tis the key that opens the human mind I most regrait. Miranda hast a pervairse fasinaytion whist the key & hast us'd ait to fill her head with all thair is to know about WAR & the SLAIYING of MEN, & she carrys an arsanall whist her whairever she goes. Yet I am less in dred of what she has put in than what she hast remov'd. Sometimes it is as if she is now without FEER and indeed is herself more man than I!

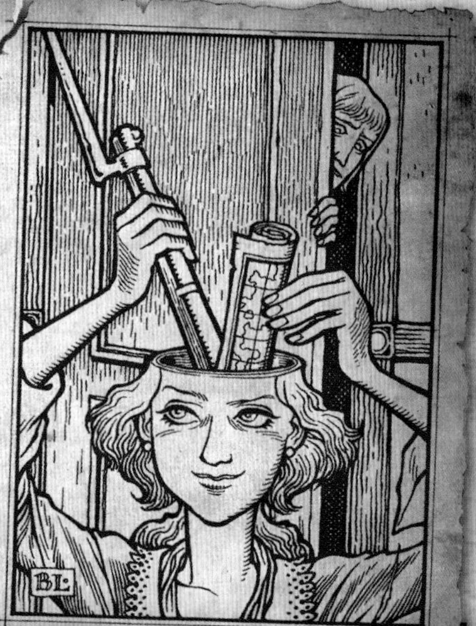

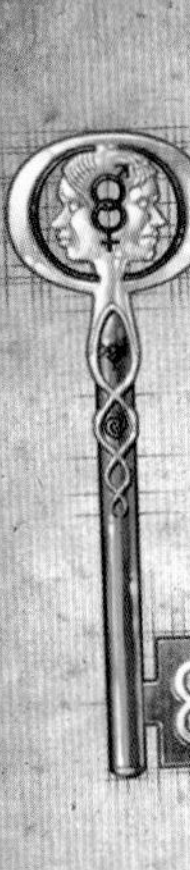

GeNDeR KEY

my sister - or should I now say my brother! - fights the shadow war with Crais in the streets of Boston whilst I wait at home, like a helpless maiden, praying to the ALLMAIGHTY! for her safe return. When first I fashin'd the key, I imagained she maight trainsform to a boy to protect her, if necessaire, from the unsavorie lusts of ENGLISHMEN should the King's foot-soldiers return to Lovecraft to abuse God fairing womain. Never did I think she wouldst WILLENGLY caist off the wardrobe of her femininitie for this ruggaid liberation among men...

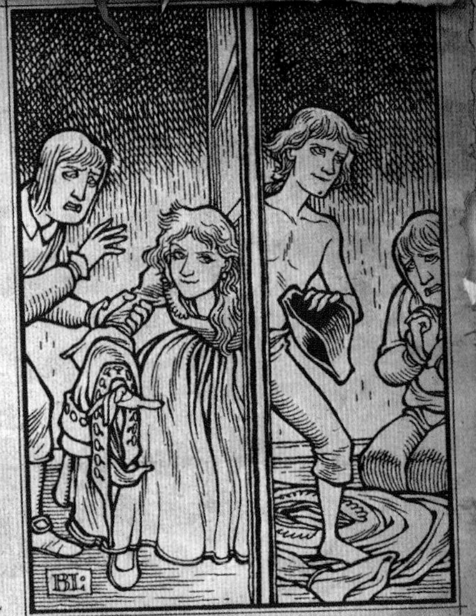

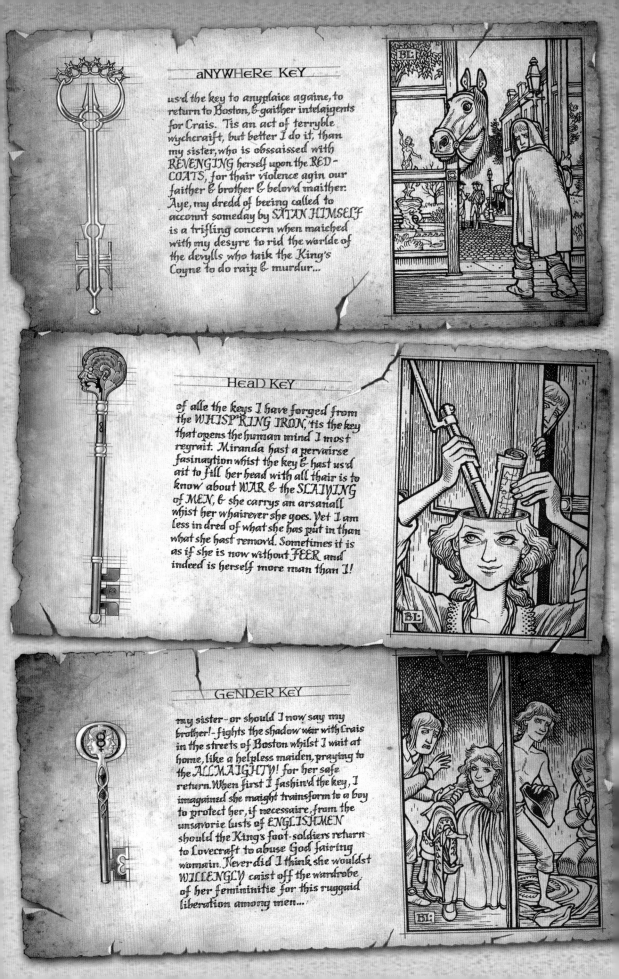

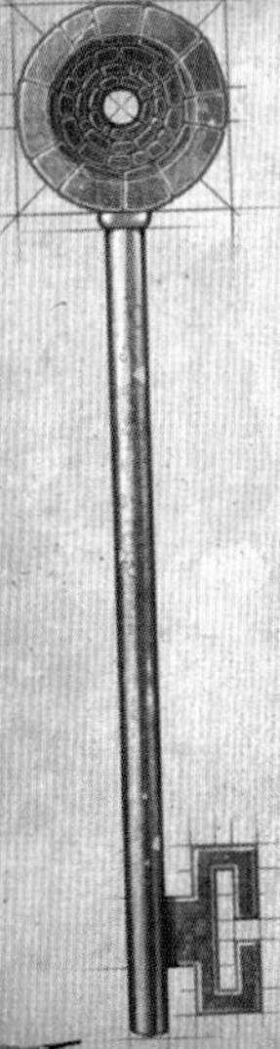

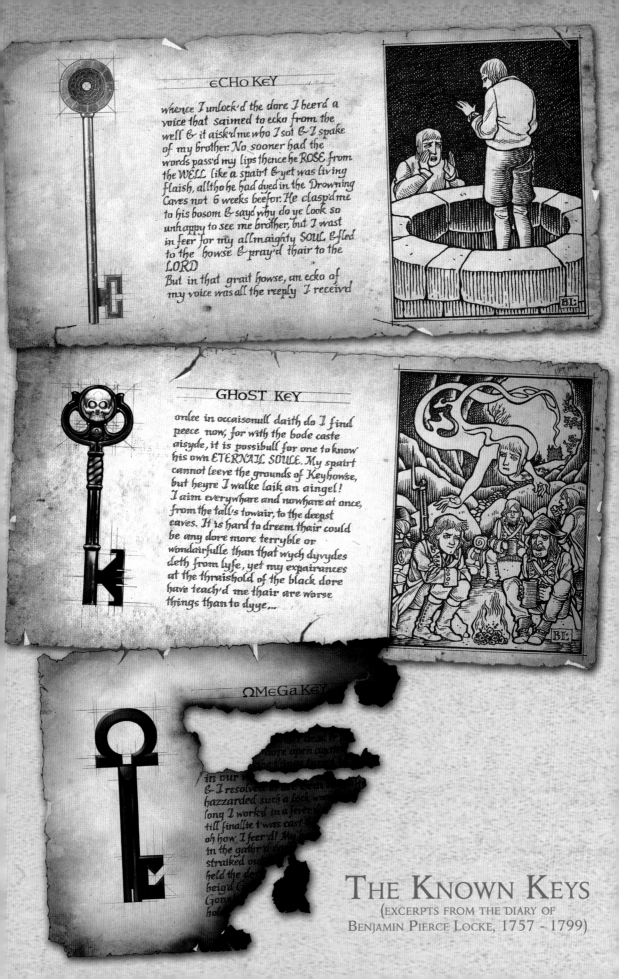

ECHO KEY

whence I unlock'd the dore I heerd a voice that saimed to ecko from the well & it aisk'd me who I sot & I spake of my brother. No sooner had the words pass'd my lips thence he ROSE from the WELL like a spairt & yet was living flaish, alltho he had dyed in the Drowning Caves not 6 weeks beefor. He clasp'd me to his bosom & sayd why do ye look so unhappy to see me brother, but I wast in feer for my allmaighty SOUL & fled to the howse & pray'd thair to the LORD

But in that grait howse, an ecko of my voice was all the reeply I receiv'd

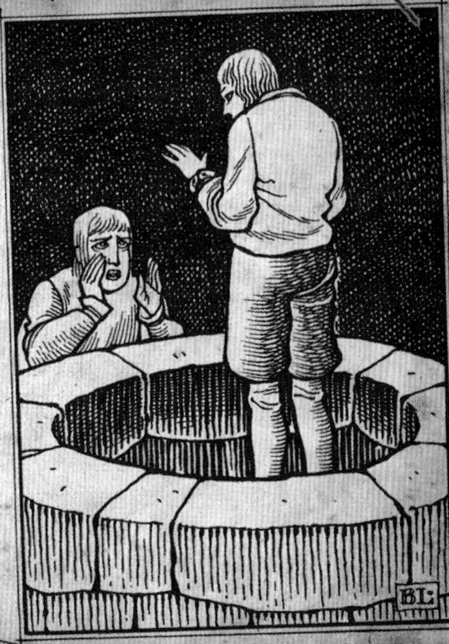

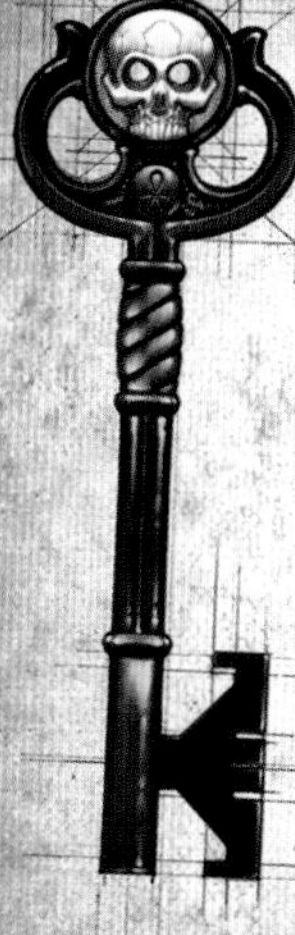

GHOST KEY

onlee in occaisonull daith do I find peece now, for with the bode caste aisyde, it is possibull for one to know his own ETERNAIL SOULE. My spairt cannot leeve the grounds of Keyhowse, but heyre I walke laik an aingel! I aim everywhare and nowhare at once, from the tall's towair, to the deepst caves. It is hard to dreem thair could be any dore more terryble or wondairfulle than that wych dyvydes deth from lyfe, yet my expairances at the thraishold of the black dore have teach'd me thair are worse things than to dyye...

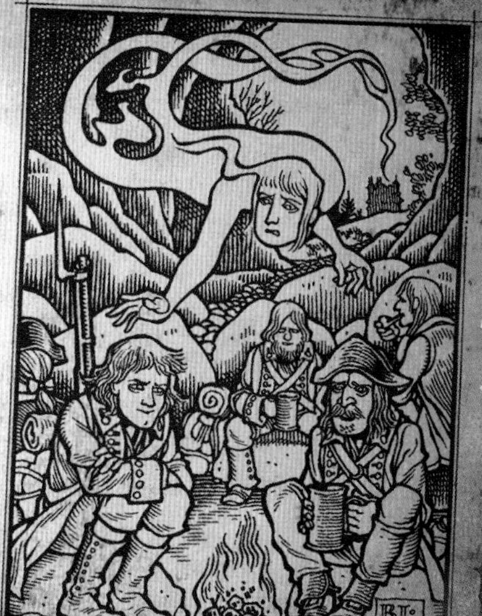

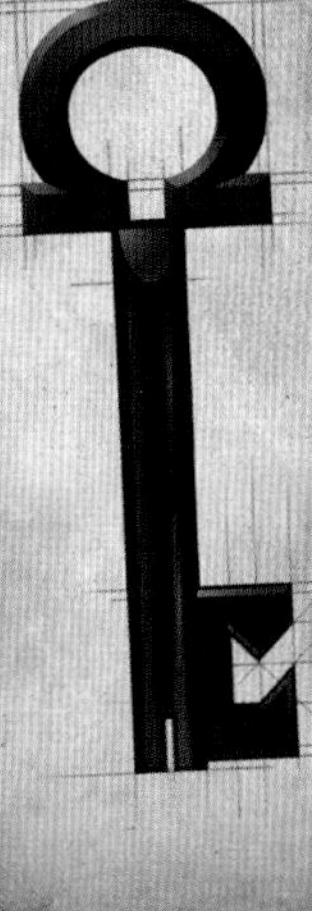

ΩMEGA KEY

dore open agai

in our w

& I resolve

hazzarded such a lock wa

long I work'd in a fever

till finallie t'was cast

oh how I feer'd! My

in the gathr'd

straiked ou

held the do

beig'd G

Gon

hol

THE KNOWN KEYS

(EXCERPTS FROM THE DIARY OF BENJAMIN PIERCE LOCKE, 1757 - 1799)

Series Illustrator and co-Creator Gabriel Rodriguez, for the first time, shares the process involved in developing a page of *Locke & Key*.

Step 1: The Script

Once a script is received, I read it two or three times, completely, BEFORE I start drawing. I'm used to receiving a new script when I'm finishing the previous issue, so this reading process is useful for me to start turning words into images, still free from the problem of drawing. It also helps me to identify the easy, the not so easy, and the extremely hard pages and sequences. Having done this mental exercise, I'm ready to face the white page.

Step 2: The Page Script and Documentation

Here we'll follow the creation of page 8, from *Locke & Key: Head Games* #6 "Army Of One." I start re-reading (again) the description of the page and the text that it will have in it. Having previously pictured it in my mind, I know the elements involved, and start imagining them turned into a comic panel.

I try to turn the visual concept into a specific shot.

During this process, I identify elements that demand research or the collection of references, external references, and elements that appear early in the story. In this scene, the key elements are: a mason jar (fortunately, I had one at hand here at home), the two keys (check *Locke & Key: Welcome to Lovecraft* #6), female Dodge's dress (check in *Welcome to Lovecraft*, too) and the shape of the hole in the bathroom wall (check early pages of this same issue). Having all those elements at hand, I know I'm able to create an image consistent with the story, and with the visual appeal we have developed for our tale.

On this specific page there is a particularly complex element: What does a hand look like holding a mason jar like the one Ellie is supposed to be holding? This kind of uncommon relation between body and object is a key element of establishing believable body language for the characters. I solve the problem by looking at photos in books, or sometimes by watching myself in the mirror, but in this case I held a mason jar in my left hand, at an angle like the one I'll draw, while working on the next step.

Step 3: Rough Line Work

The first step of drawing, finally... I try to do a fast and very synthetic, but as definitive as possible, organization of all the elements of the image. This is a chance to define the camera shot, angle, and balance between elements. In this case: Ellie, shocked, watching the mason jar; the jar, the note outside the jar, the little She Dodge, the Well Key, the note attached to the Well Key, the Gender Key, the wall, and the hole in the background. The idea here is trying to solve the outlines and overlapping of elements, the sense of space, the body language and expression of the characters, and the dramatic feeling of the scene.

Step 4: Final Pencils

The second step of drawing consists of simultaneously correcting any deficient element from the previous step, while adding, as completely as possible, the remaining graphic elements that will compose the scene.

In this particular panel, being a splash page that we want to be shocking and spectacular, I try to do detailed pencils for the complete image. Also, because I have to deal with elements of different scale that require different approaches, it is important, for example, to have a detailed perception of Ellie and her reaction, in an extreme close up, and at the same time from She Dodge, which has a small full-body shot. Here we also balance the thickness of lines to distinguish elements, and the relation of visual weight between full blacks and the rest of the line work. All this, considering that we can still make changes with the inking.

In pages with more panels, I usually don't have time to do this complete, detailed penciling. In those, I try to select the most complex elements and develop them in full detail, while elements that are easier to solve directly with the inking remain schematic.

Step 5: Main Outlines

The process of inking starts with drawing the main outline shapes of the different elements included in the shot. At this stage, the priority is working on the characters and most important objects, while the background just needs detailing on some key lines and, sometimes, the main full-black elements (on some occasions this is left for the final step, depending on the relation between elements and background...). It's important here to identify the different objects and characters clearly, and also to establish the outline of the overlapping elements, which is crucial when you're dealing with translucent objects, like the mason jar.

Step 6: Detailing Characters

It's important to give the proper relevance to the main elements of the image, in this case the characters and the keys. So, their full inking is the next step, to have it solved before inking the other elements. That helps when you need to change some details in the background inking in order to keep the relevance of the main visual elements. Also, in this example, it is time to solve one of my regular nightmares in the inking process... the HAIR. Sometimes I wish I only had to draw bald people...

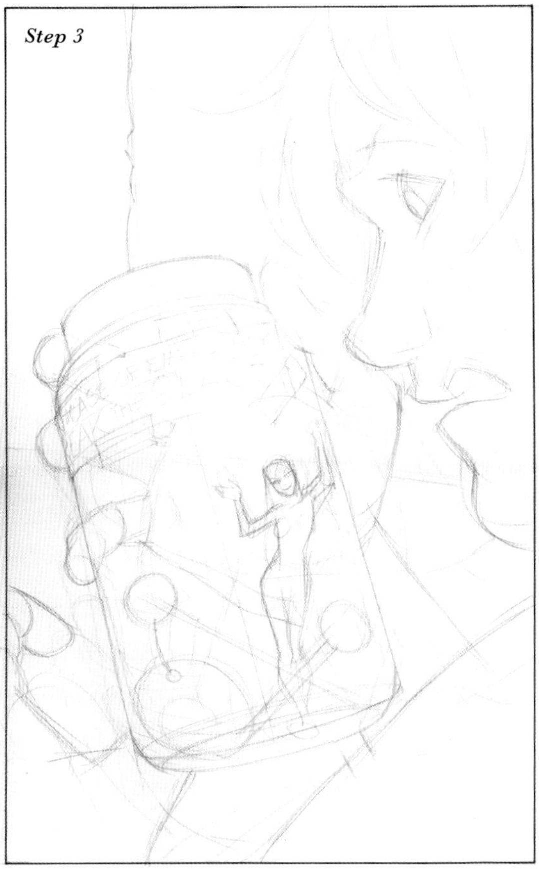
Step 3

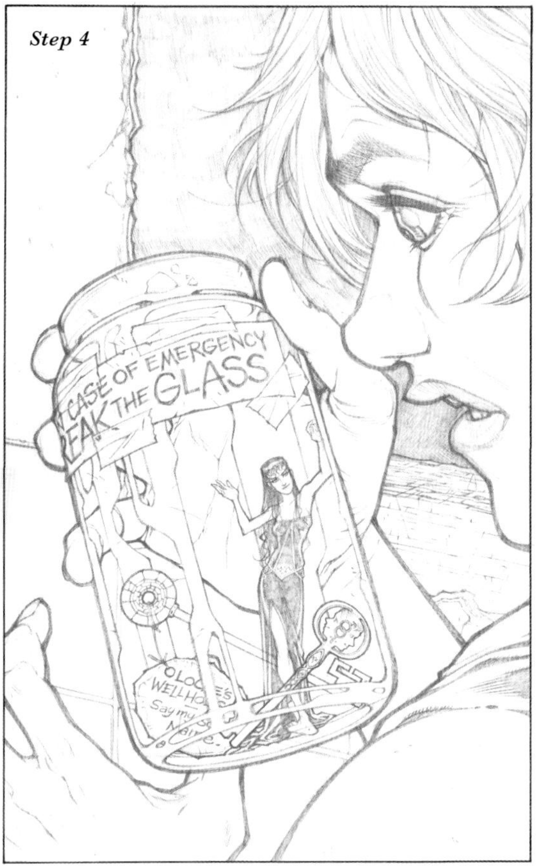
CASE OF EMERGENCY
REAK THE GLASS
Step 4

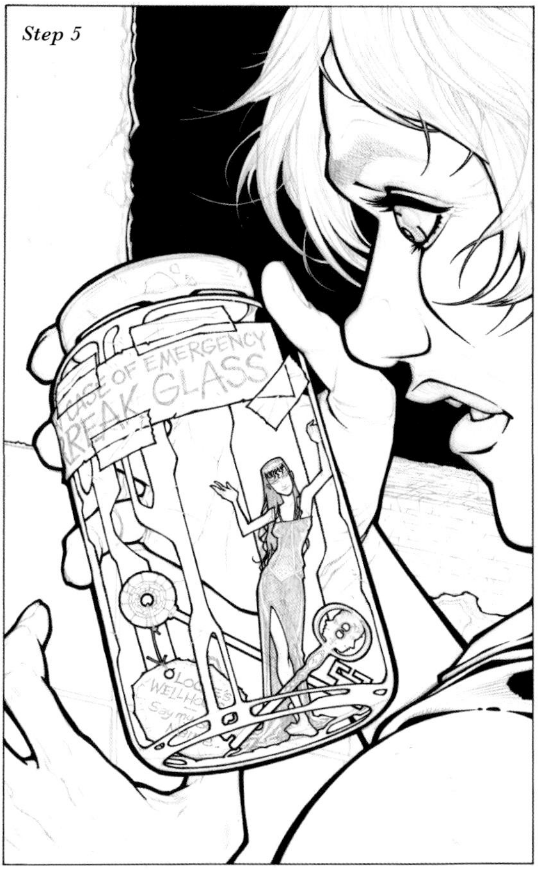
CASE OF EMERGENCY
REAK GLASS
Step 5

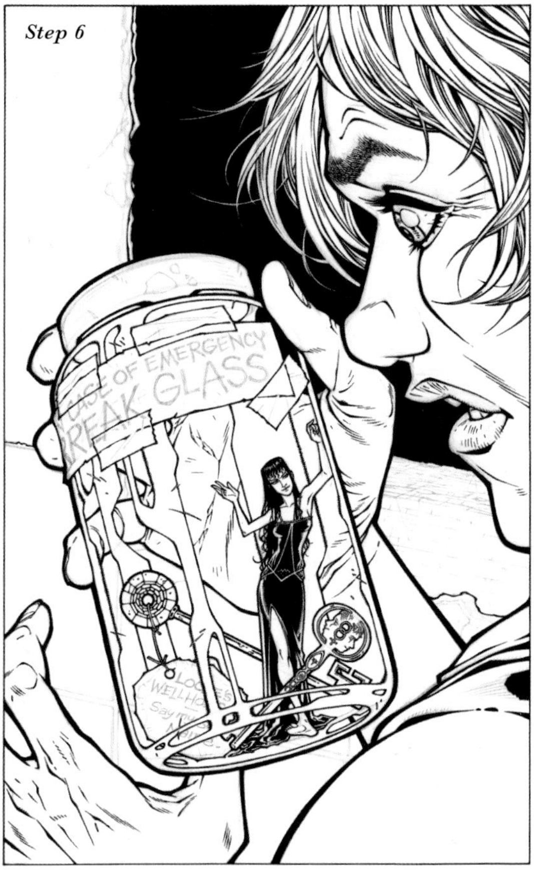
CASE OF EMERGENCY
REAK GLASS
Step 6

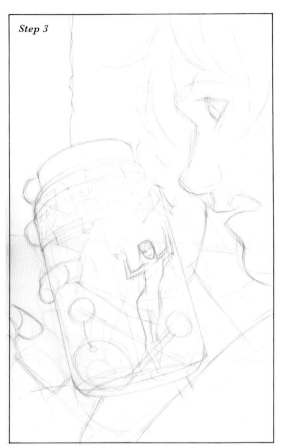

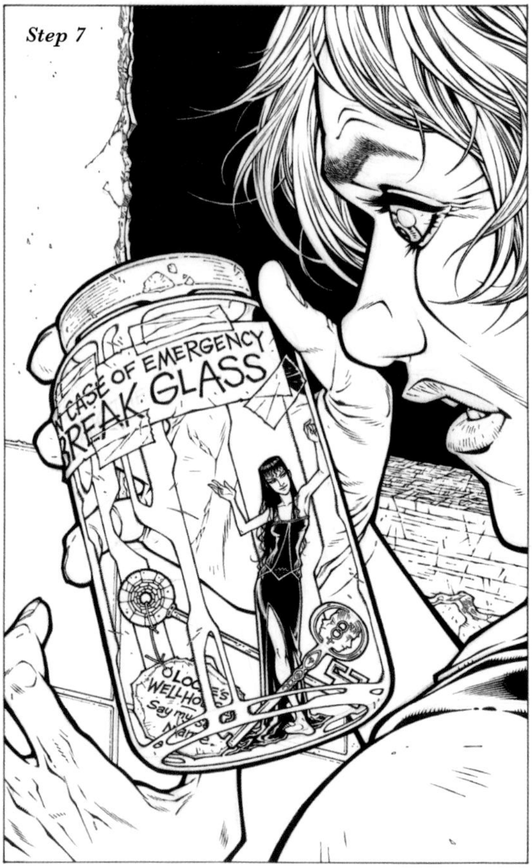
CASE OF EMERGENCY
BREAK GLASS
Step 7

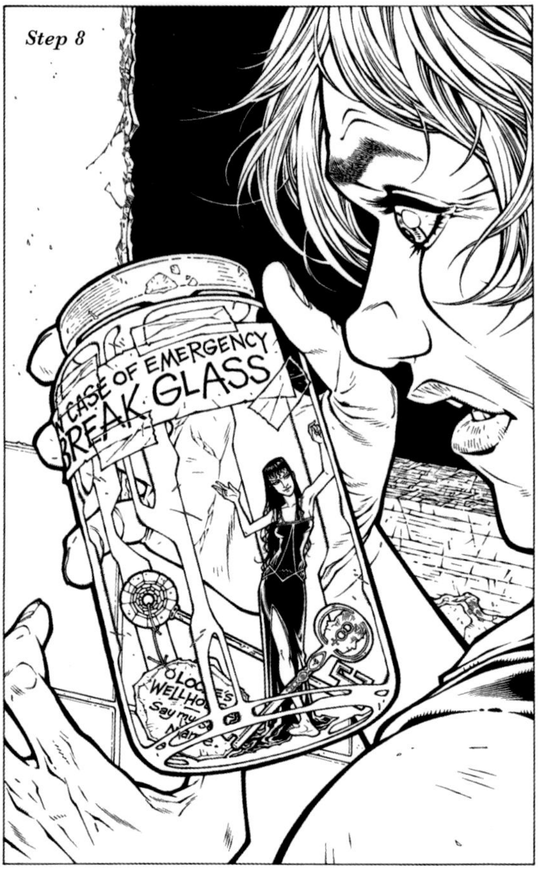
CASE OF EMERGENCY
BREAK GLASS
Step 8

Step 7: Detailing Background and Remaining Elements

And this is how we complete the handwork of the inking process, aware that there may still be some things to polish. But fortunately, we still have a post-production stage...

Step 8: Scanning and Cleaning the Lines

This is a crucial stage. We start scanning the page as a color file. Then, manipulating brightness and contrast of the image, we enhance the inking. After that, we turn the file into a CMYK color file. Next, we select the yellow channel of the color file (which shows only clean elements from the black layer of the image) and create a new file, this time in B&W, without any trace of the blue pencil lines. In this file the black lines appear gray, so we adjust the brightness and contrast of the image to get the traditional full black. Now we're almost done.

Step 9: Post-Production and Definitive File

And then we have the final lines... or do we? When we get to this part of the drawing with just the inked lines, it's common to notice some details that don't work as well as we would want. I used to repeatedly make the mistake of drawing more lines than necessary, and some elements would not look exactly as we wanted. So we have a cleaning process (in this case removing some extra lines from Ellie's face, hands, and lips), and another round of adjusting details (correcting some lines in the faces of the Gender Key, reducing Dodge's smile a little, and fixing the hole of the paper attached to the Well Key, which looks like an extra "o" in the original drawing). Having this done, we copy this drawing into the official page format and "voilá!" We have our finished inks ready to be delivered.

Steps 10, 11, and 12: Approval, Coloring, and Lettering

The last three steps are the ones that continue after my work. Once delivered, the page needs to be approved by the writer and editor. Once given the okay, the editor uploads the file on the FTP server, and from there the color artist grabs the file to proceed with the digital coloring. Once Jay's wonderful work is done, the pages are uploaded back to the server, now in full color, to be approved by editor, writer, and artist. After that, Robbie proceeds with the lettering, then it's sent to the writer for revisions, specifically to see if the text needs any changes…

And THEN, we've got a finished page, ready to go to print.

Repeat this process about 22 times (sometimes more), and you have what you need to produce a cool comic book.

Step 9

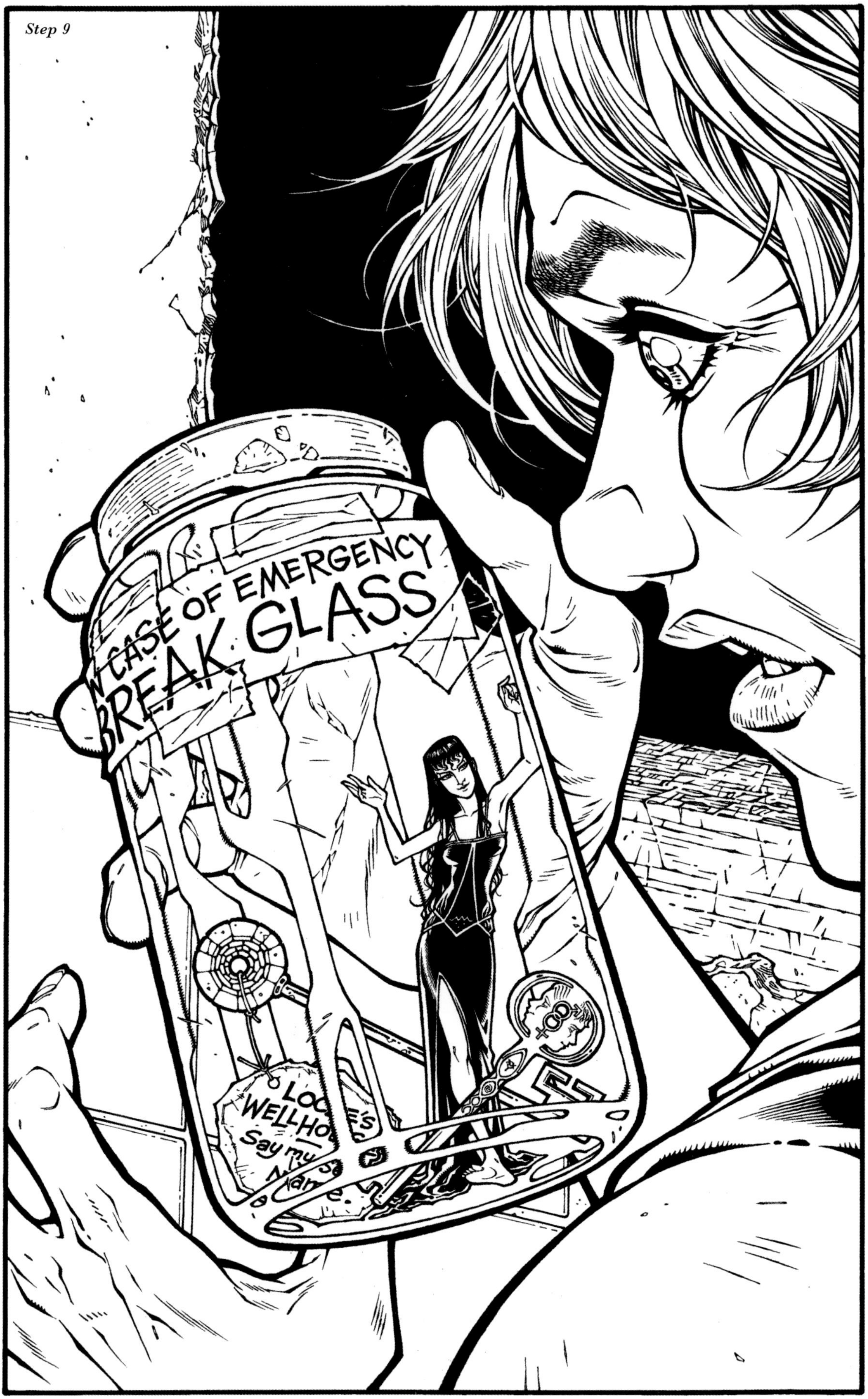
CASE OF EMERGENCY
BREAK GLASS

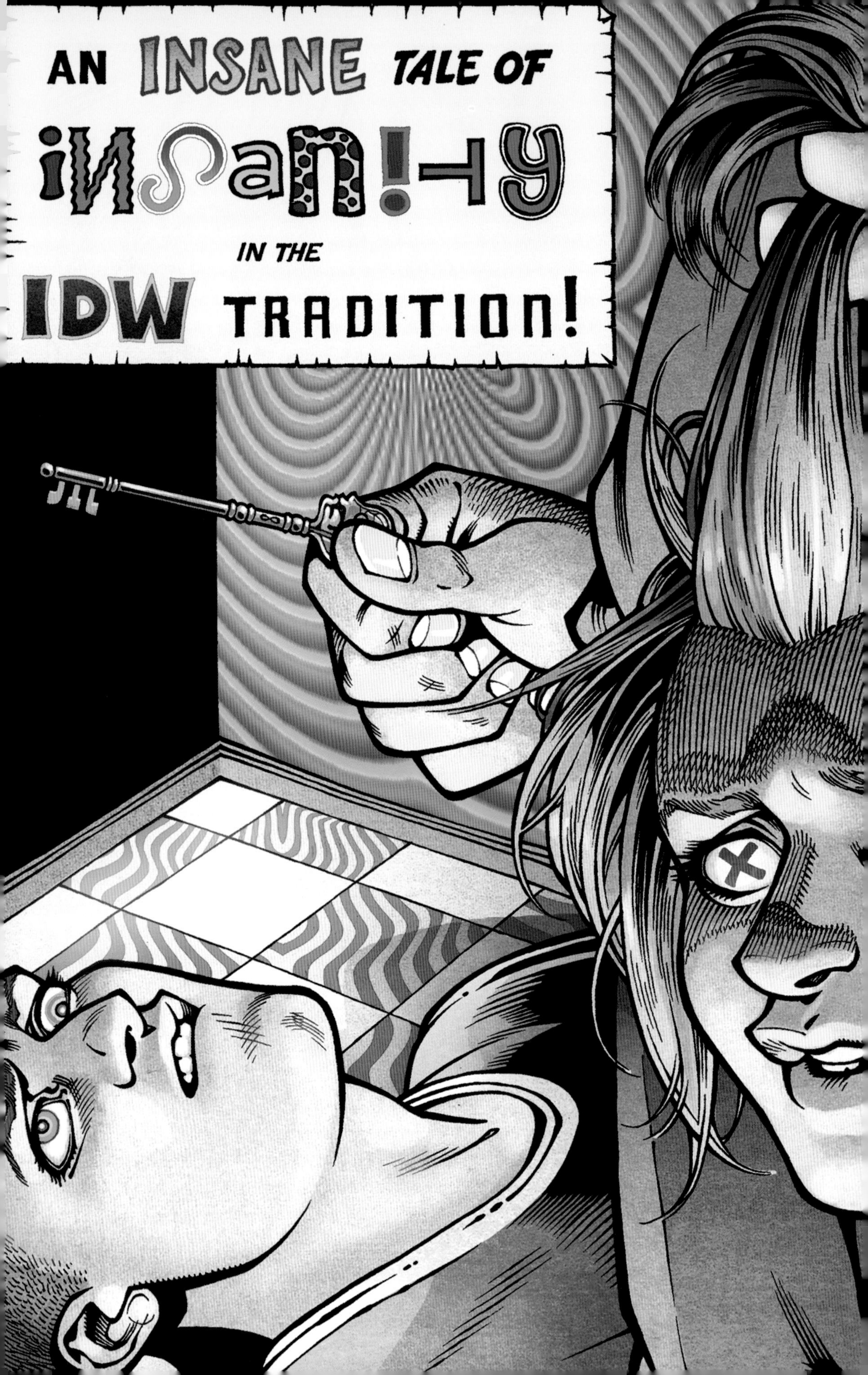
AN INSANE TALE OF
INSANITY
IN THE
IDW TRADITION!

ART
GALLERY

BY GABRIEL RODRIGUEZ

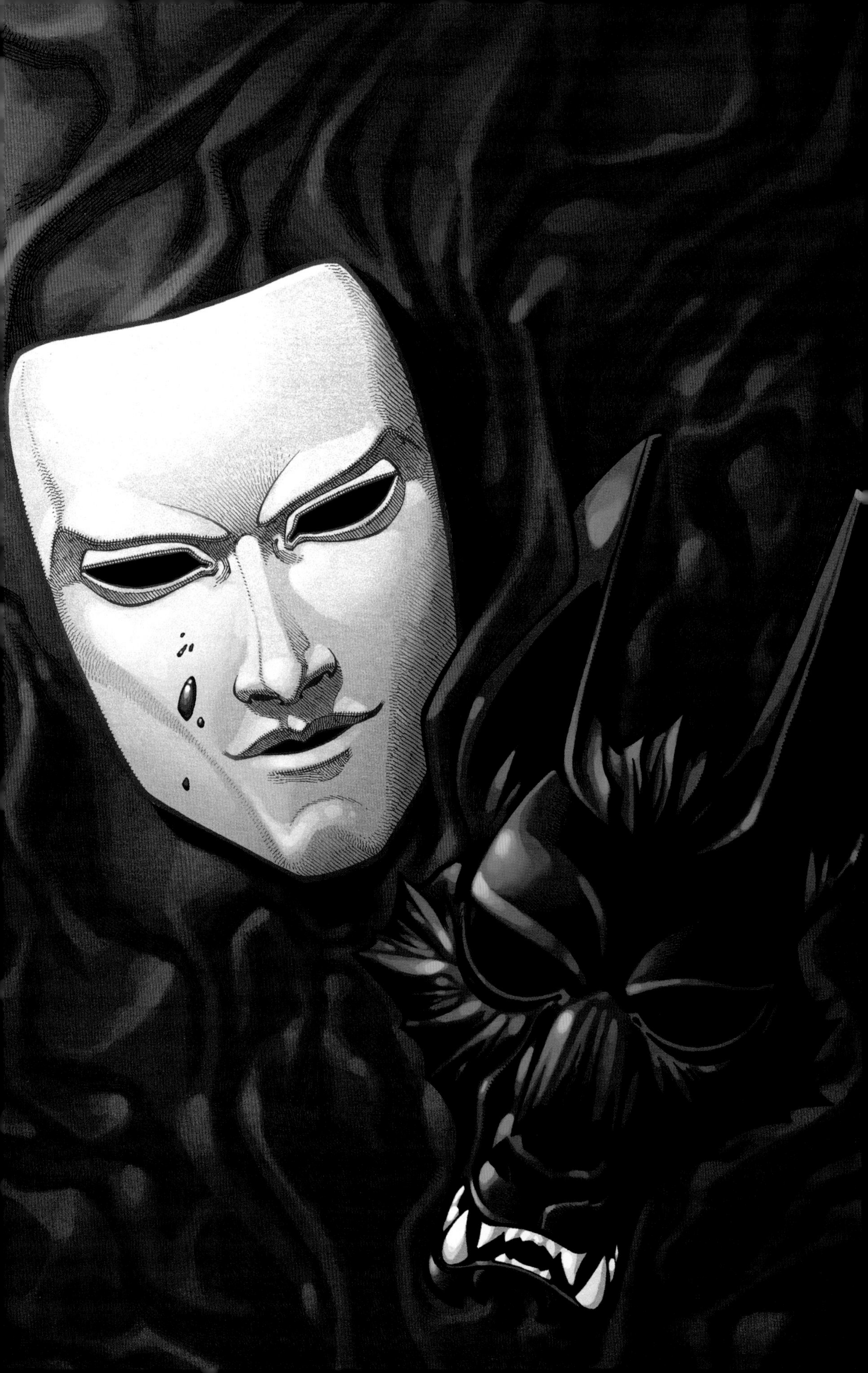

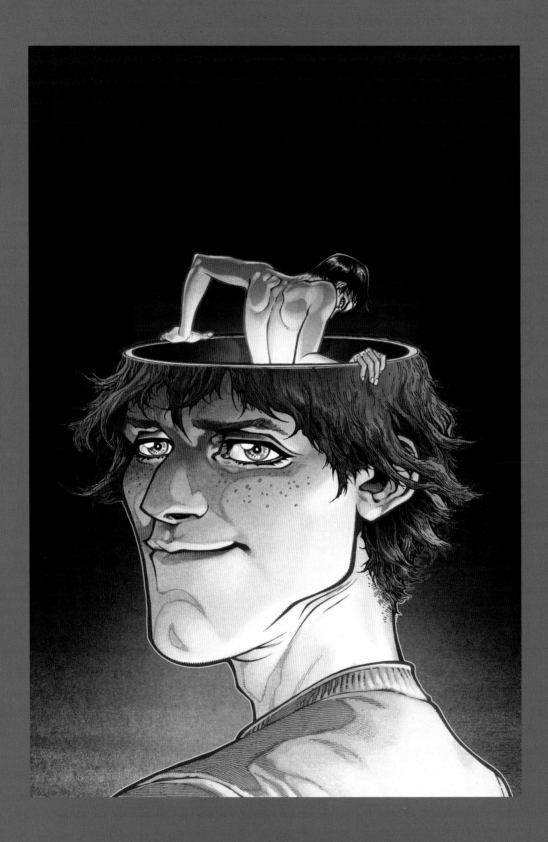

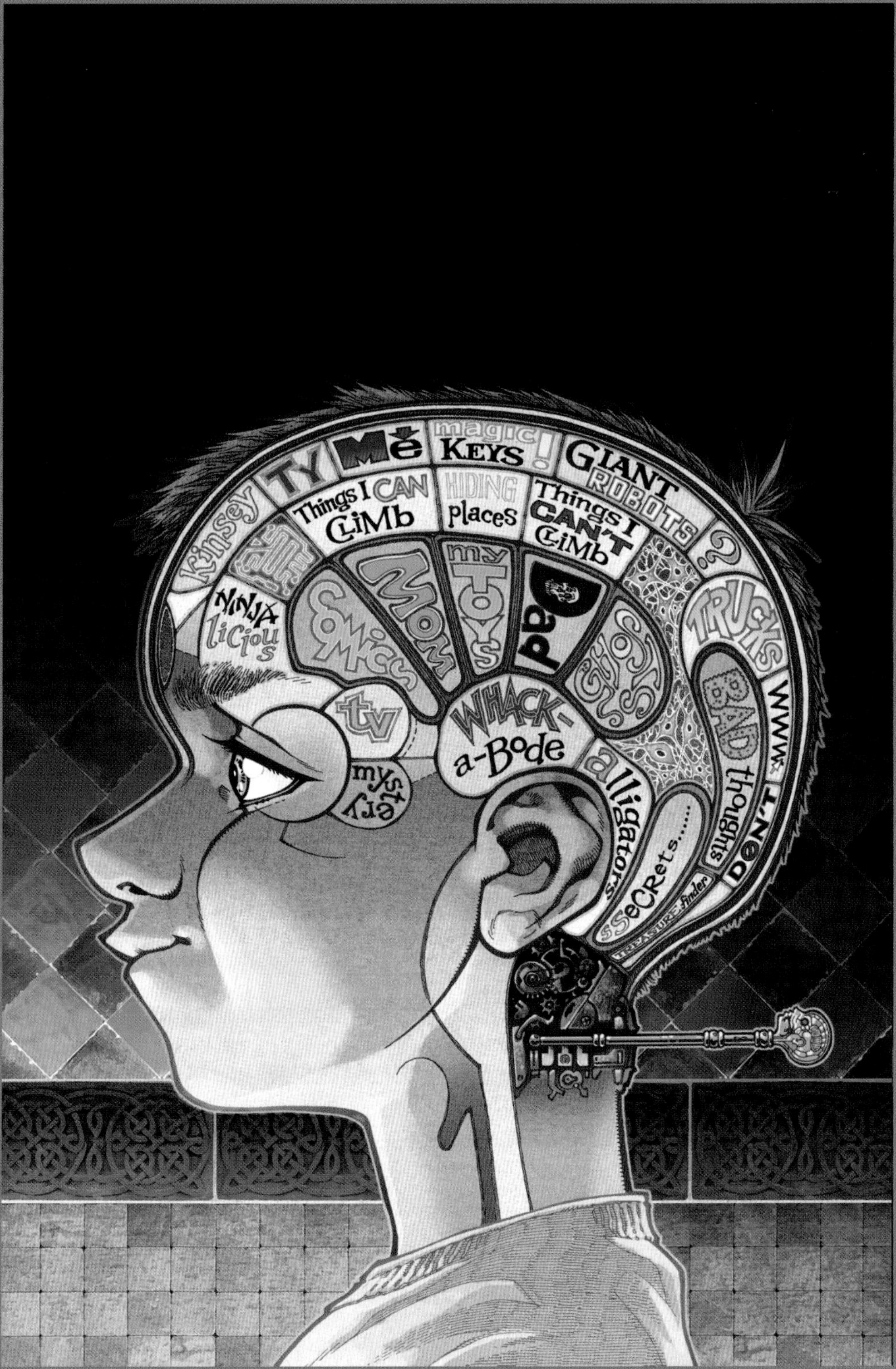
Kinsey
TY
Me
magic
KEYS
!
GIANT
ROBOTS
Things I CAN CLiMb
HIDING places
Things I CAN'T CLiMb
?
NINJA licious
Comics
Mom
my TOYS
Dad
Ghosts
TRUCKS
tv
WHACK-a-Bode
BAD thoughts
www
mystery
alligators
secrets......
DON'T
TREASURE finder

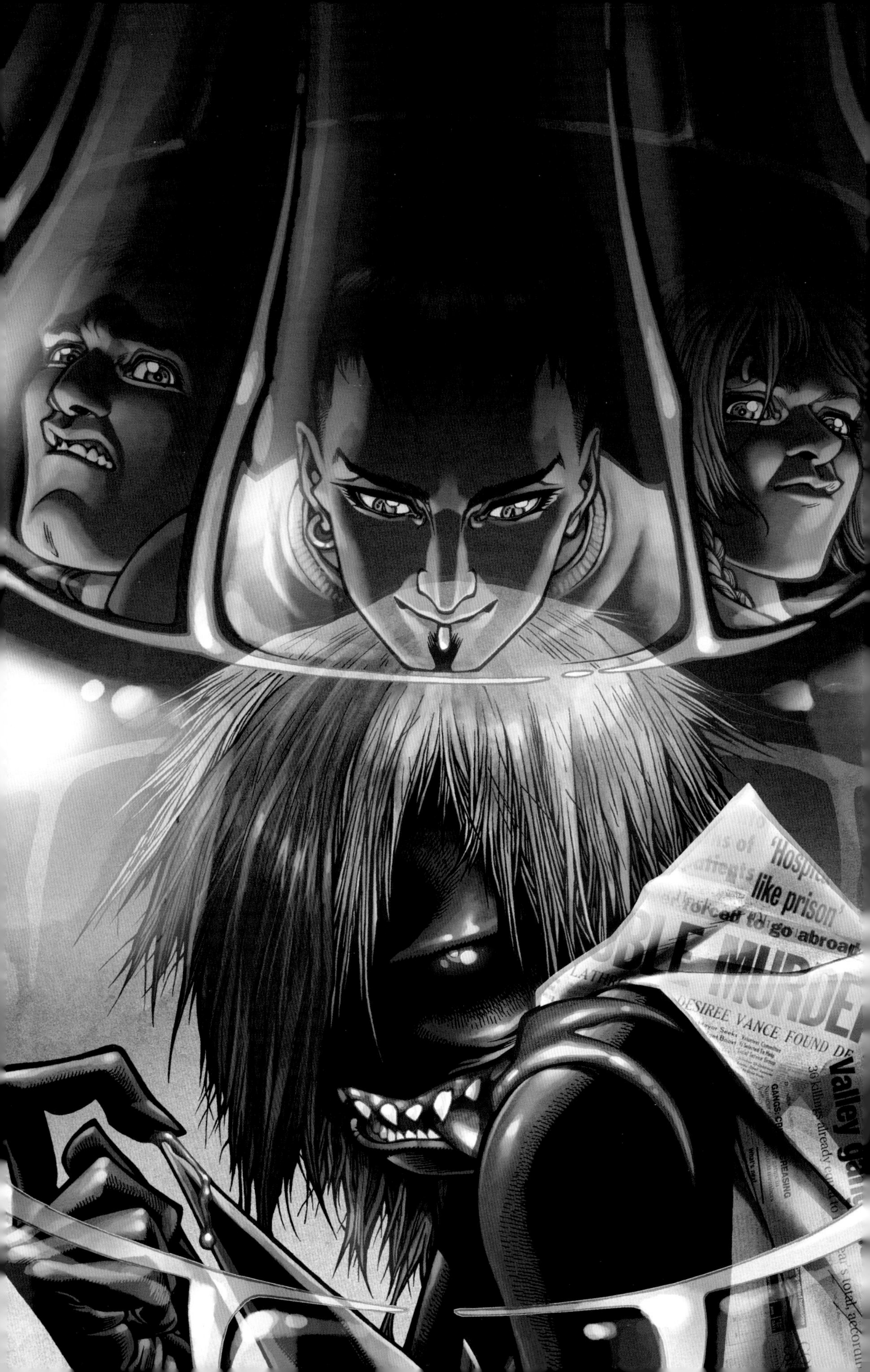

'Hospi
like prison'
go abroad
MURDE
DESIREE VANCE FOUND DE
Valley ga
36 killings already
GANGS:

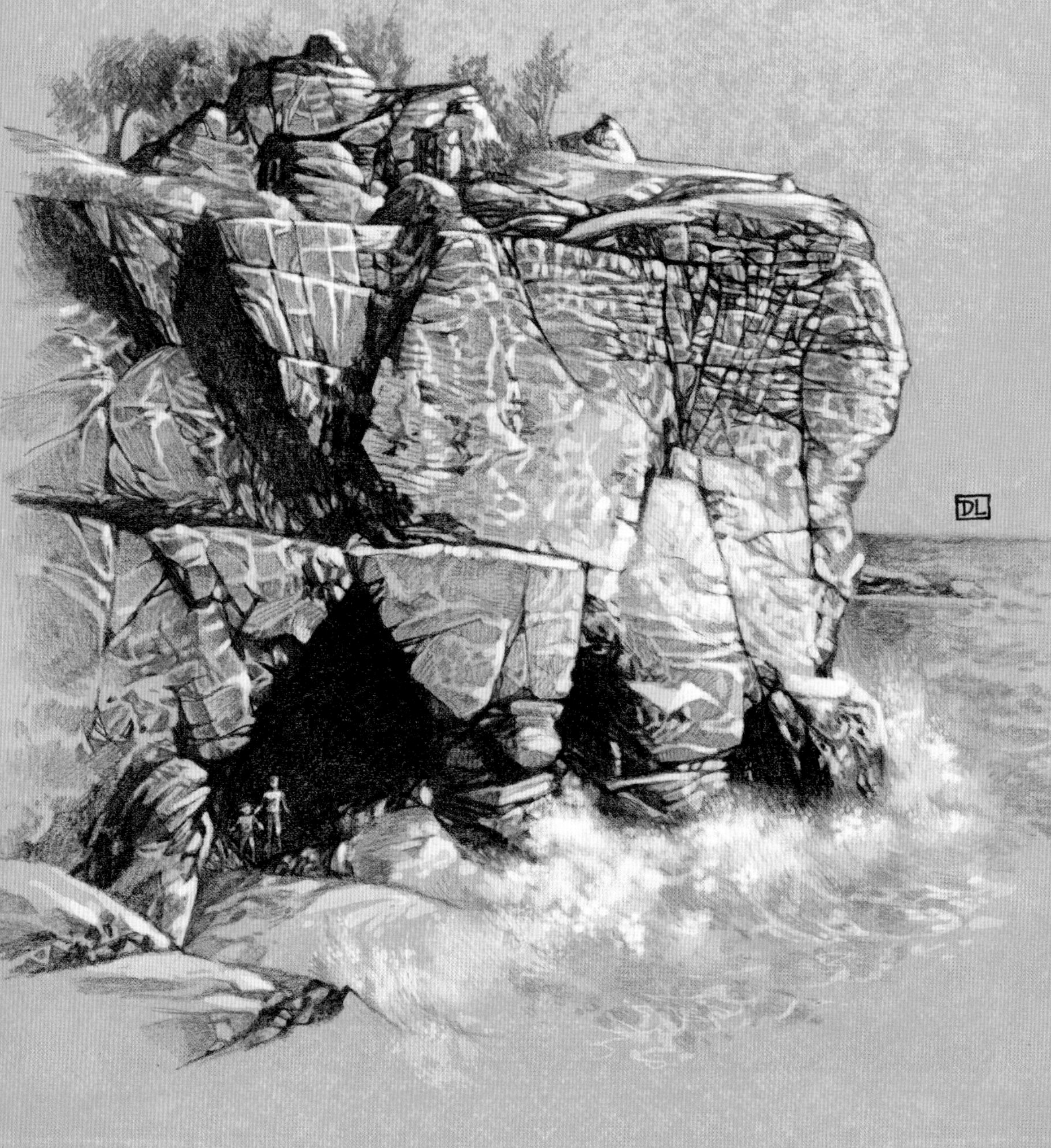
DL

Joe Hill

is the author of a novel, *Heart-Shaped Box*, and a collection of stories, *20th Century Ghosts.* He is currently at work on a new novel. The worst comic book he ever read was still a pretty good time. He has a website, joehillfiction.com, where you can find out stuff; you can also follow him on Twitter where he goes by the inspired handle of joe_hill.

Gabriel Rodriguez

is a supremely gifted Chilean artist and co-creator of the twisted but wonderful world of *Locke & Key*. The invitation to participate in the fantastic journey of the surviving members of the Locke family, conceived by Joe Hill, has become a dream project made real for Gabriel. He asks that readers unlock their hearts and minds, and accept an invitation into new realms and tales, thrilling experiences, and secret places that his efforts craft into a vivid universe.

In addition to his current work in *Locke & Key*, Gabriel has collaborated with IDW on *Clive Barker's The Great And Secret Show, Beowulf, George A. Romero's Land of the Dead*, as well as several *CSI* comics. He currently lives in Santiago, Chile, with his wife, Catalina, and their sons, José Manuel and Matías.

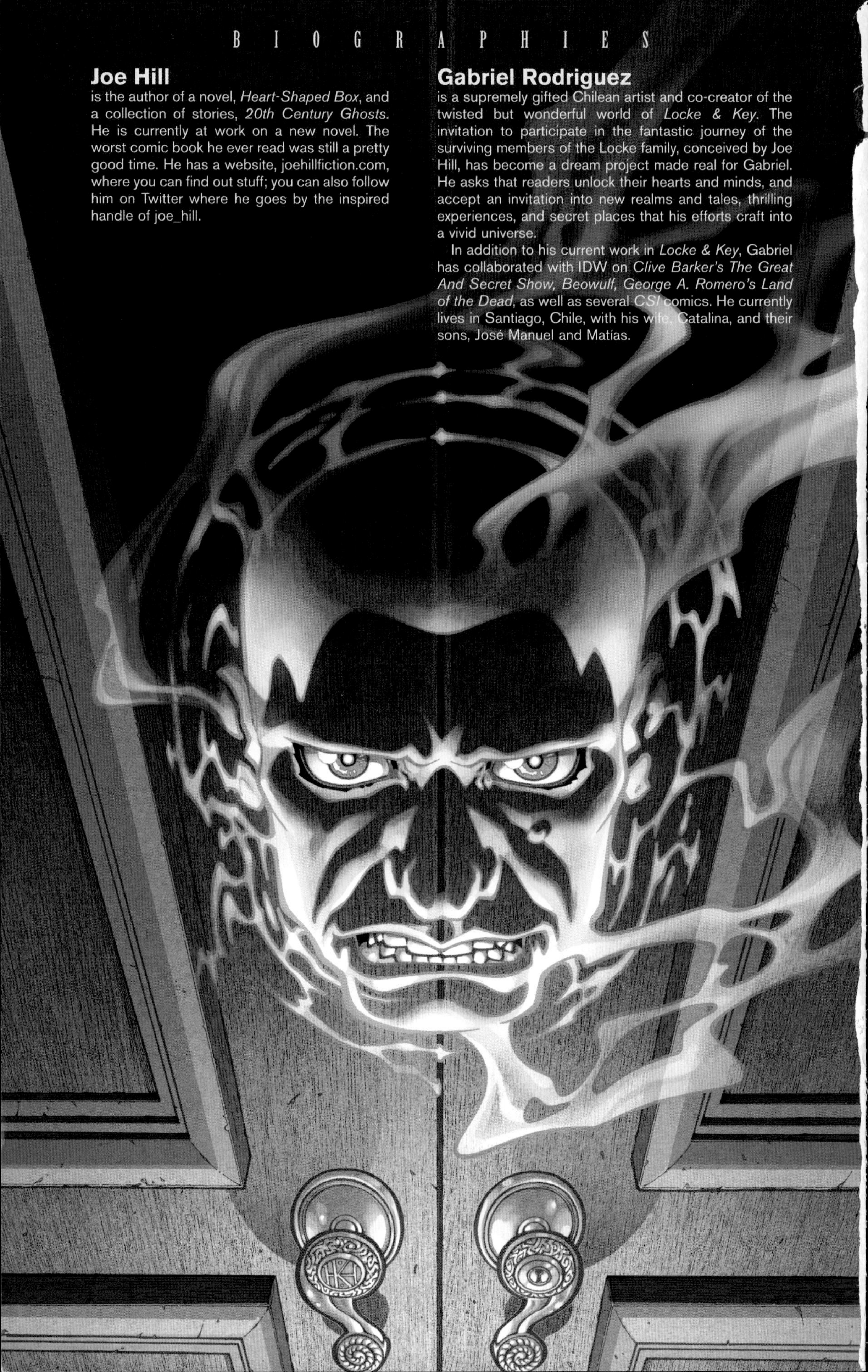

KEYHOUSE EAST ELEVATION

5/9/14

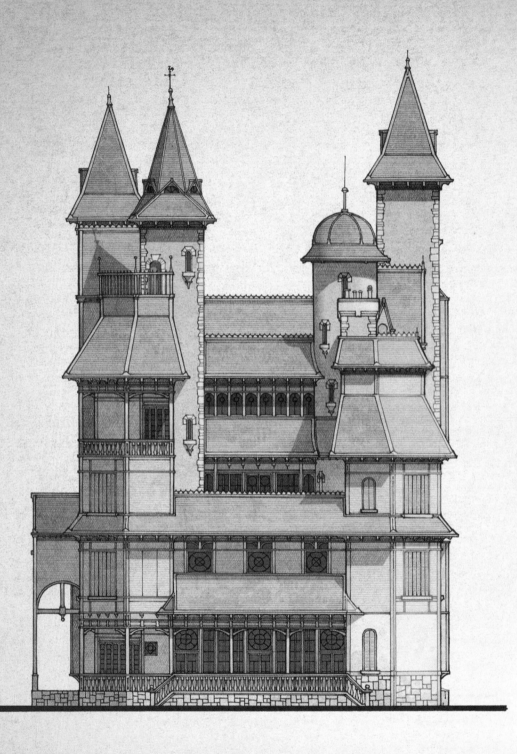

KEYHOUSE SOUTH ELEVATION